HOME OWNERSHIP AND SOCIAL INEQUALITY
IN COMPARATIVE PERSPECTIVE

HOME OWNERSHIP AND SOCIAL INEQUALITY IN COMPARATIVE PERSPECTIVE

Edited by Karin Kurz and Hans-Peter Blossfeld

STANFORD UNIVERSITY PRESS

STANFORD, CALIFORNIA

2004

Stanford University Press
Stanford, California

©2004 by the Board of Trustees of the Leland Stanford Junior
University. All rights reserved.

Printed in the United States of America on acid-free, archival-
quality paper

Library of Congress Cataloging-in-Publication Data

Home ownership and social inequality in comparative
   perspective / edited by Karin Kurz and Hans-Peter Blossfeld.
      p. cm. — (Studies in social inequality)
   Includes bibliographical references and index.
   ISBN 0-8047-4851-9 (cloth: alk. paper)
      1. Home ownership.   2. Social stratification.   I. Kurz,
   Karin.   II. Blossfeld, Hans-Peter.   III. Series.
   HD7287.8 .H65 2004
   305.5'12—dc22   2003027548

Typeset by G&S Book Services, in 10/14 Sabon

Original Printing 2004

Last figure below indicates year of this printing:
13   12   11   10   09   08   07   06   05   04

CONTENTS

TABLES AND FIGURES

Tables

Figures

CONTRIBUTORS

Irit Adler is a Ph.D. student in the Department of Sociology and Anthropology at Tel Aviv University. She is writing her dissertation on the role of the welfare state in Israel in shaping housing inequality among groups of varying ethnicity and national origin.

Fabrizio Bernardi is associate professor of social structure in the Department of Sociology II of the Universidad Nacional de Educación a Distancia in Madrid. His main research interests are social inequality and the relationship between labor market and family dynamics.

Hans-Peter Blossfeld is professor and chair of sociology at the Otto Friedrich University Bamberg, Germany. His research interests include social inequality, sociology of the family, educational sociology, labor market research, demography, social stratification, quantitative methods, and longitudinal data analysis.

Anna Cabré Pla, of the Department of Geography of the Autonomous University of Barcelona, is director of the Centre d'Estudis Demogràfics. Her main research interests lie in the field of demography.

Daniel Courgeau is an emeritus research director at the Institut National d'Études Démographiques, Paris. He is currently working on multilevel analyses of life history surveys and on the methodology and epistemology of demography and social sciences.

John Ermisch is a professor at the Institute for Social and Economic Research at the University of Essex and a Fellow of the British Academy. Formerly (1991–1994), he was Bonar-Macfie Professor in the Department of Political Economy at the University of Glasgow. His research is broadly concerned with how markets interact with household and demographic decisions.

Tony Fahey is a research professor at the Economic and Social Research Institute, Dublin. His interests include housing, the family, the quality of life in Europe, various aspects of demography, and attitudes and values.

Veerle Geurts is a researcher in the Research Group on Poverty, Social Exclusion and the City (OASES) within the Department of Sociology and Social Policy of Antwerp University. Her research interests include housing and housing policy.

Luc Goossens teaches sociology, public administration, and housing in the Faculty of Social and Political Sciences of the University of Antwerp. He is a senior researcher with OASES, and is primarily interested in housing policy, local governance, and residents' movements.

Lars Gulbrandsen is research director at NOVA—Norwegian Social Research. His research interests include housing, family, and intergenerational transfers.

Brendan Halpin is a professor at the Department of Sociology of the University of Limerick, Ireland. His research interests include social stratification and social mobility, educational inequality, methods for the analysis of longitudinal data, the dynamics of family formation and divorce, and labor market dynamics.

Karin Kurz is an assistant professor in the Faculty of Social and Economic Sciences at Otto Friedrich University Bamberg, Germany. Her research interests include social inequality, social stratification, housing, the family, the labor market, and the life course.

Søren Leth-Sørensen, a sociologist, works as a senior adviser at Statistics Denmark. Currently, his office is at the University of Aarhus. His main interests are labor market issues and family changes in Denmark. He played a role in the development of the IDA database, a longitudinal database of people and companies in Denmark.

Noah Lewin-Epstein is a professor and past chairperson of the Department of Sociology and Anthropology at Tel Aviv University. His research interests include social inequality, ethnic stratification, and labor markets. He is currently engaged in research on housing and intergenerational determinants of life chances.

Bertrand Maître is a research analyst at the Economic and Social Research Institute, Dublin. He works on a range of Irish and European projects, analyzing data from the Living in Ireland Panel Survey and the European Community Household Panel. His current research focuses on poverty and inequality, social exclusion, and income distribution.

George S. Masnick has a Ph.D. in sociology/demography from Brown University. He taught at the University of Pennsylvania from 1970 to 1974 and at Harvard University from 1974 to 1987. Since "retiring" in 1987, he has been working part-time at Harvard's Joint Center for Housing Studies, where he is a senior research fellow. Dr. Masnick has done research and writing in the areas of household and family demography, population dynamics, housing, and household forecasting.

Monique Meron works at the Direction de l'Animation de la Recherché, des Etudes et des Statistique (DARES) at the Ministère des Affaires Sociales, du Travail et de la Solidarité. The research for her work in this book was carried out while she was a member of Daniel Courgeau's research team at the Institut National d'Études Démographiques, Paris.

Juan Antonio Módenes Cabrerizo, of the Department of Geography at the Autonomous University of Barcelona, is a researcher in the Centre d'Estudis Demogràfics. His main research interests lie in the field of population geography.

Clara H. Mulder is at the Amsterdam Study Centre for the Metropolitan Environment (AME) in the Department of Geography and Planning of the University of Amsterdam. Her research interests include the connection between household formation and housing. The research for her work in this book was carried out while she was at the Urban Research Centre Utrecht in the Faculty of Geographical Sciences of Utrecht University, holding a research fellowship from the Royal Netherlands Academy of Arts and Sciences.

Teresio Poggio is a research officer and a doctorate student in the Department of Sociology and Social Research at the University of Trento, Italy. His primary interests include research on welfare and housing, social inequality, social stratification, and poverty. He is writing his dissertation on home ownership and social inequality in Italy during the twentieth century.

Moshe Semyonov is a professor of sociology and labor studies in the Faculty of Social Sciences in the Departments of Sociology and Anthropology, and Labor Studies at Tel Aviv University. He is also a professor of sociology at the University of Illinois at Chicago. His main research interests lie in the areas of comparative stratification and mobility, immigration and labor migration, and in sources of ethnic and gender inequality in the labor market.

HOME OWNERSHIP AND SOCIAL INEQUALITY IN COMPARATIVE PERSPECTIVE

CHAPTER ONE

Introduction: Social Stratification, Welfare Regimes, and Access to Home Ownership

Karin Kurz and
Hans-Peter Blossfeld

Traditional social stratification research concentrates on labor market inequalities in income, class, and socioeconomic status, and on how those inequalities are brought about through the influence of the family of origin or education (Blau and Duncan 1967; Erikson and Goldthorpe 1992). Although home ownership is the most important form of family wealth—it greatly affects both the living conditions and financial security of households—it has rarely been a topic of social stratification research. That omission is astonishing because access to home ownership might well deepen labor market inequalities (Forrest and Murie 1995a); alternatively, it might serve to level out those inequalities to some extent. The main proponent of the latter position is Saunders (1990), who describes Britain as a property-owning democracy in which a broad mass of households own homes and class position has lost much of its significance. Saunders's view is close to the popular theory that individualization in present-day society is increasing, the belief that traditional social collectives—based on class or ascribed characteristics, for example—have lost their significance in shaping the lives of individuals (Beck 1986, 1994).[1]

The study of housing and tenure type (ownership versus tenancy) has been left mostly to the specialized field of housing research, which does not have strong links to general social inequality research. Housing studies tend to concentrate on housing conditions and policies, and only rarely address stratification issues (cf. Kemeny 1992). An exception are British studies that investigate whether home ownership is a determinant of life chances independent of labor market position and whether home ownership alters class consciousness and voting behavior (Forrest, Murie, and Williams

1

1990; Saunders 1990). Discussion in this field, however, is mainly confined to the United Kingdom: it has not stimulated systematic international comparisons. In contrast, cross-national studies of housing policies in European countries and other industrialized nations have been conducted (see, for example, Boelhouwer and van der Heijden 1992; Doling 1997; and McCrone and Stephens 1995). Moreover, quite recently attempts have been made to link housing policy studies with research on welfare states (Barlow and Duncan 1994; Castles and Ferrera 1996; Doling; Kemeny).

At the same time, economists, geographers, and demographers have undertaken empirical analyses of the determinants of tenure type. Using a cost–benefit framework, economists have mainly focused on the income elasticity of housing demand and consumption, as well as on the probability of owning versus renting. Demographers and geographers have put more emphasis on linking tenure choice to regional and temporal contexts and to events in the family life cycle (cf. Clark, Deurloo, and Dieleman 1994, 1997; Mulder and Hooimeijer 1995). In these fields, recent quantitative studies increasingly use a life course framework and methods of transition data analysis (see, for example, Courgeau and Lelièvre 1992; and Mulder and Wagner 1998). But here, too, cross-national studies are rare; and in almost none of these contributions has the question of differential access to home ownership been studied in a stratification framework (cf. Mulder and Smits 1999). From these diverse research traditions, we take up, on the one hand, the social stratification perspective and, on the other, the interest in understanding country differences by referring to different cultural and institutional contexts. Moreover, we apply a life course perspective.

HOUSING TENURE AND SOCIAL STRATIFICATION

In traditional stratification research, the labor market is considered the central institution: it determines life chances. The main focus of that research, then, is on the position of the individual in the labor market and within work organizations, which is interpreted in terms of class position, social standing, or the living standard of an individual or household.[2]

Social mobility studies coming from this research tradition typically ask two related sets of questions (see, for example, Erikson and Goldthorpe 1992): First, *to what extent does class structure change between genera-*

tions? If there is mobility between generations, is it simply a function of change in the occupational structure, or is it caused by a greater openness in society? Second, *do children who come from different social backgrounds have equal opportunities*? In industrial and postindustrial societies, is there a trend away from ascription toward achievement? That is, what role does educational achievement—versus the influence of the family of origin—play in determining an individual's job and resultant position?

It is clear that understanding the mechanisms of how occupational position is attained is relevant only if labor market position actually does shape the life chances of individuals. In his individualization hypothesis, Beck (1986, 1994) attacks this proposition with several arguments. He states that, as educational opportunities expand, and as geographic and occupational mobility increases, family and class become less important determinants of the individual's life course. At the same time, he suggests, social class (and other social collectivities) loses its subjective relevance and people begin to interpret labor market risks (unemployment is one example) in terms of individual risk, not class risk. Finally, Beck expects that labor market risks, once confined to specific disadvantaged groups, spread to everyone in the labor market.

Social stratification researchers point to empirical findings that contradict Beck's assumptions, in particular the first and third arguments. Family background still plays an important role in shaping the individual's life course both directly and indirectly: family resources influence educational opportunities, which in turn influence occupational position (see, for example, Erikson and Goldthorpe 1992; Shavit and Blossfeld 1993; and Shavit and Müller 1998). At the same time, labor market risks are clearly structured by education and first occupational position (Blossfeld, Klijzing, Mills, and Kurz forthcoming; Brauns, Gangl, and Scherer 1999; Gangl 2001; Kurz, Steinhage, and Golsch 2001; Shavit and Müller).

If the labor market still structures life chances, why should home ownership be of interest to the study of social inequality? The basic argument is that household assets—including a home—affect the household's standard of living, social standing, and wealth. Social stratification researchers typically would argue that it is not necessary to consider home ownership (or, more generally, household assets) because access to home ownership closely follows the class, occupation, or earnings of individuals and households. In fact, that argument fails on at least two counts. First, it is obvious that assets can be transferred from one generation to the next, which means that a household's standard of living and wealth do not simply reflect its labor market position. Research has shown unequivocally that individuals in favorable labor market positions are more likely to receive inheritances or gifts from their families (see, for example, Forrest and Murie 1995a; Hamnett 1991; Kendig 1984; and Lauterbach and Lüscher 1996). But most people are age 40 or older when they receive an inheritance—an age at which tenure decisions typically have been made (Bonvalet 1995; Forrest and Murie; Hamnett; Lauterbach and Lüscher). On the basis of that finding, some authors have argued that intergenerational transfers have little impact on first home ownership and the household's living standard (Lauterbach and Lüscher; Munro 1988). We would still argue that inheritances are important because they can be used in various ways to improve a household's economic and social situation. In addition, it is well documented that *inter vivos* transfers play an important role in access to home ownership (Castles and Ferrera 1996; Forrest and Murie 1995b; Motel and Szydlik 1999). Family resources, then, can facilitate access to home ownership.

Saunders (1978, 1990) raised a second issue: because real property tends to gain or lose value over time, home ownership itself—independent of labor market position—can affect a household's living standard and wealth. In the three decades after World War II, inflation increased the price of housing in virtually all Western countries.[3] Hence, home ownership came to be viewed as an independent factor in the distribution of social inequality.[4]

The crucial question here is whether home ownership can alter social inequality that the labor market has produced. Three scenarios are possible:

- Capital gains closely mirror the differential class and income positions of households, and so have little effect on social inequality.
- Upper classes realize higher capital gains, widening class differences in wealth and living standards.
- Capital gains are similar across groups, reducing the distance between upper and lower classes.

Saunders (1990) found support for the third scenario in an empirical analysis of housing prices in three towns in Great Britain. But his results have been questioned by several authors. Forrest and Murie (1995a), for example, argue that Saunders's method—calculating the rate of return on the initial deposit—is faulty, that it is more instructive to refer to absolute returns on purchase price. When absolute returns are used, a relationship between class and property value (the second scenario) becomes clear.

In summary, labor market–induced inequalities in a household's standard of living and wealth are deepened to the extent that (1) intergenerational transfers increase access to home ownership, and (2) lower social classes realize smaller capital gains through home ownership than do upper social classes, which is very likely.[5] Analyzing these relationships contributes to our understanding of the relevance of family transfers and home ownership as sources of inequality independent of the labor market. Although the country-specific case studies in this book do not focus on the second issue, the role of intergenerational transfers is investigated for several nations: West Germany, the Netherlands, Denmark, Italy, and Israel.

But an even more basic question needs to be asked (Savage, Watt, and Arber 1992): To what extent does access to home ownership depend on a household's class and income? A weak relationship, like that suggested by Saunders, would support the view of an individualized society, a society in which social cleavages along class lines are losing much of their importance. Of course, this assumes that home ownership is an important determinant of living standards. So one of the main topics addressed in this volume is how the probability and timing of access to home ownership are related to occupational class.[6] Following Erikson and Goldthorpe (1992, 37), we understand *class* in terms of labor market position and position within production units. For the questions studied in this book, we believe class is more relevant than the household's current income because class typically is linked to specific expectations with respect to the development and stability of earnings over the working life.

It needs to be added, though, that even if the class position of a household proves to be unimportant for access to home ownership, class position may still play an indirect role in that access. Key here is the close relationship between class position and the likelihood of receiving intergenerational transfers. Also, even when we find a broad middle mass of homeowners, with little class differentiation, the size and quality of housing may well be class dependent. This issue is addressed in the discussion of Norway in Chapter 7.

WELFARE REGIMES AND HOUSING TENURE

In our discussion to this point, we have not touched on the role that country-specific history, cultures, institutions, and economic development play in the attainment of home ownership. It goes without saying that this omission is unrealistic. Home-ownership rates vary tremendously among countries that are similar in terms of economic development but differ in other respects. For example, in the countries under study in this book, home-ownership rates range from 42 percent in West Germany to about 80 percent in Norway and Spain. Can these differences be related to a welfare regime classification?

Although the state subsidizes housing in virtually all industrial and post-industrial nations, research has remained remarkably silent on the nature and role of housing policy in different types of welfare regimes (cf. Kemeny 1992, 79ff.).[7] Kemeny (1981) was among the first to direct attention to the relationship between a state's housing policy and the rate of home ownership. His basic argument is that the differences in the rates of home ownership in industrial societies must be understood in terms of divergent "dominant ideologies."[8] He distinguishes two fundamental ideologies: individualistic (or privatist) and collectivist. The former favors individual solutions for the welfare of citizens; the latter, solutions in which costs are pooled in some way. In nations where collectivist ideology dominates over an extended period, a well-developed welfare state arises. One area in which the differences between individual and collectivist solutions are visible in the social structure is housing tenure. In his original (1981) work, Kemeny argued that home ownership is a privatist solution to the housing problem and that renting is a collectivist solution. His thesis: in countries like Australia and the United States, where privatist ideology prevails, rates of home ownership should be higher and public spending on housing lower than they are in countries like Sweden, Germany, and the Netherlands, where collectivist ideology is dominant. He tested that thesis by looking at home-ownership rates and welfare state spending in a small number of countries, and found the expected negative correlation. Later analyses of a larger number of countries tend to confirm the relationship (cf. Castles and Ferrera 1996; Schmidt 1989).

The negative correlation between home-ownership rates and state spending on housing is further explained by the lifetime costs of home ownership. When homes are privately owned—versus rented—the lifetime costs of housing typically are skewed: initially costs are high; over time they fall slowly, becoming very low in old age. Kemeny (1992) believes that high housing costs at the start of home ownership are "a structural deterrent to both high taxes and high levels of social security (payments)" (122). In a sense, then, home ownership and pensions are alternative routes to social security in old age (Castles 1998; Castles and Ferrera 1996; Kemeny 1981, 1992). In a society where home ownership is widespread, public old-age pensions can be smaller.

Esping-Andersen (1990, 1999) used institutional contexts to differentiate among welfare states. In his typology, he does not take into account housing systems and policies. He focuses instead on the social insurance systems that buffer the risks attached to employment—unemployment, sickness, old age—and on policies directed at child care and female employment. Nor does Esping-Andersen cite ideology as a driving force behind the development of the welfare state and the social structure in general. He is a proponent of "labor movement theory," which argues that labor unions and labor parties have been more or less successful in shaping government policies.[9]

Despite differences in their basic approaches—dominant ideology on the one hand and political actors on the other—both Kemeny and Esping-Andersen identify a fundamental split in the development of social policy: a collectivist/social democratic version versus a privatist/liberal version. And Esping-Andersen refines that split by adding a third contingent, the conservatives. In a conservative welfare regime, the state exhibits less of an interest in equalizing the living conditions of its citizens and is less active in fostering equality between the sexes than the state in social democratic welfare regimes.

One of the most important developments in Esping-Andersen's more recent work is the distinction he makes among the three main societal institutions that provide welfare services—state, market, and household (also see Rose 1986a)—and their association with the three regime types.[10] In the social democratic regime, state activities are comprehensive and are intended to reduce social inequalities and to foster equality between the sexes. Neither the market nor the family is expected to be a major welfare provider. In contrast, in the liberal regime, welfare services typically are bought on the market; state support is residual and means tested. The liberal regime does not rely on the family to provide welfare; but it also does not design policies to reduce the burden on those families, as the social democratic regime does. In the conservative regime, the family is expected to be a major service provider. The state is much less active in reducing social inequalities than it is in the social democratic regime; and the market is seldom called on for welfare services.

In addition, a fourth regime type can be distinguished, the Southern European regime, in which the family plays an extremely important role in providing welfare of different kinds. Traditionally, the Southern European family is integrated in a broad kinship network with strong and intense relationships among extended family members (cf., for example, Jurado Guerrero and Naldini 1996). According to Castles and Ferrera (1996), "the southern European family tends to operate as a clearing-house for the pooling of social and material resources and for their redistribution among its members according to need: most notable those needs which arise at critical junctures of the life-cycle (housing, employment, childminding, income), not infrequently as a consequence of defective public policies" (181). In this regime, the kinship network provides services that in other countries are at least in part delivered by the state or the market.

The distinction between state and market provision of welfare fits in well with Kemeny's (1992) notion of collectivist and individualistic ideologies. Where a collectivist ideology is dominant, we are more likely to find state or other nonprofit mechanisms for solving welfare problems. Where a privatist ideology is dominant, market mechanisms (including employer-provided mechanisms) are more likely to be in place. How does the family fit into this scheme? It seems plausible that in countries where the family is a major service provider, there will typically be an ideology that supports this institutional pattern. Indeed, it is well known that in conservative Southern European welfare regimes, the Catholic Church provides an ideological foundation for reliance on the family.

Assuming that the basic ideologies that underlie regime types are reflected not only in the policy fields Esping-Andersen focused on but also in housing, we can ask what types of housing systems are likely in social democratic, liberal, and conservative welfare regimes. Departing from his earlier work, Kemeny (1992) suggests that there is not a simple one-to-one relationship between welfare regime type and housing tenure (see also Barlow and Duncan 1994). He argues that whatever the tenure, housing can vary considerably in its degree of collectivism (1992, 118).[11] But Kemeny does not develop the idea further. Rose (1986b), who is interested in the mix of institutions in the provision of welfare, is more specific. Referring to the United Kingdom, he characterized owner occupation as a mix of market and family, private rentals as strictly market, and council rentals as a mix of state and market (86ff.).[12] We would like to argue that public forms of renting can vary in the degree to which they are "marketized," a function of how close the rents are to private market rents.[13] The degree to which public-sector rents are lower than private-sector rents can vary among countries and at different times. Council rents in Britain, for example, have followed private-profit rents quite closely since the 1980s.

In the private housing sector, the degree to which rents are governed by market processes also can vary. Most European countries have introduced—at least temporarily—state measures to control private rents. Ireland, Great Britain, Italy, and Spain have all implemented rent freezes at one time or another; in Germany, the Netherlands, and Italy, control measures have been more flexible. So even in the private sector, rents are not set solely by the market.

The state also plays a role in owner occupation to the extent that it regulates the prices of houses or land or subsidizes housing costs (cf. Barlow and Duncan 1994). There is virtually no Western industrialized country where home ownership is not subsidized by the state in some way. Even in the United States, the purest example of a liberal regime, the state supports owner occupation by means of tax relief. But what matters, of course, is the level of subsidization and the question of who profits from it (see Chapter 4).

There is another tenure type that seldom shows up in official statistics. *Cooperative tenure* can be viewed as a combination of owning and renting: the household owns a portion of the property value but also pays a fee—in effect, a rent—that covers mortgage and maintenance costs. The specific conditions of cooperative tenure can vary greatly, which often makes it difficult to distinguish between owning and cost renting (Kemeny 1981, 19). Cooperative forms of tenure are common in the Scandinavian countries but are rare in Anglo-Saxon countries.

Based on these considerations, we can draw several conclusions about each regime type. First, *in a liberal regime, private home ownership should be the preferred form of housing tenure.* The main ingredients of the classic liberal ideology are individual freedom, individual property rights, and individual responsibility to provide for one's self (Lipset 1991; Vorländer 1990). The free market lies at the core of economic liberalism: that markets operate without restriction is seen as essential for both economy and society to flourish.[14] Government intervention is considered positive only insofar as it helps the market operate freely or protects individuals who—for reasons beyond their control—are unable to provide for themselves.

Clearly, home ownership and owner occupancy accord best with liberal ideology. Private rental is also compatible with liberal ideology but less so than owner occupancy—a function of the liberal emphasis on individual property. Certainly regulations to hold down rents in the private sector and rent subsidies do not accord with the liberal idea of a free market. If there are state subsidies, they should go mainly to owner-occupiers to foster private property. At the same time, a small, residual public housing sector with subsidized rents is likely, given the liberal commitment to temporarily help individuals in need.

Second, *the opposite prediction, that collectivist (social democratic) regimes should generally have a small private-ownership sector appears less cogent.* At first glance, private home ownership would seem to contradict collectivist ideology; but on closer inspection, it is clear that the ideology speaks more to method than means. Central to collectivist ideology today is the belief that housing costs should be distributed to some degree as a means of guaranteeing good housing conditions for all households. Or, to put it differently, individuals and households should be decommodified to some extent so that labor market position becomes less important for attaining a decent housing standard. In principle, this goal can be achieved by any combination of subsidies and regulations for private or public rentals, cooperative housing, or private ownership. The crucial point is simply that housing costs should be collectivized to some degree. Historically, though, this has not always seemed to be the case. The roots of the collectivist ideology lie in Europe's socialist labor movement. The basic socialist position—as put forward originally, in 1872, by Friedrich Engels—is that individual home ownership leads to the embourgeoisement of the working class, which in turn weakens the labor movement. It is not surprising, then, that the socialist movement and the social democratic parties of Europe originally chose to promote rental and cooperative housing over private ownership (cf. Häußermann and Siebel 1996). But it is also true that in the course of the twentieth century, the idea of private home ownership has gained ground in social democratic parties. We therefore can no longer assume an automatic relationship between social democratic (or collectivist) ideas, and rental and co-operative forms of housing. But if there is a public rental sector in a social democratic country, it should not be residual, stigmatized, or directed toward low-income households as is likely in liberal welfare regimes; instead, it should be large, of high quality, and open to large parts of the population.

Third, *we cannot identify a clear link between conservative welfare regimes and preferred forms of housing tenure.* According to Kemeny (1992, 97ff.), in the corporatist tradition—one of the features of conservative regimes—neither the individualistic nor the collectivist ideology has achieved dominance, making it impossible to predict a regime's housing policy. What is clear, however, is that there should be more state involvement in public and/or private renting than we would find in a liberal regime.

We also might expect that the importance of the family as a welfare provider in conservative regimes would lend distinct characteristics to the housing system, that family and household should play a large role in the provision of housing. In their study of housing in Europe in the 1980s, Barlow and Duncan (1994, 30) found strong evidence that households in conservative regimes are more involved in the house-building process than are households in other regime types. For example, in the conservative regimes of France and Germany, the majority of households initiate the house-building process (the authors call this *self-promotion*). Furthermore, in France, about 10 percent of households actually build their own homes (41). That percentage is likely to be higher in Germany, where there are fewer large building companies and less catalog building (37, 41). We should add that self-building in France and Germany tends to be a working-class tradition that enables low-income households, often with the help of extended family and friends, to keep building costs down (cf. Bonvalet 1995; Häußermann and Siebel 1996; Petrowsky 1993). By comparison, Barlow and Duncan did not find self-promotion and self-building as common in Great Britain (a liberal regime) or in Sweden (a social democratic regime) as in France and Germany.

Finally, *two distinct features of the Southern European welfare regime—the small role of government in the provision of welfare and the heavy reliance on the family—should make private home ownership and private rental the main housing alternatives.* We would expect little in the way of a public housing sector to be developed in these countries. The family should play an even larger role in the provision of housing in Southern European regimes than it does in conservative regimes; Barlow and Duncan (1994, 37) also contend that it plays, at least in part, a different role. In particular, the extended family is more important in financing home ownership (Castles and Ferrera 1996). At the same time, institutions for financing housing are less developed in the Southern European countries than in the rest of Europe, so that the extended family is needed to finance private home ownership.

THE ROLE OF CLASS AND FAMILY SUPPORT IN DIFFERENT WELFARE REGIMES

From our understanding of the relationship between housing and social stratification and the relationship between housing and regime type, we can formulate two hypotheses:

- The dependence of home ownership on the household's class and income position should vary between regime types.
- Intergenerational transfers should play different roles in different welfare regimes.

We would expect the link between home ownership and household class and income to be strongest in liberal regimes, where home ownership is clearly the favored form of housing and where other tenures are either accepted as transitional (for example, young people renting in the private sector while they are students) or socially stigmatized (public housing for low-income households). The class–income dependence is strengthened by the economics of home ownership in liberal regimes, which is less cushioned by public policies than it is in other regimes: high initial costs act as a hurdle for low-income households (Kemeny 1981). Employment security is another factor here: because poor and working-class households have less job security, they often do not have the steady income stream that is necessary to acquire and then pay off a mortgage.

In contrast, in social democratic regimes, where no stigma attaches to public housing, the public rental sector should attract both working- and middle-class households (Kemeny 1981). In addition, because land prices and house prices tend to be highly regulated in social democratic regimes (cf. Barlow and Duncan 1994), home ownership should be more accessible to households from all social classes. For both reasons, home-ownership rates should be less related to class position in these regimes than in liberal regimes.

The conservative model lies somewhere in between the liberal and social democratic models. Self-building and self-promotion activities and the support of the extended family should improve access to home ownership for working-class and low-income households beyond the access available to them in liberal countries. At the same time, the regime's reluctance to take an active role in equalizing living conditions means less accessibility in conservative regimes than in social democratic regimes.

Finally, in Southern European regimes, class differences should again loom large. The reasons: few public policies to facilitate home ownership and the prominent role family financing plays in acquiring housing.

A corollary to our second hypothesis—that the role of intergenerational transfers varies in the different welfare regimes—is a rank order of the importance of those transfers in the various regimes. We would expect family gifts and inheritances to matter least in social democratic regimes, where the government is strongly and explicitly committed to equal opportunities. Also, price regulations for buildings and land should mean less need for family support in those regimes. Intergenerational transfers should be more important in liberal and conservative regimes, where the government does less to equalize access to home ownership. And, given the traditional role of kinship networks and the less-developed mortgage credit sector in Southern European regimes, it follows that intergenerational transfers should be most important there.

We expect the effects of occupational class and intergenerational transfers to differ in different welfare regimes; we do not expect differences by country for two more-general influences on home ownership. First, people who are self-employed are more likely to live in their own home because their house is typically part of their means of production. This is particularly true for self-employed farmers, who by definition own land and buildings. Second, we expect an urban–rural dimension in all of the countries under study. Land and house prices tend to be lower in rural regions, which makes access to home ownership there easier.[15]

COHORT AND LIFE COURSE EFFECTS
ON HOME OWNERSHIP

Even when we confine the analyses to the period since World War II—a constraint adhered to in most of the analyses in this book—we find enormous variation in the historical conditions for access to home ownership. In all Western industrialized countries, the period from the 1950s until the beginning of the 1970s was one of remarkable economic growth and full employment. At that time, home-ownership rates rose in virtually all countries. Households profited from rising incomes and inflation, which reduced the real costs of their mortgages and increased the value of their houses. From the 1970s to the 1990s, economic growth slowed and unemployment rates rose in most Western industrialized countries, which in turn limited the ability of young households to buy homes of their own. We can assume that many first-time homeowners overcame these hurdles with the help of their parents, who had accumulated wealth in the decades of the economic miracle. At the same time, we suppose that family support and self-building activities may have become less common over time. The impact of these two conflicting trends on the rate of home ownership among younger birth cohorts, and differences by birth cohort, are topics examined throughout this volume.

Related to the issue of birth cohort is the timing of home ownership in the life course. At least two findings suggest that younger people are becoming homeowners increasingly later in life. First, as educational opportunities and employers' demands for a better-educated workforce increase, younger people are spending more time in school and are setting up their households later. Second, in many countries, younger cohorts need more time to get settled into the labor market (Blossfeld et al. forthcoming). Phases of unemployment and insecure employment at the beginning of their careers make long-term commitments—among them, buying a house—increasingly difficult. In a cross-sectional analysis, it is not possible to see whether different generations realize home ownership at different ages in their lives. It is essential, then, to analyze housing tenure within a longitudinal framework to be able to distinguish whether it is the timing of access to home ownership or the final probability that has changed across cohorts. The question of timing is also relevant when we study class patterns of access to home ownership. In most countries, blue-collar workers face higher risks of unemployment, which means they are more likely to postpone home ownership. Most of the analyses in the chapters that follow use a life course perspective to examine housing careers and so are able to draw a clear picture of the timing aspects of home ownership.

THE COUNTRY-SPECIFIC STUDIES

In this volume, we have assembled analyses of twelve countries to shed light on the question of how access to home ownership is related to the household's position in the social inequality structure of society. Our focus is on Western industrial (or postindustrial) countries belonging to different types of welfare regimes. West Germany, France, and Belgium represent conservative regimes; the Netherlands, Denmark, and Norway are examples of social democratic regimes;[16] Italy and Spain are examples of Southern European regimes; and Britain, Ireland, and the United States are liberal regimes. In addition, we include Israel, a country with an exceptionally high immigration rate and specific housing policies that show certain collectivist traits.

The main questions addressed in the chapters are the following:

- What are the differences between the ways in which occupational class and income affect the probability and timing of home ownership in the life course?
- What role do intergenerational transfers play in a household's access to home ownership?
- How do patterns of access to home ownership vary across birth cohorts? And how can that variation be explained?

Most of the chapters also include information on macroeconomic trends and housing policies in the country under discussion, to highlight important features of the housing system. In the studies of home ownership in the United States and Israel, the issues of race and ethnicity are raised. The study of Ireland examines the consequences of home ownership on the inequality structure. And the study of Belgium looks at the extent to which housing policy is reaching its intended target, low-income households.

Notes

1. But there are also important differences in the arguments put forward by Saunders and Beck. Most important, Saunders insists there are still important so-

cial cleavages, with home ownership playing a prominent role, while Beck sees a general individualization in which clear-cut social cleavages are not important anymore.

2. Most researchers agree that the household, not the individual, is the central unit of social stratification. However, there has been considerable debate over the method by which that unit is determined. Traditional thinking is that the man's labor market position is more important than his female partner's position, so it is sufficient to consider the man's position (Goldthorpe 1983). But that thinking has been seriously challenged by the increasing labor market attachment of women (cf. Szelényi 1994).

3. However, starting in the 1980s, housing prices fell in Germany (cf. Häußermann and Siebel 1996, 251) and several other countries. Conditions were particularly drastic in the United Kingdom between 1989 and 1993, when the housing market collapsed and the price of houses fell dramatically (see, for example, Forrest and Murie 1995a).

4. In 1978, Saunders insisted that home ownership is the basis of "housing classes," or what Weber described as *property classes*. By 1990, he argued that home ownership does not produce housing classes but instead establishes a "consumption sector cleavage."

5. The proposition that labor market inequalities are deepened by differences in the likelihood of intergenerational transfers rests on the well-supported assumptions of relatively high marital homogamy and of a positive association between an individual's class position and the class position of the family of origin in Western industrial and postindustrial societies (see, for example, Blossfeld and Timm 2003; and Erikson and Goldthorpe 1992).

6. Still, in some of the studies described in this book, household income was used as a proxy for class position.

7. State subsidies can take various forms, including tax deductions and special low-rate mortgages. For specific examples, see the country chapters.

8. Kemeny (1992) rejects the concept of *ideology* as "false consciousness" or "some distorted version of an absolute truth." Instead he offers this definition: "a loosely organized set of ideas defining human nature (the individual), the principles underlying the organisation of social life (civil society), and the values that govern the political order (state)" (87).

9. Esping-Andersen defined three welfare regime types: social democratic, liberal, and conservative. In the Scandinavian countries, social democratic parties were in office for several decades and so have been very influential. In the United States and other liberal countries, labor organizations remained relatively powerless. In conservative countries—Germany is an example—labor organizations have played a role but less so than in the Scandinavian countries.

10. A number of other authors insist that the state is not the only nonprofit provider of welfare services (see, for example, Johnson 1987). They would argue that voluntary agencies, for example, should be considered along with the state.

11. Kemeny further argues that even within the same tenure status, different strategies, collective as well as individualistic, might exist (119).

12. According to Rose, the market component of council rentals reflects the fact that tenants pay rent for this type of housing.

13. In this context the distinction between "private-profit renting" and "cost renting" introduced by Kemeny (1981) is useful. *Private-profit rents* are market rents that typically rise when house prices go up. In contrast, the *cost rents* that are common in the public housing sector are based on original construction costs (plus maintenance costs) and may well be averaged across all buildings that belong to an administrative unit. Pooled historical costs can offer two advantages for tenants: (1) rents do not go up over time as house prices rise, and (2) the problem of high initial costs can be mitigated by the practice of averaging costs across units. Cost rents, then, are typically lower than market rents.

14. Actually, the idea that markets function best when there is no state intervention is idealistic and fundamentally wrong. Markets are social institutions that work only when regulated by at least basic rules, among them individual property rights (cf. Granovetter 1985).

15. But see the results for Israel (Chapter 13), where the urban–rural pattern is heavily influenced by government policies.

16. The Netherlands could be classified as either a social democratic regime or a conservative regime, depending on the field of public policy. In terms of housing, however, the Netherlands has adopted a social democratic approach: it has a large public housing sector that does not appear to be stigmatized, and most development land in the country has been municipalized (cf. Barlow and Duncan 1994).

References

Barlow, James, and Simon Duncan. 1994. *Success and failure in housing provision.* Trowbridge, UK: Redwood Books.

Beck, Ulrich. 1986. *Risikogesellschaft. Auf dem Weg in eine andere Moderne.* Frankfurt am Main: Suhrkamp.

———. 1994. Jenseits von Klasse und Stand? In *Riskante Freiheiten*, edited by Ulrich Beck and Elisabeth Beck-Gernsheim, 43–60. Frankfurt am Main: Suhrkamp.

Blau, Peter M., and Otis Dudley Duncan. 1967. *The American occupational structure.* New York: Wiley.

Blossfeld, Hans-Peter, and Andreas Timm, eds. 2003. *Who marries whom? Educational systems as marriage markets in modern societies. A comparison of thirteen countries.* Dordrecht: Kluwer.

Blossfeld, Hans-Peter, Erik Klijzing, Melinda Mills, and Karin Kurz. Forthcoming. *The losers of globalization: Becoming an adult in uncertain times.*

Boelhouwer, Peter, and Harry van der Heijden. 1992. *Housing systems in Europe: Part I. A comparative study of housing policy*. Delft: Delft University Press.

Bonvalet, Catherine. 1995. The extended family and housing in France. In *Housing and family wealth. Comparative international perspectives*, edited by Ray Forrest and Allan Murie, 148–67. London: Routledge.

Brauns, Hildegard, Markus Gangl, and Stefani Scherer. 1999. Education and unemployment: Patterns of labour market entry in France, the United Kingdom and West Germany. *Mannheimer Zentrum für Europäische Sozialforschung—Arbeitspapiere* 6.

Castles, Francis G. 1998. The really big trade-off: Home ownership and the welfare state in the New World and the Old. *Acta Politica* 33 (1): 5–19.

Castles, Francis G., and Maurizio Ferrera. 1996. Home ownership and the welfare state: Is Southern Europe different? *South European Society & Politics* 1 (2): 163–85.

Clark, William A. V., Marinus C. Deurloo, and Frans M. Dieleman. 1994. Tenure changes in the context of micro-level family and macro-level economic shifts. *Urban Studies* 31:137–54.

———. 1997. Entry into home-ownership in Germany: Comparisons with the United States. *Urban Studies* 34:7–19.

Courgeau, Daniel, and Eva Lelièvre. 1992. Interrelations between first home-ownership, constitution of the family, and professional occupation in France. In *Demographic applications of event history analysis*, edited by James Trussell, Richard Hankinson, and Judith Tilson, 120–40. Oxford: Clarendon Press.

Doling, John. 1997. *Comparative housing policy. Government and housing in advanced industrialized countries*. Houndmills, UK: Macmillan Press.

Erikson, Robert, and John Goldthorpe. 1992. *The constant flux. A study of class mobility in industrial societies*. Oxford: Clarendon Press.

Esping-Andersen, Gøsta. 1990. *The three worlds of welfare capitalism*. Princeton: Princeton University Press.

———. 1999. *Social foundations of postindustrial economies*. Oxford: Oxford University Press.

Forrest, Ray, and Allan Murie. 1995a. Accumulating evidence: Housing and family wealth in Britain. In *Housing and family wealth. Comparative international perspectives*, edited by Ray Forrest and Allan Murie, 58–85. London: Routledge.

Forrest, Ray, and Allan Murie, eds. 1995b. *Housing and family wealth. Comparative international perspectives*. London: Routledge.

Forrest, Ray, Alan Murie, and P. Williams. 1990. *Home ownership*. London: Unwin Hyman.

Gangl, Markus. 2001. *Unemployment dynamics in the United States and West*

Germany: Economic restructuring, institutions, and labour market processes over the 1980s and 1990s. Mannheim: Fakultät für Sozialwissenschaften der Universität Mannheim.

Goldthorpe, John H. 1983. Women and class analysis. In defence of the conventional view. *Sociology* 17:465–88.

Granovetter, Mark. 1985. Economic action, social structure and embeddedness. *American Journal of Sociology* 91:481–510.

Hamnett, Chris. 1991. A nation of inheritors? Housing inheritance, wealth and inequality in Britain. *Journal of Social Policy* 20:509–36.

Häußermann, Hartmut, and Walter Siebel. 1996. *Soziologie des Wohnens. Eine Einführung in Wandel und Ausdifferenzierung des Wohnens.* Weinheim, Ger.: Juventa.

Johnson, Norman. 1987. *The welfare state in transition: The theory and practice of welfare pluralism.* Brighton, UK: Wheatsheaf.

Jurado Guerrero, Teresa, and Manuela Naldini. 1996. Is the South so different? Italian and Spanish families in comparative perspective. Special issue, *Southern European Society & Politics* 1:42–66.

Kemeny, Jim. 1981. *The myth of home ownership: Private versus public choice in housing tenure.* London: Routledge and Kegan Paul.

———. 1992. *Housing and social theory.* London: Routledge.

Kendig, Hal L. 1984. Housing careers, life cycle and residential mobility: Implications for the housing market. *Urban Studies* 21:271–83.

Kurz, Karin, Nikolei Steinhage, and Katrin Golsch. 2001. Global competition, uncertainty and the transition to adulthood. GLOBALIFE Working Paper, Faculty of Sociology, University of Bielefeld, Bielefeld, Ger.

Lauterbach, Wolfgang, and Kurt Lüscher. 1996. Erben und die Verbundenheit der Lebensverläufe von Familienmitgliedern. *Kölner Zeitschrift für Soziologie und Sozialpsychologie* 48 (1): 66–95.

Lipset, Seymour Martin. 1991. American exceptionalism reaffirmed. In *Is America different? A new look at American exceptionalism,* edited by Byron E. Shafer, 1–45. Oxford: Clarendon Press.

McCrone, Gavin, and Mark Stephens. 1995. *Housing policy in Britain and Europe.* London: University College.

Motel, Andreas, and Marc Szydlik. 1999. Private Transfers zwischen den Generationen. *Zeitschrift für Soziologie* 28 (1): 3–22.

Mulder, Clara H., and Pieter Hooimeijer. 1995. Moving into owner-occupation: Compositional and contextual effects on the propensity to become a homeowner. *Netherlands Journal of Housing and the Built Environment* 10 (1): 55–76.

Mulder, Clara H., and Jeroen Smits. 1999. First-time home-ownership of couples: The effect of intergenerational transmission. *European Sociological Review* 15 (3): 323–37.

Mulder, Clara H., and Michael Wagner. 1998. First-time home-ownership in the family life course: A West German–Dutch comparison. *Urban Studies* 35 (4): 687–713.

Munro, Moira. 1988. Housing wealth and inheritance. *Journal of Social Policy* 17 (4): 417–36.

Petrowsky, Werner. 1993. *Arbeiterhaushalte mit Hauseigentum. Die Bedeutung des Erbes bei der Eigentumsbildung.* Bremen: Universität Bremen.

Rose, Richard. 1986a. Common goals but different roles: The state's contribution to the welfare mix. In *The welfare state East and West*, edited by Richard Rose and Rie Shiratori, 13–39. Oxford: Oxford University Press.

———. 1986b. The dynamics of the welfare mix in Britain. In *The welfare state East and West*, edited by Richard Rose and Rie Shiratori, 80–106. Oxford: Oxford University Press.

Saunders, Peter. 1978. Domestic property and social class. *International Journal of Urban and Regional Research* 2:233–51.

———. 1990. *A nation of home owners.* London: Unwin Hyman.

Savage, Mike, Paul Watt, and Sara Arber. 1992. Social class, consumption divisions and housing mobility. In *Consumption and class. Divisions and change*, edited by Roger Burrows and Catherine Marsh, 52–70. New York: St. Martin's Press.

Schmidt, Stephan. 1989. Convergence theory, labour movements, and corporatism: The case of housing. *Scandinavian Housing & Planning Research* 6:83–101.

Shavit, Yossi, and Hans-Peter Blossfeld, eds. 1993. *Persistent inequality. Changing educational attainment in thirteen countries.* Boulder, CO: Westview Press.

Shavit, Yossi, and Walter Müller, eds. 1998. *From school to work. A comparative study of qualification and occupations in thirteen countries.* Oxford: Oxford University Press.

Szelényi, Szonja. 1994. Women and class structure. In *Social stratification. Class, race and gender in sociological perspective*, edited by David B. Grusky, 577–82. Boulder, CO: Westview Press.

Vorländer, Hans. 1990. "American Creed," liberale Tradition und politische Kultur der USA. In *Liberale Demokratie in Europa und den USA. Festschrift für Kurt L. Shell*, edited by Hans Vorländer and Franz Greß, 11–33. Frankfurt am Main: Campus.

CHAPTER TWO

Home Ownership and Social Inequality in West Germany

Karin Kurz

Only a few recent sociological studies address the social distribution and the attainment of home ownership in Germany (Häußermann and Siebel 1996; Kurz 2001; Mulder and Wagner 1998; Wagner and Mulder 2000). This is surprising because such studies are relevant from both a social-policy and a social-inequality perspective. It is the latter that interests us here.

From a social-inequality perspective, three issues make the study of access to home ownership particularly relevant. First, home ownership is an investment that greatly influences the household's welfare and assets. Households that built or bought a house during the decades immediately after World War II saw their housing costs go down and their house values go up over time (Häußermann and Siebel 1996, 242ff.). Second, labor market position typically skews the household's access to home ownership: the worse that position, the less accessible home ownership. If home ownership produces capital gains, class differences in access to home ownership deepen existing inequalities produced by the labor market. Third, through gifts and inheritances, wealth is kept within families over generations. Empirical studies unequivocally report that people in a favorable labor market position are more likely to receive gifts and inheritances (Kendig 1984; Lauterbach and Lüscher 1996; Szydlik 1999). So the pattern of intergenerational transfers also is likely to reinforce the inequalities produced by the labor market.

I thank Fabrizio Bernardi, Hans-Peter Blossfeld, Tony Fahey, and Thorsten Schneider for their helpful comments.

In this chapter, we consider the second and third issues for several birth cohorts in West Germany.[1] In Germany, the proportion of households that own homes is very low compared with other Western industrialized countries: in what was West Germany, just 43 percent of all households were owner-occupiers in 1998; in the area that formerly was East Germany, the rate was even lower—just 31 percent. The percentages in all of the other countries studied in this book are higher, ranging from about 50 percent in the Netherlands to about 80 percent in Norway and Spain. One question that interests us in this analysis, then, is why home-ownership rates in Germany are generally so low.

Another issue that concerns us has to do with class structure in Germany. Class differences with respect to home ownership in West Germany after World War II were not very strong: According to cross-sectional data, the proportion of homeowners among working-class and middle-class households was similar until the end of the 1970s (Geißler 1996, 66; Glatzer 1980, 248; Häußermann and Siebel 1996, 238).[2] Of course, the houses of working-class families are usually smaller and of lower quality and value than the houses of white-collar workers and civil servants, and they more often are located in less attractive neighborhoods and in smaller towns or villages (Herlyn and Herlyn 1983, 71). Still, blue-collar workers on average earn less than other workers (see, for example, Geißler 1996, 58ff.). How, then, do we explain the relatively high proportion of lower-income households that own homes in Germany?

To understand the low home-ownership rates in the country, we examined West German housing policies after World War II. What we discovered is that the high quality and affordable prices of housing in the public and private rental sectors have kept renting an attractive option for many households.

The second question—Why are the home-ownership rates of blue-collar workers comparatively high?—is more difficult to answer. The analysis here begins with a brief history of home ownership among manual laborers and an examination of what motivates home ownership within the working class. The analysis continues with data on access to home ownership drawn from three birth cohorts: people born between 1929 and 1931, between 1939 and 1941, and between 1949 and 1951. To better understand working-class home ownership, the empirical analysis addresses the following questions:

Does living in a rural community facilitate access to home ownership for working-class households? Are there differences in access to home ownership within the working class, between skilled workers and workers who are semiskilled or unskilled? Does the wife's employment increase the likelihood of home ownership in working-class households? What role do intergenerational transfers play in the transition to home ownership for those households? In addition, the cohort data and a life course perspective allow us to investigate how opportunities for home ownership have changed across generations and when in the life course the transition to home ownership typically occurs.

HOME OWNERSHIP AFTER WORLD WAR II

Official data on the distribution of housing status in West Germany are available only from 1957. They show that households headed by a self-employed worker are most likely to own a home: in each of the years listed in Table 2.1, more than 60 percent of these households were homeowners. For other groups of workers, home ownership increased from close to 20 percent in 1957 to more than 40 percent in 1998. Geißler (1996) suggests that the lower rates at the start of the period must be seen in the context of the destruction of buildings during World War II and the high numbers of refugees after the war.

Until the early 1970s, working-class households were somewhat more likely than middle-class households (headed by a nonmanual worker or civil servant) to live in their own home. That began to change in the course of the 1970s: toward the end of the period we studied, the home-ownership rate of manual workers remained around 35 percent, while the rate for middle-class workers rose to more than 40 percent (see also Häußermann and Siebel 1996, 242). This indicates that the relationship between occupational position and home ownership is highly variable over time.

Official housing data also show that married couples and households with children more often live in their own home than do others. The same is true for households in rural regions (see, for example, Glatzer 1980; Häußermann and Siebel 1996; and Lauterbach and Lüscher 1996). Furthermore, home ownership is clearly associated with household income (Laue 1995). For example, in 1993 only 30 percent of all households with income less

TABLE 2.1

Home ownership among households by occupational position of the head of household, West Germany, 1957–1998, and East Germany, 1998

	PERCENTAGE OF HOMEOWNERS										East Germany
Occupational position of head of household	1957	1960	1965	1968	1972	1978	1987	1993	1998	1998
Self-employed	64.6	67.5	66.8	69.1	66.7	67.1	64.7	61.5	60.4	55.2
Nonmanual worker/ civil servant	19.3[a]	21.8	22.3	27.0	28.7	35.5	41.2	42.6	42.5	30.3
Manual worker		26.4	27.2	32.3	31.3	34.1	35.7	35.5	35.0	36.3
Not employed	25.6	28.5	28.1	31.3	30.2	31.5	31.0	39.9	43.1	26.4
AVERAGE	28.8	32.3	31.3	35.1	33.5	36.1	37.8	41.6	42.6	31.0

SOURCES: 1957–1968: Glatzer (1980, 248); data for all other years were taken from publications of the German statistical office (Statistisches Bundesamt).

[a]Includes manual workers.

than DM 2,500 owned property or buildings, compared with 54 percent of households with income between DM 2,500 and DM 5,000, and 80 percent of households earning between DM 5,000 and DM 35,000.

THE COUNTRY CONTEXT

Macroeconomic Conditions

Economic expansion in West Germany from the 1950s through the mid-1970s provided suitable conditions for households to buy their own home: marked economic growth, rising real wages, favorable mortgage rates, and low unemployment (Ambrosius and Kaelble 1992; Häußermann and Siebel 1996, 246ff.; Miegel 1983).[3] During this period, even low-income households were increasingly able to own their home. By the early 1980s, conditions had changed—real wages were stagnant or even falling, interest rates were rising, and unemployment was increasing—making home ownership more expensive and so less accessible to low-income households.[4] We find evidence of the impact of the economic downturn on the housing market in records of new construction: between 1980 and 1985, the number of building permits was down by more than 40 percent.[5] More evidence comes from the high number of compulsory home auctions held during the first half of the 1980s (Häußermann and Siebel, 246). From the mid-1980s to the end of the decade, economic conditions improved somewhat: mortgage interest rates fell, land prices were stable, and the unemployment rate went down slightly.

Housing Policy

Since the 1950s, two components of housing policy in West Germany—the public housing program *(sozialer Wohnungsbau)* and subsidies for private home ownership—have had a significant impact on the housing situation of households (Häußermann and Siebel 1996, 146).[6] The public housing program was particularly influential in the first decades after World War II, when the country was facing a tremendous housing shortage. The program relied mainly on large nonprofit housing organizations, which received government subsidies for building public housing.[7] But a change in the law meant that private construction companies also participated in the public housing program. State subsidies for public housing were now open to anyone who observed certain regulations (Häußermann and Siebel, 152): restricting profits, maintaining certain quality standards, making low-rent flats available to low-income households, charging cost rents (versus market rents), and granting tenants the unrestricted right to stay in their flat (Häußermann and Siebel, 150–51). The obligation to observe these regulations, however, was limited to the duration of the public subsidies. A huge number of flats for the rental market were built under the public housing program during the first decades after the war (Häußermann and Siebel, 152). The relevance of the public housing program has decreased over the last few decades. In 1986, support for public housing was stopped altogether; but it was reinstated at the beginning of the 1990s, when a reunified Germany once again faced huge housing shortages.

It is important to note that the public housing sector in the Federal Republic of Germany never targeted only the poor (as is common in Anglo-Saxon countries), focusing instead on the middle mass of households. Although the size of the sector varied, at most it covered 30 percent of rentals as a whole (Häußermann and Siebel 1996, 154). This means that private rentals, which are not conditioned on charging cost rents, always have made up the majority of the rental market. It does not mean that the rents in the private market are necessarily higher than those in the public housing sector: flats in old buildings typically are cheaper than those in new buildings. Also, the comparable-rents legislation passed in 1971 restricts rent increases in the private rental sector to a prescribed annual percentage. Tenants who have lived in a flat for many years typically pay lower rents than do those with newer leases. Furthermore, tenants enjoy housing security: the law allows landlords to evict tenants only for very limited reasons. West Germany's rent and occupancy controls were designed to make renting an attractive and secure option for households and, at the same time, to allow landlords and housing organizations to make a reasonable profit. Moreover, the regulations have made it unnecessary for the country to rely on rent freezes or other drastic measures.[8]

Currently the most important—at least financially—component of German housing policy are subsidies for private home ownership. During the first decades after World War II, government support for owner occupancy was seen as synonymous with support for families. A home of one's own with a garden was thought to be the ideal place for families to raise children

(Bahrdt 1968; Häußermann and Siebel 1996, 147ff.). There was also a political motivation for home ownership: to bind the working classes more closely to the capitalist system (Bahrdt, 71; Häußermann and Siebel, 734; Herlyn and Herlyn 1983, 82). Public subsidies for private home ownership have had the unequivocal support of conservative, liberal, and social democratic parties in power since World War II.

Government support for home ownership takes the form of tax relief. One policy offers tax advantages to those who save with a building and loan association *(Bausparkassen)*. The program is an extremely popular path to home ownership in Germany. It requires the household to save at least 40 percent of the amount needed to buy or build a house. Once the 40 percent has been saved, the association loans the household the balance at a very low rate of interest. There is one main drawback to the system: time. It takes a household typically 5 to 10 years to save the required sum, which translates into a long wait for would-be homeowners.

Into the 1990s, the government also allowed home buyers tax deductions based on the price of a house or flat—a policy that favored high-income households. In 1995, a tax bonus that does not vary by income was substituted for the deduction. In addition, there has always been tax relief for families with children.

All in all, housing policy in West Germany has not undergone major changes since World War II. The official rhetoric since the 1950s—owner-occupied housing is the best housing, especially for families with children—still drives housing policy today. But extensive construction in the rental sector, especially in the first decades after the war, partially supported by a public housing program and the regulation of private rents, has contributed to high-quality yet affordable rentals for the middle mass of households. Moreover, renting is not in any way stigmatized or thought of as a transitional tenure for young people.

At the same time, becoming a homeowner is an expensive and time-consuming process in Germany today. Compared with other countries—the United States and the Netherlands, for example—construction and land prices are high (Clark, Deurloo, and Dieleman 1997; Mulder and Wagner 1998). And down payments of 20 percent to 30 percent of the purchase price can mean years of saving for a home. In sum, the relatively low home-ownership rate in Germany is a by-product of housing policies that make the decision to rent versus own a choice that many households make in favor of renting—in particular, in urban areas, where land and house prices are relatively high and where the rental sector is well developed.

HOME OWNERSHIP IN THE WORKING CLASS

Historical Background

Although home-ownership rates in Germany are relatively low, the proportion of working-class households that own homes is relatively high. This relationship predates World War II and is, at least in part, a function of the agrarian origins of the typical industrial worker, whose family often owned land and buildings (see, for example, Müller 1986).[9]

Unhappily, we have no official statistics on the distribution of home ownership by social class or occupational status for Germany as a whole throughout the nineteenth century and the first half of the twentieth century (Petrowsky 1993, 107). Research on the history of working-class housing instead has concentrated on the size and quality of workers' homes. It tells us that housing conditions in towns were much worse for low-income households than for other population groups (Niethammer 1976). And we have evidence from several towns at the beginning of the last century that manual workers were less likely to own their own homes than were other groups of workers (Petrowsky, 108ff.).[10] In the studies that do distinguish among manual workers by skill level, skilled workers owned their homes much more often than did semiskilled and unskilled workers. But the majority of the working class lived not in cities but in villages and small towns, where home ownership was (and still is) more affordable.[11]

Statistics are available for a few rural municipalities; they show that a large percentage of working-class households owned land and buildings (Petrowsky, 92ff.). Those communities were in the main rural but close to or with train connections to urban industrial areas, which enabled workers to commute daily or weekly. Commuting to work, which was quite common in the Ruhr and in Baden-Württemberg in particular, allowed workers to continue to be integrated in village life and to improve their livelihood by farming in addition to their other work. In 1925, almost a third of manual and nonmanual workers cultivated a piece of land (Stockmann quoted in Petrowsky, 125ff.).[12] In fact, certain industrial companies—particularly mining companies in the rural areas of the Ruhr and Saarland—directly supported land and home ownership (Tenfelde 1977).

In summary, at the beginning of the twentieth century, most industrial workers came from rural areas. Often they were the sons of self-employed farmers, so their family typically owned land.[13] Those workers who remained "rooted in the soil"—that is, workers who commuted to their industrial jobs—were able to keep their land and stay integrated in their village networks.

Motivations for Home Ownership

For many working-class families, owning a home is still an important life goal (Häußermann and Siebel 1996, 267). For example, Glatzer (1980) demonstrates that at the same income level, manual workers more often own houses or flats than do nonmanual workers and civil servants. And a qualitative study by Petrowsky (1993) shows that working-class families make considerable effort to realize their dream of living within their own four walls. Although much of the motivation here lies in the rural tradition—land is the most important means of earning a living—other factors are at work too. First, real estate has proved to hold its value during periods of inflation and currency reforms (Häußermann and Siebel, 267). Second, there is the real or assumed security a house offers (Häußermann and Siebel; Kaufmann 1973; Lauterbach and Lüscher 1996, 68ff.). *Security* means many things: no fear of being evicted, a haven in old age, a hedge against unemployment or disability, and, finally, the means to pass something along to one's children. Providing for the future should be of particular importance for working-class households, most of which can expect only a small pension in old age.

A third motivation is independence: the freedom to lay out one's home as one wishes (Häußermann and Siebel 1996, 229; Herlyn and Herlyn 1983, 79ff.). That this motivation is particularly relevant to manual workers makes intuitive sense. These workers usually do not have the income to rent a large, high-quality apartment, but many of them do have manual skills that can compensate, at least in part, for their lack of money (Häußermann and Siebel, 269; Herlyn and Herlyn, 71; Petrowsky 1993).

Finally, there is the need among blue-collar workers to use their skills to create something lasting of their own. Owning a home, working on it, is a project that promises manual workers security and independence. It also is evidence that they have achieved a certain standard of living and of providing for their family.

Attaining Home Ownership

A number of different resources can be used to buy a home: savings, an inheritance, gifts, as well as social capital (Glatzer 1980; Häußermann and Siebel 1996; Herlyn and Herlyn 1983; Petrowsky 1993). Working-class households generally rely on a combination of these resources. Häußermann and Siebel (259) use the term *investive lifestyle* to describe a way of organizing life and household around a central goal, home ownership. The household's time, money, and work schedules are all directed toward that goal. For example, while a couple household is saving up to buy a house, it is not unusual for the woman to work and for the man to work extra hours (Petrowsky, 45). With the funds to build or buy an existing house in hand, it is not unusual for the household to spend every free minute building or renovating the house. This is often a group effort, with relatives, neighbors, and friends helping out. "A worker builds his house over thirty years: first, his brother-in-law's house, then the neighbor's house, then with their help his own house, and finally he helps his son" (Petrowsky, 260).[14] A prerequisite of this exchange of social capital is immobility (Häußermann and Siebel; Petrowsky). It seems likely, then, that working-class households that do not live near their family of origin are less likely to own a home.

The opposite of the investive lifestyle is the *consumption lifestyle* (Häußermann and Siebel 1996, 282ff.). Here, instead of investing all of its available resources—including financial and social capital, physical labor, and manual skills—over many years to own a home, the household assumes a large mortgage to buy or build a house. Working-class households usually do not have the income to pursue a consumption strategy; the strategy is an option only for households with high incomes from market work. Notice that in the consumption lifestyle, market exchange is dominant; in the investive lifestyle, home ownership is realized primarily at a distance from the market.

Intergenerational Transfers of Wealth

Several qualitative studies on home ownership find that intergenerational transfers of wealth are often indispensable for access to home ownership in low-income and working-class households (Meinecke 1987; Neubeck 1981;

Petrowsky 1993, 23ff.).[15] But the reality is that these households are not very likely to receive large inheritances or gifts from their family: both the probability of inheriting (Lauterbach and Lüscher 1996, 83; Szydlik 1999, 90ff.) and the size of inheritances (Engel 1985; Schlomann 1991; Szydlik, 92ff.) decrease with occupational status (or income) and educational level.[16] The findings are similar for parental gifts of money to children: The likelihood and size of those gifts tend to be smaller the lower the parents' income and money capital and the lower the income and money capital of the children (Motel and Szydlik 1999).[17] Low-income households are at a double disadvantage: low earnings make it difficult for them to accumulate wealth on their own, and they are less likely to receive assets through inheritance or gifts. Ultimately, then, labor market inequalities are reinforced by the different probabilities of receiving intergenerational transfers (Lauterbach and Lüscher; Munro 1988; Szydlik)—an effect alleviated only by the self-help and mutual support that facilitate home ownership for working-class households, especially in rural areas.[18]

It could be argued that the effect of an inheritance on a household's ability to buy a home is weak because people typically become homeowners well before the time they are likely to inherit assets from their parents (Lauterbach and Lüscher 1996; Munro 1988). But Lauterbach and Lüscher found that a high proportion of individuals who received an inheritance between 1960 and 1988—45 percent—did so before their forty-first birthday, at a stage in life when it is quite common to buy a first home. Their analysis also reveals that almost two-thirds of the heirs were already homeowners. It seems likely that many households that inherit money and other assets from their parents have also been gifted while their parents were alive, which facilitates home ownership for those households.

The thesis that labor market inequalities are reinforced through intergenerational transfers appears convincing. But we suspect that a strong polarization between social classes in terms of the likelihood of home ownership has not yet evolved. The reason lies in the enormous improvement in living standards in the first few decades after World War II, which enabled a growing proportion of working-class and low-income people—primarily those born between 1930 and 1940—to buy homes. This population, which was represented in our study by two birth cohorts, was able to profit from favorable interest rates and growing real wages to a greater extent than those born around 1950 (the youngest birth cohort we studied). The economic downturn since the 1980s has worsened conditions for the later cohort, probably for low-income households in particular. But even if the younger cohort experienced worsened economic conditions, we can assume that many of its members were able to profit from the prosperity of their parents.

DATA AND METHODS

Our analyses were based on data collected for the German Life History Study (Mayer and Brückner 1989), an examination of three birth cohorts (1929–1931, 1939–1941, and 1949–1951).[19] Between 1981 and 1983, the researchers interviewed about 700 West Germans from each cohort. Using a standardized questionnaire, they asked participants retrospectively about their education, occupations, couple relationships, children, geographic mobility, and housing. Information on these different aspects of the life course was recorded in months. The housing questions asked about household composition, housing status (home ownership or form of rental), and household status (own household or another's).

In our analyses, we examined the transition from parental household (or another household where the respondent was not the householder) or own household in a rented home, to own household in an owned home. We assumed a respondent was a homeowner when he or she reported living in his or her own household and in an owner-occupied home. This operationalization was problematic when a person was living in his or her own household in a house owned by someone else—parents, for example. But given the data, we could not circumvent this problem.

The statistical models used in the analyses were continuous event history models, piecewise constant exponential models, and simple exponential models in which time dependence was taken into account by specific time-dependent variables (cf. Blossfeld and Rohwer 2001). The models predicted the rate of transition (the hazard rate) to home ownership. Whenever possible, the explanatory variables were constructed as time-dependent variables. This was done for the respondent's occupational status, the wife's employment status, the marriage phase, community size, relationship status, and children's ages. Three variables were time constant: birth cohort, living in an owned home during childhood, and father's occupational status.

Whenever the start of a marriage was used to construct a time-dependent variable or the time axis underlying an analysis, the start was set at three months before the marriage. This was done to correct for possible measurement errors and to include transitions to home ownership that occurred shortly before marriage (on the assumption that it was the upcoming marriage that led to the home purchase).

HYPOTHESES

The analyses tested several hypotheses:

- That older respondents—those born around 1930 and 1940—were able to profit from the favorable economic conditions in the first decades after World War II and so were more likely to own a home.
- That households in small municipalities are in a better position to achieve home ownership than are households in larger municipalities, especially big cities. The key factors here: access to support networks and less expensive land and housing.
- That married couples and couples who are expecting or have a child are more likely to become homeowners than single persons are.
- That the likelihood and timing of owning a home vary with the man's labor market position. If this thesis is right, then self-employed people should be most likely to own their own home, followed by white-collar workers and civil servants and, finally, blue-collar workers. We also would expect to find variation within each occupational group, a function of relative market position. So semiskilled and unskilled manual workers should be least likely to own a home.[20] Earlier studies in West Germany neglected this differentiation within the working-class in part because relevant data were lacking (Glatzer 1980; Häußermann and Siebel 1996). But British studies have shown that semiskilled and unskilled workers are far less likely to become homeowners than are skilled workers (Watt 1993).
- That the wife's employment matters for home ownership, but that the higher the husband's occupational position, the less important the wife's employment is for achieving home ownership. Petrowsky (1993) has shown that the wife's employment can be the means by which home ownership becomes possible. The data from the German Life History Study did not allow us to examine another strategy to increase household income—the husband's working overtime.
- That respondents whose fathers were blue-collar workers are more likely to become homeowners than are other persons. Increasing parts of the population were able to buy products and services on the market with the enormous rise in the living standard after World War II. Hence, the culture of mutual support in the working class probably has lost significance over

generations. The tradition is most likely to be found in households where the parents belong or belonged to the working class.

- That parents' owning a home increases the likelihood of home ownership for their adult children. This effect would seem to be more important for working-class families than for other families. Several studies show that inheritances and gifts can play an important role in the attainment of home ownership (cf., for example, Mulder and Wagner, 1998; Murphy 1984; Szydlik 1999). Unfortunately, the German Life History Study did not ask any questions about inheritances and gifts. But it did ask whether respondents' parents owned their own home, and that became our proxy for intergenerational transfers.

EMPIRICAL ANALYSES

Basic Factors in Access to Home Ownership

Birth Cohort

We expected to find higher home-ownership rates in the two older birth cohorts. Our thinking: those born at the start of the 1930s and 1940s were able to profit from the favorable economic conditions in the first decades after World War II and so were more likely to own their own homes. Although this hypothesis makes intuitive sense, we were unable to confirm it using the data from the life history study. This is visible in Figure 2.1, where the survivor function for each birth cohort is plotted.[21] The problem: the data were collected in the early 1980s, just as the youngest cohort was approaching the age at which most households buy their first home. We believe that if later data on this cohort were available, they would confirm that the likelihood of home ownership for this cohort decreased in later years with the deterioration of macroeconomic conditions.

Urban–Rural Differences

Several studies indicate that the use of support networks is a typical strategy by which working-class households realize the dream of owning a home (Häußermann and Siebel 1996; Petrowsky 1993). We could not test that hypothesis directly because the life history study did not collect data on support networks. Instead, we relied on place of residence—village, small or medium-sized town, or big city—as a proxy for the availability of support networks. Our assumption was that support networks are more common in rural areas (villages and small cities) than in urban centers (big cities). The

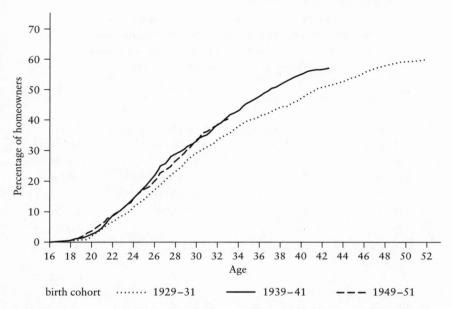

Figure 2.1. Survivor functions for the transition to home ownership, by birth cohort, West Germany

SOURCE: Author's calculations based on the German Life History Study.

results, shown in Table 2.2, indicate that home-ownership rates in villages and small cities are indeed higher than those in big cities.[22] Of course, the difficulty with using a proxy is knowing the underlying cause of the statistical effect. We expect that the availability of support networks in rural areas increases home-ownership rates in those areas; but we know that lower land prices in rural areas may also be a factor in those higher rates, perhaps the more important factor.

Another problem we faced was linking higher home-ownership rates in rural areas to what was the focus of this study: an examination of social inequality in home ownership. We expected an interaction effect with occupational class: that is, we believe working-class households in particular should profit from integration into rural communities because they are more in need of support networks and those networks are primarily found in rural areas (Bertram 1995). In the same way, we would argue that lower land prices in rural areas should make access to home ownership easier in those areas for low-income households.

TABLE 2.2

Transition to first-time home ownership by birth cohort,
place of residence, and marital status, West Germany
(piecewise constant exponential model)

Variable	Coefficient	Exp(coefficient)
Age		
16–21	−7.1867[a]	0.0008
21–26	−7.0816[a]	0.0008
26–31	−7.3454[a]	0.0006
31–36	−7.4896[a]	0.0006
36–41	−7.6304[a]	0.0005
41–46	−7.8675[a]	0.0004
>46	−8.0793[a]	0.0003
Birth cohort		
1929–1931	Ref.	
1939–1941	0.1836[a]	1.2015
1949–1951	0.1678[b]	1.1826
Place of residence		
Village	Ref.	
Small or medium-sized town	−0.7258[a]	0.4839
Big city	−1.1492[a]	0.3169
Marital status		
Unmarried	Ref.	
Married	2.4285[a]	11.3423

SOURCE: Author's calculations based on the German Life History Study.

[a]$p \leq .01$.
[b]$p \leq .05$.

Marital Status

In the birth cohorts under study, home ownership was clearly the domain of
married couples. Only 12 percent of all respondents who had never been
married had bought a home at some point, compared with 55 percent of the
ever-married respondents.[23] It seems plausible that married couples in particular would want to own a home. First, the financial and nonmaterial burdens of home ownership are more easily shouldered when two people pool
their resources. Second, a marriage is normally a long-term "project," which

facilitates the typical long-term commitment to home ownership. Finally, marriage often is linked to starting a family. Children need an environment that is suitable for their development, an environment that is easier to create in the family's own home—in particular, in a single-family house. Space is another need met more easily in a single-family house, the kind of house that is rarely available on the rental market. In addition, families with children have always been the target of government support for private home ownership in West Germany.

The results of the model in Table 2.2, with cohort and community size included, confirmed that married persons are much more likely to become homeowners. The transition rate for married respondents was more than eleven times higher than that for unmarried respondents.

Transition-Rate Models for Married-Couple Households

Because of the close association between marital status and home ownership, we restricted all further analyses to married respondents. In all of the models we describe, cohort membership and the urban–rural indicator were included to control for composition effects. Furthermore, the models were estimated solely for men, although the wife's employment position was taken into account in some models. This strategy was adopted because the labor market activities of husband and wife in the birth cohorts under study had different meanings and importance with respect to continuity and earnings. The wife was most likely to be employed when her husband's income was low or her own educational level was high (cf. Drobnič, Blossfeld, and Rohwer 1999; Kurz 1998).

Marriage and Children

We did not advance any hypotheses about the timing of the transition to home ownership within marriage. Therefore, the only requirement for our analyses was that the timing of the transition be modeled flexibly. To do this, we began with piecewise constant exponential models. We set the start of the time axis at three months before marriage. Model 1 in Table 2.3 clearly shows the time dependence of the transition to home ownership: couples move to their own home either right at the beginning of their marriage or—with slightly varying and much lower probability—during the first twenty years of marriage. Thereafter, first-time transitions to home ownership are very rare.[24]

TABLE 2.3
Transition to first-time home ownership by marriage and family stage,
married men, West Germany (piecewise constant exponential models)

Variable	MODEL 1 Coefficient	MODEL 1 Exp (coefficient)	MODEL 2 Coefficient	MODEL 2 Exp (coefficient)	MODEL 3 Coefficient	MODEL 3 Exp (coefficient)
Constant					−4.6493[a]	0.0096
Marital stage						
Marriage ± 3 months	−3.0240[a]	0.0486	−3.0235[a]	0.0486		
4–12 months	−4.9817[a]	0.0069	−4.9323[a]	0.0072		
1–5 years	−5.2660[a]	0.0052	−5.1405[a]	0.0059		
5–10 years	−5.3048[a]	0.0050	−5.1602[a]	0.0057		
10–15 years	−5.1309[a]	0.0059	−5.0220[a]	0.0066		
15–20 years	−5.4907[a]	0.0041	−5.4096[a]	0.0045		
>20 years	−6.2447[a]	0.0019	−6.2033[a]	0.0020		
Birth cohort						
1929–1931			Ref.			
1939–1941	0.1268	1.1352	0.1252	1.1334	0.3257[a]	1.3849
1949–1951	0.0787	1.0819	0.0617	1.0636	0.2766[b]	1.3186
Place of residence						
Village			Ref.			
Small or medium-sized town	−0.6940[a]	0.4996	−0.6972[a]	0.4980	−0.7752[a]	0.4606
Big city	−1.1620[a]	0.3129	−1.1706[a]	0.3102	−1.3162[a]	0.2682
Family stage						
No children under age 16			Ref.			
First child expected			0.0567	1.0583	0.6584[a]	1.9316
Youngest child <6 years			−0.1854	0.8308	−0.6974[a]	0.4979
Youngest child 6–16 years			−0.0723	0.9303	−0.6911[a]	0.5010
Log-likelihood	−2,797.88		−2,796.62		−2,939.17	

SOURCE: Author's calculations based on the German Life History Study.

[a]$p \leq .01$.
[b]$p \leq .05$.

There are good reasons to suppose that home ownership is of particular interest to families with children (cf., for example, Vaskovics 1988). Further, it can be assumed that couples aspire to home ownership especially when they are expecting a child or when their children are young because it is during these stages of the family life cycle that there is a long-term need for more space (Mulder and Wagner 1998). However, as model 2 shows (see Table 2.3), family stage did not seem to exert an independent effect when the duration of marriage was taken into account. It should be kept in mind, though, that young children tend to be present in the household only during the first fifteen years of marriage.[25]

That there is indeed a dependence on the family stage becomes evident in model 3 (Table 2.3), where family stage, but not marriage stage, was included. Married couples make the transition to home ownership even when they do not (yet) have children. The problem with model 3 is that it does not specify when during the childless stage of marriage the move to home ownership occurs. As shown by the earlier models, the likelihood of becoming homeowners is especially high at the start of a marriage. The lesser explanatory power of model 3 is indicated by its log-likelihood value, which is much lower than that of model 1 and 2.

Marriage Phase and Place of Residence

In all of the analyses that follow, we used an exponential model with dummy variables for the decisive marriage phases instead of a piecewise constant exponential model. This made it easier to test the interaction effects between the explanatory variables and the marital stages. Three stages turned out to be relevant: the beginning of the marriage (the period three months before and after the wedding month), the first through the fifteenth year of the marriage (more precisely, from the fourth month through the fifteenth year), and after the fifteenth year of marriage. In addition, we included a dummy variable to indicate periods when the respondent was divorced or widowed.

Model 1 in Table 2.4 presents the estimated coefficients for the starting model. A look at the (exp)coefficients confirms that the likelihood of becoming a homeowner is exceptionally high around the time of the wedding—almost nine times higher than it is during the subsequent period.

It seems unlikely that newlyweds would already have enough savings from work to buy a home. It make sense, then, to assume that they are rely-

TABLE 2.4
Transition to first-time home ownership by marriage stage,
married men, West Germany (exponential models)

Variable	MODEL 1		MODEL 2	
	Coefficient	Exp (coefficient)	Coefficient	Exp (coefficient)
Constant	−5.2195[a]	0.0054	−5.3079[a]	0.0050
Birth cohort				
1929–1931		Ref.		
1939–1941	0.1407	1.1511	0.1412	1.1516
1949–1951	0.0722	1.0748	0.0766	1.0796
Place of residence				
Village		Ref.		
Small or medium-sized town	−0.6919[a]	0.5006	−0.6064[a]	0.5453
Big city	−1.1631[a]	0.3125	−0.9053[a]	0.4044
Marital stage				
Marriage ± 3 months	2.1850[a]	8.8910	2.4039[a]	11.0667
1–15 years		Ref.		
>15 years	−0.6806[a]	0.5063	−0.6989[a]	0.4971
Divorced or widowed	−0.2735	0.7607	−0.3440	0.7089
Interaction of marital stage and place of residence				
Marriage ± 3 months * small or medium-sized town			−0.2056	0.8141
Marriage ± 3 months * big city			−1.0217[a]	0.3600
Log-likelihood	−2,795.810		−2,789.938	

SOURCE: Author's calculations based on the German Life History Study.

[a]$p \leq .01$.

ing heavily on the transfer of housing or money capital from their parents.
As a proxy for intergenerational transfers, we used place of residence. Our
thinking was that these transfers would be more common in rural areas,
where home ownership is less expensive and more widespread than it is in
urban areas. Model 2 in Table 2.4 supported that hypothesis: newlyweds living in villages were almost three times more likely to become homeowners

than were couples living in big cities. For couples in villages, the transition rate was about eleven times higher at the beginning of the marriage than it was between the first and fifteenth year. In contrast, for couples in big cities, the transition rate was only about four times higher in the earliest marital stage.

Husband's Labor Market Position

We started from the finding that until the beginning of the 1970s, blue-collar workers, despite their lower labor market position, were at least as likely to become homeowners as white-collar workers were (cf. Table 2.1). Would this result be supported in transition-rate models that take other explanatory factors into account? We developed two models, shown in Table 2.5, that included the respondents' occupational class plus all the covariates from the previous models. Model 1 shows that the transition rate to home ownership for white-collar workers was statistically significant and about 30 percent higher than that of blue-collar workers. It seems that white-collar workers are more often able to translate their (on average) better market position into a move to home ownership, or to do so more quickly. But when we excluded the place of residence—an indicator of differences in land and housing prices as well as of the diffusion of support networks—the positive effect for white-collar workers fell to a statistically insignificant level (model 2). That working-class households become homeowners as often as middle-class households seems to result from the fact that blue-collar workers more often live in rural areas.

In these models, we also distinguished among self-employed farmers, other self-employed persons, and those who work in a family business ("helping family members"). The high transition rate to home ownership for farmers was not surprising because land and home ownership essentially define this group in West Germany. Their transition rate was more than eight times that of blue-collar workers (model 1 in Table 2.5). The transition rate for other self-employed persons was also quite high—almost two times that of blue-collar workers. We found a slightly negative and insignificant effect for men who worked in a family business. This makes intuitive sense: this kind of job is usually temporary, a stage in the transition to self-employment; and while they are working at this kind of job, most men live in their parents' household. The effect was not significant because few men work in this kind of position after they marry.

TABLE 2.5
Transition to first-time home ownership by husband's occupational
position, married men, West Germany (exponential models)

	MODEL 1		MODEL 2	
Variable	Coefficient	Exp (coefficient)	Coefficient	Exp (coefficient)
Constant	−5.4113[a]	0.0045	−5.9217[a]	0.0027
Birth cohort				
1929–1931		Ref.		
1939–1941	0.0798	1.0830	0.1255	1.1337
1949–1951	0.0503	1.0516	0.1592	1.1725
Place of residence				
Village		Ref.		
Small or medium-sized town	−0.6575[a]	0.5181		
Big city	−0.8977[a]	0.4075		
Marital stage				
Marriage ± 3 months	2.3741[a]	10.7414	2.2821[a]	9.7977
1–15 years		Ref.		
>15 years	−0.7039[a]	0.4947	−0.7430[a]	0.4757
Divorced or widowed	−0.3274	0.7208	−0.5530	0.5752
Interaction of marital stage and place of residence				
Marriage ± 3 months	−0.9802[a]	0.3752		
Husband's occupational status				
Blue-collar worker		Ref.		
White-collar worker/civil servant	0.2622[b]	1.2997	0.1517	1.1638
Farmer	2.1293[a]	8.4089	2.5690[a]	13.0525
Other self-employed person	0.5753[a]	1.7776	0.6195[a]	1.8580
Helping family member	−0.5750	0.5627	−0.2320	0.7929
Not employed	−0.0247	0.9756	−0.1551	0.8563
Missing information	−0.2331	0.7921	−0.2719	0.7619
Log-likelihood	−2,770.26		−2,822.20	

SOURCE: Author's calculations based on the German Life History Study.

[a] $p \leq .01$.
[b] $p \leq .05$.

When we differentiated within the groups of white- and blue-collar workers by qualifications and status, the results were quite instructive. As model 1 in Table 2.6 shows, unskilled and semiskilled workers, who rank at the low end of the income spectrum, were less likely to become homeowners than were members of all the other occupational groups with the exception of those working in a family business. For skilled workers, the transition rate to home ownership was about 70 percent higher; for master craftsmen, it was more than 100 percent higher. In much the same way, white-collar workers were more likely to become homeowners as they moved up the white-collar hierarchy.[26] We also found this basic pattern between the two levels of civil servants. However, the transition rate for low- and middle-level civil servants was not significantly different from the rate we found for unskilled and semiskilled workers. This may have been a function of the relatively small number of respondents in the group of low- and middle-level civil servants.

The difference between unskilled and semiskilled blue-collar workers and other workers was reduced somewhat when we excluded place of residence from the estimation (model 2 in Table 2.6). That is, lower-level manual workers were able to compensate somewhat for their generally low likelihood of home ownership by living disproportionately in rural areas. But all in all, unskilled and semiskilled manual workers are clearly at a disadvantage in becoming homeowners. These findings demand modification of the assumption that blue-collar workers are able to become homeowners at the same rate as white-collar workers: that rule holds true only for skilled and master laborers.

Maximizing Household Income

It seems logical that having two incomes, even temporarily, would help working-class families in particular to attain home ownership. We tested the effect of the wife's employment (outside the home) in models 1 and 2 in Table 2.7.[27] The results were surprising: we found no evidence that working-class households can make up even part of their economic disadvantage through the wife's employment.

The interaction effects between wife's employment and occupational class are not significant, and the log-likelihood value for the model changed only marginally (model 1 compared with model 2 in Table 2.7). All households seemed to profit alike from the wife's employment. If anything, households headed by higher-level white-collar workers were more likely to make

TABLE 2.6
Transition to first-time home ownership by husband's
detailed occupational position, married men, West Germany
(exponential models)

Variable	MODEL 1		MODEL 2	
	Coefficient	Exp (coefficient)	Coefficient	Exp (coefficient)
Constant	−5.7833[a]	0.0031	−6.2686[a]	0.0019
Birth cohort				
1929–1931		Ref.		
1939–1941	0.0321	1.0326	0.0826	1.0861
1949–1951	−0.0054	0.9946	0.1119	1.1184
Place of residence				
Village		Ref.		
Small or medium-size town	−0.6754[a]	0.5090		
Big city	−0.9120[a]	0.4017		
Marital stage				
Marriage ± 3 months	2.3938[a]	10.9545	2.2872[a]	9.8470
1–15 years		Ref.		
>15 years	−0.6916[a]	0.5008	−0.7306[a]	0.4816
Divorced or widowed	−0.3601	0.6976	−0.5756	0.5624
Interaction of marital stage and place of residence				
Marriage ± 3 months * small or medium-sized town	−1.0016[a]	0.3673		

(*continued*)

the transition to home ownership when the wife was employed. This effect, however, was not statistically firm ($\rho \leq .10$). It seems that in all social classes, the wife's employment was used as a means to facilitate the transition to home ownership. When the wife was employed, the transition rate increased by almost 50 percent (model 1).

Support Networks: Urban–Rural Differences and Father's Occupation

Did the help of support networks increase home-ownership rates among the working-class members of the cohorts we studied? In most of the models we

TABLE 2.6
(*Continued*)

Variable	MODEL 1		MODEL 2	
	Coefficient	Exp (coefficient)	Coefficient	Exp (coefficient)
Husband's occupational position				
Unskilled or semiskilled manual worker		Ref.		
Skilled manual worker	0.5444[a]	1.7236	0.5165[a]	1.6762
Master craftsman	0.7516[a]	2.1204	0.6055[a]	1.8322
Low- or middle-level white-collar worker	0.5758[a]	1.7786	0.4376[b]	1.5489
Higher-level white-collar worker	0.8057[a]	2.2383	0.6171[a]	1.8535
Low- or middle-level civil servant	0.3825	1.4660	0.2435	1.2758
Higher-level civil servant	0.9882[a]	2.6865	0.8854[a]	2.4239
Farmer	2.5349[a]	12.6151	2.9509[a]	19.1230
Other self-employed person	0.9799[a]	2.6641	0.9904[a]	2.6924
Helping family member	−0.1996	0.8190	0.1212	1.1289
Not employed	0.3840	1.4681	0.2214	1.2479
Missing information	0.1918	1.2115	0.1159	1.1229
Log-likelihood	−2,758.13		−2,811.87	

SOURCE: Author's calculations based on the German Life History Study.

[a]$p \leq .01$.
[b]$p \leq .05$.

have discussed to this point, place of residence was a variable. Our unequivocal finding: home ownership is more likely in rural areas than in big cities. As mentioned earlier, however, the availability of social networks in rural areas is only one factor here; the rate increase also reflects differences in the price of land.

Do manual workers benefit from living in rural areas more so than other groups? Model 1 in Table 2.8 suggests the answer is yes: unskilled and semiskilled manual workers who live in a village have a significantly better chance of becoming homeowners than they would in urban areas, especially in big cities. Also, skilled manual workers or master craftsmen seem to profit

TABLE 2.7
Transition to first-time home ownership by wife's employment,
married men, West Germany (exponential models)

Variable	MODEL 1		MODEL 2	
	Coefficient	Exp (coefficient)	Coefficient	Exp (coefficient)
Constant	−5.8719[a]	0.0028	−5.7812[a]	0.0031
Birth cohort				
1929–1931		Ref.		
1939–1941	−0.0127	0.9874	−0.0101	0.9900
1949–1951	−0.0662	0.9359	−0.0684	0.9339
Place of residence				
Village		Ref.		
Small or medium-sized town	−0.6580[a]	0.5179	−0.6446[a]	0.5249
Big city	−0.8827[a]	0.4136	−0.8639[a]	0.4215
Marital stage				
Marriage − 3 months	2.9001[a]	18.1766	2.8960[a]	18.1009
Marriage + 3 months	1.3974[a]	4.0446	1.3884[a]	4.0086
1–15 years	Ref.			
>15 years	−0.7192[a]	0.4872	−0.7120[a]	0.4906
>Divorced or widowed	−0.2341	0.7913	−0.2340	0.7914
Interaction of marital stage and place of residence				
Marriage ± 3 months * small or medium-sized town	−0.9642[a]	0.3813	−0.9654[a]	0.3808
Husband's occupational position				
Unskilled or semiskilled manual worker		Ref.		
Skilled manual worker or master craftsman	0.5808[a]	1.7874	0.4935[a]	1.6381
Low- or middle-level white-collar worker or civil servant	0.4880[a]	1.6291	0.4325[b]	1.5411

(continued)

TABLE 2.7
(*Continued*)

Variable	MODEL 1		MODEL 2	
	Coefficient	Exp (coefficient)	Coefficient	Exp (coefficient)
Higher-level white-collar worker or civil servant	0.8771[a]	2.4039	0.6762[a]	1.9665
Farmer	2.7111[a]	15.0455	2.5954[a]	13.4016
Other self-employed person	0.9277[a]	2.5288	0.7383[a]	2.0923
Helping family member	−0.3574	0.6995	−0.5087	0.6013
Not employed or missing information	0.3596	1.4327	0.2045	1.2269
Wife's employment status				
Employed	0.3972[a]	1.4877	−0.0462	0.9549
Not employed		Ref.		
Missing information	−0.3144	0.7302	−0.3202	0.7260
Interaction of husband's occupational position and wife's employment status				
Skilled manual worker or master craftsman * wife employed			0.4035	1.4970
Low- or middle-level white-collar worker * wife employed			0.3025	1.3532
Higher-level white-collar worker * wife employed			0.7318[c]	2.0788
Other self-employed person * wife employed			0.6375	1.8918
Log-likelihood	−2,726.5975		2,724.3835	

SOURCE: Author's calculations based on the German Life History Study.

[a]$p \le .01$.
[b]$p \le .05$.
[c]$p \le .10$.

TABLE 2.8

Transition to first-time home ownership by access to support
networks, married men, West Germany (exponential models)

Variable	MODEL 1		MODEL 2	
	Coefficient	Exp (coefficient)	Coefficient	Exp (coefficient)
Constant	−5.6423[a]	0.0035	−5.8680[a]	0.0028
Birth cohort				
1929–1931		Ref.		
1939–1941	−0.0146	0.9855	−0.0075	0.9926
1949–1951	−0.0500	0.9512	−0.0905	0.9134
Place of residence				
Village		Ref.		
Small or medium-sized town	−1.2515[a]	0.2861	−0.6446[a]	0.5249
Big city	−1.4668[a]	0.2307	−0.8210[a]	0.4400
Marital stage				
Marriage − 3 months	2.9004[a]	18.1821	2.8914[a]	18.0190
Marriage + 3 months	1.3885[a]	4.0088	1.3933[a]	4.0280
1–15 years		Ref.		
>15 years	−0.7116[a]	0.4908	−0.7014[a]	0.4959
Divorced or widowed	−0.2387	0.7876	−0.2156	0.8061
Interaction of marital stage and place of residence				
Marriage ± 3 months * small or medium-sized town	−0.9735[a]	0.3778	−0.9490[a]	0.3871
Husband's occupational position				
Unskilled or semiskilled manual worker		Ref.		
Skilled manual worker or master craftsman	0.8661[a]	2.3776	0.6173[a]	1.8539
Low- or middle-level white-collar worker or civil servant	0.9172[a]	2.5023	0.5716[a]	1.7710
Higher-level white-collar worker or civil servant	1.3399[a]	3.8187	0.9894[a]	2.6896
Farmer	3.3056[a]	27.2636	2.5420[a]	12.7049
Other self-employed person	1.3989[a]	4.0509	0.9880[b]	2.6858

(*continued*)

TABLE 2.8
(*Continued*)

Variable	MODEL 1		MODEL 2	
	Coefficient	*Exp (coefficient)*	Coefficient	*Exp (coefficient)*
Helping family member	0.1654	1.1799	−0.5008	0.6061
Not employed or missing information	0.8066[a]	2.2404	0.4169[c]	1.5173
Wife's employment status				
Employed	0.4195[a]	1.5212	0.4105[a]	1.5076
Not employed		Ref.		
Missing information	−0.2953	0.7443	−0.2775	0.7577
Interaction of husband's occupational position and living in a village				
Skilled manual worker or master craftsman * village	−0.4592	0.6318		
Low- or middle-level white-collar worker * village	−0.8091[b]	0.4453		
Higher-level white-collar worker * village	−0.9415[b]	0.3901		
Self-employed person * village	−0.8298[b]	0.4362		
Father's occupational position				
Blue-collar worker		Ref.		
White-collar worker or civil servant			−0.3532[a]	0.7024
Farmer			0.1689	1.1840
Self-employed person			0.0581	1.0598
Not employed or missing information			−0.4342[c]	0.6478
Log-likelihood	−2,721.8587		−2,719.4787	

SOURCE: Author's calculations based on the German Life History Study.

[a]$p \leq .01$.
[b]$p \leq .05$.
[c]$p \leq .10$.

from living in rural areas—but less so than the lowest category of blue-collar workers.

A better indicator of mutual support is provided by the father's occupational status. Model 2 in Table 2.8 shows that the sons of blue-collar workers had a higher probability of becoming homeowners than did the sons of white-collar workers.[28] The transition rate for the sons of blue-collar workers was about 40 percent higher than that for the sons of white-collar workers. Other models that are not included in the tables showed that the within-group status of the father's occupational group is not relevant.

Another effect of the father's occupational status should be mentioned. We expected that the sons of farmers would be more likely to become homeowners than the sons of all the other occupational groups because farmers normally own land and buildings that can be transferred directly to the next generation. This thesis was only partially supported: the transition rate of the sons of farmers was almost 40 percent higher than that of the sons of manual workers—but only when the occupational status of the son was not included in the estimation (this model is not shown in the table). The decisive factor, then, seems to be whether the son becomes a farmer himself, not simply the fact that there is property in the family of origin.

Intergenerational Transfers

In model 1 in Table 2.9, we included a variable indicating whether the respondent had lived in an owner-occupied home during his childhood. As we expected, there was a clear effect: the transition rate to home ownership was almost 60 percent higher for respondents whose parents owned a home than for those whose parents rented a home. Clearly, intergenerational transfers influence the likelihood of home ownership; although we cannot rule out that the effect here also reflects socialization.

The important question now was whether blue-collar workers are more dependent on intergenerational transfers than are other groups of workers. According to model 2 in Table 2.9, blue-collar workers, but also low- and middle-level white-collar workers, benefit from property in the family of origin. In contrast, higher-level white-collar workers seem to be less dependent on their parents' housing tenure. However, none of the interaction effects reaches conventional levels of significance.

SUMMARY AND DISCUSSION

Our objective here was to understand the relatively low rates of home own-ership in West Germany and the comparatively high likelihood of manual workers' becoming homeowners. Why are home-ownership rates in Ger-many generally so low? The answer is simple: long-term policies of provid-ing high-quality units at affordable rents in the public housing sector and of regulating rent increases in the private rental sector have kept renting an at-tractive option for many households. This is true in particular in urban ar-eas, where land and house prices are typically high and the rental sectors are well developed. In addition, high down payments and the time it typically takes to save up for them, and the relatively high prices of land and houses are factors that reduce the attractiveness of home ownership (Clark, Deur-loo, and Dieleman 1997; Mulder and Wagner 1998).

How do we explain the relatively high proportion of lower-income households that own homes in Germany? To answer this question, we stud-ied the transition to home ownership for married couples in which the hus-bands were members of the 1930, 1940, or 1950 birth cohort. The results show, first, that there is considerable variation in the transition rates within the working class. Skilled manual workers and master craftsmen are as likely as white-collar workers to become homeowners; but unskilled and semi-skilled laborers are at a distinct disadvantage compared with almost all other occupational groups. The finding of only marginal differences between all blue-collar workers and all white-collar workers is largely the product of a composition effect: blue-collar workers more often live in rural areas, where land is less expensive and support networks are more common.

We found no evidence that working-class households in particular rely on the wife's employment outside the home to facilitate home ownership. Having a second income increases the probability of home ownership across all social classes. But we did find indications that low land prices or social networks are particularly important to working-class households, especially the households of unskilled and semiskilled laborers. This group seems to improve its chances of achieving home ownership more than other groups by living in small towns or villages. Furthermore, we found that respondents from a working-class background were more likely to become homeowners whether or not their family of origin owned a home.

TABLE 2.9
Transition to first-time home ownership by intergenerational
transfers, married men, West Germany (exponential models)

	MODEL 1		MODEL 2	
Variable	Coefficient	Exp (coefficient)	Coefficient	Exp (coefficient)
Constant	−6.0956[a]	0.0023	−6.1844[a]	0.0021
Birth cohort				
1929–1931		Ref.		
1939–1941	0.0117	1.0118	−0.0055	0.9945
1949–1951	−0.0802	0.9229	−0.0828	0.9205
Place of residence				
Village		Ref.		
Small or medium-sized town	−0.5579[a]	0.5724	−0.5303[a]	0.5884
Big city	−0.7080[a]	0.4927	−0.6968[a]	0.4982
Marital stage				
Marriage − 3 months	2.8586[a]	17.4369	2.8579[a]	17.4252
Marriage + 3 months	1.3731[a]	3.9477	1.3717[a]	3.9421
1–15 years		Ref.		
>15 years	−0.7013[a]	0.4959	−0.6947[a]	0.4992
Divorced or widowed	−0.1807	0.8347	−0.1694	0.8441
Interaction of marital stage and place of residence				
Marriage ± 3 months * small or medium-sized town	−0.9206[a]	0.3983	−0.9113[a]	0.4020
Husband's occupational position				
Unskilled or semiskilled manual worker		Ref.		
Skilled manual worker or master craftsman	0.5839[a]	1.7931	0.5707[b]	1.7694
Low- or middle-level white-collar worker or civil servant	0.5885[a]	1.8012	0.6052[b]	1.8316
Higher-level white-collar worker or civil servant	0.9538[a]	2.5956	1.2244[a]	3.4021
Farmer	2.5105[a]	12.3113	2.9423[a]	18.9602
Other self-employed person	0.9580[a]	2.6066	1.2168[a]	3.3764
Helping family member	−0.5491	0.5775	−0.1402	0.8691
Not employed or missing information	0.3941[c]	1.4830	0.6593[b]	1.9333

(continued)

TABLE 2.9
(*Continued*)

Variable	MODEL 1		MODEL 2	
	Coefficient	Exp (coefficient)	Coefficient	Exp (coefficient)
Wife's employment status				
Employed	0.4081[a]	1.5040	0.4189[a]	1.5203
Not employed		Ref.		
Missing information	−0.2566	0.7737	−0.2326	0.7925
Father's occupational position				
Blue-collar worker		Ref.		
White-collar worker or civil servant	−0.3651[a]	0.6941	−0.3872[a]	0.6790
Farmer	−0.0337	0.9669	−0.0516	0.9497
Other self-employed person	−0.0455	0.9555	−0.0488	0.9524
Not employed or missing information	−0.4676[c]	0.6265	−0.4621[c]	0.6300
Lived in owner-occupied home during childhood (for at least 3 years)				
Parents rented home		Ref.		
Parents owned home	0.4458[a]	1.5617	0.6008[b]	1.8235
Interaction of husband's occupational position and parents' housing tenure				
Skilled manual worker or master craftsman * parents owned home			0.0085	1.0086
Low- or middle-level white-collar worker * parents owned home			−0.0126	0.9874
Higher-level white-collar worker * parents owned home			−0.4901	0.6126
Self-employed person * parents owned home			−0.4694	0.6254
Log-likelihood	−2,710.066		−2,707.3584	

SOURCE: Author's calculations based on the German Life History Study.

[a]$p \le .01$.   [b]$p \le .05$.   [c]$p \le .10$.

There is clear evidence of the importance of intergenerational transfers. Parents' home ownership increases the probability of home ownership across social classes—in particular for lower-income households. Of course, as other studies have shown, it is exactly these groups that are less likely to receive intergenerational transfers (Lauterbach and Lüscher 1996; Szydlik 1999). Hence, there is some evidence of the cumulative disadvantage facing unskilled and skilled manual laborers and low- and middle-level white-collar workers.

In sum, the analyses showed that the likelihood of owning a home is structured along the lines of the respondents' labor market position on the one hand and of the wealth position of the family of origin on the other. The result: in terms of home ownership, as in other aspects of life, unskilled and semiskilled workers are disadvantaged (cf. Blossfeld and Timm 1997). What ameliorates their housing situation somewhat is the fact that they are more likely to live in rural areas and so more often have the help of family and friends to achieve home ownership.

Finally, we should stress that the empirical analyses here examined developments only until the beginning of the 1980s. In the two decades since, it is likely that access to home ownership for manual workers has become more difficult with the increasing risk of unemployment in this population. Results from Wagner and Mulder (2000) point in this direction, although Kurz (2001) found no clear indication of this trend. Further research is needed to understand how younger birth cohorts are making the transition to home ownership today.

Notes

1. The analyses described in this chapter focus on West Germany: they relied on historical data that followed the members of three birth cohorts until the beginning of the 1980s. Reunification of the two Germanys did not begin until 1989.

2. We use the adjectives *working-class* and *blue-collar* to describe couple households in which the man is a manual laborer. We do not use the woman's occupational position as an indicator of class because in the birth cohorts under study, employment of married women was relatively rare and usually was interrupted for a relatively long period (Lauterbach 1994; Tölke 1989). See Goldthorpe (1983), Handl (1993), and Szelényi (1998) on the problem of assigning social class solely on the basis of the man's occupational position.

3. This overview on macroeconomic conditions covers the 1950s through the

1980s, the period that is most important to the examination of home ownership among the birth cohorts we studied. See Berger (1998) for an overview into the 1990s.

4. For example, Herlyn and Herlyn (1983, 136) cite mortgage rates of, on average, 6.4 percent in 1978 and 11.1 percent in 1981.

5. Our calculation is based on data in Manzel (1995, table 8).

6. Rent subsidies for low-income households *(Wohngeld)*, although they affect only a small fraction of households, are another important component of German housing policy.

7. Nonprofit housing organizations (and housing cooperatives) had played an important role during the Weimar Republic (1918–1933) in providing afford-able housing to white- and blue-collar workers (cf. Häußermann and Siebel 1996, 119ff.). During the Nazi regime, these organizations were centralized, which made it administratively easy after the war to base the public housing program on them. The biggest nonprofit housing organization after the war was Neue Heimat (New Home), which was owned by the labor unions.

8. In contrast, in the Weimar Republic, rents were frozen at their 1914 level (cf. Häußermann and Siebel, 108).

9. It needs to be stressed that not all industrial workers were sons of self-employed farmers. Many were sons of farm laborers who did not own their home (cf. Häußermann and Siebel 1996). Still, owning property is traditionally an im-portant goal in rural cultures whatever the individual's situation.

10. The comparison of groups by occupational status is problematic though. At the beginning of the twentieth century, the urban population of manual workers was comprised primarily of young unmarried men. Young unmarried people in general—regardless of occupational position—are unlikely to be homeowners (Petrowsky, 108).

11. In 1925, 28 percent of the manual workers in Germany lived in cities, and 58 percent lived in municipalities with fewer than 20,000 inhabitants. In 1978, the respective proportions were 30 percent and 44 percent (Häußermann 1984, 651).

12. There were large regional differences.

13. Over time, the division of the land into increasingly small parcels would make it impossible to feed and support a family through farming (Petrowsky 1993, 100).

14. Translated from the German by the author.

15. These studies are restricted to three large cities—Stuttgart, Munich, and Bremen, respectively. So their findings are not representative of Germany as a whole.

16. At the same time, the likelihood of inheriting in Germany is especially fa-vorable for households that already own a home (Engel; Lauterbach and Lüscher). Similar results have been found for the United Kingdom (Hamnett 1991, 525ff.).

17. Motel and Szydlik do not take into account land and buildings. However,

it is likely that income and money capital are positively correlated with land and building assets.

18. Labor market inequalities also are reinforced through marriage homogamy (Blossfeld and Timm 1997; Wirth 1996; Wirth and Lüttinger 1998) and through the influence of social origin (parents' social class and education) on children's educational level and labor market position (cf., for example, Hall 1997; Müller 1986).

19. For simplicity, we refer to them as the 1930, 1940, and 1950 birth cohorts.

20. Studies in West Germany on social inequality found that people without occupational qualifications face the greatest challenges in the labor market: they are more often unemployed and seldom advance in their work (see, for example, Blossfeld 1985, 1989; Blossfeld and Mayer 1988; and Shavit and Müller 1998). Furthermore, they usually cannot improve their situation by marrying "up" (see, for example, Blossfeld and Timm 1997).

21. The survivor functions in Figure 2.1 are based on all respondents. When the functions are estimated separately for men and women, the basic pattern remains very similar. We conducted a log-rank test and diverse Wilcoxon tests to measure the differences among survivor functions for statistical significance (Blossfeld and Rohwer 2001, 79ff.). The tests revealed that the difference between the 1930 birth cohort and both of the younger cohorts is significant, but that the difference between the 1950 cohort and the older cohorts is not.

22. This result remained basically the same in later more-complex statistical models.

23. The number of never-married respondents was 195.

24. More-detailed breakdowns of the duration of marriages led basically to the same conclusion.

25. See Mulder and Wagner (1998) for more-detailed results on the link between family phase and the transition to home ownership.

26. The fact that the transition rate increases with status within a worker group could be a function of income; but it also could relate to life cycle. That is, blue-collar workers over time might become master craftsmen, and white-collar workers might move up to managerial or executive positions, and, yes, their income would grow—but they would also have more time in which to save money to buy a home.

27. Because we had no information on the wife's employment status in the three months leading up to the wedding, we divided the first marital stage into the three months before and the three months following the wedding.

28. It seems that working-class parents try harder than their middle-class peers to help their adult children become homeowners. This is true whether the parents own property or not (see model 1 in Table 2.9).

References

Ambrosius, Gerold, and Hartmut Kaelble. 1992. Einleitung: Gesellschaftliche und wirtschaftliche Folgen des Booms der 1950er und 1960er Jahre. In *Der Boom 1948–1973. Gesellschaftliche und wirtschaftliche Folgen in der Bundesrepublik Deutschland und in Europa*, edited by Hartmut Kaelble, 7–32. Opladen, Ger.: Westdeutscher Verlag.

Bahrdt, Hans Paul. 1968. *Humaner Städtebau. Überlegungen zur Wohnungspolitik und Stadtplanung für eine nahe Zukunft*. Hamburg: Christian Wegner Verlag.

Berger, Johannes. 1998. Wirtschaftssystem. In *Handwörterbuch zur Gesellschaft Deutschlands*, edited by Bernhard Schäfers and Wolfgang Zapf, 710–20. Opladen, Ger.: Leske & Budrich.

Bertram, Hans. 1995. Regionale Vielfalt und Lebensformen. In *Das Individuum und seine Familie: Lebensformen, Familienbeziehungen und Lebensereignisse im Erwachsenenalter*, edited by Hans Bertram, 157–95. Frankfurt am Main: Campus.

Blossfeld, Hans-Peter. 1985. *Bildungsexpansion und Berufschancen. Empirische Analysen zur Lage der Berufsanfänger in der Bundesrepublik*. Frankfurt am Main: Campus.

———. 1989. *Kohortendifferenzierung und Karriereprozeß—Eine Längsschnittstudie über die Veränderung der Bildungs- und Berufschancen im Lebenslauf*. Frankfurt am Main: Campus.

Blossfeld, Hans-Peter, and Karl-Ulrich Mayer. 1988. Arbeitsmarktsegmentation in der Bundesrepublik Deutschland—Eine empirische Überprüfung von Segmentationstheorien aus der Perspektive des Lebensverlaufs. *Kölner Zeitschrift für Soziologie und Sozialpsychologie* 40:245–61.

Blossfeld, Hans-Peter, and Götz Rohwer. 2001. *Techniques of event history modeling. New approaches to causal analysis*. Mahwah, NJ: Lawrence Erlbaum.

Blossfeld, Hans-Peter, and Andreas Timm. 1997. Der Einfluß des Bildungssystems auf den Heiratsmarkt. Eine Längsschnittanalyse der Wahl von Heiratspartnern im Lebenslauf. *Kölner Zeitschrift für Soziologie und Sozialpsychologie* 49:440–76.

Clark, William A. V., Marinus C. Deurloo, and Frans M. Dieleman. 1997. Entry into home-ownership in Germany: Comparisons with the United States. *Urban Studies* 34:7–19.

Drobnič, Sonja, Hans-Peter Blossfeld, and Götz Rohwer. 1999. Dynamics of women's employment patterns over the life course: A comparison of the United States and Germany. *Journal of Marriage and the Family* 61:133–46.

Engel, Bernd. 1985. Stetige und diskrete private Transfers: Zur Bedeutung von Erbschaften und privaten Unterhaltszahlungen für die Einkommens- und Vermögensverteilung. In *Soziale Sicherung und Einkommensverteilung. Empirische Analysen für die Bundesrepublik Deutschland*, edited by Richard Hauser and Bernd Engel, 239–55. Frankfurt am Main: Campus.

Geißler, Rainer. 1996. *Die Sozialstruktur Deutschlands*. Opladen, Ger.: Westdeutscher Verlag.

Glatzer, Wolfgang. 1980. *Wohnungsversorgung im Wohlfahrtsstaat*. Frankfurt am Main: Campus.

Goldthorpe, John H. 1983. Women and class analysis: In defence of the conventional view. *Sociology* 17:465–88.

Hall, Anja. 1997. Abbau sozialer Barrieren? Zur Entwicklung der Muster sozialer Mobilität in Westdeutschland. In *Soziale Ungleichheit. Neue Befunde zu Strukturen, Bewußtsein und Politik*, edited by Walter Müller, 111–35. Opladen, Ger.: Leske & Budrich.

Hamnett, Chris. 1991. A nation of inheritors? Housing inheritance, wealth and inequality in Britain. *Journal of Social Policy* 20:509–36.

Handl, Johann. 1993. Zur Berücksichtigung von Frauen in der empirisch arbeitenden Mobilitäts- und Schichtungsforschung. In *Soziale Ungleichheit und Geschlechterverhältnisse*, edited by Petra Frerichs and Margareta Steinrücke, 13–29. Opladen, Ger.: Leske & Budrich.

Häußermann, Hartmut. 1984. Wandel der Wohnverhältnisse von Arbeitern. Eine Problemskizze. In *Das Ende der Arbeiterbewegung in Deutschland*, edited by R. Ebbinghausen and F. Tiemann, 646–60. Opladen, Ger.: Westdeutscher Verlag.

Häußermann, Hartmut, and Walter Siebel. 1996. *Soziologie des Wohnens. Eine Einführung in Wandel und Ausdifferenzierung des Wohnens*. Weinheim, Ger.: Juventa.

Herlyn, Ingrid, and Ulfert Herlyn. 1983. *Wohnverhältnisse in der Bundesrepublik. 2. Überarbeitete Auflage*. Frankfurt am Main: Campus.

Kaufmann, Franz-Xaver. 1973. *Sicherheit als soziologisches und sozialpolitisches Problem*. Stuttgart: Enke.

Kendig, H. L. 1984. Housing careers, life cycle and residential mobility: Implications for the housing market. *Urban Studies* 21:271–83.

Kurz, Karin. 1998. *Das Erwerbsverhalten von Frauen in der intensiven Familienphase—Ein Vergleich zwischen Müttern in der Bundesrepublik Deutschland und den Vereinigten Staaten von Amerika*. Opladen, Ger.: Leske & Budrich.

———. 2001. Klassenlage und Wohneigentum. Ungleichheitsstrukturen 1980 bis 1998. In *Blickpunkt Gesellschaft Band 6*, edited by Achim Koch, Martina Wasmer, and Peter Schmidt, 247–75. Opladen, Ger.: Leske & Budrich.

Laue, Evelyn. 1995. Grundvermögen privater Haushalte Ende 1993. Ergebnisse der Einkommens- und Verbrauchsstichprobe. *Wirtschaft und Statistik*, no. 7: 488–97.

Lauterbach, Wolfgang. 1994. *Berufsverläufe von Frauen: Erwerbstätigkeit, Unterbrechung und Wiedereintritt*. Frankfurt am Main: Campus.

Lauterbach, Wolfgang, and Kurt Lüscher. 1996. Erben und die Verbundenheit der Lebensverläufe von Familienmitgliedern. *Kölner Zeitschrift für Soziologie und Sozialpsychologie* 48 (1): 66–95.

Manzel, Karl-Heinz. 1995. Zur Entwicklung des Wohnungsbaus in Deutschland in der ersten Hälfte der 90er Jahre. *Wirtschaft und Statistik* no. 5: 350–60.

Mayer, Karl Ulrich, and Erika Brückner. 1989. *Lebensverläufe und Wohlfahrtsentwicklung. Konzeption, Design und Methodik der Erhebung von Lebensverläufen der Geburtsjahrgänge 1929–31, 1939–41, 1949–51.* Teil 1. Berlin: Max-Planck-Institut für Bildungsforschung.

Meinecke, B. 1987. Eigenheim und Eigentumswohnung. In *Wohnungsversorgung und Wohnungspolitik in der Großstadtregion*, Beiträge zur Stadtforschung der Robert-Bosch-Stiftung 5, edited by Heik Afheldt, Walter Siebel, and Thomas Sieverts, 132–59. Gerlingen, Ger.: Bleicher.

Miegel, Meinhard. 1983. *Die verkannte Revolution. Einkommen und Vermögen der privaten Haushalte.* Stuttgart: Bonn Aktuell.

Motel, Andreas, and Marc Szydlik. 1999. Private Transfers zwischen den Generationen. *Zeitschrift für Soziologie* 28 (1): 3–22.

Mulder, Clara H., and Michael Wagner. 1998. First-time home-ownership in the family life course: A West German–Dutch comparison. *Urban Studies* 35 (4): 687–713.

Müller, Walter. 1986. Soziale Mobilität in Deutschland: Die Bundesrepublik im internationalen Vergleich. In *Politische Wissenschaft und politische Ordnung*, edited by Max Kaase, 339–54. Opladen, Ger.: Westdeutscher Verlag.

Munro, Moira. 1988. Housing wealth and inheritance. *Journal of Social Policy* 17 (4): 417–36.

Murphy, M. J. 1984. The influence of fertility, early housing-career, and socioeconomic factors on tenure determination in contemporary Britain. *Environment and Planning A* 16:1303–18.

Neubeck, Klaus. 1981. Eigentumsbildung im Wohnungsbau. In *Wohnen zur Miete*, edited by J. Brech, 111–25. Weinheim, Ger.: Beltz.

Niethammer, Lutz, with Franz Brüggemeier. 1976. Wie wohnten die Arbeiter im Kaiserreich? *Archiv für Sozialgeschichte* 16:61–134.

Petrowsky, Werner. 1993. *Arbeiterhaushalte mit Hauseigentum. Die Bedeutung des Erbes bei der Eigentumsbildung.* Bremen: Universität Bremen.

Shavit, Yossi, and Walter Müller. 1998. *From school to work. A comparative study of educational qualifications and occupational destinations.* Oxford: Oxford University Press.

Schlomann, Heinrich. 1991. Der Einfluß von Erbschaften auf die Vermögensausstattung privater Haushalte im Jahr 1988. Diskussionspapier 39, Deutsches Institut für Wirtschaftsforschung, Berlin.

Szelényi, Szonja. 1998. Women and the class structure. In *Social stratification. Class, race, and gender in sociological perspective*, edited by David B. Grusky, 577–82. Boulder, CO: Westview Press.

Szydlik, Marc. 1999. Erben in der Bundesrepublik Deutschland. Zum Verhältnis von familialer Solidarität und sozialer Ungleichheit. *Kölner Zeitschrift für Soziologie und Sozialpsychologie* 51 (1): 80–104.

Tenfelde, Klaus. 1977. *Sozialgeschichte der Ruhrbergarbeiterschaft im 19. Jahrhundert.* Bd. 125. Bonn-Bad Godesberg: Schriftenreihe des Forschungsinstituts der Friedrich-Ebert-Stiftung.

Tölke, Angelika. 1989. *Lebensverläufe von Frauen. Familiäre Ereignisse, Ausbildungs- und Erwerbsverhalten.* München: Juventa.

Vaskovics, Laszlo. 1988. Veränderungen der Wohn- und Umweltbedingungen in ihren Auswirkungen auf die Sozialisationsleistungen der Familie. In *Wandel und Kontinuität der Familie in der Bundesrepublik Deutschland,* edited by Rosemarie Nave-Herz, 36–60. Stuttgart: Enke.

Wagner, Michael, and Clara H. Mulder. 2000. Wohneigentum im Lebenslauf. *Zeitschrift für Soziologie* 29:44–59.

Watt, Paul. 1993. Housing inheritance and social inequality: A rejoinder to Chris Hamnett. *Journal for Social Policy* 22:527–34.

Wirth, Heike. 1996. Wer heiratet wen? Die Entwicklung der bildungsspezifischen Heiratsmuster in Deutschland. *Zeitschrift für Soziologie* 25:371–94.

Wirth, Heike, and Paul Lüttinger. 1998. Klassenspezifische Heiratsbeziehungen im Wandel? Die Klassenzugehörigkeit von Ehepartner 1970 und 1993. *Kölner Zeitschrift für Soziologie und Sozialpsychologie* 50:47–77.

CHAPTER THREE

Home Ownership and Social Inequality in France

Monique Meron and
Daniel Courgeau

In France, the percentage of homeowners among households increased rapidly in the 1980s, rising from approximately 46 percent at the start of the decade to 54 percent at its close (Figure 3.1).[1] By 1984, more than 50 percent of all households in France owned their own home. The growth in home ownership slowed in the 1990s. According to the French labor force survey, approximately 55 percent of households owned a home in 2002.

In this chapter, we trace the evolution of home ownership in France since World War II. Then we examine how class differences that affect opportunities for home ownership have been growing and try to explain why.

For our empirical analyses, we relied on population censuses from 1975, 1982, and 1990 (INSEE 1993); housing surveys from 1973, 1978, 1984, 1988, 1992, and 1996 (INSEE 1998); and annual labor force surveys that offer precise information on home ownership from a sample of about 75,000 households. For our longitudinal analysis, to complement the labor force surveys, we used the Youth and Careers (*Jeunes et Carrières*) Survey, a face-to-face survey carried out by Institut National de la Statistique et des Études Économiques (INSEE) interviewers in March 1997 (Meron 1997). The study reflects the job-related experiences of 20,770 individuals aged 19 to 45. The interviewers asked each respondent to remember family events, changes of residence, and educational and economic activities dating back to when the individual was 16.

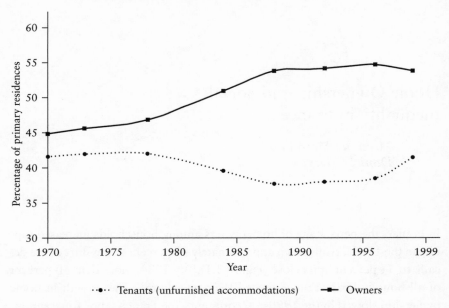

Figure 3.1.   Distribution of housing by households, France, 1970–1999

SOURCE: Authors' calculations based on population and housing surveys (INSEE 1993, 1998) and the French labor force survey (1999).

HOUSING IN FRANCE SINCE 1946:
AN INCREASE IN NUMBER AND QUALITY

Since the end of World War II, new housing in France has been built faster than the country's population has grown. According to census and housing survey data, from 1946 through 1998, the number of new homes (primary residences) almost doubled, from 13 million to 23 million, a growth rate of 77 percent; in the same period, the population grew by just 45 percent.[2] In France, as in many other countries, the growth of households is a function of three factors: young people are leaving their parents' households earlier; an increase in separations and divorces; and the fact that elderly people are living in their own homes longer than previous generations of the elderly did (Ascher 1995).

The quality of housing in France also has improved (Segaud, Bonvalet, and Brun 1998). In 1970, 49 percent of primary residences did not have modern conveniences; in 1996, only 4 percent of homes were lacking complete sanitary installations. Also, according to housing surveys, homes have become bigger: the living space per person increased from 22 square meters in 1970 to 35 square meters in 1996.[3] At the same time, housing has become the household's main expense: 22.5 percent of the household budget in 1996 compared with 10.4 percent in 1960.

At the end of 1996, 56 percent of households lived in houses—13 million houses versus 10 million flats—up from 51 percent in 1970 (Laferrère 1999). Houses are more often occupied by homeowners than rented out: in 1996, 80 percent of owners lived in houses; just 23 percent of tenants lived in houses. Also, the number of second homes experienced a spectacular increase over the period: there were almost three times more second homes in 1996 than in 1962 (Omalek and Le Blanc 1998). According to the 1996 housing survey, owner-occupied housing represents the largest proportion of the household's property: primary residences make up 49 percent, and other homes account for 16 percent.

One consequence of more comfortable homes and easier access to ownership is that households are showing more appreciation for their homes: according to housing surveys, almost 73 percent of households reported being satisfied with their housing conditions in 1996, up from just 52 percent in 1973. Among homeowners with mortgages, 87 percent expressed satisfaction in 1996 versus 77 percent in 1973.

After a period of growth between 1946 and 1990, the proportion of homeowners has remained at about 54 percent. Initially growth was fueled by tax advantages that supported the demand for home ownership among French families. Between 1950 and 1963, the proportion of households living in their own home increased rapidly, from 35 percent to 42 percent (see Topalov 1987, 301). Over the next fifteen years, growth was slower: the proportion had reached 47 percent in 1978 (cf. Figure 3.1). During the 1980s, the rate increased again; by 1990, though, it had reached a plateau. Access to home ownership had once again become more difficult.

Figure 3.2 depicts another trend: throughout much of the postwar period, the age of access to home ownership moved downward. The median age at which people born in 1910 bought their first home, for example, was 56; for those born in 1950, the median age had dropped to 34. For those born after 1950—people approaching home-buying age in the mid-1980s—the median age began to move upward. In fact, from 1984 to 1996, the rate of home ownership among people under 40 fell.

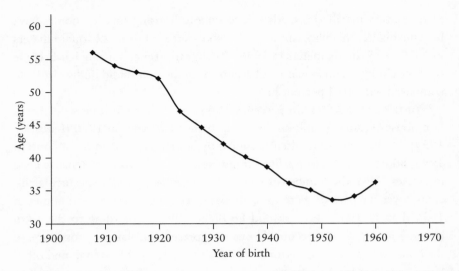

Figure 3.2.   Median age at access to home ownership by year of birth, France
SOURCE: Authors' calculations based on population and housing surveys (INSEE 1993, 1998).

One possible reason that the rate of home ownership among younger people has fallen is that they are delaying the transition to home ownership (Laferrère 1997). Montgomery (1992) cites the fact that unemployment is more common among younger people, which in turn has lowered this population's earnings and created more uncertainty about the future, both of which may prevent younger people from borrowing money to pay for a home. In addition, jobs today often require more mobility, which makes buying a house or a flat more difficult. Education, too, may contribute to a delay in home ownership. The fact that young people are in school longer means they arrive on the job market later.[4] More education also has contributed to the delay in forming first partnerships—a committed relationship or marriage—which in turn leads to a delay in having children. In the 1970s, the average age of women having their first child was 24; by the 1990s, it was 28 (Galland 2000). Marriage (or a long-term relationship) and the birth of children often motivate a couple to buy a home. If couples are putting off marriage and children, it makes sense, then, that they are putting off home ownership. Another factor here is the instability of relationships: couples break up more often today. Knowing that, they may well delay making a long-term commitment to buy a home.

Since the 1960s, government regulations in France have played an important role in increasing access to home ownership. A policy adopted in 1963 helped low-income households buy new housing.[5] Through the 1970s, housing prices increased, but inflation made real interest rates comparatively lower. The government encouraged the construction of new houses and gave subsidies for the purchase of housing. Since 1981, however, real interest rates have grown faster than the rate of inflation, increasing the cost of loans. Although housing prices have gone down, higher interest rates have made other forms of investment more attractive.

Today, 75 percent of people over 40 are homeowners. In the next few decades, many of their homes will be inherited, either directly or indirectly, by members of younger generations. This trend could well exclude from home ownership those people who have nothing to receive by inheritance.

HOME OWNERSHIP AND SOCIAL INEQUALITIES

As Table 3.1 shows, the percentage of homeowners varies by the age and occupational category of the head of household.[6] These differences are linked

TABLE 3.1

Home ownership by age and occupational category
of the head of household, France, 2002

| | PERCENTAGE OF HOMEOWNERS | | | | | |
| | Head of household's age | | | | | |
Head of household's occupational category	< 30 years	30–39 years	40–49 years	50–59 years	≥ 60 years	Average rate
Farmers	23.5	71.7	82.8	88.2	91.4	81.2
Craftspeople and tradespeople	23.2	55.4	72.3	79.5	80.7	69.6
Senior executives	14.5	47.3	71.6	77.1	75.5	60.8
Middle-level professionals	12.3	45.5	66.8	73.8	57.7	54.1
Office and service staff	9.1	25.6	42.9	50.7	47.7	33.0
Blue-collar workers	12.3	39.1	53.7	61.2	52.4	44.3
Retired workers	—	—	—	78.6	71.0	71.3
Other unemployed	3.0	15.0	27.4	47.8	55.3	32.4
AVERAGE	10.0	39.6	58.2	66.7	69.6	54.9

SOURCE: Authors' calculations based on the French labor force survey (2002).

to differences in income, behavior, and lifestyle among occupational categories as well as to constraints in the economic environment.

The table confirms that younger workers in all occupational categories are less likely to own a home. In 2002, just 10.0 percent of those under 30 and just 39.6 percent of those ages 30 to 39 were estimated to own homes; the rate increased to 58.2 percent for workers between ages 40 and 49, and to 66.7 percent for workers between ages 50 and 59. We know that unemployment is a factor here: younger workers generally are less secure in their jobs than older workers are. We know, too, that mobility is a factor in home-ownership rates by age: younger workers are more mobile than older workers are, which means they may also be more reluctant to set down roots. Mobility also appears to be a factor in rates by occupation. For instance, despite comparable incomes and across all ages, blue-collar workers are more likely to own homes than are office and service workers. The greater mobility demanded by white-collar jobs may well explain that variation. We found the highest proportion of homeowners in 2002 among self-employed workers—farmers (81.2 percent) and craftspeople and tradespeople (69.6 percent).

Between 1990 and 1999, the rate of home ownership decreased generally, but the relative proportion represented by each category of worker did not change markedly (Figure 3.3). Rates remained highest among farmers, and the rate for blue-collar workers continued to outpace that for office and service workers.[7] But part d of the figure shows that the transition to home ownership for both manual laborers and clerical and service workers became more difficult over the decade, especially among younger and middle-aged workers. This inequality may reflect the relatively high cost of housing for lower-income households: the vast majority of these workers buy their home on credit, and the cost of housing represents a higher proportion of their income than the cost of housing for executives and middle-level professionals. Table 3.2 shows the *rate of effort*—the proportion of household income spent on housing—for different categories of workers. Looking only at the net rates (mortgage costs alone), clerical and service workers and manual laborers spend between 24.5 and 25.0 percent of their income on housing, while other groups of workers spend just 20.7 to 24.0 percent.

More evidence of social inequality in the housing market in France comes from an examination of where homeowners live (Figure 3.4). Ownership rates vary greatly depending on the size of the community (Martin-Houssart and Tabard 2003). For example, it is relatively rare for office and

a. Average of all occupational categories

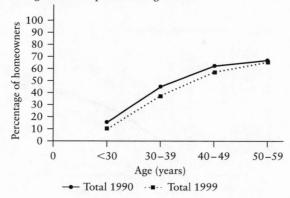

b. Farmers and other self-employed workers

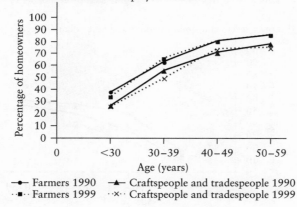

Figure 3.3. Home ownership by age and occupational category of the head of household, France, 1990 and 1999

S O U R C E : Authors' calculations based on the 1990 census (INSEE 1993) and the French labor force survey (1999).

service workers and manual laborers to buy homes in large towns or in the urban area of Paris: in 1990, only 30 percent of these workers owned homes in Paris, compared with 60 percent of senior executives. In contrast, in rural areas, all occupational groups have home-ownership rates of approximately 80 percent.

Figure 3.3.   (Continued)

c. Senior and middle-level professionals

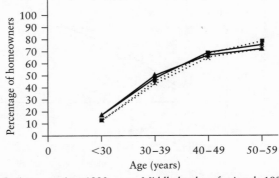

—•— Senior executives 1990   —▲— Middle-level professionals 1990
··■·· Senior executives 1999   ··×·· Middle-level professionals 1999

d. Lower-level white-collar workers and blue-collar workers

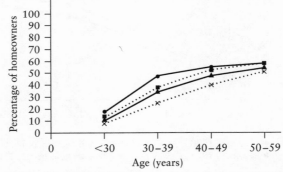

—▲— Office and service staff 1990   —•— Blue-collar workers 1990
··×·· Office and service staff 1999   ··■·· Blue-collar workers 1999

DELAY IN ACCESS TO HOME OWNERSHIP: INCREASED
DISPARITIES BY AGE AND OCCUPATIONAL CATEGORY

Using data from the Youth and Careers Survey (Meron 1997), we examined access to home ownership for couple households in which the head of household was born between 1952 and 1963. Our focus was the interval between the end of schooling and the date the first home was bought. Although we

TABLE 3.2
Home ownership and rate of effort by the occupational
category of the head of household, France, 1996

Head of household's occupational category	Number of households (1,000s)	RATE OF EFFORT		AVERAGE RATE OF EFFORT	
		Raw	Net	Raw	Net
Farmers	100	19.2	17.1	24.9	22.8
Craftspeople and tradespeople	447	19.5	18.9	24.6	24.0
Senior executives	709	16.6	16.5	20.8	20.7
Middle-level professionals	1,194	18.1	17.6	23.0	22.5
Office and service staff	671	20.0	18.8	26.0	24.8
Blue-collar workers					
Skilled	1,131	21.2	19.2	27.0	25.0
Semi- and unskilled	418	21.4	18.6	27.3	24.5
Retired persons					
No pension	58	22.8	22.0	29.8	29.0
Pension	388	15.7	15.2	21.9	21.4
Other unemployed	77	19.6	16.6	27.4	24.5
TOTAL/AVERAGE	5,193	18.8	17.8	24.1	23.1

SOURCE: Authors' calculations based on the 1996 housing survey (INSEE 1998).

NOTE: The rate of effort is the proportion of household income spent on housing. The raw rate includes running costs; the net rate does not.

could have used the date of marriage as our starting point, the survey had very precisely measured the interval between schooling and home purchase, making it a more useful measure for our purposes. The variation among age groups and occupational categories is more pronounced for men than for women; for the following analyses, then, we focused only on men.

In our analyses, we saw a strong link between occupation and the timing of home ownership. For example, half the senior executives waited 9.1 years after ending their studies to make the transition to home ownership; by comparison, service workers waited, on average, 14.5 years. Within any occupational category, men born between 1952 and 1957 bought homes more rapidly than did men born between 1958 and 1963 (Figure 3.5):

- Among senior executives, the median duration increased from 9.0 years for the older cohorts to 9.2 years for the younger ones.

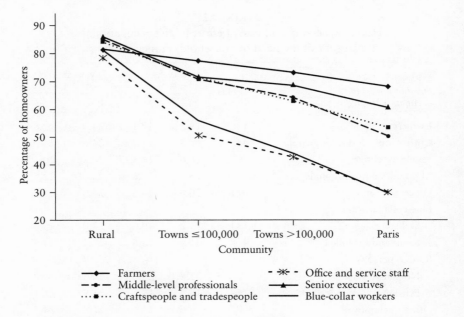

Figure 3.4. Home ownership by occupational category and community, France, 1990

s o u r c e: Authors' calculations based on the Youth and Careers Survey (Meron 1997).

- Among craftspeople and tradespeople, the median duration grew from 11.1 years to 12.8 years.
- Among middle-level professionals, the median duration went from 11.1 years to 13.3 years.
- Among service workers, the duration increased from 12.3 to 19.2 years.
- Among manual laborers, the interval went from 12.7 to 18.0 years.

Clearly this trend did not affect all occupational groups to the same extent. It touched members of lower occupational groups in particular and increased the dispersion among occupational groups in the younger cohorts. During the period the younger cohorts became homeowners, the French government was cutting back the number and scope of policies that supported home ownership.

Clerical and service workers were most affected: it was becoming increasingly difficult for them to buy a home. In fact, analyses with more-detailed birth cohorts (intervals of three years) showed that for men born between 1955 and 1957, the likelihood of owning a home had begun to shift. It was now greater for manual laborers than it was for office and service workers. In Figure 3.6, we present the survival distributions for the 1958–1960 birth cohort. That office and service workers had become less likely to make the transition to home ownership is clear. In the older birth cohorts, office employees became homeowners more quickly than blue-collar workers did; in the cohorts born after 1955, the rate for office workers began falling.

Behind the change in access to home ownership for younger clerical and service workers are changes in the makeup and skills of the labor market in France over the last few decades. In that period, the number of manual workers decreased, and those who continued as blue-collar workers generally became better qualified. At the same time, office and service employees were working at jobs that required fewer skills and offered less stability (Meron 1997).

In addition to the survival analyses, we conducted a Cox analysis, which allowed us to introduce several explanatory variables at the same time. The

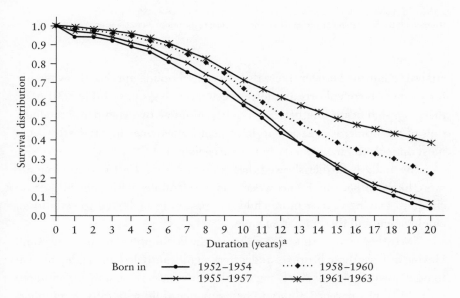

Figure 3.5.   Transition to home ownership by birth cohort, France

SOURCE: Authors' calculations based on the Youth and Careers Survey (Meron 1997).
[a]Duration is the interval in years from the end of schooling to the transition to home ownership.

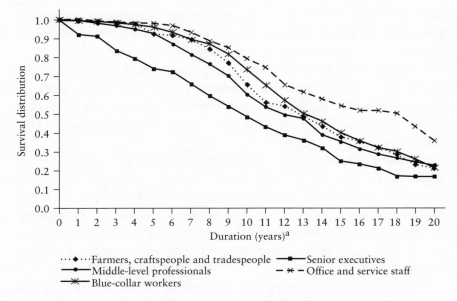

Figure 3.6. Transition to home ownership by occupational category, 1958–1960 birth cohort, France

SOURCE: Authors' calculations based on the Youth and Careers Survey (Meron 1997).
[a]Duration is the interval in years from the end of schooling to the transition to home ownership.

analysis confirmed longer intervals between schooling and home ownership for younger birth cohorts and lower occupational groups (Table 3.3). Also, there is a significant link between the rate of home ownership and the location of the home: it is easiest to become a homeowner in rural areas; it is most difficult to buy property in the Paris district.

The analysis further showed that couples with at least two children are more likely to become homeowners than are couples with one child or no children. Having two or more children appears to be linked to stability in employment and therefore in income.

Two other factors appear to influence the likelihood of home ownership. Having at least three brothers and sisters significantly lengthens the interval to home ownership, all else being equal. In this case, the number of children probably limits parents' ability to help any one child with gifts or an inheritance. A previous marriage also lengthens the wait for home ownership.

Further analyses revealed the influence of birth cohort in combination

TABLE 3.3
The likelihood of becoming a homeowner,
assorted variables, France (Cox analysis)

Variable	Parameter estimate		Risk ratios
Birth cohort			
1952–1954	0.11[b]		1.12
1955–1957		Ref.	
1958–1960	−0.35[c]		0.71
1961–1963	−0.61[c]		0.54
Occupational category			
Senior executives	0.36[c]		1.43
Farmers, craftspeople and tradespeople, and middle-level professionals		Ref.	
Office and service staff	−0.37[c]		0.69
Blue-collar workers	−0.21[c]		0.81
Location of home			
Rural district	0.18[c]		1.19
Urban district		Ref.	
Paris district	−0.12[a]		0.89
Number of children			
0		Ref.	
1	0.19[c]		1.22
2	0.38[c]		1.47
Number of siblings			
0 or 1	0.09[a]		1.09
2		Ref.	
3	−0.16[c]		0.85
Marital status			
Not previously married		Ref.	
Previously married	−0.17[b]		0.84

SOURCE: Authors' calculations based on the Youth and Careers Survey (Meron 1997).

NOTE: Location and number of children were treated as time-dependent variables.
[a] $p < .10$.
[b] $p < .05$.
[c] $p < .001$.

with other factors. We have already discussed the increased delay in home ownership for younger workers generally and low-income workers specifically. We also found that homeowners under age 40 (respondents born between 1958 and 1963) lived mainly in rural areas. The number of children was also an important factor for the younger birth cohorts. And we found that having three or more siblings or a father born abroad often increased the interval to home ownership, although the effects differed by occupational category.

In fact, the circumstances that are favorable or unfavorable to home ownership are not necessarily the same across occupational categories (Table 3.4). For example, birth cohort has a very slight effect on the home-ownership rates of senior executives; its effect is more pronounced on the other categories of workers, especially office and service workers. Living in Paris has a strong negative effect on craftspeople and tradespeople and middle-level professionals; living in a rural area is particularly motivating for manual workers. Having two or more children encourages home ownership among most categories except the self-employed (farmers, craftspeople, and tradespeople). Having many siblings reduces access to home ownership across all groups of workers, especially middle managers and the self-employed—workers for whom parental help probably plays an important role. Finally, having a father born abroad appears to play a significant negative role only for senior executives.

CONCLUSION: STRONG INFLUENCES OF
BIRTH COHORT AND OCCUPATIONAL CLASS

Rates of home ownership clearly are linked to birth cohort. Younger workers, facing insecurity in the labor market and jobs that demand travel, are forced to put off home ownership. Contributing to that delay are the educational process and the reality of relationships today. Occupational class is another important factor in access to home ownership: as labor market position improves, the size and stability of income increase and, in turn, so does the ability to buy a home.

In France, differences among social classes still loom large. Because many adult children remain in the same social class as their parents, it is likely that their behavior continues to be distinguished by occupational class. And access to home ownership depends not only on own earnings, but also

TABLE 3.4

The likelihood of becoming a homeowner by occupational category, France (Cox analysis)

	HEAD OF HOUSEHOLD'S OCCUPATIONAL CATEGORY									
	Senior executives (n = 563)		Farmers and craftspeople and tradespeople (n = 462)		Middle-level professionals (n = 780)		Office and service staff (n = 375)		Blue-collar workers (n = 1,441)	
Variables	Parameter estimate	Risk ratio	Parameter estimate	Risk ratio	Parameter estimate	Risk ratio	Parameter estimate	Risk ratio	Parameter estimate	Risk ratio
Birth cohort										
1952–1954	0.29[c]	1.33	0.11	1.11	0.08	1.09	0.43[b]	1.53	−0.08	0.92
1955–1957					Ref.					
1958–1960	−0.01	0.99	−0.43[c]	0.65	−0.37[c]	0.69	−0.67[c]	0.51	−0.44[c]	0.65
1961–1963	0.053	1.06	−0.63[c]	0.53	−0.67[c]	0.51	−0.93[c]	0.40	−0.88[c]	0.41
Location of home										
Rural district	0.127	1.14	0.04	1.04	0.06	1.06	0.03	1.03	0.35[c]	1.42
Urban district					Ref.					
Paris district	−0.07	0.93	−0.49[a]	0.61	−0.21[a]	0.81	−0.06	0.94	−0.11	0.89
Number of children										
0 or 1					Ref.					
≥2	0.15[b]	1.16	0.06	1.07	0.30[c]	1.36	0.29[a]	1.34	0.28[c]	1.33

(*continued*)

TABLE 3.4
(Continued)

| | HEAD OF HOUSEHOLD'S OCCUPATIONAL CATEGORY | | | | | | | | | |
| | Senior executives (n = 563) | | Farmers and craftspeople and tradespeople (n = 462) | | Middle-level professionals (n = 780) | | Office and service staff (n = 375) | | Blue-collar workers (n = 1,441) | |
Variables	Parameter estimate	Risk ratio	Parameter estimate	Risk ratio	Parameter estimate	Risk ratio	Parameter estimate	Risk ratio	Parameter estimate	Risk ratio
Number of siblings										
0–2					Ref.					
≥3	−0.22	0.80	−0.47	0.63	−0.19[b]	0.82	−0.19	0.83	−0.10	0.91
Marital status										
Not previously married					Ref.					
Previously married	−0.19[a]	0.82	−0.21	0.81	−0.30[a]	0.74	−0.28	0.76	−0.08	0.92
Father's citizenship										
Foreign	−0.28[b]	0.75	0.24	1.28	−0.16	0.85	0.11	1.11	−0.08	0.93
French					Ref.					
Number of events	440		334		572		200		855	
Censored episodes	123 (21.85%)		128 (27.71%)		208 (26.67%)		175 (46.67%)		586 (40.67%)	

SOURCE: Authors' calculations based on the Youth and Careers Survey (Meron 1997).

NOTE: Location and number of children were treated as time-dependent variables.

[a] p < .10.
[b] p < .05.
[c] p < .001.

on intergenerational transfers. Does this mean that there are no modifications in class differences between generations in the French population? No. Inequalities have been growing, particularly among younger cohorts. Job insecurity is a special problem that is more severe for those who are less educated; they have more difficulties with economic integration; they postpone family formation; and many of them extend the time of training. Also, the institutional features of the French housing system do not support young people whose savings are limited by income. All of these factors contribute to strengthening spatial and socioeconomic inequalities (Martin-Houssart and Tabard 2003) and to delaying home ownership. Access to home ownership has changed across generations. But those changes have not reduced the differences among occupational classes; they have widened them.

Notes

1. A historical note: at the end of World War II, the proportion of homeowners among households in France was just 31 percent.

2. If not otherwise stated, all numbers are based on the authors' calculations using data from the housing surveys (INSEE 1998).

3. Housing surveys also tell us that homeowners today are more likely to buy an older home than a newer one. At the beginning of the 1980s, 68 percent of new housing was owner occupied; in 1996, that rate had dropped to 45 percent.

4. More years of education also means that the younger population makes up an increasing proportion of managerial and executive staff, people who are more mobile than those in other professions, especially at the beginning of their careers. And, again, that contributes to a delay in home ownership.

5. In 1997, a less-favorable policy—Allocation Personalisée pour le Logement (APL)—was adopted to help low-income households become homeowners.

6. The type of housing purchased (flat versus house) also varies by occupational group (Laferrère 1999).

7. According to the housing survey of 1996, which is more precise, 86 percent of farmers and 74 percent of craftspeople owned their home. This was also the case for 56 percent of senior managers, 59 percent of middle-level professionals, and 55 percent of office and service staff, versus more than 60 percent of blue-collar workers.

References

Ascher, François, ed. 1995. *Le logement en questions*. Paris: Édition de l'Aube.
Courgeau, Daniel, and Eva Lelièvre. 1992. Interrelations between first homeowner-

ship, constitution of the family, and professional occupation in France. In *Demographic applications of event history analysis*, edited by James Trussell, Richard Hankinson, and Judith Tilson, 120–40. Oxford: Clarendon Press.

Galland, Olivier. 2000. *Entrée dans la vie adulte: Des étapes toujours plus tardives mais resserrées*. Économie et Statistiques 337–338. Paris: INSEE.

Institut National de la Statistique et des Études Économiques (INSEE). 1993. *Logements immeubles, recensement de la population 1990*. INSEE résultats coll. Démographie et Société 28–29. Paris.

———. 1998. *Les conditions de logement des ménages enquête logement 1996–1997*. INSEE résultats coll. Consommation Modes de Vie 97–98. Paris.

Laferrère, Anne. 1997. Les ménages et leurs logements. *INSEE—Première*, no. 562 (Décembre).

———. 1999. *L'occupation des logements depuis 1945*. Données Sociales 333–340. Paris: INSEE.

Martin-Houssart, Gèraldine, and Nicole Tabard. 2003. *Inégalités et disparités entre les quartiers en 1999*. Données Sociales 2002–2003 489–500. Paris: INSEE.

Meron, Monique. 1997. *Dossier sur "Les trajectoires des jeunes: Distances et dépendances entre générations."* Économie et Statistiques 304–305. Paris: INSEE.

Montgomery, Mark. 1992. *Household formation and home-ownership in France. Demographic applications of event history analysis*, edited by James Trussell, Richard Hankinson, and Judith Tilson, 94–119. Oxford: Clarendon Press.

Omalek, Laure, and David Le Blanc. 1998. Les conditions de logement fin 1996. *INSEE—Première*, no. 563 (Janvier).

Segaud, Marion, Catherine Bonvalet, and Jacques Brun, eds. 1998. *Logement et habitat: L'état des savoirs*. Paris: Editions La Découverte.

Topalov, Christian. 1987. *Le logement en France. Histoire d'une marchandise impossible*. Paris: Presses de la Fondation Nationale de Sciences Politiques.

CHAPTER FOUR

Home Ownership and Social Inequality in Belgium

Veerle Geurts and Luc Goossens

Studies on the connection between home ownership and income inequality often produce conflicting conclusions. For example, Kemeny (1980, 1981) suggested that there is an inverse relationship, a trade-off, between welfare-state spending and the incidence of home ownership in Western industrialized nations. Castles (1998) examined Kemeny's trade-off hypothesis more rigorously and over a longer time. The overall implications of his findings supported Kemeny's basic insight: since the 1970s, high levels of home ownership in Western societies have been linked to weakly developed welfare states.[1] But Castles drew a very different conclusion. Kemeny had argued that the distribution of home ownership reinforces social inequalities; Castles argued that home ownership, at least for the elderly, actually levels out the distribution of final income.

The outcome in these studies and others seems to depend primarily on the incidence of home ownership across social categories. To resolve the disagreement over the relationship between home ownership and inequality, then, more research in this area is necessary. Because Belgium is an exception to the trade-off hypothesis—the rate of home ownership there is high, particularly in Flanders, and the country has a well-developed welfare state—it constitutes a valuable case study.[2]

Our analysis is in four sections. In the first, we give an overview of general socioeconomic conditions in the postwar period. We also summarize the most important housing policies and regulations, briefly noting their ideological bases. In the second, we outline trends in home ownership since 1945 as they relate to housing policies. In Belgium, home ownership has always been a widespread phenomenon. Furthermore, housing policy in the country, officially at least, has always supported home ownership in general and home ownership for low-income families in particular. So we would expect a somewhat equal distribution of home ownership across social categories. Changes in housing tenure for important social groups are the main focus of this second section. In the third section, we look at several aspects of the relationship between home ownership and social inequality. We begin with an examination of the role government support plays in the attainment of home ownership. Who benefits from housing subsidies for home ownership? How effective is housing policy? How selective is it? Then we focus on housing tenure: renting versus owning. Are there differences in housing quality and comfort? What is the relative impact on the household budget of paying rent versus a mortgage? Finally, we explore the effects of tenure and housing costs on income inequality and poverty. In the fourth section, we summarize and discuss our findings.[3]

CONTEXT

Economic Developments

Since World War II, general socioeconomic conditions in Belgium have moved through four phases (Cantillon 1999; Cantillon et al. 1999; Meulemans, Geurts, and De Decker 1995):[4]

- *From World War II until the mid-1970s.* The economic expansion experienced by most European countries after the war provided favorable economic conditions in Belgium for home ownership. That expansion was marked by rising wages, low mortgage interest rates, low unemployment rates, and positive feelings about the future.
- *From the mid-1970s to the mid-1980s.* In this period, economic conditions began to deteriorate. Average household welfare fell slightly, and unemployment rose.[5] But the period was also marked by an equalization of income rooted largely in significant increases in standardized income (actual income adjusted by household size) for the elderly, particularly for the least-affluent elderly. Furthermore, relative poverty dropped sharply in this period, from about 10 percent in 1976 to 6 percent in 1985.
- *From 1985 to 1992.* During this period, equalization came to an end. Relative poverty remained more or less constant at about 6 percent, and there was only a slight increase in income disparities. Nevertheless, all income groups saw a strong improvement—about 17 percent on average—in their

standard of living. Rich and poor shared almost equally in the growth of household welfare. Furthermore, unemployment dropped visibly in this period.

- *From 1992 to 1997.* In this period, inequalities continued to grow slowly. Because the average increase in standardized income was very low (just 3 percent), the least-affluent households made barely any progress in real terms. The biggest losers were households surviving exclusively on unemployment benefits. Unemployment in Flanders increased again, although it seemed to peak in 1996.

The years from 1970 to 2000 were characterized by very rapid increases in housing costs (Van Dam and Geurts 2000). Both rents and the price of houses rose about five times faster than the price of other goods and services. However, rents increased steadily over the years, while the prices of owner-occupied houses fluctuated.[6] After spectacular growth in the mid-1970s, the purchase price of housing dropped in real terms between 1980 and 1985. With the economic revival, purchase prices recovered and quickly rose above the general rate of inflation. Also, mortgage rates went up dramatically between 1976 and 1983; reached their low for the period in 1988; and then peaked in 1992. After 1992, the rates dropped to historically low levels.

Housing Policy

In Belgium, the focus of housing policy generally has always been on home ownership among private households. The broader purpose of housing policy has been "to achieve a balance between the housing stock on the one hand and the quantitative and qualitative housing needs on the other, while paying special attention to the plight of the 'less well-off'" (Deleeck, Huybrechs, and Cantillon 1983). In practice, though, the scope of Belgian housing policy often has been narrowed to the stimulation of home ownership, particularly through newly built houses, among lower-income social groups. Industrial workers were the earliest target. The first housing legislation, which was passed in 1889 in response to a labor uprising in 1886 that had been inspired by the socialist movement, must be seen as a means to counter socialism and to integrate manual laborers. The idea was that home ownership would bind the working classes more closely to the capitalist economic system. Over the next eighty or so years, new legislation was passed to extend support to all low-income families, especially to large families. The widespread belief in Belgium, as in many other countries, was that a family's own home with a garden was the ideal place to raise children (Goossens 1983, 1986, 1993).

The economic recession of the 1970s and 1980s inspired the Belgian government to no more than a few—not even successful—alternative readings of the classic Keynesian housing policy of home ownership and/through new construction. After the reorganization of the country in 1980, housing policy was decentralized. In the years that followed, the Flemish government held on to the primary goal of supporting private home ownership: 58 percent of that government's spending on housing went to stimulate home ownership; 23 percent, to the public rental sector; and 17 percent, to improving and renovating housing (*Economisch Financiële Berichten* 2000; Peeters and De Decker 1997).[7] Only recently has there been a cautious shift in policy toward more local and democratic involvement, housing quality, and the rental sector.

Housing policy in Belgium historically had three main characteristics. First, it centered on subsidies for the construction of new houses. The subsidies were directed at individual households, which took responsibility for purchasing land, contracting with an architect, and organizing the building process. Until recently, the policy only gave lip service to renovation. At work here was the *filtering-up principle*: large-scale construction projects not only produce new houses for middle- and upper-income households; they also enable lower-income households to rent better-quality accommodations. That the principle does not hold can be seen in the lack of substantial urban renewal to date and the fact that a large quantity of poor-quality housing remains in use (De Decker and Raes 1996).

Second, the target of housing policy—in particular, support for home ownership—has always been very broadly defined. Income limits, if any, traditionally have been high: at least theoretically, more than 80 percent of renters are eligible for one or more subsidies to help them buy a home (Meulemans et al. 1995).

Third, housing policy was (and continues to be) characterized by small financial incentives in both macro- and microeconomic terms. The historical policy option was to give as many households as possible relatively limited support instead of giving a limited number of households substantial support. It has repeatedly been demonstrated that the amount of intervention at the household level remains low in comparison to necessary investment. Subsidies or grants, therefore, rarely influence the decision to buy a home.

In 1979, the national planning office highlighted the limited scope and effect of subsidies (Planbureau 1979). Several years later, criticism of subsidy levels and their effectiveness was voiced by researchers who argued that "the limited amount of the premium (less than 4 percent of the purchase price of a newly-built house) can in itself provide no encouragement for building" (Deleeck et al. 1983). G. Verscheure (1988) of the national planning office confirmed that opinion, stating that there was no significant relationship between the demand for housing and the number of subsidies granted. In fact, households that built or bought with the aid of a cheap loan from the Housing Fund for Big Families received premiums, on average, that varied from just 2.3 percent to 8.9 percent of their total investment (De Decker, Goossens, and Beirens 1994).

In the three regions of Belgium, there is a wide range of government support for home ownership: cheap loans, cheap land, and mortgage deductions among them. However, since 1984, the dominant form of help for low-income families who want to buy a home has been a combined housing grant for the construction of a new dwelling, the purchase of a subsidized dwelling, or the renovation of an older dwelling. In the years since the program was introduced in 1948, thousands and thousands of Belgian households with limited earnings—the equivalent of €19,850—obtained a grant.[8] The grants could be very substantial: in 1992, for example, €13,900 for a married couple with four children and a net taxable income below €9,900 (Hubeau, Lancksweerdt, and Vandenberghe 1992).

In 1993, the Flemish government replaced the federal grant system with a monthly allowance toward mortgage payments. The subsidy program was available to households for an initial three-year period, which could be extended for another three years. Qualifying households had to meet both income and dwelling-size criteria. The level of the subsidy was means tested; but for the 9,860 households that qualified in 1995, the average value per year was a maximum of €610 (De Decker 2000). At the beginning of 2000, the Flemish government abolished the program, by its own account because low interest rates and a public insurance system against income loss had reduced its effectiveness.[9]

Another instrument of direct government intervention is the cheap loan, a loan with a low interest rate. In principle, cheap loans are targeted at low-income households. The interest rates are means tested and correspond to the household's number of children, and the loans are restricted generally to families with a net taxable income of less than €29,750 to €37,200 a year (with an increase for encumbrances).

The federal government also supports home ownership indirectly, through subsidies to public housing associations for the construction of houses and through tax measures. The latter encompass reduced registration fees, income tax relief, and preferential value-added tax (VAT) rates.[10] Most important, mortgage payments are deductible in part for all homeowners regardless of household income.[11]

TRENDS IN HOME OWNERSHIP

The Rate of Home Ownership Since 1945

Like home-ownership rates in most Western European countries—for example, West Germany/Germany, Norway, and Britain—rates in Belgium have increased steadily over the postwar decades, especially in Flanders. In fact, home ownership has always been more common in Flanders than in the other regions of Belgium and in other European countries. In 1947, more than 40 percent of Flemish households owned their own home; fifty years later, the rate was over 70 percent (Figure 4.1). Of neighboring countries, only Luxembourg has had a comparable share of owner-occupied housing. And only the rates of countries in the south of Europe, which are strongly oriented toward agriculture and often are referred to as residual (less developed) welfare states (Barlow and Duncan 1994), rival the Flemish rate.

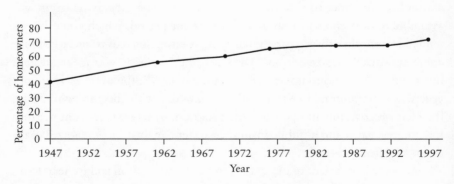

Figure 4.1. Proportion of homeowners, Flanders, 1947–1997

SOURCE: Authors' calculations based on data from censuses (Nationaal Instituut voor de Statistiek 1947, 1961, 1971, 1981, 1991) and the Belgian SEP, and supplemented with survey data (see the appendix).

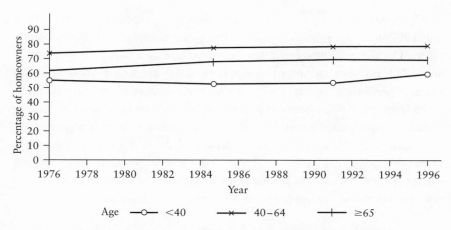

Figure 4.2.   Proportion of homeowners by age of head of household, Flanders, 1976–1997

SOURCE: Belgian SEP, Flanders.

It follows that the rental sector has always been relatively small in Flanders; and the sector has further decreased in size since World War II. But this trend has affected public rental stock more than private rental stock, which nearly equals the EU average of 21 percent. By comparison, public rental units account for only 6 percent of the region's total housing stock.[12]

Some would argue that the high level of home ownership in Flanders results from a stable policy of supporting home ownership. But others would argue that households buy homes because there has never been a realistic alternative: there simply isn't enough public rental stock, and the lack of regulation in the private rental sector means no security or rent controls for tenants (De Decker 2000).

Government policy has an important impact on the rate of home ownership. So do economic conditions. If we look again at Figure 4.1, we can see the slowdown in the growth of home ownership during the economic crisis that started in the mid-1970s and continued into the 1980s. When the economy improved, the incidence of home ownership picked up again.

Figure 4.2 shows the strong relationship between age and home ownership. The highest proportion of home-owning households—approximately 80 percent in 1997—is found among those ages 40 to 64. Between ages 65 and 70, the rate gradually falls (to below 70 percent for those over age 70 in

1997). Although the figure indicates that ownership rates rose between 1976 and 1997 in all age groups, it is clear that younger people were particularly affected by the economic crisis that began in the mid-1970s.[13] Between 1976 and 1992, the proportion of homeowners in this age group actually fell by about 3 percentage points.[14] After 1992, the rate rose again, surpassing its 1976 level: by 1997, about 60 percent of households in which the head of household was under age 40 were owner–occupiers. Furthermore, since the 1990s, the rates for older cohorts—those who drove the overall increase in ownership attainment between 1976 and 1992—appear to have peaked. The proportion of owners has more or less stabilized since 1985 at 79 percent for 40- to 64-year-olds and at 69 percent for those age 65 and over.[15]

The Distribution of Home Ownership

In Belgium, as in most other European countries, economic expansion after the war encouraged home ownership. During this period, even low-income households were able to build or buy their own house, and, in the absence of an alternative, many did so. Table 4.1 shows that in 1976, rates of home ownership differed little in terms of household occupation, income, and education. This was true for elderly people (age 65 or older) and even more so for active people (under age 65).[16] One- or more-income families, low- or high-income families, blue- or white-collar families, uneducated or well-educated families, all had more or less the same home-ownership rate—about 65 percent. We found just two exceptions: unemployed people (44 percent) and single persons (50 percent).

But after 1976, a gap began widening between low-income and higher-income households, especially among homeowners under age 65. For example, a remarkable increase in home-ownership rates occurred between 1976 and 1997 among couples with two or more incomes from work, households belonging to the two highest income quintiles, and households whose head had higher education. In addition, for the first time ever, there was a substantial drop in the owner-occupancy rate for households headed by an unskilled manual worker and those whose head received only a primary school education.[17]

HOME OWNERSHIP AND SOCIAL INEQUALITY

Subsidized Ownership

Housing subsidies in Flanders could be described as selective because subsidy policies are aimed primarily at lower-income households. To understand the extent to which those policies realize their objective, we looked at the distribution of subsidized owners across income deciles and examined profiles of the various segments of the housing market.[18]

Data from the Belgian Socio-Economic Panel (SEP) indicate that in 1997, almost 30 percent of Flemish households (just under 42 percent of all homeowners) relied on direct incentives to purchase or make payments on a home. For most, that incentive took the form of a purchase and building grant: about 70 percent of all subsidized owners have claimed a government grant for the acquisition (approximately 20 percent) or construction (approximately 80 percent) of a dwelling. Some 26 percent have a loan at a reduced rate of interest, while 20 percent have claimed a renovation, redevelopment, or improvement grant. About 12 percent of subsidized owners have purchased a cheap dwelling (approximately three-quarters of these owners) or building lot (approximately one-quarter) from a social housing association or other government institution. And, finally, close to 3 percent have claimed the recently introduced and even more recently abolished rent subsidy. Many households combine two or more measures.

Figure 4.3 shows that subsidized home ownership in 1997 actually was not selective. When we correct income for differences in household size, just 16 percent of all subsidized owners belong to the lowest income groups (deciles 1 and 2). Participation is spread widely over the other decile groups, with a slight concentration in the higher middle groups (deciles 6 to 8).

Sociodemographic data tell us that subsidized owners do vary somewhat from nonsubsidized owners along several dimensions (Table 4.2):

- Subsidized owners are less likely to be single (a total of 13.9 percent versus 21.3 percent) and are more likely to have a household with three or more children (9.2 percent versus 4.6 percent).
- Almost two-thirds (66.2 percent) of subsidized owners are between the ages of 35 and 64; the equivalent rate for nonsubsidized owners is 57.3 percent.
- Although multiple-income households are represented more strongly in the category of subsidized owners than in that of nonsubsidized owners, and

TABLE 4.1

Proportion of homeowners by age and socioeconomic characteristics, Flanders, various years 1976–1997

PERCENTAGE OF HOMEOWNERS

Socioeconomic characteristics	Active persons (<65)				Elderly persons (≥65)				Average			
	1976	1985	1992	1997	1976	1985	1992	1997	1976	1985	1992	1997
All households	66.2	67.2	67.0	71.6	62.1	68.1	69.6	69.7	65.1	67.4	67.6	71.1
Number employed												
0	64.7	60.1	65.2	61.3	60.5	67.3	68.6	69.4	61.6	64.9	67.4	66.6
1	66.9	65.0	63.4	65.6	*a*	*a*	*a*	*a*	67.1	65.5	64.4	65.8
2	65.6	71.9	70.4	80.1	*a*	*a*	*a*	*a*	65.9	72.0	70.5	80.2
Labor market status (head of household)												
Employed	66.5	68.4	67.0	73.4	*a*	*a*	*a*	*a*	66.7	68.4	66.9	73.2
Not employed	64.2	62.5	67.4	66.0	61.7	67.9	69.7	70.0	62.4	65.8	68.7	68.4
Retired	73.9	77.9	79.3	82.2	61.8	67.9	69.7	70.0	63.8	70.4	72.3	73.2
Unemployed	44.4	35.1	47.2	37.8	*a*	*a*	*a*	*a*	44.7	35.1	47.2	37.8
Disabled	67.5	67.8	64.8	69.7	*a*	*a*	*a*	*a*	65.4	67.8	64.8	69.7
Occupational status (head of household)												
Unskilled manual worker	63.5	58.0	56.6	50.5	56.7	63.4	66.2	65.2	61.5	59.9	60.1	55.6
Skilled manual worker	64.3	69.9	65.4	68.9	56.0	74.6	78.7	72.1	63.2	70.5	67.1	69.5
Clerical worker, middle manager	64.9	67.6	69.3	76.3	59.8	70.7	61.7	67.3	64.4	68.0	67.7	74.3
Executive	69.3	73.7	75.6	81.9	73.0	80.1[b]	86.9[b]	79.3	69.7	74.5	76.9	81.5
Farmer or other self-employed worker	73.8	67.6	69.8	70.0	75.8	77.5	76.9	84.2	74.5	69.9	71.8	74.7

Number of incomes (from work)

1, single-person household	49.8	36.0	41.0	44.7	49.8	60.3	57.3	53.5	49.9	50.3	48.6	48.6
1, couple household	71.4	71.8	74.5	75.1	72.6	79.9	81.9	79.2	71.6	73.4	76.4	76.4
2, couple household	64.7	70.2	71.3	79.3	67.7	70.4	78.8	86.0	65.2	70.3	72.3	80.3
Standardized income quintile												
1 (lowest)	61.2	55.6	53.9	52.0	60.6	67.2	64.0	65.6	60.9	61.0	59.0	58.8
2	67.0	64.6	65.9	65.1	61.9	65.7	72.6	69.3	65.6	64.9	67.9	66.7
3	69.4	68.5	67.4	69.7	64.8	68.0	71.5	69.7	68.9	68.4	68.2	69.7
4	66.3	71.6	68.4	78.4	67.9	70.3	77.0	77.0	66.3	71.4	69.2	78.2
5 (highest)	64.0	70.6	73.5	81.7	75.9	76.9	78.6	84.2	64.7	71.2	74.0	81.9[b]
Relative poverty status (EU benchmark)												
Poor	56.3	51.9	39.9	39.7	64.7	63.3	62.4	64.1	62.1	57.7	51.7	53.4
Not poor	66.6	67.8	68.2	73.0	61.3	68.7	70.8	70.6	65.6	68.0	68.7	72.4
Education (head of household)												
Primary school	68.5	71.3	67.3	64.3	61.2	67.8	70.7	63.7	65.7	69.7	69.1	64.0
Lower secondary	64.9	66.1	67.8	70.7	67.8	62.0	64.5	74.4	65.2	65.4	67.2	71.6
Advanced secondary	66.6	64.8	66.1	67.3	60.3	73.7	68.3	79.3	66.1	65.8	66.4	68.9
Higher education	61.8	67.3	66.5	79.6	72.3[b]	79.5[b]	76.3[b]	79.0	62.8	68.3	67.2	79.5
Number of households	4,154	2,850	1,741	2,003	1,255	906	538	722	5,419	3,756	2,279	2,725

SOURCE: Authors' calculations based on the Belgian SEP, Flanders.

[a] Fewer than 20 cases, so not presented.
[b] Fewer than 50 cases.

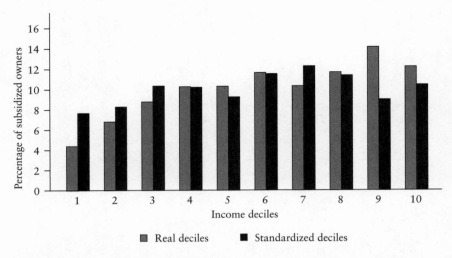

Figure 4.3. Distribution of subsidized owners across income deciles, Flanders, 1997

SOURCE: Belgian SEP, Flanders, wave 1997.

the employment rate among household heads is also higher, the average standardized household income is only €50 lower.

- In terms of education, subsidized owners are slightly more prominent in the lower categories: 53 percent did not study beyond secondary school, compared with 43 percent of nonsubsidized owners.
- Subsidized owners are more likely to be manual workers: 39.7 percent versus 30.9 percent.

The results indicate that subsidized home ownership is most common in the middle class, especially in the upper middle class, and is less common among lower-income households. This modest degree of selectivity might be explained by two factors: on the one hand, the high financial burden of becoming an owner–occupier and, on the other hand, the relatively low amounts of subsidies. Furthermore, the income ceilings for government subsidies are high: theoretically, three out of four nonowners are eligible. It seems that government supports home ownership for households that could manage it financially anyway—that subsidies are in large part a bonus—and that home ownership remains the privilege of middle- and upper-income groups. Consequently, low-income households in the main have to turn to the private and public rental sectors.

TABLE 4.2
Sociodemographic profiles of nonsubsidized and
subsidized owners and tenants, Flanders, 1997

Sociodemographic characteristics	PERCENTAGE OF				Average of all owners and tenants (%)
	Non-subsidized owners	Subsidized owners	All owners	All tenants	
Household type					
1 elderly person	11.0	8.0	9.8	20.3	12.8
1 active person	8.3	4.0	6.5	22.1	11.0
Single-parent family	2.0	1.9	1.9	4.6	2.7
2 elderly persons	20.2	18.2	19.3	9.8	16.6
2 active persons, 0 children	15.4	15.5	15.4	17.5	16.0
2 active persons, 1 child	11.0	11.9	11.4	10.0	11.0
2 active persons, 2 children	15.4	14.5	15.0	7.0	12.7
2 active persons, 3 children	4.6	9.2	6.5	2.6	5.3
Others, 0 children	8.5	10.3	9.2	3.9	7.7
Others, ≥ 1 child	3.6	6.7	4.9	2.1	4.1
Age (head of household)					
<35	14.9	10.3	12.9	30.9	18.1
35–44	21.5	24.9	23.0	19.5	22.0
45–64	35.8	41.3	38.1	21.8	33.4
≥ 65	27.8	23.5	26.0	27.8	26.4
Number of incomes (from work)					
1, single-person household	21.2	13.9	18.1	47.1	26.5
1, couple household	21.6	24.5	22.8	17.3	21.2
2 or more, couple household	57.2	61.6	59.0	35.6	52.3
Relative poverty status (EU benchmark)					
Poor	6.6	3.3	5.2	11.2	7.0
Not poor	93.4	96.7	94.8	88.8	93.0
Standardized income quintile					
1 (lowest)	17.2	15.1	16.3	28.9	20.0
2	16.8	21.5	18.8	23.2	20.0
3	18.3	21.6	19.7	20.8	20.0
4	22.5	21.4	22.0	15.0	20.0
5 (highest)	25.3	20.3	23.2	12.1	20.0

(*continued*)

TABLE 4.2
(*Continued*)

Sociodemographic characteristics	PERCENTAGE OF				Average of all owners and tenants (%)
	Non-subsidized owners	Subsidized owners	All owners	All tenants	
Education (head of household)					
Primary education	22.5	25.6	23.8	32.3	26.3
Lower secondary	20.9	27.1	23.5	22.4	23.2
Advanced secondary	27.9	25.7	27.0	29.3	27.6
Higher education	28.7	21.7	25.8	16.0	22.9
Occupational status (head of household)					
Unskilled manual worker	10.0	12.8	11.2	22.6	14.4
Skilled manual worker	20.9	26.9	23.4	25.9	24.1
Clerical worker, middle manager	32.2	33.4	32.7	28.6	31.5
Executive	21.1	15.1	18.6	10.7	16.3
Farmer or other self-employed worker	14.4	10.2	12.6	10.8	12.1
Number of households	1,124	811	1,935	787	2,725

SOURCE: Authors' calculations based on the Belgian SEP, Flanders.

Inequalities: Owners Versus Tenants

Since 1993, decent housing has been a basic right in Belgium. In 1997, the Flemish government decreed that *decent housing* speaks to dwellings that are comfortable and of good quality, reasonably priced, and in a safe environment, and that offer owner or tenant housing security.[19] In this section, we deal with the question of whether home ownership, in particular subsidized home ownership, contributes to the quality, comfort, and affordability of housing, especially for lower-income families.[20]

Housing Quality and Comfort

The quality of a dwelling is measured in terms of the defects noted by interviewers (exterior) and respondents (interior).[21] The degree of comfort is measured primarily by means of two indicators: Does a structure have a bath or a shower, and does it have central heating? If the answer to both questions is yes, then we rated the structure "full comfort."[22]

Quality is strongly related to the age of a structure, which is why the year of construction is the first variable listed in Table 4.3. There appears to be a marked difference between nonsubsidized owners and tenants on the one hand and subsidized owners on the other: about 55 percent of the former live in housing that predates the 1960s, whereas 58 percent of subsidized owners live in houses that were built between 1961 and 1990. Although nonsubsidized owners occupy slightly more dwellings constructed after 1990, we can conclude that the dwellings occupied by subsidized owners tend to be more recently constructed than those occupied by nonsubsidized owners or tenants.

Owner occupancy seems to have a greater impact than subsidies do on the defects in housing. If we look at the overall number of defects, we find no significant differences between nonsubsidized and subsidized owners: about 61 percent report no defects.[23] Only 44 percent of tenants report no defects in their housing.

Our criterion for poor-quality housing was three or more defects on the interior and exterior of the dwelling.[24] In general, 15 percent of all households rent or own housing with three or more defects. But when we compare owners and renters, we find that the percentage of tenants living in poor-quality housing is more than twice that of homeowners: 26 percent versus 11 percent. And among homeowners, it is clear that subsidized owners are better off than nonsubsidized owners, with 9 percent versus 12 percent living in a dwelling with three or more defects.[25]

Between 1976 and 1997, housing in Flanders generally underwent continuous and pronounced improvement in comfort (Van Dam and Geurts 2000). For example, in 1997, 74 percent of housing met our full-comfort criterion: the dwellings had both a shower or a bath, and central heating. The rate was 43 percent in 1976. The improvement in terms of comfort applied to both owners and tenants fairly evenly until 1992, when improvements in owner-occupied housing began to outpace improvements in rental housing. By 1997, owner-occupied dwellings were appreciably more comfortable than rented dwellings: almost 79 percent met the full-comfort criterion versus 64 percent of rental units. Rental housing is particularly likely to suffer from a lack of double-glazed windows and central heating.

TABLE 4.3
Housing quality and comfort, Flanders, 1997

| Variable | PERCENTAGE OF | | | | Average of all owners and tenants (%) |
	Non-subsidized owners	Subsidized owners	All owners	All tenants	
Year of construction					
Before 1919	10.8	3.3	7.7	10.3	8.6
1919–1945	23.1	14.5	19.4	19.3	19.8
1946–1960	20.8	19.3	20.1	25.6	21.7
1961–1970	12.1	20.7	15.8	19.3	16.6
1971–1980	15.8	20.6	17.8	12.1	16.0
1981–1990	6.6	16.2	10.7	6.8	9.5
After 1990	10.8	5.4	8.6	6.8	7.9
Number of defects					
0	60.3	61.2	60.7	43.7	56.0
1	17.9	22.3	19.7	19.3	19.5
2	9.6	7.7	8.8	11.1	9.4
3	3.9	3.2	3.6	5.7	4.1
4	4.1	2.4	3.3	8.8	4.8
≥ 5	4.1	3.3	3.8	11.8	6.2
Amenities					
Double-glazed windows	55.0	64.4	59.0	36.5	52.5
Kitchen size at least 4 square meters	95.0	96.4	95.6	83.6	92.1
Indoor flush toilet	96.9	97.3	97.1	95.6	95.5
Hot running water	97.0	98.9	97.8	94.6	96.9
Central heating	76.1	82.8	78.9	65.0	74.9

(*continued*)

In the owner-occupied sector, the homes of subsidized owners are better equipped than the homes of nonsubsidized owners. Here, too, the largest discrepancies have to do with double-glazed windows and central heating, but the pattern holds true across all comfort indicators.

Finally, an examination of the socioeconomic variables in Table 4.3 indicates that almost without exception, subsidized owners enjoy better quality and more-comfortable housing than do nonsubsidized owners and renters in the same low socioeconomic categories. What the table does not show,

TABLE 4.3
(*Continued*)

| | PERCENTAGE OF | | | | *Average of all owners and tenants (%)* |
Variable	*Non-subsidized owners*	*Subsidized owners*	*All owners*	*All tenants*	
Bath or shower	97.0	98.9	97.8	94.4	96.8
Full comfort[a]	75.5	82.6	78.6	64.0	74.4
Rate of poor-quality housing among					
Single persons	17.6	25.9	20.3	25.8	23.3
Single-income couples	8.6	4.2	6.6	25.8	11.3
Lowest standardized income quintile	17.5	10.3	14.7	31.3	21.8
People with only a primary school education	22.9	8.1	16.2	23.7	19.0
Unskilled workers	28.0	11.6	20.0	33.5	26.4
Rate of full-comfort housing among[a]					
Single persons	69.8	64.7	68.2	64.0	66.0
Single-income couples	68.7	84.7	75.9	60.4	72.3
Lowest standardized income quintile	51.1	73.1	59.7	52.5	56.7
People with only a primary education	50.3	74.9	61.4	55.4	59.3
Unskilled workers	41.0	80.9	60.5	52.6	57.0
Number of households	1,124	811	1,935	787	2,725

SOURCE: Authors' calculations based on the Belgian SEP, Flanders, wave 1997.

[a]A structure having both a bath or a shower, and central heating.

however, is that nonsubsidized owners in upper socioeconomic categories also live very comfortably—in fact, more comfortably than subsidized owners in the same socioeconomic categories.[26]

Housing Costs and Affordability

As mentioned earlier, the Flemish housing market saw significant price increases between 1976 and 1997. Housing costs have gone up much faster than consumer prices generally.[27] Survey data show that the average monthly mortgage payment in real terms was 73 percent higher in 1997 than it was in 1976; and the average rent increased by 65 percent. Moreover, this trend was amplified by an increase in the proportion of homeowners with house loans, from less than 20 percent in 1976 to more than 30 percent in 1997. In a period of just twenty-one years, general housing costs (calculated for all households, including those without housing costs) went up 95 percent.

Over the same period, the disposable income of nonsubsidized home-owners rose by less than 6 percent. As households grew increasingly smaller, average household welfare (measured in terms of standardized income, which corrects actual income for household size) increased more rapidly (by 18.6 percent) but was still well below the rate at which housing expenditures rose.[28] Consequently, the average *housing burden*—housing costs expressed as a percentage of income—almost doubled for all households between 1976 and 1997, from 6.5 percent to 11.6 percent (see Table 4.4).

Although the average housing burden for renters increased less than the average for homeowners, the gap between tenants and owner-occupiers widened between 1976 and 1997, especially in the last five years of the period. Until 1992, the increase was virtually identical for renters and owners (up 6.4 percentage points): both groups were spending an average of 18 percent of their income on housing. However, between 1992 and 1997, the average housing burden for renters rose sharply: up 5.6 percentage points versus an increase of just 1.8 points for owners. There were two factors behind this development. First, renters' disposable income (both real and standard-ized) fell; second, the proportion of owners who owned their house outright (with no mortgage payments) increased for the first time since 1976.

The problem of affordability increased for owners and renters between 1976 and 1985, and between 1992 and 1997. In the intervening years, there was stability. Not surprisingly, that period of stable housing prices was marked by a strong increase in household welfare: the average standardized household income went up 16 percent.[29]

When social scientists and policymakers talk about *affordable housing*, they use a housing burden of 20 percent as the criterion of affordability. Following this standard, in 1997 affordable housing was a problem for 23 percent of Flemish households (Table 4.4). Here, too, renters were especially disadvantaged: by 1997, over half of them—51.2 percent—were paying more than 20 percent of their income to cover the basic cost of housing; the

TABLE 4.4
Income and housing costs by
housing market segment, Flanders, 1997

Variable	Non-subsidized owners	Subsidized owners	All owners	All tenants	Average of all owners and tenants
Average disposable monthly income					
Households with housing costs					
Real income	2,620	2,560	2,590	1,530	2,110
Standardized income	1,440	1,280	1,360	1,050	1,220
All households					
Real income	2,150	2,200	2,170	1,530	1,990
Standardized income	1,270	1,220	1,250	1,050	1,190
Average monthly housing cost					
Households with housing costs	450	360	410	300	450
All households	180	160	170	300	200
Average housing burden (%)[a]					
Households with housing costs	20.8	16.2	18.8	23.6	21.0
All households	8.1	7.2	7.7	23.6	11.6
Relative housing burden (%)					
Households with no housing costs	61.0	55.5	58.7	0.0	44.8
< 15%	15.1	23.8	18.7	28.0	20.6
15%–20%	8.2	9.4	8.7	20.8	11.6
> 20%	15.7	11.3	13.9	51.2	23.0
> 33%	3.7	1.8	2.9	17.0	6.4
Comfort and affordability (%)[b]					
Households that lack comfort and have a housing burden above 20%	3.0	2.0	2.6	13.2	5.6
Households that lack comfort and have a housing burden above 33%	0.7	0.2	0.5	4.2	1.5
Households with affordability problems (%)[c]					
All households					
Single persons	13.4	11.6	12.8	71.6	39.0
Single-income couples	10.6	12.3	11.3	49.1	19.0
Lowest standardized income quintile	10.8	16.6	13.1	65.9	31.5
People with only a primary school education	3.2	2.0	2.7	50.8	18.2
Unskilled workers	10.5	16.7	13.5	50.1	28.0

(*continued*)

TABLE 4.4
(*Continued*)

Variable	Non-subsidized owners	Subsidized owners	All owners	All tenants	Average of all owners and tenants
Households with housing costs					
Single persons	55.2	46.4[d]	53.6	71.6	67.7
Single-income couples	42.2	34.3	38.0	49.1	44.7
Lowest standardized income quintile	70.9[d]	64.3[d]	67.5	65.9	66.4
People with only a primary school education	32.6[d]	10.3[d]	18.9	50.8	48.3
Unskilled workers	45.6[d]	43.2[d]	44.1	50.1	44.3
Number of households	1,124	811	1,935	787	2,725

SOURCE: Authors' calculations based on the Belgian SEP, Flanders, wave 1997.

[a]The average housing burden is the average cost of housing expressed as a percentage of average income.
[b]Again, the full-comfort criterion is a structure with both a bath or a shower, and central heating.
[c]Affordable housing places a housing burden of no more than 20% on the household.
[d]Fewer than 50 cases.

equivalent rate for homeowners was less than 14 percent. That disadvantage is also reflected in the average housing burden for renters: almost 24 percent. In fact this average and the average housing burden for nonsubsidized owners with housing costs (close to 21 percent) both fall outside the affordable standard.

Banks in Flanders use a different standard for assessing affordability: that is, they are willing to grant mortgages up to a 33 percent housing burden. In 1976, just 2.3 percent of households exceeded that standard; by 1997, 6.8 percent of Flemish households were spending more than 33 percent of their disposable income on bare housing costs. And again, the gap between owners and renters was considerable: 2.9 percent versus 17.0 percent.

Table 4.4 also shows that the average mortgage payment in the nonsubsidized sector (€450) is €90 higher than it is in the subsidized sector, while disposable real income is just €60 higher. This discrepancy explains why the average housing burden among nonsubsidized owners who are paying off a mortgage is 4.6 percentage points higher than the burden for subsidized owners. That there are more households without a mortgage among non-subsidized owners explains why the difference in the average housing burden for all nonsubsidized households is just 0.9 point higher than it is for subsidized owners. Moreover, 3.7 percent of nonsubsidized owners exceed the affordability limit set by financial institutions, compared with 1.8 percent of subsidized owners.

On average, the disposable (real) income of tenants in 1997 was €1,060 lower than that of owners with mortgages, but renters paid just €110 less for rent on average. The result: 51.2 percent of tenants spent more than a fifth of their disposable income on rent, and 17.0 percent spent more than a third of their disposable income. And when we examine comfort with affordability, it is clear that renters have the worst of the housing market: more than 13 percent of tenants live in housing that meets neither the comfort nor the affordability criterion.

Finally, for households with housing costs, in every socioeconomic category, subsidized owners are less likely than nonsubsidized owners and renters to have a problem with affordable housing.

Housing Costs, Income Inequality, and Poverty

The cost of housing often is one of the largest items in the household budget. The affordability of housing by definition is a function of household income. Obviously, it is also a function of housing circumstances: homeowners without a mortgage are better off, other things being equal, than are tenants or homeowners with a mortgage (Van den Bosch 1998). Put simply: households with no housing costs have more money for nonhousing consumption.

To understand the connections among housing costs, income inequality, and poverty, we could begin by deducting bare housing costs (the household's monthly rent or mortgage payment) from the household's disposable income. Clearly outright owners, because they do not have to pay rent or make mortgage payments, immediately have a higher standard of living than do tenants or mortgaged owners with the same disposable income. But that calculation ignores important differences between tenants and mortgaged owners. Mortgages eventually are paid off; rent is forever. In addition, a house is part of a household's wealth. In other words, when a household has paid off its mortgage, it has the benefit of free housing *and* the value of its property. Therefore, we deduct only interest payments, not payments for principal. The repayment of capital is a form of wealth accumulation.[30]

Table 4.5 displays the mean disposable income of households before and after the deduction of rent or of mortgage interest. In 1997, disposable income decreased in real terms by about 7 percent when housing costs were subtracted. Among elderly households (head of household age 65 or older), the difference was somewhat smaller because of the high proportion of mortgage-free owners. Moreover, although the standard deviation falls after the deduction of housing costs, the coefficient of variance and the Theil coefficient, two measures of inequality, indicate a greater disparity in income.[31] This is true for real income as well as for standardized income and for both active and elderly households.[32]

The effects on real and relative poverty rates of deducting housing costs are shown in Table 4.6. The adjustment of disposable income for the cost of rent or mortgage interest produced poverty rates about 2.5 percentage points higher than the unadjusted rates. The table shows real and relative poverty rates by age and housing tenure. In active and elderly households, poverty rates among outright owners drop considerably—about 45 percent in relative terms. Although the adjustment produced a 19 percent increase in the relative poverty rate of mortgaged owners, that rate remained far below average.

Where housing costs seem to have dramatic effects is among tenants. When we deducted the cost of rent from their disposable income, poverty rates for tenants in both age groups rose significantly, by about 44 percent in relative terms. Remember that poverty rates for tenants start out quite high. That disparity was strengthened when we adjusted their disposable income for housing costs: tenants in active households were almost two times more likely than the average household to fall below the poverty threshold, and tenants in elderly households were more than three times more likely to meet the poverty criterion.

CONCLUSION

In Flanders, home-ownership rates have always been high. Furthermore, housing policy there—at least officially—focused on supporting home ownership for low-income families. Therefore, we would expect a rather equal distribution of home ownership across different social categories. And survey data suggest that until the mid-1970s, that was the case: home-ownership rates were little affected by income, education, or occupational status.

TABLE 4.5
The impact of monthly housing costs on mean disposable income
(in euros) and income inequality, Flanders, 1997

Household type	Mean	Standard deviation	Coefficient of variance	Theil coefficient	N
Total population					
Disposable income					
Real	1,990	1,150	0.579	0.149	2,725
Standardized	1,190	550	0.462	0.093	2,725
Disposable income − housing costs					
Real	1,850	1,130	0.611	0.168	2,716
Standardized	1,100	550	0.497	0.109	2,716
Active households (<65)					
Disposable income					
Real	2,240	1,170	0.521	0.121	2,003
Standardized	1,270	550	0.431	0.082	2,003
Disposable income − housing costs					
Real	2,080	1,160	0.556	0.141	1,998
Standardized	1,170	550	0.467	0.098	1,998
Elderly households (≥65)					
Disposable income					
Real	1,280	740	0.578	0.138	722
Standardized	960	490	0.505	0.102	722
Disposable income − housing costs					
Real	1,220	760	0.625	0.162	718
Standardized	910	500	0.552	0.123	718

SOURCE: Authors' calculations based on the Belgian SEP, Flanders, wave 1997.

NOTE: For mortgaged owners, housing costs in this table were limited to interest payments.

TABLE 4.6

Real and relative poverty rates before and after
adjusting for housing costs, Flanders, 1997

Type of household and housing tenure	UNADJUSTED RATES (%)		ADJUSTED RATES (%)		Percentage in sample
	Real	Relative[a]	Real	Relative[a]	
All households	7.0	100	9.5	100	100
Active households (< 65)					
Owners with a mortgage	1.8	26	2.9	31	30.6
Owners without a mortgage	3.0	43	2.3	24	21.9
All owners	2.3	33	2.7	28	52.6
All tenants	8.8	126	17.2	181	20.9
All owners and tenants	4.2	60	6.8	72	73.5
Elderly households (≥ 65)					
Owners without a mortgage	13.6	194	10.2	107	8.0
All tenants	17.4	249	34.1	359	18.5
All owners and tenants	14.7	210	17.3	182	26.5

SOURCE: Authors' calculations based on the Belgian SEP, Flanders, wave 1997.

NOTE: For mortgaged owners, housing costs in this table were limited to interest payments.
[a]In proportion to the overall poverty rate.

That would change in the last decades of the century, as the gap between rich and poor widened. General economic conditions certainly played a part. In Belgium, as in most European countries, the economic expansion after World War II had created very favorable conditions for home ownership: even lower-income families were able to build or buy their own houses. But the economic downturn that began in the mid-1970s and continued with just one abatement through 1997 made the transition to home ownership more difficult, especially for younger people.

The data also point to important differences in housing conditions for different segments of the housing market. Subsidized owners—even in lower socioeconomic groups—typically live in newer, higher-quality, and more-comfortable housing than do nonsubsidized owners. Furthermore, the average housing burden for subsidized owners is below the critical 20 percent standard. Although home ownership offers nonsubsidized owners a security that renters lack, affordability is a problem for these homeowners and for renters: both segments shoulder housing burdens above 20 percent.

Given these observations, can we conclude that housing policy in Flanders has been successful? Our answer is a qualified no, not if the goal of that policy is to increase home-ownership rates among lower-income groups. Our findings indicate that subsidized home ownership is most common among middle-class households, which might be explained by the high financial burden of buying a house and the relatively low amount of subsidies. Furthermore, the income ceilings for government support are so high that theoretically three out of four nonowner households are eligible. In general, then, housing policy in Flanders promotes home ownership for households that could manage it anyway. The subsidies are for the most part an added incentive, and home ownership remains the privilege of middle- and upper-income groups.

The effects of current housing policy in Flanders are particularly harsh for renters. Even the small bias in housing programs has forced low-income households to turn to the rental sector. And because those programs focus on home ownership, there are few public rental options for tenants. This, too, increases the economic burden on tenant households, especially older households. The result: a growing inequality in disposable income when housing costs are taken into account, and a relative poverty rate almost double that of homeowners.

Albeit more by setting a norm than by financing housing, the Flemish government's support of home ownership seems to have produced a high rate of home ownership and considerably better housing conditions for homeowners. Still, an important segment of the population remains excluded from home ownership and must contend with poor housing conditions and housing costs that push these households over the threshold of poverty.

APPENDIX: SOME METHODOLOGICAL REMARKS

Samples and Data Collection

The Center for Social Policy (CSP) conducts research into social policy issues. The key questions invariably are "What are the effects of this policy, and is the policy meeting its objectives?" The research primarily uses quantitative methods. Data are collected by means of surveys of a representative sample of households. The first such survey, encompassing 5,419 Flemish households, was conducted in 1976. It was repeated in 1982 with 4,840 Flemish households participating.

In 1985, the survey was extended to the whole of Belgium. That was the first of four rounds of interviews—called *waves*. It also marked the start of the Belgian Socio-Economic Panel (SEP). Of the 6,471 Belgian households that were surveyed in 1985 (first wave), 3,779 were surveyed again in 1988 (second wave), and 2,821 were surveyed again in 1992 (third wave). The 1997 survey (fourth wave) encompassed 4,632 households, including 2,802 in Flanders. In 1992 and 1997, the panel was replenished with an additional sample. The initial sample was a stratified two-step sample from the registers of the population. Both replenishments were identified in roughly the same way using the National Registry (*Rijksregister*).

The data were collected by means of face-to-face interviews. Household data, including housing indicators, were provided by the head of household or possibly the partner. Within each household, information was gathered about every member. All household members age 18 or older were asked to respond to an individual questionnaire; basic information about those under 18 was provided by the household head.

Key Measures and Concepts

Unit of Analysis

The unit of analysis in the SEP is the private household. The adjective *private* indicates that the household lives independently. Homeless people and those residing in institutions were excluded from the research population. All persons living under the same roof and largely combining their incomes are considered members of the same household. Also included were students and working children who live at home and other persons living in.

Income

In the SEP, the term *income* refers to monthly disposable income. It includes the net income from chief and secondary occupations and the net earnings of self-employed individuals. It also includes social benefits that replace income (disability, retirement, unemployment) and allowances at the household level (child benefits, scholarships). Although the SEP also considers property and earnings from property to be part of the household's disposable income, we for the most part did not include these items in our income calculations. The only exception: in the analyses relating exclusively to the 1997 data, we added income from rental property to household income.

Household Welfare

The *welfare* of a household is a function of the household's total income and the number of individuals living on that income. To compare the standard of living of households of different sizes, we used equivalence factors to convert household income into *standardized income*—income that takes into account household size and economies of scale in consumption. The first adult constitutes the base and so was assigned a factor of 1. Each additional adult and child in the household was assigned an equivalence factor of 0.5 and 0.3 respectively.

EU Benchmark

We used the EU benchmark to determine whether or not a given household was poor. That relative standard fixes the poverty line at 50 percent of the average household income. Otherwise, we applied the equivalence scale described above.

Inequality Measures

To measure income and welfare inequality, we used three traditional inequality measures. The first was the *coefficient of variation* (V):[33]

$$V = \frac{s}{\overline{X}}$$

in which s = the standard deviation, and
$\overline{X}$ = the mean.

The second and third were the *Theil coefficient* and the *Gini coefficient*:

$$\text{Theil coefficient} = \frac{1}{n} * \sum_{i}^{n} \left(\left(\frac{y_i}{m} \right) * \log \left(\frac{y_i}{m} \right) \right)$$

$$\text{Gini coefficient} = \frac{2}{n^2 m} * \sum_{i}^{n} i y_i - \frac{n+1}{n}$$

in which
n = the number of income units,
i = the income unit,
$y_i \ldots y_n$ = the income of the income unit, and
m = the average income in the sample.

Both Theil and Gini coefficients obtain a value of 0 if the total income volume is distributed equally over the sample—that is, if every income unit gets the same share of the total income volume. Both measures also attain their maximum value when all income is concentrated in one household. For the Theil coefficient, this maximum is log n; for the Gini coefficient, the maximum is ~ 1 (approximating 1).

Tenure

We began by identifying four basic types of tenure: owner occupancy with a mortgage, owner occupancy with no mortgage (outright ownership), rental, and free occupancy (living rent-free in a dwelling one does not own).

On the basis of the information supplied in 1997, it was possible to distinguish between *nonsubsidized* and *subsidized housing markets*. In the analyses, we classified all households that made use of one or more of the following provisions as subsidized owners: (1) a construction or purchase subsidy; (2) a renovation subsidy; (3) a loan at a reduced rate of interest from the Flemish Housing Association (*Vlaamse Huisvestingsmaatschappij*) or the Flemish Housing Fund (*Vlaams Woningfonds*); (4) purchase of a dwelling or building lot from a registered public housing association or any other public body; and (5) an interest subsidy.

Housing Conditions

We measured the *degree of comfort* primarily by means of two indicators: "bath or shower" and "central heating." We defined *full comfort* as the presence of both. Because we used only two indicators here, the conclusions we've drawn regarding the degree of comfort should be interpreted with caution.

A number of indicators for the quality of housing were first incorporated in the 1997 survey. Because one of the samples in that survey was taken from private households on the National Registry, the figures are not representative of the entire housing stock: vacant dwellings and dwellings occupied by collective households or by individuals who are not included in the National Registry are outside the research population.

Housing quality was evaluated in two ways. Interviewers assessed the exterior of structures, while respondents provided information about the interior. Among the exterior indicators were type of dwelling, breadth of the facade, and neighborhood. Interviewers were also asked to try to identify defects in the roof, gutters, walls, windows, and doors. Each building element was marked on a three-point scale: 1 indicated a major defect to the element in question; 2, a minor defect; and 3, no defect. In addition, the interviewers were asked to use the same scale in making a general assessment of each structure's state of repair. Finally, they were asked to categorize the exterior of each dwelling using one of five labels, ranging from "dwelling without defects" to "slum, fit for clearing."

The respondents were asked to report the quality of and amenities in the interior of the dwelling, among them the year of construction; total surface area; and the presence of a separate kitchen measuring at least four square meters, hot running water, central heating, double-glazing on all windows, a bath or a shower, and a flush toilet. In terms of quality, respondents were asked about the occurrence of the following defects:

- Drafts through cracks or doors and windows that do not close well
- Dampness or water seeping through windows, doors, or windowsills
- Damp or moldy patches on walls, floors, or ceilings
- Cracks in a wall or damaged plastering

For each of these defects, respondents were asked whether they occurred in the living room, bedroom(s), bathroom, or kitchen. Finally, they were asked whether power was ever lost when several electrical appliances were used at once.

Housing Costs

Housing costs consist of the actual monthly rent in the case of tenants and of monthly mortgage payments for homeowners. These costs are "bare" costs—they do not include taxes or expenses for water, heat, electricity, and maintenance. A household's *housing burden* is the percentage of household income it spends on housing. In our analyses, we calculated the housing burden—the housing-cost-to-income ratio—using the bare housing costs.

Affordability

To answer the question of whether a given level of housing costs was affordable, we needed an affordability criterion. But we found no consensus in the international literature on such a criterion (Meulemans, Geurts, and De Decker 1996).

In Belgium, two measures are commonly used. One is the one-third standard applied by banks in determining a household's ability to repay a housing loan: a household may spend up to one-third of its income on mortgage payments. Public housing authorities use 20 percent of household income to determine the maximum a household should spend on rent. As a rule, we used the 20 percent standard throughout the analysis.

Income Inequality and Poverty

To incorporate housing tenure into the measurement of income inequality and poverty, we had to deduct housing costs from disposable income. The process involves several steps. To begin, we had to convert mortgaged owners' monthly mortgage payment to a monthly interest payment:

$$\text{Interest payment} = \frac{a * [1 - (1 + i)^{k-n-1}]}{12}$$

in which a = the household's monthly mortgage payment * 12,
    i = the average interest rate of current mortgages,
    k = 1997 − the year when the mortgage was granted, and
    n = the term of the mortgage (number of years).

Second, we deducted the monthly rent or mortgage interest payment from the household's real monthly disposable income. Third, we standardized the real net income by means of the equivalence factors described above. Finally, we recalculated the EU poverty benchmark using the adjusted income figure.

Notes

1. Castles also noted that this correlation appeared to be fading in the 1990s.

2. Belgium is divided into three regions. The Brussels–Capital Region is in the center of the country, and the people there are bilingual: they speak both French and Dutch. The Flemish Region is in the north, and Dutch is spoken there. The people in the Walloon Region, in the south, speak French. (For more information about the structure of Belgium, see www.belgium.be/eportal/application?origin= navigationBanner.jsp&event=bea.portal.framework.internal.refresh&pageid= indexPage&navId=2679.) Throughout this chapter, our focus is on Flanders.

3. Part of the analyses reported in the following sections comes from a study financed by the Flemish Community on the profile of the tenant in the social sector. More results of this study can be found in Van Dam and Geurts (2000).

4. Because data are available only from certain years, we could not determine the exact beginning and end of trends—a fact that readers should bear in mind here and throughout. Our observation years were 1976, 1985, 1992, and 1997. See the appendix to this chapter for more information on the data we used.

5. Household welfare is a function of the household's total income and the number of individuals living on that income. See the appendix for the calculation of this standardized income measure.

6. Owner-occupied houses include existing houses and newly built houses. The price of new houses includes the price of land and of construction.

7. The remaining 2 percent was allocated to administrative costs.

8. An encumbrance increase was made in 1993 for people with handicaps, for example.

9. The insurance went into effect on December 5, 1998. Its terms: for a period of ten years, eligible families receive a subsidy, which is paid directly to the mortgage loan office, as insurance against the head of household's becoming unemployed or disabled. During the first year, the maximum monthly subsidy is €250 per month; during the second year, the amount is reduced by 20 percent; in the third year, it is reduced by 40 percent. The income limit is €29,750, and the maximum mortgage loan is €49,580. The actual amount paid depends on the household's net taxable income and the amount of the loan.

10. The VAT rate is based on the nature of the transaction. In Belgium, the standard VAT rate is 21 percent, and that is the rate applied to the building industry. Reduced rates—generally, just 6 percent to 12 percent—are available for work done on private dwellings that are at least fifteen years old (there have been excep-

tions for houses that are newer), that house people with handicaps, and that are temporary or small; and for public housing.

11. This provision dates back to the first housing law (1889). The deductions include all mortgage expenses: principle, interest, and insurance premiums. This policy represents 80 percent of all government benefits for housing, and it is not selective at all—that is, higher-income taxpayers benefit the most (De Decker 2000). Because the policy makes no income restrictions and is funded by the federal government, it was beyond the scope of our study.

12. It is difficult to compare social housing rates in Europe: "Unfortunately, figures on 'social' renting are not comparable across EU countries, as the national definitions of 'social' rental dwelling vary considerably. From the information that exists, it can be said that in many countries, including Denmark, France, the Netherlands and the United Kingdom, this 'public' rental accommodation represents roughly half or more of the total rental sector" (European Central Bank 2003, 30).

13. For details, see www.ufsia.ac.be/CSB/about_en.htm.

14. Although this drop in itself is not statistically significant, it points to the turnaround in the economy during the period. The increases in the different time spans are also not significant, but the overall increase between 1976 and 1997 is.

15. In addition, among single elderly people, the proportion of homeowners actually fell significantly in the late 1990s (Van den Bosch 1998, 11–16).

16. We made the distinction between the two groups on two grounds: first, because the generalization by birth cohort masks the real increase in home ownership, and, second, because labor market status, income quintiles, and levels of education are biased by including the elderly.

17. Over the period studied, membership in both of these categories decreased, especially among people under age 65. Therefore, the overall home-ownership rates were not much affected.

18. It is important to bear in mind that household income relates to the year the data are collected, not necessarily to the year the household bought a home. Also, by *subsidized owners*, we mean households that received support from the Flemish government in purchasing their home. See the appendix for further details.

19. Some would argue that owning a home within its means is the only guarantee of a household's housing security (see, for example, Gennez 2003).

20. We focused on these three dimensions—omitting the environment and housing security—because quality, comfort, and affordability seem better indicators of individual family welfare.

21. For more on the quality of housing, see the policy note of former housing minister Bert Anciaux (2000).

22. See the appendix for more information on the measurement of housing quality and comfort.

23. We do find a difference between nonsubsidized and subsidized owners in terms of the nature of defects. Nonsubsidized owners report fewer defects inside

their homes; subsidized owners typically have no visible defects on the exterior of their homes.

24. Our results were similar when we used a five-defect criterion, as Table 4.3 shows.

25. A more-detailed analysis indicated that the difference between subsidized and nonsubsidized owners can be explained by the difference in the age of their homes; but the difference between renters and owners cannot.

26. In this comparison, households were in the two highest income quintiles, and they were headed by a college-educated individual who was either self-employed or an executive. The nonsubsidized-owner advantage also showed up in households with three or more children, including single-parent households.

27. All references to housing expenses here are to the "bare" costs of housing: principal and interest for homeowners, rent for tenants. Taxes and the costs of decoration, maintenance, utilities, water and sewer, and the like have not been taken into account. See the appendix for more details.

28. See the appendix for more information on the measurement of income and household welfare.

29. See the discussion of general economic development above.

30. See the appendix for more information on the adjustment of income and poverty thresholds for housing costs.

31. The Gini coefficient, another measure of inequality, produced similar results. See the appendix for the calculation of inequality measures.

32. Results not shown here indicate that the disparity between active households and elderly households was slightly smaller after the deduction of housing costs.

33. It is also called the *coefficient of dispersion*.

References

Anciaux, Bert. 2000. *Beleidsnota 2000–2004*. Available at http://www.wvc .vlaanderen.be/jeugdbeleid/beleid/beleidsnota/

Barlow, James, and Simon Duncan. 1994. *Success and failure in housing provision. European systems compared*. Oxford: Pergamon.

Belgian Socio-Economic Panel (SEP). Available online at www.ufsia.ac.be/CSB/ sep_nl.htm.

Cantillon, Bea. 1999. *De welvaartsstaat in de kering*. Kapellen: Pelckmans.

Cantillon, Bea, Lieve De Lathouwer, Ive Marx, Rudi Van Dam, and Karel Van den Bosch. 1999. *Sociale indicatoren 1976–1997, Berichten*. Antwerpen: Centrum voor Sociaal Beleid, UFSIA.

Castles, Francis G. 1998. The really big trade-off. *Acta Politica* 33 (1): 5–19.

De Decker, Pascal. 2000. Wie geniet van de overheidsuitgaven voor wonen in Vlaanderen? *Ruimte en Planning* 20 (1): 8–35.

De Decker, Pascal, Luc Goossens, and Kristin Beirens. 1994. *Naar een eerste Vlaamse Wooncode: Achtergrondnota*. Antwerpen: Vlaamse Wooncode-Commissie, UFSIA.

De Decker, Pascal, and Koen Raes 1996. *Access to housing, processes of exclusion and tenure (in)security in Belgium. The 1995 Belgian national report for the European Observatory on Homelessness*. Brussels: European Federation of National Organisations for Homeless People.

Deleeck, Herman, Johan Huybrechs, and Bea Cantillon. 1983. *Het Mattheüseffect*. Antwerpen: Kluwer.

Economisch Financiële Berichten. 2000. Tendensen op de Belgische woningmarkt. Vol. 55, no. 2: 1–20.

European Central Bank. 2003. *Structural factors in the EU housing market*. Frankfurt am Main.

Eurostat. 1999. *European Community Household Panel (ECHP), selected indicators from the 1995 wave*. Luxemburg: European Community.

Gennez, Caroline. 2003. Luyten Anna and Gilbert Roox, Breinstorm 2003. Wordt het straks allemaal minder? *De Standaard*, December 27 (interview).

Goossens, Luc. 1983. Het sociaal huisvestingsbeleid in België. Een historisch-sociologische analyse van de woonproblematiek sinds 1830. *Tijdschrift voor Sociale Wetenschappen* 8 (2): 83–110.

———. 1986. Het sociaal huisvestingsbeleid in Vlaanderen (1972–1986): Op het breukvlak van een traditie. *Ruimtelijke Planning* 17:1–11.

———. 1993. De middelpuntvliedende en -zoekende krachten in de Vlaamse huisvestingswereld. *Ruimtelijke Planning* 1 (1): 39–58.

Hubeau, B., E. Lancksweerdt, and J. Vandenberghe, 1992. *Huisvestingszakboekje*. Deurne: Kluwer Rechtswetenschappen.

Kemeny, John. 1980. The political economy of housing. In *Essays in the political economy of Australian capitalism*, vol. 4, edited by E. L. Wheelwright and Ken Buckley. Sydney: Australia and New Zealand Book Company.

———. 1981. *The myth of homeownership*. London: Routledge and Kegan.

Meulemans, Bert, Veerle Geurts, and Pascal De Decker. 1995. *Onderzoek naar de doelgroepen van het woonbeleid*. Antwerpen: Centrum voor Sociaal Beleid—Steunpunt Wonen en Woonbeleid, UFSIA.

———. 1996. *Het onbereikbare dak. Eigendomsverwerving, wooncomfort, prijsontwikkelingen en betaalbaarheid in dynamisch en geografisch perspectief*. Antwerpen: Centrum voor Sociaal Beleid, UFSIA.

Nationaal Instituut voor de Statistiek (NIS). Various years. Volkstellingen. Brussels.

Peeters, Leo, and Pascal De Decker. 1997. *Het woonbeleid in Vlaanderen op een tweesprong*. Berchem: EPO.

Planbureau. 1979. *Ontwikkelen van sociale indicatoren: Naar een sociaal verslag*. Brussels.

Van Dam, Rudi, and Veerle Geurts. 2000. *De bewoners van gesubsidieerde en niet gesubsidieerde woningen in Vlaanderen*. Antwerpen: Centrum voor Sociaal Beleid, UFSIA.

Van den Bosch, Karel. 1998. Hoe rijk zijn de armen? Het vermogen van huishoudens beneden de armoedegrens. *CSB-Berichten*, December.

Verscheure, G. 1988. *Fonction sociale et dimension économique du logement en Belgique*. Bruxelles Bureau du Plan.

CHAPTER FIVE

Home Ownership and Social Inequality in the Netherlands

Clara H. Mulder

In the past few decades, the Netherlands has quickly developed from a renter society into a society where over half of the homes are occupied by their owners. This change can be attributed to changes in housing and tax policies, which have left the country with a strong public rental sector and full tax deductions for mortgage interest. Other factors here include changes in real income and lifestyle (dual earnership and postponement of childbearing, for example).

AN OVERVIEW

Trends in Home Ownership

The Netherlands has traditionally been a society of renters. Compared with most industrialized countries, its share of homeowners was low. In 1955, for example, the proportion of owner-occupied homes in the Netherlands was under 30 percent; it was between 35 percent and 40 percent in France, West Germany, and Great Britain (Martens 1985). From the 1950s on, however, the percentage of owner-occupied homes has grown continuously (Table 5.1). The 50 percent divide was passed in 1998, and there are as yet no signs of a slowdown.

An indication of the changing position of owner-occupied housing in the market comes from the distribution of new construction across housing sectors (Figure 5.1). The proportion of new owner-occupied units varied considerably over the 1970s, 1980s, and 1990s. The main trend in those decades was a decrease of construction in the public and private rental sectors, while

TABLE 5.1
Number of dwellings and rate of home ownership,
the Netherlands, 1947–1999

Year	Number of dwellings (1,000s)	Percentage owner occupied	Year	Number of dwellings (1,000s)	Percentage owner occupied
1947	2,126	28	1990	5,802	45
1956	2,567	29	1994	6,116	48
1964	3,072	34	1995	6,192	48
1971	3,787	35	1996	6,276	49
1977	4,480	41	1997	6,358	50
1982	4,957	42	1998	6,441	51
1986	5,384	43	1999	6,521	52

SOURCE: Ministerie VROM (1999).

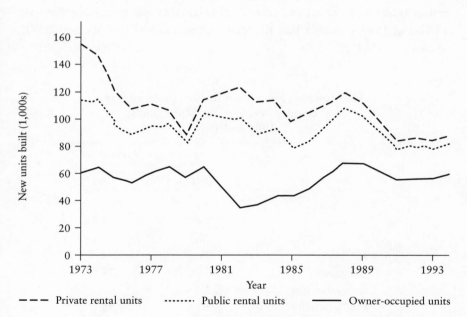

--- Private rental units   ·········· Public rental units   —— Owner-occupied units

Figure 5.1.   New construction by housing market sector, the Netherlands, 1973–1993

SOURCE: Statistics Netherlands.

construction in the owner-occupied sector remained almost constant. The early 1980s were an exception: private construction of owner-occupied housing plummeted in reaction to a collapse of the owner-occupied market in 1979 (see the section below about the costs of owner-occupied housing). The government reacted with an anticyclical construction policy, encouraging construction in the public sector, while private companies shifted their focus from the owner-occupied sector to the private rental sector.

As is the case in most countries, home ownership is not spread equally across the population of the Netherlands. Table 5.2, for example, shows the enormous variation in home ownership among income groups: in 1994, just one-fifth of the households in the lowest income quartile were homeowners; that same year, almost three-quarters of the households in the highest income quartile owned their homes. The table also shows the impact of country of origin on home ownership: in 1994, a household headed by a native-born resident was more than twice as likely to own its home than was a household headed by a foreign-born resident. The differences in home ownership in terms of income and country of origin increased markedly between 1981 and 1994 (see also Van Kempen, Schutjens, and Van Weesep 2000).

TABLE 5.2

Homeowning households by household income
and country of origin, the Netherlands,
1981 and 1994

Variable	PERCENTAGE OF HOME-OWNING HOUSEHOLDS	
	1981	*1994*
Income quartile		
1 (lowest)	30.3	20.4
2	30.3	31.2
3	39.3	54.7
4 (highest)	57.9	74.5
Country of origin		
The Netherlands	42.0	48.1
Elsewhere	26.6	23.6

SOURCE: Author's calculations based on Housing Demand Surveys (1981, 1994).

The increasing disparity in home ownership among income groups reflected a widening income gap in the 1980s and 1990s (see also Van Kempen et al. 2000). Two factors here were decreases in social security benefits and the implementation of a less-progressive tax policy, both of which adversely affected lower-income households. Also, construction subsidies for owner-occupied housing were abolished in the course of the 1980s. In the 1970s and early 1980s, those subsidies had promoted the construction of affordable homes in the owner-occupied sector. And, finally, it is possible that the introduction and growing popularity of new types of mortgages in the 1980s and early 1990s played a role in the growing inequality. The new mortgages were designed to make optimal use of tax relief for homeowners. Because tax relief benefits most those who pay higher taxes, changes in the mortgage system may well have encouraged upper-income households to buy homes.[1]

Housing Policy

Housing policy is crucial to the relative positions of owner-occupied and rental housing in a country. Börsch-Supan (1993) suggested this on the basis of a comparison of policies in the United States, Germany, and Japan; Mulder and Wagner (1998) came to the same conclusion from a comparison of the transition to home ownership in West Germany and the Netherlands.

Traditionally, the housing market in the Netherlands was characterized by strong government intervention. That intervention took three forms: extensive regulations, investment in public housing, and individual subsidies. Since the early 1980s, however, we have witnessed a trend toward less intervention. Housing policy in the Netherlands has always had two major goals: to provide affordable housing to lower-income groups and to encourage home ownership. In the last two decades of the twentieth century, emphasis shifted to owner occupancy.

A major policy instrument that influences the relative importance of renting versus owning is rent control. In the Netherlands, rents were frozen after World War II. Then the government set limits on annual rent increases and on the amount of rent landlords could charge (a function of the quality of the dwelling): annual rent increases were permitted at rates below inflation, and renting a home of a certain quality was often cheaper than buying one. That changed in 1980, when the government allowed rent increases to exceed inflation.

The Netherlands also has strict regulations governing spatial planning. That long-standing policy may well limit the number of households that build homes themselves or hire a private contractor: most new construction is initiated by real estate developers or large construction companies.

The second major instrument is investment in public housing. This takes the form of construction initiated by local governments and subsidies for housing construction. Several local governments, particularly those in the largest cities, had their own housing departments, which built and managed public housing. In the 1980s and 1990s, all of those departments were turned into private housing associations. And, after a temporary increase in the early 1980s, construction subsidies have been cut back.

The third major instrument is individual subsidies. For lower-income renters, the Netherlands provides rent subsidies. For homeowners, probably the most significant individual subsidy the government offers is a tax deduction on mortgage interest.[2] Until 2002, there were no constraints on that deduction; that year, a change in the tax rules limited the interest deduction to a period of thirty years. Although the government levies other taxes on housing—a value-added tax on new houses, a tax on the purchase price of existing houses, and a tax on imputed rent (a fictitious value owner-occupiers have to add to their taxable income)—the interest deduction more than offsets them. Furthermore, local governments in the Netherlands offer mortgage guarantees for dwellings up to a certain purchase price.

Tax relief for homeowners applies only to owner-occupiers, not to landlords. A by-product of that policy is that private landlords have become increasingly rare. The only private parties that own housing for investment purposes in substantial numbers today are institutions (pension funds and insurance companies). The bulk of rental housing is in the public sector, and those units are owned by nonprofit housing associations.[3]

A Note on Norms

It is not easy to make firm statements about the extent to which a norm of home ownership exists in a given country. The fact that the proportion of homeowners varies widely even among countries with similar prosperity, and the fact that the most prosperous countries do not necessarily have the highest ownership proportions, suggest that home ownership is not a universal goal. Elsinga (1995) studied motives for home ownership in the

Netherlands and found that financial advantage—notably, tax advantage—is crucial to choosing to buy a home. The greater accessibility and the higher quality of owner-occupied housing, the idea of having something of one's own, and the fact that ownership is an investment were important too. Respondents also mentioned the freedom to make changes to the structure. Of these motives for ownership, the idea of having something of one's own is the only one that points to a feeling that owning is intrinsically better than renting, a feeling that might be influenced by social norms. This motive was mentioned by 14 percent of the respondents in the survey. It seems reasonable to think that the decision to buy a home to a large extent depends on the country's housing market—the supply, price, and quality of owner-occupied versus rental housing.

The Costs of Owner-Occupied Housing

The average prices in euros of existing owner-occupied homes (1970–1993) and newly constructed homes (1984–1998) are given in Table 5.3. Boelhouwer, Mariën, and De Vries (1999) found that the evolution of prices in the Netherlands—both in nominal and in real terms—was much like that in other Western countries, with two exceptions.[4] The first was the peak in the price of existing homes in 1978. Only in Belgium and Sweden did house prices peak around that time, but not as sharply as they did in the Netherlands. Price peaks in several other countries around 1990 (for example, in Finland, Japan, and the United Kingdom) were about as sharp as the 1978 peak in the Netherlands in nominal terms but not in real terms. The second exception was the strong growth in the prices of new homes between 1990 and 1998. Prices did grow in other countries but generally not to the degree they did in the Netherlands.

To understand the affordability of owner-occupied dwellings, we have to relate prices to household income. Between 1970 and 1993, the average price of an existing structure was about 4.5 times the average annual household income in the Netherlands (Mulder and Wagner 1998). At one point in the late 1970s, the average price peaked at about 6.5 times annual income. The lowest average prices—around 4.1 times the average annual income—were reached in the mid-1970s and mid-1980s, just before and after the peak. Between 1970 and 1993, house prices in West Germany fluctuated between 6.0 and 7.7 times annual income. Why were home prices in the

TABLE 5.3

Inflation, mortgage interest, and home prices,
the Netherlands, 1970–1998

| | | | PRICES (€1,000) | |
Year	Inflation (%)	Mortgage interest (%)	Existing homes	New homes
1970	3.6	8.0	34.9	
1971	7.5	8.3	35.6	
1972	7.8	7.9	38.2	
1973	8.0	8.0	40.5	
1974	9.6	9.6	44.5	
1975	10.2	9.3	46.6	
1976	8.8	8.8	59.8	
1977	6.4	8.7	83.6	
1978	4.1	8.3	90.2	
1979	4.2	9.1	85.0	
1980	6.5	10.2	77.6	
1981	6.7	10.9	69.6	
1982	5.9	10.0	62.6	
1983	2.7	8.3	64.5	
1984	3.3	8.3	63.3	70
1985	2.3	7.8	63.6	71
1986	0.1	7.0	66.7	70
1987	−0.7	7.0	69.9	72
1988	0.7	6.9	72.6	76
1989	1.1	7.6	77.9	82
1990	2.4	6.3	79.2	86
1991	4.0	9.3	81.9	91
1992	3.7	8.8	88.4	96
1993	2.1	7.5	96.4	100
1994	2.7	7.3		108
1995	2.0	7.1		110
1996	2.1	6.3		113
1997	2.2	5.8		129
1998	2.0	5.6		135

SOURCES: Inflation rates: Organisation for Economic Co-operation and Development (various publications); interest rates and the price of new construction: Ministerie VROM (1999); the price of existing homes: Golland (1996).

Netherlands so much lower? First, lot sizes are smaller and so cheaper; also the government places fewer quality restrictions on builders (Mulder and Wagner).

Homeowners in the Netherlands paid an estimated 20.6 percent of their income in 1990 for housing; in 1994, they paid 23.1 percent; in 1998, 24.5 percent (Ministerie VROM 2000). Those proportions were appreciably higher for renters: 28.3 percent in 1990, 30.0 percent in 1994, and 33.2 percent in 1998. With the exception of the period from 1976 to 1978 and the period from 1995 to 1998, rents have risen more than purchase prices (Figure 5.2). Consequently, renting has lost much of its attraction over the course of time.

Quality also has an impact on the prices of housing. Using a standardized quality valuation system, it was estimated that, on average and taking dwelling type into account, owner-occupied homes received 194 "quality

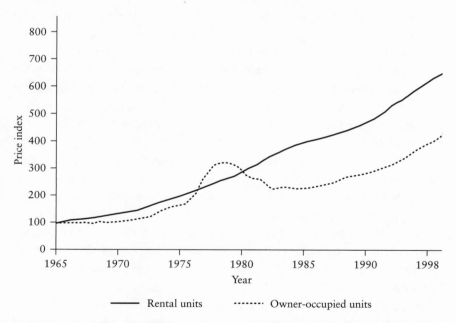

Figure 5.2. A comparison of rent and purchase prices, the Netherlands, 1965–1998

SOURCE: Ministerie VROM (2000).

points" compared with 125 points for rented homes in 1998 (Ministerie VROM 2000).[5] For the average dwelling, the cost per month was €482 for homeowners versus €393 per month for renters. Per quality point, that worked out to €2.49 for homeowners and €3.14 for renters. In other words, homeowners pay more for housing, but they spend a lower share of their income on housing, enjoy better-quality homes, and pay less for the quality of their homes.

Mortgage costs in the Netherlands have varied considerably over time (see Table 5.3). The nominal mortgage interest rate was well over 7.5 percent during the 1970s and the first half of the 1980s.[6] When we consider mortgage interest in relation to inflation, mortgages were exceptionally cheap between 1972 and 1976. The high inflation that occurred in the early 1970s also boosted the demand for owner-occupied housing and so its price.[7] In contrast, after 1976, lower rates of inflation and higher mortgage interest rates led to a drop in demand for owner-occupied housing.

Falling interest rates in the 1990s were one of the factors underlying the strong growth in demand for home ownership and, consequently, housing prices in that period. But certain long-term changes in income, age, and household structure also played a role, among them the growth of real income and dual earnership, the fact that many baby boomers (born between 1946 and, in the Netherlands, 1970) were reaching prime home-buying age (30 to 40), and the postponement of childbearing, which prolongs the period in which couples have two incomes and do not have to bear the cost of rearing children.

For would-be homeowners with stable and sufficient income, mortgages have become increasingly easy to obtain in the Netherlands, and they are being offered for as much as 100 percent of the purchase price or even more.[8] Moreover, mortgage lenders have redesigned the structure of mortgages to allow borrowers to take full advantage of the mortgage interest tax deduction. The general feeling is that mortgage debt—because of the tax savings on the interest—is a good investment. This is in sharp contrast with attitudes and policy in West Germany, where down payments of 20 percent to 30 percent of the purchase price are required (Tomann 1996) and where at least one housing policy *(Bausparen)* encourages households to save instead of borrow.

The cost of buying and selling a home in the Netherlands is high.

A transfer tax of 6 percent is levied on the sale price; and the transaction costs, including the cost of a notary and real estate agent, add another 4 percent or so.

Intergenerational Transmission of Home Ownership

According to Mulder and Smits (1999), home ownership tends to run in families: the children of homeowners are almost 1.5 times more likely to be homeowners themselves than are the children of tenants.[9] Several factors may be at work here. The first seems obvious: children whose parents own a home are more likely to inherit a home after the death of their parents. Although we have no data on the impact of inheritance on home ownership in the Netherlands, we expect it is small. Research in other countries tells us that most children do not inherit from their parents before the age of 40, by which time they are likely to be homeowners themselves (Lauterbach and Lüscher 1996; Munro 1988).[10] Tax policy, housing prices, and the structure of mortgages in the Netherlands also may limit the effect of intergenerational transfers on the proportion of homeowners. Mulder and Wagner (1998) found the association between parents' and children's home ownership to be considerably stronger in West Germany. They suggest that the German tax system is much friendlier to parent–child transfers than is the system in the Netherlands.[11] They also suggest that differences in house prices and in mortgage and down payment practices create greater reliance on parents' help in West Germany than in the Netherlands.

Second, parents who own a home can more easily give financial help to their children. They are likely to have higher earnings and, in the case of outright owners, more disposable income. They also have the option of transferring equity from their home to their children. In their study, Mulder and Smits (1999) found that children of homeowners were more than four times more likely to report a substantial financial gift from their parents, including help buying a home.

Third, a preference for home ownership might be the result of socialization (Henretta 1984)—to a certain standard of living or to the idea that home ownership is advantageous or obvious. Finally, the association between home-owning parents and children who are homeowners might reflect a shared environment: that is, both operate in the same regional housing market.

Changing Life Courses

Home ownership is strongly connected with the course of family life, with forming a couple, getting married, and having children (Clark, Deurloo, and Dieleman 1994; Mulder and Wagner 1998). Certain factors appear to facilitate or impede home ownership for families. Owning a home is facilitated by putting off parenthood: couples can use the longer interval between marriage and having children to earn two full incomes without bearing the cost of child rearing. Having fewer children also lowers household costs and, consequently, increases the amount available to spend on housing. Instability in the partner relationship—for example, the perceived threat of divorce—most likely discourages home ownership too.

In the Netherlands, as in most Western countries, the course of family life has changed substantially over the past few decades. For example, women's age at marriage started to rise in the 1970s and has continued to do so since, as has the age at which they have a first child (Table 5.4). The difference between women's ages at marriage and first childbirth increased from 1960 to 1980, indicating that, on average, women were putting off having children after marriage. That the difference began to decrease after 1980

TABLE 5.4
Marriage, fertility, and divorce, the Netherlands, 1960–1995

Year	WOMAN'S AGE (YEARS)		Total fertility (number of children per woman)	Divorces per 1,000 marriages
	At first marriage	At first childbirth		
1960	24.5	25.6	3.11	2.2
1965	23.5	24.7	3.03	2.2
1970	22.9	24.3	2.58	3.3
1975	23.0	25.0	1.67	8.0
1980	23.2	25.6	1.60	7.5
1985	24.4	26.5	1.51	9.9
1990	25.9	27.6	1.62	8.1
1995	27.3	28.6	1.53	10.2

SOURCES: Age at first marriage and childbirth, and fertility: Statistics Netherlands (various publications); divorces: Van Praag (1997); last divorce figure is for 1994 instead of 1995).

TABLE 5.5
Household composition, the Netherlands, 1960–1995

Household composition	PERCENTAGE OF HOUSEHOLDS					
	1960	1971	1981	1985	1990	1995
Single person	12	17	22	27	29	31
One-parent family	5	5	6	7	7	5
Married couple	22	22	23	25	22	23
Married couple with 1 or more children	56	52	43	38	35	31
Unmarried couple	—	—	4	5	6	8
Unmarried couple with 1 or more children	—	—	1	1	1	2
Other	5	4	1	1	1	0
N (1,000s)	3,130	3,990	5,111	5,565	5,955	6,516

SOURCE: Van Praag (1997).

does not mean women were choosing to have children sooner; it indicated that for more and more couples, marriage marked the formalization of an existing union, not the start of a new one (cf. Manting 1994). From the 1960s through the mid-1980s, total fertility fell; it remained low but more or less stable through the mid-1990s. Strong growth in the number of divorces per 1,000 marriages occurred in the 1970s; since then, growth has been modest.

Table 5.5 shows changes in household structure in the Netherlands between 1960 and 1995. Three major changes stand out: the growth in the share of single-person households, from 12 percent at the start of the period to 31 percent at the end; the decline in the percentage of married couples with children, from 56 percent to 31 percent; and the growth in the proportion of unmarried couples (the proportion doubled between 1981 and 1995). The data in Table 5.6 indicate that in large part these changes resulted from changes in the behaviors of young people (age 35 or younger) who had just left the parental home. In 1977, 53 percent of young people left their parents' home to get married; 34 percent lived alone or with roommates; and just 13 percent cohabited. In 1994, in contrast, 53 percent of young people

TABLE 5.6
Household composition, children leaving the parental home
to live independently, the Netherlands, 1977–1994

	PERCENTAGE OF HOUSEHOLDS			
Household composition	*1977*	*1981*	*1985*	*1994*
Married	53	43	27	14
Cohabiting	13	21	26	33
Living alone or with others	34	36	46	53

SOURCE: Author's calculations based on Housing Demand Surveys (1977, 1981, 1985, 1994).

NOTE: This population is age 35 or younger.

left their parents' home to live alone or with roommates; 33 percent left to live with an unmarried partner; and just 14 percent left to live with a spouse.

BECOMING A HOMEOWNER IN THE NETHERLANDS: FINDINGS AND QUESTIONS

A major purpose of this book is modeling the transition to first-time home ownership in different countries. In two earlier papers written with colleagues, I presented results from analyses of this transition. One focused on a comparison between the Netherlands and West Germany in the transition to home ownership (Mulder and Wagner 1998); and one focused on the intergenerational transmission of home ownership in the Netherlands (Mulder and Smits 1999).

In the first study, we developed a theoretical framework that stressed the benefits and costs of home ownership and their evolution over the life cycle (for example, as family status changes); the different resources needed to meet the costs of home ownership at different stages of the family life cycle; and the spatial and temporal context, which changes with the supply and price of owner-occupied versus rental housing, financing costs, the perceived risks of home ownership, the distribution of resources in the population, and the amount of resources needed to become a homeowner (Mulder and Wagner 1998). The paper documented the importance of family status, education, unemployment, socioeconomic status, parental home ownership, degree of urbanization, and birth cohort for the transition to home ownership in the Netherlands:

- Many households in the Netherlands make the transition to home ownership in the first year of marriage, particularly if the marriage is not followed rapidly by the birth of a first child. By contrast, in West Germany, marriage followed by childbirth is even more strongly associated with the purchase of a home than is marriage as such.
- Among couples, the transition to home ownership became less likely after the birth of the first child.[12]
- Single persons are not very likely to become homeowners.
- People who are highly educated are somewhat more likely to become homeowners than are those with less education.
- Not surprisingly, unemployment has a negative effect on the likelihood of becoming a homeowner.
- Socioeconomic status is positively associated with the likelihood of becoming a homeowner.
- People whose parents were homeowners are more likely to become homeowners themselves.
- As the degree of urbanization increases, the likelihood of becoming a homeowner decreases.
- Younger birth cohorts (particularly those born after 1950) are more likely to become homeowners than are older birth cohorts.

We did not find any significant effects for self-employment, work experience, and father's education.

The second paper reported additional findings on the impact of resources from male and female partners and from their parents (Mulder and Smits 1999). We found that the socioeconomic status of male and female partners was of almost equal importance in the transition to home ownership, but that the male partner's employment status was much more important. We also found that the likelihood of home ownership was enhanced when both partners came from a family where the father was self-employed.

All of these findings are relevant to the issues discussed in this book. But one issue that is central to this volume was not addressed in the earlier papers: inequality between social (occupational) classes. We were left, then, with this research question: To what extent can the transition to home ownership in the Netherlands be explained by the social class of prospective homeowners and their parents? We expected two aspects of social class to be important for the transition to home ownership. The first has to do with resources: skilled workers on average earn more than unskilled workers do, which means they generally have more resources available for buying a home. The second is about the means of production: farmers and other self-employed workers are more likely to own their farm or company and, consequently, their homes.

DATA AND METHOD

The data were taken from two retrospective life history studies: the ESR/Telepanel Survey (ESR/STP 1992) and the Netherlands Family Survey (NFS; Ultee and Ganzeboom 1993).[13] Both samples were more or less representative of the Dutch population age 18 and older (ESR) and ages 21 to 64 (NFS). The data from the two samples were pooled.

The ESR survey was conducted in 1993 among 3,000 members of about 1,600 households. It was a single-round retrospective survey of participants in a longer-term study.[14] The NFS was conducted in 1992 and 1993 among a sample of 1,000 primary respondents.[15] Both sets of data contain information about the respondents' housing, migration, education, household history, and work experience, as well as some information on their families of origin.

The analyses focused on respondents who had ever lived in a marital or cohabiting union, and were carried out separately for males and females. Although we wanted to ensure the comparability of our findings with those in the analyses of West Germany (Chapter 2), we decided to include respondents from their first cohabitation rather than from their first marriage. This was done because cohabiting couples in the Netherlands are more likely to become homeowners than are cohabiting couples in West Germany.

We observed the respondents from the year they formed their first union (at age 18 or older) until the year they moved into the first home they owned. Once respondents owned a home, they were removed from the analysis. As respondents reached age 50, they also were removed from the analysis: few transitions to first-time home ownership occur after age 50. We defined *transition to home ownership* as a move into an owner-occupied dwelling. The data did not tell us how the actual transition to home ownership was made: through purchase, inheritance, or gift, or by moving in with a partner who already owned a home. Nor did they tell us whether transitions to home ownership were made by buying a dwelling that the respondent was already inhabiting.

Where possible, we coded the independent variables after the West German example. Variables that were likely to change over the life course were updated annually. The only exceptions: education (which was simply measured as the highest level of general education reached) and parental resources.

The central independent variable in the analyses was social (occupational) class. We identified six occupational categories: unskilled manual workers; skilled manual workers; lower- and middle-level nonmanual workers; higher-level nonmanual workers; farmers and farm laborers; and self-employed people and employers who were not farmers. Where possible, the occupational category of the job held in the year of observation was used. If the respondent was not working, we used the category of the previous job or, if there was no previous job, that of the next job. For those who never worked during the period of observation, we used the partner's occupational category if available (this solution was applied for fewer than 5 percent of the respondents). In this way, we were able to reduce the proportion of person-years for which no occupational status was available at all to about 3 percent.

Another variable distinguished those who held jobs in the year of observation from those who did not. It certainly is not uncommon for people who are not employed to have a partner who is employed. This holds particularly true for women: one-earner families in which the female partner is a housewife are still rather common in the Netherlands. Employment, therefore, has a different meaning for females than for males. For females, employment is often connected with dual earnership.

We used a partner-status variable to distinguish those in their first marriage (but not in the first year of that marriage) from those who were cohabiting, those who were in the first year of their first marriage, those who were divorced and widowed, and those who were in a second or later partnership. The variable child status had four categories: no children, expecting the first child (the variable took this value in the year before the first child was born), youngest child under 6 years of age, and youngest child age 6 or older.

Age was measured in five categories: 18–24; 25–29; 30–34; 35–39;

and 40–49. The temporal context was expressed in cohort differences (cf. Chapter 2). We examined five birth cohorts: those born between 1900 and 1924, 1925 and 1934, 1935 and 1944, 1945 and 1954, and 1955 and 1964.

Degree of urbanization was included as an indicator of the local housing market. Respondents were asked to name the municipality where they lived. All of the municipalities were then assigned one of four degrees of urbanization using a measure designed by Statistics Netherlands.

Two measures of parental resources were used. The occupational status of the father was measured in the same way as the respondent's occupational status. If available, the father's status when the respondent was age 15 was taken. Otherwise, the category of the father's first or last job was used. A separate category was reserved for respondents who had no information about their father's occupation. This category comprised respondents who did not answer the question as well as respondents whose father was unknown, had left, or had died. Another important measure was whether the parents owned a home. In the NFS, this information was obtained for respondents at age 15; in the ESR data, no information on parental home ownership was available.

The method we used was logistic regression, applied as discrete-time event history analysis. As Yamaguchi (1991) has shown, this method gives a satisfactory approximation for continuous-time models. The unit of analysis was person-years. The dependent variable was whether (1) or not (0) the respondent moved to the first dwelling he or she owned (and inhabited independently of his or her parents) within a certain year.

The parameter for parental home ownership was derived from a model using the NFS respondents only; the other parameters were derived from a model that included all respondents but did not include parental home-ownership.

THE RESULTS: MODELING THE TRANSITION
TO HOME OWNERSHIP IN THE NETHERLANDS

Table 5.7 shows the results of separate bivariate models. The expected resource effect of a person's own occupational status is clearly discernible. Although the difference between skilled and unskilled manual laborers is not statistically significant, the difference between all manual laborers and non-manual workers is marked: white-collar workers are considerably more

TABLE 5.7
Parameters of separate bivariate logistic regression models of the
transition to home ownership, males and females, the Netherlands

	MALE		FEMALE	
Variable	Parameter	Standard error	Parameter	Standard error
Occupational status				
Unskilled manual laborer		Ref		
Skilled manual laborer	0.17	0.14	0.08	0.22
Nonmanual worker, low and middle levels	0.43[c]	0.13	0.53[c]	0.11
Nonmanual worker, high level	0.51[c]	0.15	0.93[c]	0.24
Farmer	0.32	0.23	0.89[c]	0.30
Other self-employed/employer	−0.13	0.21	0.38[b]	0.18
Father's occupational status				
Unskilled manual laborer		Ref		
Skilled manual laborer	−0.03	0.13	0.20	0.14
Nonmanual worker, low and middle levels	0.34[b]	0.13	0.57[c]	0.14
Nonmanual worker, high level	0.38[b]	0.16	0.53[c]	0.17
Farmer	0.73[c]	0.14	0.94[c]	0.15
Other self-employed/employer	0.19	0.14	0.59[c]	0.14
Not available	−0.39[c]	0.15	−0.10	0.16
Parents owned a home[d]	0.51[c]	0.13	0.56[c]	0.13

[a]$p < .10$.
[b]$p < .05$.
[c]$p < .01$.
[d]From a model with NFS respondents only; the other parameters are from models with both NFS and ESR respondents.

likely to become homeowners than are blue-collar workers. This is particularly true of women in higher-level occupations. Bear in mind that most respondents in the research population were partners in a couple and that
partners in couples tend to have similar occupations. The strong positive parameter for women with higher-level jobs, then, may point to the strong likelihood of home ownership among high-income dual-earner couples.

Remarkably, the effect of being a farmer is very strong for women but smaller and not even statistically significant for men. This may be because more men than women take over their parents' farm never having left it, so the transition to ownership may have gone unreported; at the same time, more women move onto a farm owned by their husband.[16] A similar line of reasoning might be put forward to explain the gender variation for self-employment. Also consistent with this line of reasoning are the effects of the father's being a farmer and the father's self-employment: again, stronger for females than for males. Moreover, apparently the impact of a man's father's being a farmer is greater than that of a male respondent's being a farmer himself.

Finally, it makes a substantial difference whether the respondents' parents owned a home. Males with parents who were homeowners, for example, were more than 1.5 times as likely to become homeowners themselves than were men whose parents did not own a home. Table 5.8 shows somewhat different results for the full model. Some effects were weakened by the inclusion of other independent variables; others were strengthened. The impact of the father's occupational status is still substantial. Apparently, father's occupational status has a direct effect on home ownership, not just an effect running via the respondent's own work category. Another notable finding is that the effect of parental home ownership is smaller and no longer statistically significant. It may well be that the effect of parental ownership is explained by the father's occupational status (in the farmer or self-employed categories). We could interpret this finding to mean that socialization is not the main mechanism underlying the intergenerational transmission of home ownership, or that socialization has less to do with parental home ownership and more to do with some combination of parents' home ownership and father's occupational status.

The other findings largely conform with those identified in the two earlier papers (Mulder and Wagner 1998; Mulder and Smits 1999):

- Being out of work has a negative impact on the likelihood of moving into a home of one's own, but more so for men than for women.
- The transition to home ownership is more likely in the first year of a first marriage than in later years of that marriage or in years spent cohabiting.
- The transition to home ownership is not common following a divorce or the death of a spouse, but it is substantially more likely again after a second or later partnership is formed. (This was actually a new finding: in the previous work, respondents were removed from the analysis after a divorce.)

TABLE 5.8
Multivariate logistic regression of the transition
to home ownership, males and females, the Netherlands

Variable	MALE		FEMALE	
	Parameter	Standard error	Parameter	Standard error
Occupational status				
Unskilled manual laborer			Ref.	
Skilled manual laborer	0.21	0.15	0.16	0.25
Nonmanual, low and middle levels	0.52[c]	0.14	0.34[c]	0.11
Nonmanual worker, high level	0.87[c]	0.17	0.94[c]	0.27
Farmer	0.08	0.25	0.12	0.35
Other self-employed/employer	0.18	0.22	0.39[a]	0.20
Not employed	−0.52[c]	0.13	−0.29[c]	0.10
Partner status				
In first marriage			Ref.	
Cohabiting	0.23	0.16	−0.15	0.19
First year of first marriage	1.28[c]	0.12	1.12[c]	0.13
Divorced/widowed	−0.81[b]	0.32	−0.89[c]	0.30
In second or later partnership	0.38[a]	0.23	0.27	0.23
Child status				
No children			Ref.	
Expecting first child	−0.06	0.15	0.16	0.14
Youngest child under 6	−0.60[c]	0.11	−0.32[b]	0.13
Youngest child age 6 or older	−0.95[c]	0.16	−0.83[c]	0.17
Age group				
18–24 years			Ref.	
25–29 years	0.31[b]	0.13	0.10	0.11
30–34 years	0.43[c]	0.15	0.23[a]	0.14
35–39 years	0.35[a]	0.18	0.21	0.19
40–49 years	0.07	0.22	−0.18	0.23
Birth cohort				
1900–1924			Ref.	
1925–1934	0.35	0.26	0.53[a]	0.31
1935–1944	0.67[c]	0.25	0.79[c]	0.30
1945–1954	0.97[c]	0.25	0.86[c]	0.30
1955–1964	1.02[c]	0.26	1.02[c]	0.30

(*continued*)

TABLE 5.8
(*Continued*)

Variable	MALE		FEMALE	
	Parameter	Standard error	Parameter	Standard error
Urbanization				
Lives in countryside		Ref.		
Weakly urbanized	−0.05	0.10	−0.02	0.11
Urbanized	−0.52[c]	0.13	−0.79[c]	0.14
Strongly urbanized	−1.23[c]	0.14	−1.41[c]	0.15
Father's occupational status				
Unskilled manual laborer		Ref.		
Skilled manual laborer	0.09	0.14	0.17	0.16
Nonmanual worker, low and middle levels	0.27[a]	0.15	0.45[c]	0.16
Nonmanual worker, high level	0.35[a]	0.18	0.64[c]	0.19
Farmer	0.55[c]	0.16	0.64[c]	0.17
Other self-employed/employer	0.33[b]	0.15	0.55[c]	0.16
Not available	−0.13	0.16	0.09	0.17
Parents owned a home[d]	0.16	0.16	0.23	0.16
Constant	−3.79[c]	0.33	−3.66[c]	0.36
N person-years/N transitions	12,873/717		12,965/660	
Model −2 log likelihood	4,864		4,557	
Improvement,[e] df, p	671/30/0.00		659/30/0.00	

[a]$p < .10$.
[b]$p < .05$.
[c]$p < .01$.
[d]From a model with NFS respondents only; the other parameters are from models with both NFS and ESR respondents. The model for NFS respondents only was similar to the model here but with larger standard errors.
[e]Compared with the null model.

- The child-status results were in line with the previous findings: in the Netherlands, the prime time for transition to home ownership is in the first year of marriage, before the first child is born.
- Moving into a home of one's own is most common between the ages of 25 and 39.

- Younger birth cohorts have a higher probability of becoming homeowners than do older birth cohorts.
- Home ownership is less likely with higher degrees of urbanization.

DISCUSSION

Our findings confirm previous findings on the transition to home ownership in the Netherlands: they tell us that the likelihood of owning a home is not the same across occupational categories. Those in nonmanual occupations, particularly those in higher-level jobs, are considerably more likely to become homeowners than are manual workers and clerical workers.[17] The major factor underlying these differences in the likelihood of home ownership seems to be income.

From different data sources, we know that the income gap that defines home ownership in the Netherlands has grown (see the first section of this chapter). It is also likely that the home-ownership income gap in the Netherlands is larger than it is in many other countries. We base that statement on four factors: First, that mortgage interest is fully tax deductible offers higher-income groups a disproportionate advantage—a function of progressive tax rates in the Netherlands. Second, a mortgage structure that allows low down payments makes income more important than savings. Third, lower- and middle-income groups have an alternative to home ownership in the public sector: reasonable-quality housing at affordable rents and rent subsidies for those in need of help. And fourth, because the Netherlands does not have a tradition of do-it-yourself construction, the vast majority of those who become homeowners have to rely on financial resources rather than the non-financial help of family and friends.

Although income-based differences among occupational classes seem to be more important than the ownership of the means of production, we did find support for the latter effect. Those whose fathers were farmers or were otherwise self-employed were more likely to become homeowners. Parental home ownership, which previous studies determined was a factor in the home ownership of adult children, was no longer statistically significant after controlling for the father's occupational status.

We know that access to home ownership is affected by income and occupational status. We also know that there is an inequality between homeowners and renters. Homeowners are better off in several ways: they have greater control over their own housing situation; the money they pay for housing is an investment, an opportunity to accumulate wealth, not just a cost of living; they have housing of higher quality; and they pay less than renters in relation to their income and in relation to the quality of their home.

For a country in which just over 50 percent of households own a home, the quality of the housing stock is quite good. In a European Commission (1999) study of thirteen European countries, the Netherlands had the second lowest percentage of dwellings without a bath or a shower (1 percent), the second/third lowest percentage of dwellings without hot running water (1 percent), and the lowest percentage of dwellings that are too small (10 percent).[18] Apparently, a low proportion of owner-occupied homes does not necessarily hamper the quality of housing; nor, for that matter, does a high proportion of owner occupation guarantee better quality.

Like many governments, the government of the Netherlands has adopted policies that promote home ownership. In the process, it has reduced its investment in the public housing sector and no longer prohibits the sale of what were public rental units. The danger here is of moving too quickly away from the housing system on which the country traditionally has relied. It may be too easy to overlook the advantages of a large public housing sector and the disadvantages of home ownership.

What are those advantages and disadvantages? The public housing sector in the Netherlands generally has provided good-quality affordable housing for lower- and middle-income households. The sector is not marginalized; and the emergence of ghettoes is unlikely. Moreover, it offers sufficient housing opportunities for people who cannot afford home ownership or who would rather rent, among them singles and the newly divorced, students, temporary and migrant workers, the elderly, and people with disabilities. A primary disadvantage for homeowners is the risk that the price of housing could drop. As Forrest, Kennett, and Leather (1999) have shown for the United Kingdom, falling prices can create serious problems for homeowners, especially for recent home buyers and those forced to sell. An often-overlooked disadvantage is that homeowners are less inclined to move than renters are (Mulder 1993). Ultimately this can lead to lower job mobility or to longer commutes.

Much of the text of this chapter was written at the beginning of 2000, when the prices of owner-occupied housing had been rising sharply for several years in the Netherlands. The optimism generated by the growth in home ownership was just beginning to be tempered somewhat by concerns about affordability. Over time, would home ownership be limited to dual-income households? In the intervening time, house prices stabilized and even decreased somewhat in certain areas. Nobody knows what will happen next: Will there be another serious downturn in the owner-occupied market? Will prices remain stable, or will they start rising again but at a slower pace?

Notes

1. Unfortunately, our discussion of the increased disparity in home ownership by income group is limited by a data set that is much smaller than that of the Housing Demand Surveys.

2. The Netherlands is one of the few countries in the world that makes mortgage interest fully deductible (Haffner 1993; Van Weesep and Van Velzen 1994).

3. Into the 1990s, they were owned by local governments.

4. The study examined housing in Austria, Belgium, Canada, Denmark, Finland, France, Germany, Ireland, Italy, Japan, Spain, Sweden, the United Kingdom, and the United States.

5. In the quality valuation system, quality points are given for such factors as the size of the dwelling, the presence and size of a garden or balcony, the presence of a bathtub, the presence of central heating, and the presence of insulation.

6. The typical mortgage term is thirty years, although other repayment periods are available. In addition, mortgage interest rates can be fixed or variable or a combination of both, depending on the mortgage contract. The extremes—a rate that changes each year or a rate that is fixed throughout the life of the loan—are least common. Usually rates are fixed for a period of five or ten years.

7. Home ownership is regarded as a hedge against inflation, and this hedge is valued more in times of high inflation.

8. This is a departure from common practice in most other countries and from the norm in the Netherlands itself in the 1950s, 1960s, and 1970s.

9. In their study, the authors controlled for the socioeconomic status of both parents and children, the degree of urbanization in the local housing market, and other relevant factors. They determined socioeconomic status using an international socioeconomic index rather than occupational status.

10. More support for the relatively small role inheritance plays in home ownership comes from an examination of children who never leave their parents' home, and who eventually—through purchase, gift, or inheritance—come to own that home. According to Mulder and Manting (1994), only a small proportion of young people in the Netherlands never leave the parental home.

11. This holds even more for the transfer of land and homes; the taxed value of those transfers is kept artificially low in West Germany.

12. In West Germany, by contrast, no negative effect of the birth or presence of a first child was found, and the birth of a second child had a positive effect.

13. The text in this section was adapted from the data and methods section in Mulder and Wagner (1998).

14. The longer-term study asked respondents to answer questions weekly about a wide variety of topics. The sample for that study would change as several tens of respondents left or entered the sample between rounds of questions.

15. Information was also gathered from the respondents' current partners. The partners' data were not used in the analysis here.

16. Actually, the data do indicate that a son is more likely to stay on his parents' farm without ever leaving home. Sons of farmers contributed 1,095 person-years to the analysis. In 19.6 percent of those person-years, respondents never reported leaving the parental home. In contrast, daughters of farmers contributed 1,197 person-years to the analysis, and only 5.7 percent of them reported never leaving the parents' farm.

17. This conforms to findings in analyses where socioeconomic status, rather than occupational category, was taken as an independent variable and was shown to have a substantial effect (Mulder and Wagner 1998; Mulder and Smits 1999).

18. In addition to the Netherlands, the countries studied were Austria, Belgium, Denmark, France, Germany, Greece, Ireland, Italy, Luxembourg, Portugal, Spain, and the United Kingdom.

References

Boelhouwer, Peter J., A. A. A. Mariën, and P. De Vries. 1999. *Koopprijsontwikkeling in internationaal perspectief.* Delft: DGVH/Nethur.

Börsch-Supan, Axel. 1993. Housing market regulations and housing market performance in the United States, Germany, and Japan. In *Social protection versus economic flexibility*, edited by Rebecca Blank, 119–56. Chicago: University of Chicago Press.

Clark, William A. V., Marinus C. Deurloo, and Frans M. Dieleman. 1994. Tenure changes in the context of micro level family and macro level economic shifts. *Urban Studies* 31:137–54.

Elsinga, Marja G. 1995. *Een eigen huis voor een smalle beurs: Het ideaal voor bewoner en overheid?* Delft: Delftse Universitaire Pers.

ESR/STP. 1992. Data file. Owner: Stichting Economische, Sociaal-culturele en Ruimtelijke Wetenschappen (ESR) of the Nederlandse Organisation for the Advancement of Scientific Research, The Hague. Data collection: Stichting Telepanel, Amsterdam. Data management: Steinmetz Archive, Amsterdam.

European Commission. 1999. *Living conditions in Europe.* Brussels.

Forrest, Ray, Patricia Kennett, and Philip Leather. 1999. *Home ownership in crisis? The British experience of negative equity.* Aldershot: Ashgate.

Golland, Andrew. 1996. Housing supply, profit and housing production: The case of the United Kingdom, the Netherlands and Germany. *Netherlands Journal of Housing and the Built Environment* 11:5–30.

Haffner, Marietta E. A. 1993. Fiscal treatment of owner-occupiers in six EC-countries: A description. *Scandinavian Housing & Planning Research* 10: 49–54.

Henretta, John C. 1984. Parental status and child's home ownership. *American Sociological Review* 49:131–40.

Lauterbach, Wolfgang, and Kurt Lüscher. 1996. Erben und die Verbundenheit der Lebensverläufe von Familienmitgliedern. *Kölner Zeitschrift für Soziologie und Sozialpsychologie* 48:66–95.

Manting, Dorien. 1994. *Dynamics in marriage and cohabitation. An inter-temporal, life course analysis of first union formation and dissolution.* Amsterdam: Thesis Publishers/PDOD.

Martens, Maartje. 1985. Owner-occupied housing in Europe: Postwar developments and current dilemmas. *Environment and Planning* A 17:605–24.

Ministerie VROM. 1999. *Volkshuisvesting in cijfers 99.* The Hague: Ministerie van Volkshuisvesting, Ruimtelijke Ordening en Milieubeheer.

———. 2000. *Perspectief op wonen. Rapportage van het WoningBehoefte Onderzoek 1998.* The Hague: Ministerie van Volkshuisvesting, Ruimtelijke Ordening en Milieubeheer.

Mulder, Clara H. 1993. *Migration dynamics: A life course approach.* Amsterdam: Thesis Publishers.

Mulder, Clara H., and Dorien Manting. 1994. Strategies of nest-leavers: "Settling down" versus flexibility. *European Sociological Review* 10:155–72.

Mulder, Clara H., and Jeroen Smits. 1999. First-time home-ownership of couples: The effect of inter-generational transmission. *European Sociological Review* 15:323–37.

Mulder, Clara H., and Michael Wagner. 1998. First-time home-ownership in the family life course: A West German–Dutch comparison. *Urban Studies* 35:687–713.

Munro, Moira. 1988. Housing wealth and inheritance. *Journal of Social Policy* 17:417–36.

Tomann, Horst. 1996. Private home-ownership finance for low-income households. *Urban Studies* 33:1879–89.

Ultee, Wout C., and Harry B. G. Ganzeboom. 1993. *Netherlands Family Survey 1992–93* [machine readable data set]. Codebook prepared by Harry B. G. Ganzeboom and Susanne Rijken (September 1993); changes and additions made by Harry B. G. Ganzeboom and Roland Weygold (January 1995). Nijmegen, Netherlands: Department of Sociology, Nijmegen University.

Van Kempen, Ronald, Veronique A. J. M. Schutjens, and Jan Van Weesep. 2000. Housing and social fragmentation in the Netherlands. *Housing Studies* 15:505–31.

Van Praag, Carlo S. 1997. Demografie. In *Het gezinsrapport*, edited by Carlo S. Van Praag and M. Niphuis-Nell, 13–41. Rijswijk: Sociaal en Cultureel Planbureau.

Van Weesep, Jan, and R. Van Velzen. 1994. *A comparative study of financial housing instruments in selected industrialized countries: Inventory and prospects.* Utrecht: Faculty of Geographical Sciences. (Also published in *Expertenkommission Wohnungspolitik im Auftrag der Bundesregierung: Materialband mit Sondergutachten im Auftrag der Kommission.* Bundesministerium für Raumordnung, Bauwesen und Städtebau, 1995.)

Yamaguchi, Kazuo. 1991. *Event history analysis.* Applied Social Research Methods Series 28. Newbury Park: Sage.

CHAPTER SIX

Home Ownership and Social Inequality in Denmark

Søren Leth-Sørensen

In Denmark, 53 percent of households and 62 percent of the total population live in owner-occupied dwellings (Danmarks Statistik 1998). Both owners and tenants have experienced major economic changes over the years. The 1980s in particular saw substantial change in the conditions for households wanting to buy their own home. The new conditions made it considerably more difficult for first-time buyers to purchase a dwelling.

The Danish government uses housing as an instrument of its economic policy. For example, it controls the number of new buildings and the conditions applying to the sale of real property. During an upturn in economic activity, it takes measures to reduce private consumption and the number of new buildings by restricting credit and by curbing housing prices and sales. Conversely, during an economic recession, the government's focus shifts to stimulating building and construction activities.

There is a growing degree of segregation in the Danish housing market: "insiders" own their home; "outsiders" rent housing. The status accorded home ownership has fueled debate in the country; it has also raised the issue of how to integrate immigrants in Denmark.

We begin this chapter with an overview of the Danish housing market and forms of ownership. Then we examine the housing market and government policies regulating that market. Next we look at the nature of households and housing in Denmark. The chapter ends with a discussion of the empirical analysis—the data and our findings on the factors that may well influence the transition to home ownership (Kurz 1999).

THE DANISH HOUSING MARKET: TYPES OF OWNERSHIP

Ownership is divided into three main categories: a property can be privately owned, owned by a nonprofit housing association, or owned by a housing cooperative:[1]

- *Privately owned dwellings* are typically single-family houses occupied by the owner. However, privately owned structures also can be properties constructed for the purpose of letting out.
- *Nonprofit housing associations* are organizations established to provide rental housing for their members. A housing association might own one or more apartment buildings or houses within close proximity of one another. Because these associations rely on government subsidies for construction, they are subject to comprehensive government regulation. For example, although nonprofit housing associations initiate projects, the government sets an annual quota on the number of projects. This usually means a waiting list for members who want access to inexpensive and attractive dwellings.
- *Housing cooperatives* typically are made up of a small group of people who jointly own and run a property, each with the right to use a specific dwelling on the property. Government subsidies for interest and installment payments are also available for construction of this type of housing; in addition, members of a housing cooperative must contribute to construction costs. That contribution—subject to some degree of price regulation—is returned when a member moves. Cooperatives that accept government subsidies are also subject to an annual quota. There has been a sharp increase in the number of housing cooperatives over the past decades. That growth reflects an increase in both new construction and tenants' forming a housing association and buying the apartment building in which they live.

In 1998, 1.3 million (53 percent) of Danish households lived in an owner-occupied dwelling.[2] Almost 1.1 million (46 percent) of households lived in rented housing.[3] That year the stock of private rental housing reached 457,000 units; the stock of nonprofit housing association rental units was larger, a total of 466,000 units.[4] About 70 percent of rented dwellings were in apartment buildings (Danmarks Statistik 1998).

A REGULATED MARKET

The Danish housing market has for many years been the focus of political attention and the subject of much regulation. Legislation (tax and social) and policies (for example, housing subsidies) have had a major influence on the housing tenure of Danish households.

Political Ideologies

The right- and left-wing political parties in Denmark think very differently about housing policy. Right-wing parties generally support private property rights and the market economy: they want to encourage private ownership and rentals, and they want the price of housing to be determined by the market. The left wing of the political spectrum—including the Social Democratic Party—believes that public housing is an important alternative to private ownership and rentals.

The first nonprofit housing association was formed in 1865 by the shipbuilders of Copenhagen. Driving that organization was the belief that by working together, people could help one another build suitable housing. The goal was affordable housing, not profit. The housing policies that originated from those ideas found strong support in Denmark's labor unions and Social Democratic Party (Arbejderbevægelsens Erhvervsråd 1999).

Over the last decades, the number of people in Denmark living on public assistance has increased considerably. That growth reflects the fact that social support has gradually come to be considered a responsibility of the state rather than an obligation of, for instance, the family. The allocation of housing to people who are unable to find or afford a home of their own is one form of social support provided by the government. Local authorities, assigned the task of ensuring that everybody has a home, rely almost exclusively on public housing. One by-product of the process is that public housing is populated by the most vulnerable in society.

Esping-Andersen (1990) suggested that the social democratic welfare state is characterized by two criteria: a high degree of decommodification and a high degree of universalism. In its disregard of profit and its commitment to provide good and affordable housing to all people, housing policy in Denmark fully meets those criteria.

Housing and Economic Conditions

The choice between renting and buying a home depends on the financial situation of the family. Often, low-income families do not have the liquidity to consider part of the expense of home ownership as savings. Furthermore, home ownership for these households can mean the loss of rental housing benefits.

Major costs are involved in buying and selling real property in Denmark. It follows, then, that people who are buying a home must feel somewhat secure about the household's future income and the permanence of the move.

Purchases of single-family houses and apartments are financed by long-term—up to thirty years—mortgage loans.[5] In Denmark, these loans are issued by mortgage credit institutions, using the property as security. The interest rate on the loan is fixed for the entire term of the loan. The rate is determined by prices in the bond market at the time the loan is written. The borrower can choose to pay the loan off with fixed principal and interest payments (an annuity loan) or with progressively smaller payments (a serial loan).

The conditions applying to mortgage loans are regulated by legislation that prescribes, for instance, the type of loan, the amount of the loan (the allowable percentage of the selling price), and the term of the loan. As a consequence of fluctuations in the rate of interest, substantial changes can occur in the economic terms of a purchase, even over a short period of time. This fluctuation means that mortgage terms can vary considerably from generation to generation.

The government also influences home ownership through its tax policies—in particular the deductions it allows for mortgage interest payments. At the beginning of the 1980s, households were able to deduct up to 71.9 percent of their mortgage interest payments; by 1998, the maximum deduction had been reduced to 46.4 percent (Kuula and Bang 1999). Much of that reduction was the result of comprehensive tax reform implemented in 1986. In practical terms, it has become more difficult for people to buy a home, especially a first home. Homeowners also are subject to property taxes: a general assessment of the property is made, and its value is treated as taxable income.[6] This, too, limits the financial advantage of home ownership.

Low-income families living in rented or cooperative housing are entitled to claim rent subsidies. Rent subsidies are provided as a grant; their size is determined primarily by the amount of rent paid, the household income, dwelling size, and the number of children in the household. Moreover, households with one or more pensioners may qualify for a rent allowance.

Intergenerational Transfers

One of the characteristics of the social democratic welfare model is the relatively small role the family plays in supporting its members. Implicit in the state's undertaking greater responsibility for its citizens is the expectation that each generation will take care of itself. In Denmark, then, traditionally children do not expect an inheritance from their parents to change their own financial situation noticeably. In fact, many elderly people today have little income beyond their old-age pension; and, unless they own their own home, their net wealth is likely to be small.

For elderly people who own a home, the situation is very different. The boom in housing prices has increased the value of their estate, which can mean a large inheritance for their children. Of course, many of those children are likely to be adults and to own a home of their own. One option available to them is to use their inheritance to help their own children find housing. A not uncommon scenario: adult children decide to keep their parent's home, or to sell it and buy another home, and then rent that home to their own children, who, because they are tenants (of their parents' second home) may be eligible for rent subsidies. There are two issues here. First, even families with an ordinary income can amass substantial wealth by virtue of their owning a home and the increase in the price of housing. Second, inherited wealth can create new social disparities.

When the state assumes responsibility for the care of elderly people, families' members are free to live at a distance from older generations. It may be difficult, then, for parents of adult children to help their children with the practical matters of buying a house—helping them move, for example, or paint and make repairs. Instead, they may choose to help their children financially.

THE NATURE OF HOUSEHOLDS AND DWELLINGS

Trends

In 1955, the number of households in Denmark was 1.4 million; in 1998, the number of households had reached 2.4 million.[7] The increase in the number of households naturally was matched by a corresponding increase in the number of dwellings.[8]

In 1955, 43 percent of all Danish households lived in owner-occupied homes, and 53 percent rented their homes.[9] Following a sharp rise in the number of dwellings in the 1970s, largely the result of the construction of private single-family houses, the proportion of households living in owner-occupied housing had increased to 55 percent by 1981. Between 1986 and 1998, the rate of owner-occupied homes fell slightly, to 53 percent (Danmarks Statistik and Socialforskningsinstituttet 1997; Danmarks Statistik 1998). At the same time, the proportion of households living in rented dwellings decreased from 53 percent in 1955 to 46 percent in 1998.

From 1948 to 1994, private household expenditures on housing (as a percentage of total private consumption) increased from 5.1 percent to 21.8 percent. Today, on average, private households spend more than one-fifth of their disposable income on housing—a considerable amount. As the cost of home ownership increased, so did housing standards. By the mid-1990s, almost all private homes had central heating and more than 90 percent of them were fitted with a bath or a shower (Danmarks Statistik 1995). Better housing is the result of urban renewal and a sharp increase in new buildings completed.

The Changing Composition of the Home-Owning Population

Economic and other conditions are changing the characteristics of the home-owning population. Consider age: today, people are buying their first homes later than before. A couple of economic factors can explain this: The purchase price of an accommodation has increased and so have the transaction costs of buying a home. Also contributing to the delay is an increase in the duration of education. Another important factor has to do with the logistics of a move: finding new jobs, for example, and day care for children. Buying a house is a decision with consequences. It is not surprising, then, that time is spent making that decision.

Figure 6.1 shows the proportion of homeowners among persons in four age groups—20 to 24, 25 to 29, 30 to 34, and 35 to 39—between 1981 and 1999. What is immediately obvious from the figure is a decline from 1981 in all four groups.[10]

As mentioned earlier, once people buy a home, the decision to buy another is a difficult one. Certainly the transaction costs are a factor here. So are increasing job specialization and increased uncertainty about employment. Instead of moving with every new job, people tend to stay where they

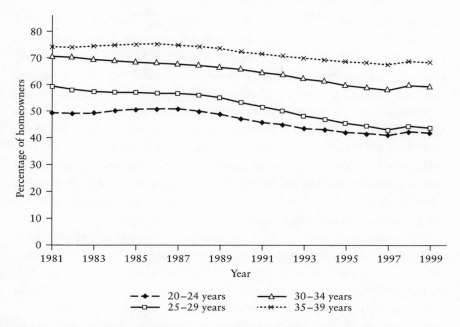

Figure 6.1.   Homeowners by age group, Denmark, 1981–1999

SOURCE: www.statistikbanken.dk

are and to commute longer distances. The expansion of areas of detached houses and the growing number of private cars in Denmark are related. Lower-income people once solved the commuting-to-work problem by living close to the workplace, often in large cities; today, they are buying a house and a car.

Although Denmark has witnessed an increase in the number of single-adult households (with or without children)—from 33 percent in 1980 to 41 percent in 1998—these households are less likely to own a home. Moreover, the disparity between population share and home-ownership share among single-person households has grown over the period. Not unexpectedly, couple households are increasingly overrepresented among owners of single-family houses (Danmarks Statistik and Socialforskningsinstituttet 1997).

We have data to compare socioeconomic (occupational) position and type of housing tenure for the years 1970, 1981, and 1991 (H. Christoffersen and Rasmussen 1995). The statistics were compiled for the *head of household*, the oldest economically active person in the household.[11] The most significant change among economically active households was a drop over the period in the proportion of households headed by unskilled manual workers, from 22 percent to 12 percent. The lower proportion can be attributed to a general increase in education levels and to changes in occupational structure: that is, the percentage of unskilled manual laborers in the workforce fell. Another group that experienced a sharp reduction in the percentage of homeowners, from 16 percent to 8 percent, was self-employed persons. Among the reasons for this change were a decrease in the number of retail shops in Denmark and structural changes in Danish agriculture (H. Christoffersen and Rasmussen).

Both unskilled workers and economically inactive households were overrepresented among tenants. Conversely, self-employed and upper-level salaried employees were overrepresented in owner-occupied dwellings. This pattern implies that households with a more stable labor market attachment and those with higher incomes live in owner-occupied housing, while households with low incomes live primarily in rented housing. Furthermore, when we examine the trends over the period, we see that the differences among occupational groups grew stronger (H. Christoffersen and Rasmussen).

New Construction

In the early 1970s, the number of new dwellings completed each year was approximately 50,000, roughly 2 percent of the total number. By comparison, fewer than 11,000 new dwellings were completed in 1996.

In the early 1970s, a large number of new buildings completed were single-family houses. Moreover, they tended to be comparatively large dwellings, with an average floor area of 125 square meters. There are many explanations for the sharp increase in the number of privately owned single-family houses (detached houses). At the time, young mothers were beginning to work in larger numbers, which meant additional income for their family. Also, increased deductions for mortgage interest made home ownership more attractive. Another factor was the widespread belief that the relatively high rate of inflation meant that large nominal expenses would rapidly become easier to pay. With the first oil crisis (1973–1974) came a decrease in the number of new houses completed; and the number of new houses completed has not reached the 1970s level since.

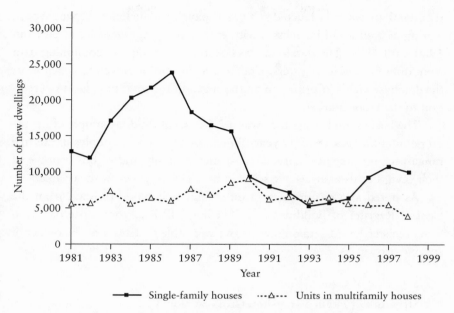

Figure 6.2.   Construction of new dwellings, Denmark, 1981–1998

SOURCE: www.statistikbanken.dk

Trends in the construction of single-family and multifamily houses appear in Figure 6.2. The figure clearly shows the sensitivity of the construction of single-family houses to economic fluctuations. The number of new buildings completed in 1993, the lowest in the period, was only about one-fifth the number completed in 1986.

After World War II, housing investments estimated at constant prices increased steadily until 1973. Subsequently, housing investments decreased until 1995, when investments accounted for one-third the level in 1973 (Danmarks Statistik 1995).

DATA

The IDA Database and the Central Register of Buildings and Dwellings

The data used here were based on a random sample from Statistics Denmark's IDA database (Danmarks Statistik 1991; Leth-Sørensen 1997). The

IDA database was constructed as a yearly panel, and includes the whole population as well as all businesses with employees. Data were collected from 1980 until 1997. The database was constructed using and combining data from different public registers. Updated at the end of November each year, the database yields information on the status of the total population in relation to the labor market.

The basic sample used here was a 2.5 percent random sample of the total population ages 18 to 39 years. We chose to examine couples in this age range because they are most likely to start a family and to buy a home of their own. In this analysis, we selected the man to represent the couple.

As noted above, information on dwellings is based on data from the Central Register of Buildings and Dwellings (BBR). From those data and other register-based data on owners, we were able to determine the owner of specific properties.[12]

Selection of Cases

Structure of Homeownership: Cross-Sectional Data

To monitor trends among owners and tenants between 1980 and 1993, we used the sample of men ages 18 to 39 in 1980 and 1993. The number of men in the two years was 24,177 and 23,853 respectively.

Transition Analysis: Longitudinal Data

Because we had data starting in 1980 and wanted to avoid left censoring, we selected a random sample of men between 18 and 20 years old in 1980 from the IDA database. We followed this group until 1993, during which time a majority bought a home of their own. In a few instances, people who owned a home in 1980 were excluded from the sample.

We were interested in one event—buying a first home—and one population—couple households. In the sample, then, we included men who had not previously been homeowners, from the year in which they started living with a partner. Men who already owned their home before they started cohabiting were excluded from the sample. We followed each man until he bought an owner-occupied dwelling alone or with a partner; until he left the population; or, in the case where no home was bought, until the end of the period. The last two cases were treated as right-censored episodes.

The number of selected men in 1980 was 2,193; the number of person-years was 10,164.

Variables

Information on Partners

We adapted operational definitions for Danish statistics on families for the register data:

- The definition of *family unit* was based not only on people's legal relationship but also on their sociological relationship: they had to live at the same address to belong to the same family unit. This means that a married couple living apart constituted two families.
- *Cohabiting couples* were also defined by means of information from the population registers.
- *Number of children* was the number of children living at the same address as their parents.
- *Household* was defined as all persons living at the same address.
- A *partner* was either cohabiting with or married to the selected man. Information on the civil registration number of the person's partner was extracted from the population registers. In this instance, we did not take the age of the partner into account. Using the civil registration number as a key, we were able to derive information for this group of women at a later time.

Information on Fathers

The population registers contain information on the fathers of the cohorts born after 1960. Therefore, we were able to obtain information on most of the fathers. But it should be remembered that a small number of people in the sample did not have information on the identity of their father. At the same time, it is uncertain whether the father would have been present in the population at the time when each subject or couple bought a first home.

Home Ownership

If the owner in question had his permanent address at the property, we considered the dwelling in question to be an owner-occupied home. One disadvantage of this method is that it is the dwelling that was classified owner occupied or rented. If a household consisted of several adults, it was not possible to establish actual ownership. In the present analysis, then, we limited our examination of home ownership to households consisting of just one or two adults. We treated people in households with more than two adult members as tenants.

Urbanization

To determine the degree of urbanization, we distinguished among three categories: Copenhagen, including the suburbs; municipality with more than 10,000 inhabitants; and rural area.

Partner Relationship

For men living in a consensual union, information on the partner's civil registration number was available. Because we were monitoring the probability of becoming a homeowner, we limited our examination to a range of characteristics in the previous year. In some cases, the female partner had not lived in Denmark in the previous year. We made a distinction between cases where information on the partner was retrieved and those where it was not. Moreover, we also saw cases in which no partner was present because the man was living alone after having lived in a consensual union.

Cohabitation Phase

We compiled the number of years that the couple lived together, married or in a consensual union. We counted each time a man began to live with a new woman as a new phase and compiled the number of years again. We assigned one of three categories to the term of each relationship: the first year in a new relationship, one to five years in a relationship, or six years or more.

Family Phase

In this context, we made a distinction between couples with no children and those expecting their first child. For families with children, we made a distinction by the youngest child's age: from birth to age 6, and age 7 and older.

Male Partner's Occupation

This variable indicated the occupation and activity status in the labor market of the selected man at the end of November of each year.

Female Partner's Labor Market Attachment

We used three classifications: employed, unemployed, and economically inactive.

Father's and Partner's Father's Occupation

The fathers of both partners were classified according to their employment status: self-employed, employee, unemployed, or economically inactive. This information was collected for the year before the owner-occupied dwelling was bought.

Father's Home Ownership

We had information about the housing situation of the selected person's father the year before the purchase of an owner-occupied dwelling until the father reached age 75. Therefore, we lacked information on the housing situation of a small group. We defined each father's housing status as tenant or homeowner.

RESULTS

The Structural Aspects of Home Ownership in 1980 and 1993

The following results were based on cross-sectional data for men ages 18 to 39 in 1980 and 1993 respectively.

Age

Figure 6.3 shows the percentage of male homeowners by age. As expected, the rate increased until age 40. But the figure also shows a slight decrease in the percentages from 1980 to 1993. This probably was related to a trend over the last decade for adult children to delay leaving the family home (M. Christoffersen 1993).

Urbanization

Urbanization is an important variable in the context of home ownership. In 1980, the home-ownership share among men ages 18 to 39 was 27 percent in Copenhagen, 41 percent in cities with more than 10,000 residents, and 53 percent in rural areas. In 1993, the proportions had fallen to 20 percent, 31 percent, and 44 percent respectively. The lower rates generally in 1993 reflected increasing difficulties in becoming a homeowner. The variation between urban and rural percentages primarily reflected the fact that there are fewer rental units available in rural areas. Also a factor here is that prices for owner-occupied dwellings are considerably lower in rural areas.

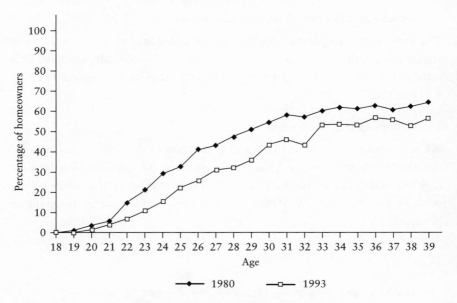

Figure 6.3.   Age and home ownership, Denmark, 1980 and 1993

SOURCES: Cross-sectional data from the IDA database and the BBR.

Living Arrangements

Over the last several decades, there has been a transition from couples living together in marriage to living together in a consensual union.[13] Figure 6.4 shows the proportion of homeowners by type of family in 1980 and 1993. It appears that only a small percentage of single persons lived in an owner-occupied dwelling. Married couples accounted for the highest home-ownership share in 1980; the percentage for cohabiting couples was slightly lower, regardless of whether they had children or not. By 1993, the share of home ownership among couples living in a consensual union with joint children was almost the same as that of married couples, while the proportion fell among cohabiting couples with no joint children.

Occupational Position

As expected, we found a close relationship between occupational position and home ownership (Figure 6.5). Self-employed persons and salaried employees at upper levels had the highest shares of home ownership; unemployed and economically inactive persons, the lowest.

All groups except for unskilled manual workers and a residual group of people who were working but did not specify the nature of their employment were affected by a decline in home ownership from 1980 to 1993. Considering the fact that self-employed persons frequently have to buy real property as a precondition for carrying out their work, it is notable that the share of home ownership in this group did not differ markedly from that of upper-level salaried employees.

Cohort Perspective: Time-Dependent Effects

Structure of the Data and the Statistical Model

The data we used in this analysis were based on annual observations.[14] Therefore, to model the rate of transition to home ownership, we used a discrete-time logistic transition rate model (Allison 1995).[15] According to our state space, we had the following origin state: not living in an owner-occupied dwelling (for example, living in one's own household in rented housing or not living in one's own household). We had one type of event: transition to living in an owner-occupied dwelling. Of course, the possibility of no transition also existed. The unit of analysis was person-years.

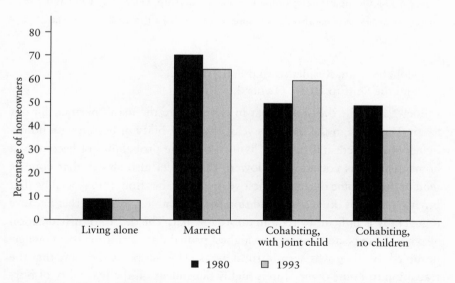

Figure 6.4.   Type of family and home ownership, Denmark, 1980 and 1993

SOURCE: Author's calculations based on cross-sectional data from the IDA database and the BBR.

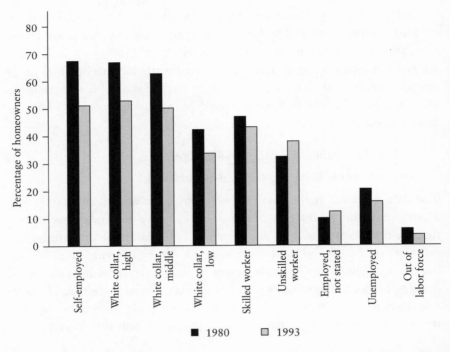

Figure 6.5.   Occupational group and home ownership, Denmark, 1980 and 1993

SOURCE: Author's calculations based on cross-sectional data from the IDA database and the BBR.

Cohabitation, Residence, and Family Phase, and the Shift to Home Ownership

Model 1 in Table 6.1 shows that in cases where the man's partner did not live in Denmark in the previous year, the probability of becoming a home-owner was lower, and for men living alone, the probability of becoming a homeowner was considerably lower. The model also shows that couples tend to buy a home during the first years of cohabitation. It may well be that buying a home is often a precondition for being able to live together because it generally is difficult to rent an affordable flat. The degree of urbanization also has the expected impact: the highest probability of shifting to an owner-occupied dwelling was seen in rural areas. This supports the view that the transition to home ownership is highly dependent on the feasibility of buy-ing a home: housing is cheaper and more readily available in rural areas

TABLE 6.1
Transition to first-time home ownership,
coupled men, Denmark, I

| Variable | COEFFICIENT | |
	Model 1	Model 2
Constant	−0.2649[a]	−0.4006[a]
Partner		
Partner present	Ref.	
No partner	−2.3671[a]	−2.2928[a]
Partner not found	−1.0515[a]	−0.9718[a]
Cohabitation phase		
First year	Ref.	
1–5 years	−0.5877[a]	−0.6330[a]
6 or more years	−0.8950[a]	−0.9625[a]
Year		
1980	−0.6146[a]	−0.6360[a]
1981	−0.4124[a]	−0.3670[a]
1982	−0.2588[a]	−0.2129
1983	−0.2134	−0.1637
1984	−0.2636[a]	−0.2019
1985	−0.1503	−0.1418
1986	Ref.	
1987	−0.1023	−0.0917
1988	−0.4283[a]	−0.4131[a]
1989	−0.3985[a]	−0.3639[a]
1990	−0.4767[a]	−0.4788[a]
1991	−0.7217[a]	−0.7086[a]
1992	−0.4763[a]	−0.4687[a]
Place of residence (origin)		
Copenhagen and suburbs	−0.9547[a]	−0.9279[a]
Municipality with more than 10,000 inhabitants	−0.4906[a]	−0.4558[a]
Rural area	Ref.	
Family phase		
No children	Ref.	
First child expected	−0.0496	
Youngest child <7 years	−0.0123	
Youngest child ≥7 years	−0.3050	

(*continued*)

TABLE 6.1
(*Continued*)

| | COEFFICIENT | |
Variable	Model 1	Model 2
Occupational status		
Self-employed		0.1666
White collar, high		0.4419[a]
White collar, middle		0.2802[a]
White collar, low		0.3103[a]
Skilled worker		0.4315[a]
Unskilled worker	Ref.	
Employed, not stated		−0.2330
Unemployed		−0.4921[a]
Out of labor force		−0.8067[a]
Log-likelihood	−3848.8349	−3778.2432
df	20	25

SOURCES: Author's calculations based on longitudinal data from the IDA database and the BBR, 1980–1997.

[a] $p < .05$.

(Mulder and Smits 1999). There was no significant interaction between the duration of the couple relationship and urbanization, and the shift to home ownership. Furthermore, it can be seen that family phase had no effect on the transition rate.

The Male Partner's Labor Market Position

Looking at the significance of the man's labor market position, it is clear that the probability of becoming a homeowner is lower if he is either unemployed or economically inactive (see model 2 in Table 6.1). This was also true for men employed in more-marginal jobs. Among employed persons, the probability of becoming a homeowner was particularly high for skilled manual workers. We have several explanations for this. Skilled manual workers often serve their apprenticeship at a relatively young age, which means they have a long time in which they can save up for a home of their own. Also, it is likely that many of the 18- to 20-year-olds in 1980 tried to buy their own home before the tax reform of 1986, which substantially changed the conditions for buying an owner-occupied dwelling. Moreover, skilled craftspeople can repair and make home improvements themselves, and they frequently have a network of colleagues in other trade groups to help them—all of which saves them money. This implies relatively greater advantages for skilled manual workers within these cohorts.

It may seem surprising that self-employed persons were far less likely to become homeowners than were skilled manual workers. But we should note that this group consisted of young men who had been self-employed for a relatively short period. The rate of home ownership among upper-level white-collar workers was the only rate similar to that of skilled manual workers. Again, this finding indicates that a person's resources are key to becoming a homeowner (Mulder and Smits 1999).

When the interaction effects between occupation and place of residence were included, we found significant effects in three cases (model 1 in Table 6.2). First, salaried employees who lived in Copenhagen were more likely to become homeowners than were members of other occupational groups. That is, the general tendency toward low transition rates to home ownership in Copenhagen was moderated for white-collar workers. The advantage was most pronounced for upper-level white-collar workers. Second, in contrast, the rate was similar for all occupational groups when we looked at home ownership in municipalities outside Copenhagen. Third, in rural areas, the probability of skilled manual workers' becoming homeowners was considerably higher than for the other occupational groups, but the effect was not significant. The differential advantages of the occupational groups are captured in Figure 6.6, which shows the interaction effects of occupational group and place of residence.

Partner's Occupation, Father's Occupation, and Father's Home Ownership

There is no tradition in Denmark for women to leave the labor market when they have children. Most women return to their jobs when they finish their maternity leave.

Model 2 in Table 6.2 indicates that the probability of a couple's becoming homeowners was higher when the woman was working. Obviously, by pooling their resources, a couple improves their chances of buying a home (Mulder and Smits 1999).

TABLE 6.2
Transition to first-time home ownership,
coupled men, Denmark, II

	COEFFICIENT	
Variable	Model 1	Model 2
Constant	−0.3699[a]	−1.2051[a]
Partner		
Partner present	Ref.	
No partner	−2.2910[a]	
Partner not found	−0.9349	
Cohabitation phase		
First year	Ref.	
1–5 years	−0.6227[a]	−0.6257[a]
≥6	−0.9482[a]	−0.9352[a]
Missing partner		−1.6054[a]
Year		
1980	−0.6440[a]	−0.6173[a]
1981	−0.3758[a]	−0.3216[a]
1982	−0.2192	−0.1861
1983	−0.1693	−0.1365
1984	−0.2063	−0.2183
1985	−0.1443	−0.1465
1986	Ref.	
1987	−0.0953	−0.0925
1988	−0.4155[a]	−0.4040[a]
1989	−0.3706[a]	−0.3674[a]
1990	−0.4863[a]	−0.4930[a]
1991	−0.7090[a]	−0.6903[a]
1992	−0.4681[a]	−0.4486[a]
Place of residence (origin)		
Copenhagen and suburbs	−1.1551[a]	−1.0559[a]
Municipality more than 10,000 inhabitants	−0.4408[a]	−0.4065[a]
Rural area	Ref.	
Occupational status		
Self-employed	0.1741	0.0540
White collar, high	0.1841	0.1000
White collar, middle	0.1488	0.0593
White collar, low	0.1904	0.1512
Skilled worker	0.4323[a]	0.4018[a]
Unskilled worker	Ref.	

(*continued*)

TABLE 6.2
(*Continued*)

	COEFFICIENT	
Variable	Model 1	Model 2
Employed, not stated	−0.2004	−0.2696[a]
Unemployed	−0.4840[a]	−0.4145[a]
Out of labor force	−0.7953[a]	−0.7721[a]
*Interaction: occupational status * urbanization*		
White collar, high * Copenhagen and suburbs	0.7576[a]	0.6956[a]
White collar, middle * Copenhagen and suburbs	0.5725[a]	0.6086[a]
White collar, low * Copenhagen and suburbs	0.4796[a]	0.4452[a]
Partner's employment status		
Employed		0.7211[a]
Unemployed		0.4311[a]
Out of labor force	Ref.	
Missing	−0.2322	
Father's employment status		
Self-employed		0.1574
Employee		−0.0261
Unemployed		−0.0711
Out of labor force	Ref.	
Missing		0.1930
Partner's father's employment status		
Self-employed		0.0025
Employee		−0.0490
Unemployed		−0.0027
Out of labor force	Ref.	
Missing		−0.1241
Father's tenure		
Tenant	Ref.	
Owner		0.3526[a]
No information		0.6770[a]
Log-likelihood	−3769.8919	−3719.4302
df	28	40

SOURCES: Author's calculations based on longitudinal data from the IDA database and the BBR, 1980–1997.

[a]$p < .05$.

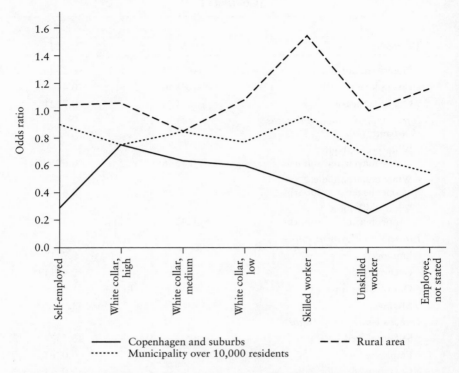

Figure 6.6. Determinants of home ownership: The effect of occupation and place of residence, Denmark

SOURCE: Author's estimates of interaction effects based on longitudinal data from the IDA database and the BBR.

There were no significant interaction effects on home-ownership rates when we examined men's occupational position and women's employment status together.

We also included information in the analysis on the home-ownership status and employment status of the male partner's father. For the latter, we used the categories self-employed, employed, unemployed, and economically inactive. We found that a man whose father owns a home is much more likely to buy a home himself; but the father's employment status did not seem to have any impact on the couple's transition to home ownership. We would have expected men with self-employed fathers to have higher transition rates than the other groups. It is reasonable to interpret the findings to mean that self-employed fathers more often live in their own home, and in that way their occupational position affects the likelihood that their adult children will live in their own home.

CONCLUSIONS

In Denmark, almost two-thirds of the population live in an owner-occupied dwelling. However, the percentage of home ownership among younger generations has dropped, a response, at least in part, to the fact that changes in tax laws and general economic conditions have made it more difficult to acquire real property. Our analysis also shows that men ages 18 to 39 are much more likely to own their own home in rural areas than in Copenhagen. Married couples, especially, and couples living in consensual unions are also more likely to own a home, whereas single persons tend to live in rented dwellings. Occupational position too plays a role in home ownership: not surprisingly, economically active persons—in particular self-employed persons and upper-level salaried employees—account for the highest home-ownership share. What is more surprising, however, is that skilled manual workers have only a slightly lower rate of home ownership than do self-employed and high-level salaried employees.

A longitudinal analysis of men ages 18 to 20 in 1980, which followed them until 1993, shows that many of them bought a home when they married or began to live in a consensual union. In this context, the effects of urbanization and occupational position just noted are still significant. When we look at the interaction effects of urbanization and occupational position, we find that in Copenhagen, upper-level salaried employees were more likely to live in their own home. In rural areas, on the other hand, skilled manual workers had the highest probability of becoming homeowners. There is a positive effect on the probability of moving to an owner-occupied dwelling if the female partner is working. Another important factor seems to be the employment status of the man's father but only by way of the father's housing tenure: the sons of self-employed fathers (who are more likely to own their own home) are more likely to become homeowners. The employment position of the partner's father is of no importance.

Housing tenure plays a significant role in inequality in Denmark. Today, Danish society is increasingly segregated: homeowners have many resources, and tenants have few resources. From our analysis, it seems that a range of factors contribute, most having to do with the decisions young people make

for themselves about education and career, for example. Much less important are the contributions of their parents.

Notes

1. See also Bolig- og Byministeriet (1998).

2. Looking at the proportion of persons—instead of households—living in owner-occupied dwellings, we observed a slightly higher rate: 62 percent of the population (Danmarks Statistik 1999).

3. For about 1 percent of households, ownership was not known.

4. The balance was owned by housing cooperatives and the state.

5. At present, it is possible to remortgage.

6. Until the late 1990s, this policy had only a minor effect on homeowners' tax liability.

7. A household consists of one or more persons living at the same postal address. All persons living in the same dwelling are considered to belong to the same household, regardless of family ties. If the owner of the dwelling belongs to the household, all persons living in the household are classified as persons "who live in an owner-occupied dwelling."

8. Until 1970, statistics on housing conditions in Denmark were compiled in conjunction with population censuses. In 1977, a register of all buildings and dwellings, the Central Register of Buildings and Dwellings (BBR) was set up, and that is the source of our housing data after 1970. The statistics relating to households and families are also compiled from a register, specifically the Central Office of Civil Registration (CPR). In our analysis, we at times combined information from the two registers to describe the housing situation for individual population groups.

9. The balance was owned cooperatively or by the state.

10. The figure probably overstates the rate of home ownership in the youngest group. Some of these young people were still living at home with their parents: the data do not distinguish between living in a home one owns and living in a home one's parents own.

11. Where no member of the household was economically active, the oldest person in the household was treated as the head of household. This methodology may explain, at least in part, an increase in the rate of home ownership among economically inactive households, from 22 percent in 1970 to 38 percent in 1991.

12. A property may consist of one or more separated dwellings.

13. We should note that the proportion of people living alone has increased as well.

14. See also Danmarks Statistik (1994).

15. The author thanks statistician Esben Agerbo of the National Centre for Register-Based Research for his helpful discussions of methods and results.

References

Allison, Paul D. 1995. *Survival analysis using the SAS system: A practical guide.* Cary, NC: SAS Institute.

Arbejderbevægelsens Erhvervsråd. 1999. Fremtidsudsigter for den almene sektor (The future of nonprofit housing associations). Available online at http://www .ae-dk.dk/dokument/analyse/nyea/Sep99/bygge_a0999.pdf (accessed February 20, 2004).

Bolig- og Byministeriet (Ministry of Housing and Urban Affairs). 1998. *Bygge- og boligpolitisk oversigt 1997–1998 (Survey of housing policies 1997–1998).* Kbhvn.

Christoffersen, Henrik, and Lars E. Rasmussen. 1995. *Danskernes bomønster siden 1970 (Housing patterns in Denmark since 1970).* Kbhvn: AKF Forlaget.

Christoffersen, M. Nygaard. 1993. *Familiens ændring (Family change).* Rapport 93:2. Kbhvn: Socialforskningsinstituttet (Danish National Institute of Social Research).

Danmarks Statistik. 1991. *IDA—en integreret database for arbejdsmarkedsforsk- ning. Hovedrapport (IDA—an integrated database for labor market research. Main report).* Kbhvn.

———. 1994. *Personstatistik i Danmark. Et registerbaseret statistiksystem (Statis- tics on persons in Denmark. A register-based statistical system).* Kbhvn.

———. 1995. *50-års oversigten (50-year review).* Kbhvn.

———. 1998. Boligtællingen 1998 (Housing census 1998). *Befolkning og Valg 1998 Population and Elections 1998),* 18.

———. 1999. *Statistisk tiårsoversigt 1999 (Statistical ten-year review 1999).* Kbhvn.

Danmarks Statistik and Socialforskningsinstituttet (Danish National Institute of Social Research). 1997. *Levevilkår i Danmark. Statistisk oversigt 1997 (Living conditions in Denmark 1997).* Kbhvn.

Esping-Andersen, Gøsta. 1990. *The three worlds of welfare capitalism.* Princeton, NJ: Princeton University Press.

Kurz, Karin. 1999. *Social inequality and homeownership attainment in West Ger- many.* Bielefeld: University of Bielefeld, Department of Sociology.

Kuula, Dorte, and Orla Bang. 1999. Det første huskøb er blevet sværere (Buying a first house has become more difficult). *Jyllands-Posten,* October 31.

Leth-Sørensen, Søren. 1997. The IDA database—a longitudinal database of estab- lishments and their employees. Working paper, Danmarks Statistik, Kbhvn.

Mulder, Clara H., and Jeroen Smits. 1999. First-time homeownership of couples. *European Sociological Review* 15 (3): 323–37.

CHAPTER SEVEN

Home Ownership and Social Inequality in Norway

Lars Gulbrandsen

Throughout the postwar period, a central aim of Norwegian housing policy has been to enable as many people as possible to own their own home, either individually (most common in rural areas and in small- and midsized towns) or as a member of a housing cooperative (most common in larger towns and cities). Underlying that policy at the outset was a hostility toward landlords. Housing policy was designed to combat the property rights of the few (the landlords) by spreading ownership among the many (the tenants). That thinking was expressed most clearly by Trygve Brattelie in the early 1950s, when he told the Norwegian parliament that people's housing needs should be completely shielded from profit and commercial gain.[1]

Universal property rights became an important part of a policy that in Norway was generally known as *social housing policy*. The state played a key role, not least by financing a substantial share of new construction, channeled primarily through the Norwegian State Housing Bank. Between 1945 and the end of the millennium, 1 million new homes were financed by loans from the bank. The significance of that investment is reflected in the fact that Norway entered the new millennium with a total of about 2 million homes accommodating 4.45 million inhabitants, and with about 80 percent of households owning a home. This very large element of private ownership in the Norwegian housing sector is to a large extent a product of public support in the form of low-interest state loans.[2]

To achieve the government's goal of equalization, the State Housing Bank set size (floor area) and cost limits as a condition for granting subsidized loans to individuals and housing cooperatives. In the largest towns and surrounding districts, the housing cooperative played a major role. Norwegian housing cooperatives are members of a nationwide organization with a cooperative building association in most municipalities. The association's task is to acquire homes for its members. As each housing development is completed, the new flats or houses are organized into one or more housing cooperatives, each of which is jointly owned by the residents. The building association sees to it that the homes meet state loan criteria for size and price, and that they are distributed fairly (usually on the basis of a queue scheme). Price controls and fair distribution also applied to resale flats in housing cooperatives. The goal, to put all households in a financial position to buy their own house or flat, was largely achieved. Hence in Norway, in contrast to Sweden, it was not considered necessary to maintain a supply of local-authority housing. Several thousand municipal rental flats were built in Oslo between the world wars; in the 1950s, most were sold cheaply to the tenants and organized as housing cooperatives. Today, only 3 percent of households live in a home owned by the local authority. These homes are dispersed around the ordinary housing stock. Local-authority housing in the traditional mold is virtually nonexistent.

With the exception of the years immediately following World War II, no upper limit was imposed on the consumption of housing. However, consumption that exceeded the limits set by the State Housing Bank had, at least in theory, to be paid for in full by the owner–occupier. Until 1995, the State Housing Bank granted subsidized loans to anyone willing to live in a house that did not exceed the area and cost limits set by the housing bank (which in time became fairly generous). The most luxurious houses were almost without exception individually owned. In the towns, the broad mass of social housing was in the form of flats in housing cooperatives. In smaller towns and communities and in rural areas, with the help of state loans, the vast majority of households were able to afford an owner-occupied detached house of moderate size.

The state's policy of encouraging home ownership proved problematic as homeowners acquired a taste not only for living in low-cost secure housing but also for reselling at a high price without hindrance. The problem was not diminished by the fact that government regulation drew a line dividing the housing market by nuances in the owner segment. Price controls were applied to flats in housing cooperatives but not to individually owned houses and apartments. By the time price regulation on cooperatively owned flats was removed in the mid-1980s, it had long been ineffectual; in fact, it probably served more to keep lower-income groups out of the market than to bring them into it (Gulbrandsen 1980). The way was now open for the conversion of housing cooperatives and rental flats into individually owned units (Wessel 1995).

One result of price regulation was the lack of reliable data on actual market prices. Because public authorities imposed limits on prices, they could not employ other, more realistic prices as a basis for property or inheritance taxes. Accurate nationwide statistics on house prices were not compiled in Norway until the start of the 1990s. By then, prices had been falling steadily since the spring of 1988 and would continue to do so until the spring of 1993. Over that period, prices fell about 30 percent in nominal terms and 15 percent in real terms. Between 1993 and 2000, nominal house prices doubled, while real prices rose about 85 percent, movements that reflected the general economic climate.

Despite reliable statistics on house prices based on actual sales, there are still no comprehensive register-based statistics on the market value of all Norwegian homes. Since the beginning of the 1970s, it has not proved possible to gain a political majority for any one of the many calls for more-realistic property valuations as a basis for property taxes (Torgersen 1996). In the mid-1990s, valuations of homes for tax purposes averaged 25 percent of the homes' actual value. Because house prices have risen so steeply since 1993, it is not unreasonable to assume that houses are being taxed on the basis of a valuation between 15 percent and 20 percent of market value.

An important issue in connection with home ownership is the degree, if any, of positive correlation between home ownership and social position. Kurz (see Chapter 2) cites a lack of recent studies in Germany on the social distribution of home ownership. The same seems very much the case for Norway. It may be that the success of Norwegian housing policy in terms of producing many owners would seem to make the study of social inequality in owner distribution moot. But the truth is that housing distribution since the mid-1980s has been controlled almost exclusively by the market. Individually owned dwellings, which make up about 65 percent of the housing stock, in general might be expected to show a more skewed social distribution than cooperatively owned dwellings, which make up about 15 percent. This expectation can be justified on the grounds that individually owned dwellings are more likely to be detached houses; cooperative housing far more often is found in apartment buildings and row houses. Moreover, individually owned dwellings, because they are not financed by loans from the State Housing Bank, are not subject to limits in size, quality, and standards. Also, the distribution of individually owned dwellings, particularly resale dwellings, was almost exclusively controlled by the market even before the mid-1980s.

Although price controls were ineffectual and by no means captured all house sales, the deregulation raises several questions: Has the social distribution of ownership become more skewed since the mid-1980s? Is social inequality in the housing market greater among those who became adults after the housing market was deregulated or among older segments of the population? (Above all, the marked increase in the real prices of housing in the second half of the 1990s makes this a legitimate question.) And in light of the high incidence of home ownership in Norway, are social differences more likely to be reflected in differences in housing consumption (defined on the basis of the market value of individually owned homes) than in differences in ownership rates?

We begin our analysis of these questions with a history of home ownership in Norway in the 1900s. Our attention then shifts to homeowners themselves: At what age do they buy homes, and what role does socioeconomic position play in the transition to home ownership? Next we look at the factors that determine housing tenure—individual ownership versus cooperative ownership—in Norwegian households today. In that connection, we focus on those who were between 25 and 37 years old in 1997, a population that came of home-buying age after deregulation. Finally, armed with data, we examine the distribution of housing consumption and housing wealth (gross and net housing capital).

HOME OWNERSHIP IN NORWAY. DEVELOPMENTS IN THE TWENTIETH CENTURY

Historical data on forms of home ownership in Norway come from comprehensive population and housing censuses. The last population and housing census available to us was taken in 1990. Since the end of the 1960s, the census has been supplemented with sample surveys of housing conditions. In the 1990s, Norwegian Social Research carried out several major sample surveys in which questions on housing figured prominently (Gulbrandsen and Hellevik 1998).[3] Although our focus was on household finances, we also asked a substantial number of questions on form of ownership; age, size, and type of house; year purchased; and estimated market value. In addition, we asked retrospective questions to ascertain when respondents left their parents' home and when they became homeowners for the first time.[4]

The population and housing census from 1920 provides the first good data on forms of home ownership. As early as 1920, more than half of the houses in Norway were individually owned. There were clear differences between town and country. For example, in Oslo (at the time known as Kristiania), only 5 percent of residents owned their home (Gulbrandsen 1988); in the countryside, more than 65 percent of households were homeowners. Nationwide, there were just a few hundred cooperatively owned flats, almost all of them in Oslo. In the interwar period, particularly in the years immediately following World War I, cooperatively owned flats were the main contributor to increased home ownership in the largest cities. Just after World War II, the individual-ownership rate in Norway as a whole was slightly higher than it had been in 1920 (Wessel 1995).

Since the end of World War II, home-ownership rate has risen steadily. In the same period, housing stock has doubled, from just under 1 million units to about 2 million units. In absolute figures, then, the number of new homeowners has risen by about 1 million. Table 7.1 shows the overall proportion of homeowners in Norway and the breakdown by owner type from 1920 to 1997. Although individual ownership continued to grow through much of the 1990s, survey data suggest that the growth had ended by the end of the

TABLE 7.1

Home ownership among households by owner type,
Norway, 1920–1997

	PERCENTAGE OF HOMEOWNING HOUSEHOLDS					
Owner type	*1920*	*1960*	*1970*	*1980*	*1990*	*1997*[a]
Individual owners	53	53	53	55	59	65
Cooperative owners	—	11	13	19	19	16
Total ownership	53	64	66	74	78	81

SOURCES: Figures from 1920 to 1990 are based on Norwegian population and housing censuses; figures for 1997 are based on a sample survey conducted by Norwegian Social Research.

[a]Because these data were taken from a different source, they may overstate the proportion of homeowners somewhat.

TABLE 7.2
Owner occupancy by head of household's age,
Norway, 1973, 1988, 1992, and 1997

Year	PERCENTAGE OF OWNER-OCCUPIERS						
	25–29 years	30–34 years	35–39 years	40–49 years	50–59 years	60–69 years	>69 years
1973	50	60	83	85	81	78	64
1988	60	81	89	90	90	85	68
1992[a]	67	84	87	92	94	91	81
1997[a]	62	75	84	88	92	93	90

SOURCES: Author's calculations based on surveys of housing conditions and a sample survey conducted by Norwegian Social Research.

[a]The surveys in 1992 and 1997 asked the respondent's age, not the head of household's age.

decade; and the ownership rate for cooperative owners actually had dropped by 1997.[5]

The groups most affected by the slowdown in home ownership were younger people—those under age 35 (Gulbrandsen 1999a). In the earliest data in Table 7.2, the link between age and ownership status produces an inverse U-curve—rates are lower for the younger and older age groups, and higher for the age groups in between.[6] In 1988 and even in 1992, although the curve is changing, a U is still visible. By 1997, the U-curve has disappeared. Members of the oldest age group had achieved a very high level of owner occupancy earlier in life, and they were holding on to their homes. The two youngest groups saw their ownership rates rise through 1992; by 1997, the rates had fallen sharply, in what may well have been the first indication of a turnaround in the trend toward steadily higher levels of home ownership (Gulbrandsen 1999a).

OWNERSHIP STATUS AND THE LIFE COURSE

Ideally, we would have used longitudinal data to describe changes in home ownership at different life stages. But long-term studies of home ownership in Norway were not started until the late 1990s. We were compelled to turn to less adequate data, then, namely a representative national survey taken in

TABLE 7.3

Home ownership before age 30, by birth cohort, Norway, 1992

	BIRTH COHORT				
Variable	*Before 1923*	*1923–1932*	*1933–1942*	*1943–1952*	*1953–1962*
Reached age 30 in the period	Before 1953	1953–1962	1963–1972	1973–1982	1983–1992
Became homeowners before age 30	17%	30%	43%	57%	65%
N	308	331	329	536	609

SOURCE: Author's calculations based on a sample survey conducted by Norwegian Social Research.

the fall of 1992 by Norwegian Social Research. That survey asked respondents a retrospective question: When did you become a homeowner for the first time? One weakness of this approach was that we were unable to record the date of purchase for those in 1992 who had owned a home but no longer did so. But this was the case for only 5 percent of respondents, and they were evenly distributed across age groups, so we decided to disregard the possible error.

Table 7.3 shows for each ten-year cohort the percentage that had become homeowners before the age of 30. Notice how the rate increased in each successive birth cohort. After World War II until 1992, the age at which Norwegians bought their first home steadily went down.

The data in Table 7.3 are from 1992. Since then, the trend has shifted: current data indicate a slight tendency among people under 30 to postpone buying their first home (Gulbrandsen 2002). Several factors are cited for the change. First, younger people are spending more time in the educational system, which delays their full-time employment and their ability to afford a home of their own. Second, in the early 1990s, unemployment was growing in Norway, particularly among younger workers. Third, a steep drop in house prices created severe financial problems for people who had bought a home when prices were substantially higher. Those problems were the focus of much media attention and no doubt led some young people to put off home ownership. Also an incentive for delay was a growing supply of rental housing. By the end of the decade, young people were again buying homes in larger numbers, but not in numbers large enough to lower the average age of first-time ownership (Gulbrandsen and Sandlie 2000).

A major problem when analyzing the impact of other variables on the age of first-time ownership is that year of birth is the only variable describing the respondents at the time ownership status was attained for the first time. With the exception of social background and possibly education, most characteristics will have changed between the time a respondent buys his or her first home and the time of the interview.[7]

Acknowledging our strong reservations, we examined by means of logistic regression the degree to which attainment of home ownership before the age of 30 is conditioned by birth cohort and other relevant variables. In Table 7.4, we show the results both for age (birth cohort) alone and for the overall models. We wanted to investigate the extent to which the correlation we demonstrated in Table 7.3 is influenced by drawing other variables into the analysis.

As we see, the probability of home ownership for the various birth cohorts changes very little, even though place of residence and household income have a marked effect on the likelihood of buying a home at an earlier age. Controlling for the other variables, the likelihood of becoming a homeowner is appreciably greater in rural areas than in urban communities; that likelihood also increases with family income (model 2). The likelihood of early home ownership is smallest among those with the most education.[8] To register the occupation of as many respondents as possible, we recorded the husband's occupation in couple households and the respondent's occupation in one-person households. Even so, the number of persons with no reported occupation was so large that we were compelled to include this group in the analysis. It turned out that this group mainly comprised old-age pensioners, and, as can be seen in the table, there is no difference between those with no reported occupation and the reference group in the model (unskilled workers). We found no significant effect for any occupational group.

In the third model, we excluded household income to see whether occupational group would exert an effect. It did not. In Norway, it seems that financial resources, not some kind of class-specific behavior, are key to home ownership. Given all the reservations we noted above, our conclusion is that attaining home-ownership status early in life does not seem to be correlated with social background.

TABLE 7.4
Likelihood of home ownership before age 30, Norway, 1992
[logistic regression: Exp(B)-coefficients]

Variable	EXP(B)-COEFFICIENTS		
	Model 1	Model 2	Model 3
Birth cohort			
Before 1923	0.11^b	0.14^b	0.13^b
1923–1932	0.22^b	0.22^b	0.24^b
1933–1942	0.40^b	0.38^b	0.39^b
1943–1952	0.71^b	0.64^b	0.69^b
1953–1962	Ref.		
Place of residence			
Country's 3 largest cities		Ref.	
Other towns/urban areas		1.04	0.92
Thinly populated areas		1.70^b	1.50^b
Household income			
1st quartile (NOK 0–150,000)		Ref.	
2nd quartile (NOK 151,000–240,000)		1.30	
3rd quartile (NOK 241,000–350,000)		1.57^b	
4th quartile (> NOK 350,000)		2.13^b	
Education			
Primary school		Ref.	
Secondary school		0.93	1.02
University/college		0.72	0.84
Occupation			
Unskilled worker		Ref.	
Skilled worker		1.20	1.21
White-collar worker, lower level		1.10	1.08
White-collar worker, upper level		0.98	1.12
Self-employed		1.39	1.25
No occupation stated		1.04	0.80

$^a p < .05.$
$^b p < .01.$

WHAT DETERMINES OWNERSHIP STATUS
IN NORWAY TODAY?

In the preceding analysis we employed data from 1992 simply because the 1992 survey was the only one of our surveys that asked questions about the age at which a first home was purchased. We have since carried out several other surveys, the most recent in the fall of 1997. We used the data from the 1997 survey to study the factors that determine home ownership in present-day Norway. Unlike the 1992 survey, the 1997 survey did not collect data on respondents' occupation; on the other hand, it did ask respondents about their father's level of education.

Table 7.5 shows the results of logistic regression to determine the factors that influence home ownership generally and within categories of ownership. In model 1 (individual owners), we found clear and significant effects for all of the variables except father's education, which had no significant effect on the likelihood of becoming an individual owner. The two variables that pertain to life stage—age and marital status—both had a clear and strong effect on the likelihood of becoming an individual owner. Compared with members of the youngest group (the reference group), members of every other age group were significantly more likely to become individual home-owners. (That likelihood increased through middle age and then began to fall slightly, though it remained substantially higher than the likelihood of home ownership in the reference group.) Entering a couple relationship, especially a marriage, also increased the likelihood of home ownership. Ending a marriage reduced the likelihood of private home ownership, probably in large part a function of the economics of divorce (Gulbrandsen 1999b). Here, too, higher income had a positive effect on ownership status, as did living outside the country's three largest cities, particularly living in a rural area.

About 10 percent of Norwegian households live in a home they have inherited. All together, 20 percent of households report having inherited a dwelling. This is about half of what might be expected on the basis of the incidence of households in which the husband or wife reports the death of parents who owned a home. One explanation for the disparity here is that most inherited homes are sold, and the proceeds are considered inherited financial capital, not inherited housing capital (Gulbrandsen and Langsether 1999a). All the same, an inheritance in whatever form should increase the possibility of home ownership. Where individual ownership is concerned, Table 7.5

TABLE 7.5

Likelihood of becoming a homeowner by category of ownership,
Norway, 1997 [logistic regression: Exp(B)-coefficients]

| | EXP(B)-COEFFICIENTS | | |
Variable	Model 1 (individual owner)	Model 2 (cooperative owner)	Model 3 (total ownership)
Age (years)			
20–29 (born 1968–1977)		Ref.	
30–39 (born 1958–1967)	2.23[b]	1.23	2.56[b]
40–49 (born 1948–1957)	3.14[b]	1.14	4.37[b]
50–59 (born 1938–1947)	6.81[b]	0.53	6.63[b]
60–69 (born 1928–1937)	5.94[b]	1.28	13.65[b]
> 69 (born before 1928)	4.94[b]	2.01[a]	13.60[b]
Father's education			
Primary school		Ref.	
Secondary school	1.23	1.05	1.48
University/college	0.93	1.57[a]	1.83[b]
Inheritance or gift			
Nonrecipient		Ref.	
From parents or parents-in-law	1.24	1.10	1.60[a]
From parents and parents-in-law	1.53	0.67	1.55
Own education			
Primary school		Ref.	
Secondary school	1.50[a]	0.81	1.73[b]
University/college	1.52[a]	0.44[b]	0.80

(continued)

does show a relationship, albeit not a statistically significant one. Labor market position (as reflected in household income) matters more than intergenerational transfers.

We find fewer clear-cut significant results when it comes to factors that determine cooperative ownership (model 2). Old-age pensioners are far more likely to own a flat in a housing cooperative than are people in their twenties. Cooperative ownership appears least likely among those in their forties and fifties. The overrepresentation of the elderly in cooperative ownership seems to be a cohort phenomenon: retirees in 1997 came of age just after the last world war, and many of them were still living in the coopera-

TABLE 7.5
(*Continued*)

Variable	EXP(B)-COEFFICIENTS		
	Model 1 (individual owner)	Model 2 (cooperative owner)	Model 3 (total ownership)
Marital status			
Unmarried		Ref.	
Cohabitant	2.77[b]	0.96	2.36[b]
Married	5.31[b]	0.47[b]	4.19[b]
Previously married	2.38[b]	1.45	2.94[b]
Household income			
1st quintile (NOK 0–150,000)		Ref.	
2nd quintile (NOK 151,000–230,000)	1.13	1.72[a]	1.65[a]
3rd quintile (NOK 231,000–330,000)	2.58[b]	1.65	4.30[b]
4th quintile (NOK 331,000–450,000)	3.68[b]	1.53	7.23[b]
5th quintile (> NOK 450,000)	4.37[b]	1.40	9.31[b]
Place of residence			
Country's three largest cities		Ref.	
Other towns/urban areas	3.09[b]	0.37[b]	1.36
Thinly populated areas	8.68[b]	0.06[b]	1.62[a]

[a] $p < .05$.
[b] $p < .01$.

tive homes they bought then. By the time members of younger birth cohorts —in their forties and fifties in 1997—were ready to buy their first home, cooperative housing had become almost transitional, a step on the path to individual ownership for those with the resources to buy another type of dwelling.

We found this same reverse effect when we examined other variables: that is, variables that seemed to play a role in individual ownership were much less important to cooperative ownership, and vice versa. Married couples were least likely to be cooperative owners, as were those living in rural areas and those with the most education. In terms of social distribution (household income), the results can reasonably be interpreted to indicate that the distribution of cooperative ownership has to some extent a compensatory effect for the distribution of individual ownership. Also, we found no significant effects for intergenerational transfers, which tallies with earlier findings that inheritance has little bearing on household wealth in Norway (Gulbrandsen 1996).

Finally, when we looked at overall ownership (model 3 in Table 7.5), we found little variation from individual ownership: the variables that determine home ownership generally are largely the same as those that determine individual home ownership. This wasn't surprising given the proportion of individual owners among all homeowners.

As we mentioned at the start of this chapter, the home-ownership sector in Norway since the mid-1980s has come increasingly under the sway of market forces. The deregulation of prices, especially for cooperatively owned flats, was followed by substantial conversion of housing cooperatives and rental flats into individually owned units (Wessel 1995). That being the case, we expected the distribution between individual ownership and cooperative ownership to be skewed by purchasing power, particularly among the younger people who became first-time homeowners after deregulation. We confined our analysis, then, to those who turned 25 after the mid-1980s.

Our findings for individual ownership (model 1) and total ownership (model 2) are presented in Table 7.6. Our results for individual ownership closely match those shown in Table 7.5. That education had no effect on the rate among younger homeowners probably reflects the fact that this population had spent more time in school before entering the labor force. Notice that here, as in Table 7.5, the positive effects of income and social background (measured by means of father's education) are strengthened when we look at overall ownership. At the same time, when we added cooperative ownership to individual ownership, the effects of place of residence largely disappeared. Overall, we found no strong indication that household income had a more significant impact on home ownership after deregulation.

FORM OF OWNERSHIP, HOUSING CONSUMPTION, AND HOUSING WEALTH

In a population in which 80 percent of households own a home, homeowners necessarily are going to show wide variation. In fact, we are likely to find more social and economic inequality among owners than we might find between owners and tenants. Our research question: To what extent are

TABLE 7.6
Likelihood of becoming a homeowner, individually or generally,
ages 25 to 37, Norway, 1997 [logistic regression: Exp(B)-coefficients]

	EXP(B)-COEFFICIENTS	
Variable	Model 1 (individual owner)	Model 2 (total ownership)
Age (years)		
25–31	Ref.	
32–37	2.26[b]	2.73[b]
Father's education		
Primary school	Ref.	
Secondary school	1.21	1.42
University/college	1.12	1.95[a]
Inheritance or gift		
Nonrecipient	Ref.	
From parents or parents-in-law	1.17	1.71
From parents and parents-in-law	1.26	0.93
Own education		
Primary school	Ref.	
Secondary school	1.06	1.09
University/college	0.82	0.39[a]
Marital status		
Unmarried	Ref.	
Cohabitant	2.22[a]	1.84
Married	3.47[b]	2.78[b]
Previously married	2.06	1.78
Household income		
1st quintile (NOK 0–150,000)	Ref.	
2nd quintile (NOK 151,000–230,000)	1.68	1.68
3rd quintile (NOK 231,000–330,000)	3.43[b]	4.90[b]
4th quintile (NOK 331,000–450,000)	5.90[b]	8.07[b]
5th quintile (> NOK 450,000)	4.51[b]	7.47[b]
Place of residence		
Country's three largest cities	Ref.	
Other towns/urban areas	2.62[b]	1.61
Thinly populated areas	3.97[b]	1.31

[a]$p < .05$.
[b]$p < .01$.

variations in housing consumption and housing wealth determined by the same variables that affect the frequency of home ownership?

In this context, we defined *housing consumption* as the value of the household's home. As mentioned earlier, Norway lacks good-quality data on the market value of housing. Tax assessment values, for example, are unrealistically low. In our 1997 survey, we asked individual and cooperative owners for their estimate of the market value of their home, and about 90 percent responded.[9] It is this answer that we defined as *gross housing capital* and as an indicator of housing consumption. Tenants were given a value of zero—a completely erroneous estimate of tenants' housing consumption, but one of little consequence to our analysis because our primary concern was variation in owners' consumption. We defined *net housing capital*, or *housing wealth*, as the amount obtained after housing debt is deducted.

In Table 7.7, we show how gross and net housing wealth are distributed by age. Gross housing capital expressed by the median values rose rapidly among those in their thirties, the time when most people undertake a major housing investment. It continued rising gradually, peaking among those in their fifties, and then began edging down. Net housing capital rose more evenly, peaking among those in their sixties—quite simply because it takes time to repay a home loan. The decrease in the oldest group was to a great degree a cohort effect. Elderly people today usually own homes that are a bit less valuable than those owned by middle-aged owners. The reason: the elderly never reached as high a housing standard. (There is no evidence that the decrease in net value here has anything to do with the elderly "living off" their housing wealth.)

On the bivariate level, we found a clear positive correlation between household income and gross housing wealth, and we found that the ownership rate also increased with income (Table 7.8). Some of this correlation may be due to a underlying correlation between age and income; we have not tried to sort out this effect.

Table 7.9 shows the results of regression analysis in which gross and net housing wealth, respectively, were dependent variables. To compensate for the inverse U-curve that was generated by the relationship between age and both gross and net housing wealth, in addition to ordinary age we employed age squared, which we expected to produce negative regression coefficients.[10] Apart from overall family income, the remainder of the variables were dummies.

TABLE 7.7

Gross and net housing wealth by respondent's age, Norway, 1997

Housing wealth	AGE (YEARS)						
	20–29	*30–39*	*40–49*	*50–59*	*60–69*	*>69*	*All*
Gross housing wealth (NOK 1,000)							
1st quartile	0	300	500	600	450	300	250
Median	110	700	800	900	750	600	655
3rd quartile	700	1,000	1,200	1,100	1,000	900	1,000
Net housing wealth (NOK 1,000)							
1st quartile	0	0	160	385	400	300	10
Median	0	300	470	650	700	588	400
3rd quartile	230	580	800	900	1,000	800	750
N	478	542	502	389	265	352	2,555

NOTE: In 1997, the exchange rate was approximately NOK 7 to $1.

TABLE 7.8

Gross housing wealth and home ownership
by gross household income, Norway, 1997

Variable	HOUSEHOLD INCOME				
	1st quintile	*2nd quintile*	*3rd quintile*	*4th quintile*	*5th quintile*
Median gross housing wealth (NOK 1,000)	300	550	700	850	1,100
Proportion of homeowners	61%	75%	84%	91%	95%

In terms of gross housing wealth, the model did not provide a particularly good fit with the data (multiple $R = .19$). We can also see that age and income were the only variables with significant effects. The fit in the model analyzing net housing wealth was far better (multiple $R = .44$). Although only age and income showed a significant relationship with gross housing capital, it is clear from the table that the only variable that had no significant impact on net housing capital was father's education. From the standardized

TABLE 7.9

Gross and net housing wealth conditioned by age, household income,
own and father's education, place of residence, and inheritance,
Norway, 1997 (regression analysis)

Variable	GROSS HOUSING WEALTH (NOK 1,000)			NET HOUSING WEALTH (NOK 1,000)		
	B	β	ρT	B	β	ρT
Age in years	21.99	.16	.00	9.34	.29	.00
Age squared	−.23	−.03	.26	−.31	−.16	.00
Household income (NOK 1,000)	.47	.08	.00	.17	.13	.00
Own education (dummy: 1 = university, college)	34.70	.01	.80	79.24	.06	.00
Father's education (dummy: 1 = university, college)	97.17	−.02	.47	37.14	.03	.21
Place of residence (dummy: 1 = country's 3 largest cities)	−204.01	−.04	.13	−133.57	−.11	.00
Receipt of inheritance or advance (dummy: 1 = yes)	−22.26	−.00	.86	174.67	.16	.00
Constant	1,324.63	—	.00	391.93	—	.00

regression coefficients, we can see, too, that age had the greatest explanatory power. Also an inheritance or an advance on an inheritance seemed to increase net housing wealth but did not have the same effect on gross housing wealth. This indicates that inheritances or advances are used either to make a down payment on the purchase of a house or to pay down housing debt.

The survey also asked questions about other components of wealth—debt related to the home and other debt, the total value of bank deposits, the value of cars owned by the household, the value of recreational property, and the estimated value of a second home (almost 10 percent of Norwegian households own more than one home). Housing wealth constitutes a substantial component of households' total wealth. The correlation coefficient between housing wealth and total wealth measured in our surveys was .70. When we analyzed household wealth using the same model we used in Table 7.9 and employing housing wealth as an additional explanatory variable (model 1 in Table 7.10), we obtained a good fit with the data (multiple $R = .66$). Even when we used net housing capital as an explanatory variable, we observed significant positive effects for age and income; the negative and significant effect of age squared disappears, however. Reduced net wealth among the oldest birth cohorts seems to be the result of lower-valued housing. This can be seen in model 2 in Table 7.10, where we omitted net housing capital so that total net wealth was analyzed based on the same model as net housing capital in Table 7.9 (multiple $R = .39$). All vari-

TABLE 7.10
Household wealth conditioned by age, household income,
own and father's education, place of residence, inheritance,
and net housing capital, Norway, 1997 (regression analysis)

Variable	MODEL 1		MODEL 2		MODEL 3	
	B	β	B	β	B	β
Age in years	4.87	.07[b]	17.18	.25[b]	13.79	.20[b]
Age squared	−.02	−.01	−4.3	−.10[b]	−.28	−.07[a]
Household income (NOK 1,000)	.25	.09[b]	.47	.17[b]	.41	.15[b]
Own education (dummy: 1 = university, college)	31.26	.01	135.63	.05[a]	152.10	.06[a]
Father's education (dummy: 1 = university, college)	104.12	.04[a]	153.04	.06[a]	134.10	.05[a]
Place of residence (dummy: 1 = country's 3 largest cities)	37.67	.01	213.59	.08[b]	240.53	.09[b]
Receipt of inheritance or advance (dummy: 1 = yes)	59.04	.03	289.10	.12[b]	249.65	.11[b]
Net housing capital (NOK 1,000)	1.32	.63[b]	—	—	—	—
Form of homeownership (dummy: 1=owner)	—	—	—	—	528.09	.18[b]
Constant	32.01	—	548.21	—	91.48	—

[a] $p < .05$.
[b] $p < .01$.

ables had a significant effect. We should also note that age had the strongest effect. In model 3 we included a dichotomous variable that separates households into owners and tenants. That produced a modest increase of multiple *R* (.42). Age still had the greatest effect; the effect of other variables on net housing wealth was either weakened or the same as in model 2.

CONCLUSIONS

In a country with such a high level of home ownership as Norway, there is little room for social inequality between owners and tenants. Instead, evidence of inequality must come from within the owner group, primarily from an analysis of housing wealth. The distribution of housing wealth is determined in part by social background (variables like family income and own and father's education). An inheritance or advance on an inheritance from parents also has an independent positive effect on housing wealth. Moreover, housing wealth is greatest in the largest cities. Age, however, has the greatest explanatory power. Housing wealth is clearly the most important component of households' wealth; naturally, then, the same variables determine the distribution of households' total wealth and the distribution of housing wealth. Norway has for half a century pursued a policy aimed at turning the entire population into homeowners. It has done so in a period of substantial economic growth. Today, for most Norwegians, the most important wealth is real wealth in the form of equity in their homes. This type of wealth increases through the course of life. Although household income and intergenerational transfers also seem to be important, household wealth is distributed to an even greater degree by age.

Notes

1. Brattelie would later become prime minister.
2. The loans were subsidized until the mid-1990s. In 1995, in an attempt to make the loans more selective, the interest subsidy was removed. Today, general loans for new construction and home purchases are granted on market terms. For low-income groups, the loans are supplemented by loans on special terms and by grants (subject to the means testing of borrowers).
3. The data were representative of households: only one adult from each household was interviewed.
4. The last question was asked only in the survey we carried out in 1992.

5. That the data for 1997 were collected using a different methodology (they were taken from sample surveys rather than population and housing censuses) suggests that they may actually overstate the growth experienced that year.

6. With few exceptions, we used a lower age limit of 25 years. This was done to avoid the measurement problems caused by young people (ages 20 to 24) still living in the parental home, problems that are particularly apparent when change is measured over time. In some surveys, for example, it is impossible to separate out those living with their parents and so to determine the actual size of the group. Moreover, it is difficult to identify long-term trends because the extent to which people ages 20 to 24 live with their parents probably changes with economic conditions and educational trends. But by age 25, more than 90 percent of adult children have left their parents' home.

7. The respondent's own education is still a variable whose direct use is problematic because of the almost continual increase in the Norwegian population's level of education.

8. As the table shows, the education variable is not significant at the 5 percent level, but the coefficient for those with university or college education is close to being so ($p = .053$).

9. For a detailed assessment of the age distribution of real capital and financial capital among Norwegian households, see Gulbrandsen and Langsether (1999b, 71ff.).

10. To avoid problems that can arise with a zero point outside the area of observation, we recoded age by assigning the variable a new zero point, age 45.

References

Gulbrandsen, Lars. 1980. *Fra marked til administrasjon? Boligpolitikk og bolig-marked i Oslo i det tjuende århundre.* Oslo. Institutt for Sosialforskning.

———. 1988. Norway. In *Between owner-occupation and rented sector. Housing in ten European countries,* edited by Kroers Hans, Frits Ymkers, and Andre Mulder, 121–43. Delft: The Netherlands Christian Institute for Social Housing.

———. 1996. Er arvens betydning overvurdert? *Tidsskrift for Samfunnsorskning* 1: 28–47.

———. 1999a. Boligkonsum i et livsløps- og generasjonsperspektiv: Fortsatt konsumvekst eller reduksjon? Paper presented at Bostads och Urbanitetsforskningsseminariet, Institutet för Bostadsforskning, Uppsala Universitet, Gävle, April 14–16.

———. 1999b. *Gjeld og økte rentekostnader. Renteøkningene i 1998 sett i lys av utviklingen av husholdningenes gjeld på 1990-tallet.* Skriftserie 3/99. Oslo: Norsk Institutt for Forskning om Oppvekst, Velferd og Aldring (NOVA).

————. 2002. Aldri hard et vært så ille som akkurat nå. *Tidsskrift for Ungdoms-forskning* 2 (1): 33–49.

Gulbrandsen, Lars, and Tale Hellevik. 1998. *Norske husholdningers økonomiske situasjon. Resultater fra en undersøkelse høsten 1997.* Oslo: Norsk Institutt for Forskning om Oppvekst, Velferd og Aldring (NOVA).

Gulbrandsen, Lars, and Åsmund Langsether. 1999a. Housing wealth as inheritance. Paper presented at the New European Housing and Urban Policies Conference, Balatonfured, Hungary, August.

————. 1999b. Wealth distribution between generations: A source of conflict or cohesion? In *The myth of generational conflict. The family and state in aging societies,* edited by Sara Arber and Claudine Attias-Donfut, 69–87. London: Routledge.

Gulbrandsen, Lars, and Hans-Christian Sandlie. 2000. Alt som før? Boligkonum i Norge ved årtusensskiftet. Paper presented at the Nordic Seminar on urban and housing research, Copenhagen, September.

Torgersen, Ulf. 1996. *Omstridt boligskatt. Ut- og avviklingen av skatt av inntekt fra å bo i egen bolig 1882–1996, med særlig vekt på de tre siste tiår.* Rapport 96:5. Oslo: Institutt for Sosialforskning.

Wessel, Terje. 1995. *Eierleiligheter. Framveksten av en ny boligsektor i Oslo, Bergen og Trondheim.* Oslo: Universitetet i Oslo.

CHAPTER EIGHT

Home Ownership and Social Inequality in Italy

Fabrizio Bernardi and
Teresio Poggio

A home provides shelter. In this sense, like food and water, housing is essential to survival. In modern societies, housing also satisfies more complex cultural, social, and economic needs. Many of those societies recognize decent housing as a basic human right in their constitutions. But the means by which they translate that right in practice varies. In some countries, the state provides housing; in others it subsidizes rentals or purchases; in still others, it leaves the distribution of housing—and the choice of tenure—to market forces.

Our focus here is on social inequality and housing, in particular on access to home ownership. Why home ownership? First, because there is evidence that home ownership generally correlates with better living conditions: owner-occupied homes tend to be larger and of better quality than rented homes; they also are more likely to meet the needs and wants of the people who live in them.[1] Second, an owner-occupied home is an asset; it

Previous versions of this chapter were presented at the International Sociological Association (Research Committee 28) meeting in Oxford, April 11–14, 2002, and at a seminar of the Centro de Estructuras Sociales Comparadas based at the Universidad Nacional de Educación a Distancia, Madrid. Thanks are due the participants at these seminars for their valuable comments and suggestions. Teresio Poggio's contribution is based on work carried out during a visit to the European Centre for Analysis in the Social Sciences at the Institute for Social and Economic Research, University of Essex, supported by the Access to Research Infrastructure action under the EU Improving Human Potential Programme. An earlier version of the manuscript was published as a working paper of the Department of Sociology and Social Research at the University of Trento in 2002. The chapter is based on a secondary analysis of data from the Bank of Italy's Survey of Household Income and Wealth. The authors, not the Bank of Italy, are personally responsible for the research.

also is an investment that generates real income in the form of *imputed rent*.[2] Home ownership, then, can accentuate or compensate for the effects of economic inequalities associated with labor market status or preexisting socioeconomic assets. Finally, if intergenerational transfers play an important role in facilitating home ownership, then home ownership may be a factor in the reproduction of social and economic inequalities.

If we accept that home ownership generally is associated with better living conditions, that it is an asset that generates income—albeit in kind—independently from the labor market, and that it may well be a medium for reproducing social and economic inequalities, then it becomes crucial to investigate how home ownership is actually achieved. To that end, in this chapter we study the relationship between social class and home ownership in Italy. In particular, we address three research questions:

- Does social class influence the likelihood of becoming a homeowner?
- Have class differences in the likelihood and the process of becoming a homeowner changed over generations?
- What role do intergenerational transfers and family support play in the attainment of home ownership?

These questions are important in the field of social inequality because they speak to two related theories on the significance of social class in contemporary society. The first, which focuses on consumption classes, has been debated since the early 1980s, mostly in Britain (Saunders 1990). It centers on the idea that owning or not owning a home has become one of the most crucial determinants of the individual's life chances, independent from the individual's social position. If that is true, and home ownership is no longer a function of social class, we could see a society divided into a large majority of homeowners and a residual minority of "not owners" who have to rely on public support for their housing. The inadequacy of the class concept to describe patterns of inequality in contemporary society is one emphasis that this theory shares with the theory on the so-called risk or globalized society (Beck 1992; Giddens 1994).[3] According to this view, social class is losing significance, giving place to a generalized individualization and a temporalized inequality. Critics of both theories would argue that home ownership is an intervening factor in the structuration of inequality. In other words, social class determines the likelihood of home ownership; and home ownership, by affecting living conditions and increasing real income, in turn strengthens social inequalities (Forrest and Murie 1995).

The analysis in this chapter enables us to assess the validity of these different perspectives in the Italian case. Our examination begins with a sketch of the socioeconomic context of home ownership in Italy over the second half of the twentieth century and a more-detailed discussion of certain institutional features of the Italian housing system. Then we describe the data and methods used in our study. We end with a discussion of our findings and the tentative conclusions we've drawn from those findings.

THE EXPANSION OF HOME OWNERSHIP IN ITALY

According to the Istituto Nazionale di Statistica (ISTAT), the rate of home ownership increased from 40 percent in 1951 to about 71 percent in 2002 (Table 8.1). Most of that growth took place during the 1970s and the 1980s; the rate stabilized during the 1990s. As a rough estimate, in 2002, only about 1 percent of the housing stock was owned through housing cooperatives. In 2002, about 19 percent of Italian households rented their home (4 percent to 5 percent in the public sector). The remaining 10 percent occupied their home in other tenures, most at no charge through family or informal networks.

TABLE 8.1
Housing tenure, Italy, 1951–2002

Year	PERCENTAGE OF OCCUPIED HOUSING			Year	PERCENTAGE OF OCCUPIED HOUSING		
	Owner occupied	*Rented*	*Other*[a]		*Owner occupied*	*Rented*	*Other*
1951	40.0	48.7	11.3	1981	58.9	35.5	5.6
1961	45.8	46.6	7.6	1991	68.0	25.3	6.7
1971	50.8	44.2	5.0	2002[b]	71.1	19.2	9.7

SOURCES: Figures for 1951 through 1991 are based on ISTAT data taken from the general censuses in the year cited; figures for 2002 are from ISTAT (2003).

[a]Includes dwellings that are not owned but for which no rent is charged.

[b]Estimated household distribution (versus distribution of occupied housing in the other years).

To understand and compare the institutional characteristics of the Italian housing system, we examine the three key factors in that system: market, state, and family. Here we discuss the functioning of the housing and credit markets, the most important housing-related policies in Italy, and the role played by family. We also examine important changes in the socioeconomic context that affect both the housing system and households' living conditions.

The Housing and Credit Markets

Housing Demand and Supply

During the economic boom of the 1950s and the 1960s, there was extensive new-housing construction in both public and private sectors—much of it without substantial planning constraints.[4] The building activity was undertaken both to expand the housing stock and to improve housing conditions. Housing shortages derived from war damage and from new demand in major urban areas—Milan, Turin, and Genoa, in particular—a response to rapid industrial development and massive migration from the countryside and the south of Italy (Padovani 1996; Tosi 1990). Speculation in both rental and ownership market segments—and, to some extent, self-construction by prospective homeowners—drove development into the metropolitan areas. Public investment contributed to the expansion of home ownership too: some 850,000 dwellings were privatized between 1951 and 1971 (Padovani, 202). Moreover, by the middle of the 1960s, investors began to withdraw from the rental market in metropolitan areas. In many cases, they sold occupied flats to the tenants (Delle Donne 1978; Padovani).

From the 1970s on, new employment opportunities, and so the demand for housing, started shifting from metropolitan and traditional industrial areas to smaller cities and industrial districts, mainly in what became known as the "Third Italy" (Tosi 1990).[5] Property was more available there, and urban planning was still tolerant of new construction.

Unauthorized building was common: it was estimated that about 30 percent of the housing built between 1971 and 1984 was illegal (Tosi, 216).

Conditions changed again in the 1980s. Most cities had begun implementing planning policies and taking action against unauthorized housing and buildings that did not meet codes.[6] It became more difficult to build cheaply, and the cost of housing began to go up. Figure 8.1 shows trends in

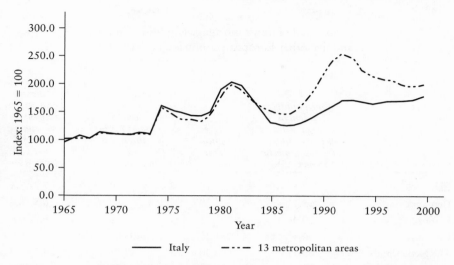

Figure 8.1.   Trends in the price of new housing, Italy, 1965–2000 (constant 2001 prices)

SOURCE: Authors' calculations based on data from Nomisma and ISTAT (2002b).
NOTE: The trends shown are for new housing only; they do not reflect prices for existing housing. They also do not reflect the cost of housing built by homeowners themselves. Although we make a distinction between countrywide prices and prices in the largest metropolitan areas, readers should be aware of the great variability that exists both among and within geographic areas.

the average price of new housing between 1965 and 2000.[7] Notice the steep increases in the 1970s and the sharp rise in the price of new housing in metropolitan areas in the late 1980s and early 1990s.

The Mortgage Market

In a departure from common practice in other European countries, the mortgage market in Italy traditionally has not been an important resource for funding home ownership. Credit in this sector is rationed by law, which until 1980 limited home mortgages to 50 percent of the property's overall value. Although the loan-to-value threshold was increased to 75 percent in 1980 and to 80 percent in 1993, banks continued to ration credit at the 50 percent maximum (Villosio 1995). Their reasoning: an undeveloped system of information on loans and the inability of the Italian judicial system to deal with mortgage defaults (Chiuri and Jappelli 2000).

TABLE 8.2
A comparison of home mortgage conditions in Italy
and five other European countries, mid-1990s

Country	1 Outstanding residential mortgage debt as a percentage of gross domestic product, 1997	2 Typical term (years)	3 Typical loan-to-value threshold (% of housing value)	4 Estimated average real interest rate on new mortgages during the first year, 1991–1997[a]
Italy	7.3	10	50	7.2–7.3
Denmark	65.1	20	80	6.5–6.6
France	20.4	15	80	6.7–6.9
Germany	50.9[b]	25–30	60–80[c]	4.8–5.0[d]
The Netherlands	60.1	30	75	4.7–4.9
United Kingdom	57.0	25	100	5.0

SOURCES: The data in columns 1–3 are from the European Mortgage Federation (EMF; 1998); the calculations in column 4 are based on the EMF data and data from the Organisation for Economic Co-operation and Development (2000).

[a]Generally, the nominal interest rate in the first year of the mortgage less any increase in the cost of living the same year (based on the consumer price index of all items). The estimate does not include the effects of allowances and tax benefits.

[b]Includes all loans to fund home purchases.
[c]Includes all housing-related loans.
[d]Includes additional costs.

In the mid 1990s, home mortgage conditions in Italy were among the worst in Europe (Table 8.2). Only at the end of the 1990s, when the Italian credit sector began to implement European Union norms, did the mortgage market in Italy move toward a more efficient model. Loans to Italian households today include thirty-year terms and pay for up to 80 percent of a property's total value.

The State: Housing Policies

Traditionally, Italy has had few policies in support of home ownership; and the few policies it had tended in large part targeted a credit market that most households were not using. The government at one time subsidized mortgage interest rates for developers of low-cost housing.[8] Similar subsidies have been available under certain conditions to help households buy new homes; since the 1980s, they also have been available for the purchase of existing housing (Villosio 1995). Limited grants *(buoni casa)* to low-income mortgagees were introduced in 1982 (Tosi 1990), as was a policy that allows employees to use—just once—up to 70 percent of their accumulated severance funds to finance the construction or purchase of a home.[9]

Fiscal policies treat home ownership rather favorably. There is no wealth tax in Italy, and imputed rents are taxed on the basis of an administrative value *(rendita catastale)* that is notably below market value. The same below-market value is also the basis for other taxes, including transaction duties (stamp taxes and registry fees, for example), taxes on *inter vivos* transfers, and local real property taxes. And additional allowances are made on all of these taxes when the property in question is the household's primary residence. In addition, there are tax rebates of up to 19 percent of the mortgage interest paid yearly on a primary residence;[10] and taxes on property transfers to a partner or a child are low. In fact, the transfer of a modest dwelling is almost tax-free.[11] The exemptions for inheritances and gifts were increased in the late 1990s; and taxes on both were recently abolished.

Private rental remains the most important alternative to home ownership for existing households. But this sector of the housing market began collapsing in the 1960s, after rent freezes for standing leases in urban areas went into effect (Delle Donne 1978). A reform passed in 1978, which established a "fair rent" regime *(equo canone)*, introduced regulations that were intended to protect both investors in the rental sector and tenants, but it failed on both counts: it did not allow landlords to consider any revaluation of their property in setting rents, and it allowed the eviction of tenants when the term of their lease ended (Tosi 1990).[12] End-of-lease evictions almost immediately became a serious social problem: the courts ordered more than 600,000 evictions between 1983 and 1992.[13] Overwhelmed by the number of eviction notices, public authorities were repeatedly forced to postpone action on them. This generated so much uncertainty that many landlords decided to keep their lodgings vacant rather than risk a drawn-out eviction process. Indeed, an unintended effect of rent control measures has been to reduce the supply of housing in the "official" rental sector while promoting a black market in very expensive rentals (Tosi). In 1992, rent controls were eased; and, in 1998, lawmakers formally acknowledged the failure of *equo canone* by repealing the law.[14]

The focus of public housing in Italy is on meeting the housing needs of poor households. But this source of housing has almost always been marginal in the country. The reasons are threefold:

- Although funds are available specifically for low-cost housing, the government has been reluctant to invest in this sector.[15]
- There are no effective policies or regulations to control the costs of developing public housing.
- From the outset, privatization was an important component of public housing policy.[16]

Although the policy model has been a residual one—the public housing sector was to serve only the more disadvantaged households, while the market would provide for the majority of households—eligibility also depends on factors other than economic and social need. There are several issues here. First, eligibility criteria were distorted to tackle the eviction emergency that followed the passage in 1978 of the *equo canone*. Second, the public housing sector has become what Tosi described as a "protected reserve" (1990, 211). Once a household qualifies for public housing, its official status does not change; there are no effective mechanisms in place to update information on households' current income or needs. At the same time, certain social categories—young singles, new households, and immigrants, for instance—are de facto excluded (Tosi 1994). Finally, in many other countries, housing allowances are an alternative means of providing low-cost housing. Italy has had a general housing allowance only since 1998, and it is too soon to evaluate its impact.[17]

The Role of the Family

Family is a primary resource in the Italian housing system (Castles and Ferrera 1996; Guiso and Jappelli 1996; Tosi 1987). Family support generally takes three forms: the labor provided on a reciprocal basis to help family members build their own home; the property (possibly including a structure) transferred to family members when they are ready to form their own household; and intergenerational transfers that allow family member to buy or build a home via market processes. The last has been of particular importance in light of the imperfections in Italy's home mortgage market.

On the basis of data from the Banca d'Italia's Survey on Household Income and Wealth (SHIW) for 1991, Guiso and Jappelli (1996) estimated that about 30 percent of Italian households relied on some sort of intergenerational transfer—an inheritance, a gift, a loan, or a discounted price—to attain their primary residence.[18] At an aggregated level, they estimated that *inter vivos* transfers funded 11 percent of the housing value of primary residences, and that overall transfers—including inheritances—funded 21 percent of that value.[19]

Furthermore, young adults in Italy increasingly are delaying leaving their parents' home (ISTAT 1997). Among other reasons, they are using that time to accumulate savings to buy a home of their own. According to ISTAT estimates (2000, 28–30), in 1998, 59 percent of Italians between the ages of 18 and 34 were not married and were living with at least one parent in the family of origin.[20] Of course, some of these young people were still in school or were looking for their first job; but 43 percent of them were working. Of that group—young unmarried people living in the family of origin with their own economic resources—19 percent cited the "unaffordability of expenditures related to a new accommodation" (for rent or for purchase) as one of the reasons they continued to live with their parents.

A Synthesis of Country Context and Important Changes

It seems that in the Italian case, incentives for home ownership have largely been created through nonpolicies—a laissez-faire attitude toward new-house construction, the failure to regulate the rental market, and a public housing sector that to a large extent is unable to meet the needs of low-income households. Moreover, until recently, the credit market has not offered feasible solutions for financing home ownership. In this context, would-be homeowners have been forced to depend on themselves and their families for the financial and other resources needed to buy and maintain a home.

In previous pages, we sketched the key roles played by the market, the state, and the family in shaping the housing system in Italy. But in the last fifty years, it is possible to observe both changes in their roles and transformations in the broader socioeconomic context in which they operate.

During the 1950s and 1960s, low housing standards and poor living conditions coexisted with a developing economy that guaranteed employment and income growth—conditions that created a demand for housing. In this context, the government's failure at both national and local levels to adopt and enforce comprehensive housing policies, and the privatization of public housing units combined to expand the home-ownership sector. Self-development also played a major role in the growth of home ownership in the countryside and in major suburbs.[21] Intergenerational transfers were less important during this period: earlier generations had little to give after a half a century of economic malaise and two world wars; and the land and in-kind resources they were able to give could not begin to meet the demand for new housing coming from the massive migration of people to industrialized areas in the north of Italy.

By the mid-1960s, labor market regulation and an expansion of welfare policies to protect those at social and economic risk meant households could begin to accumulate savings. And rising inflation in the 1970s created incentives for investing in home ownership. In those years, access to home ownership was increased by the development of new housing areas outside major cities, areas where land and building costs were lower; tolerance for unauthorized building; and the sale in urban areas of existing dwellings to tenants.

Since the 1980s, the context has changed. First, regulations began to set constraints on self-development. Second, the collapse of the rental market and the limitations of the public housing sector have left few alternatives to home ownership, especially for new entrants into the housing market. The problem for younger people has been compounded by their high rate of unemployment and their lack of employment security (Bernardi 2000), which undermine this population's ability to accumulate the economic resources needed to buy a home.

THE RESEARCH

Data

The analysis was based on data from the Survey on Household Income and Wealth for 1998 (Banca d'Italia 2000), which was conducted on a nationally representative sample of 7,147 households. We limited the analysis to married or cohabiting couples, with or without children, in which the male partner was between 33 and 67 years old. Our reasoning was twofold: to counteract the selection bias for younger households;[22] and to counteract the confounding effect of the "horizontal transfer" of home ownership, from one partner to the other, among the elderly.[23] We also dropped a few cases that would have created consistency problems with dependent variables. Our final sample was of 3,791 couples.

SHIW data were far from optimal for our purposes. First, they do not give us retrospective information on family and employment.[24] This means that it was not possible to reconstruct the stage in the family life course or to know the exact employment position and occupation when the couple first became homeowners. The survey simply asked about current occupation (in 1998) and the last occupation of those respondents who were retired or unemployed. But this missing information is not crucial when we consider the low level of career mobility in Italy (Pisati and Schizzerotto 1999). Moreover, our analysis focused on an age interval (33 to 67 years old) in which people likely had established their careers. It seemed rational, then, to assume that the subjects' current or last occupation was not too different from the occupation held at the time they became homeowners.

A second, related, problem arose because the survey asked about the age at which the respondent took possession of the current home, not the first home. Here, again, we were helped by the Italians' fondness for staying put: according to Guiso and Jappelli (1996), given the proverbial immobility of Italian homeowners, the age at which the current home was acquired can be considered a proxy for the age at which the first home was acquired.

Finally, we had a number of difficulties with the way in which information about occupational categories was collected in the survey.[25] From our perspective, the main problem here is that no distinction was made between skilled and unskilled manual workers, two groups that have been shown to have very different home-ownership rates (see Chapter 2 in this volume). In our analysis of home ownership among members of the working class, then, we likely overestimated the effects on the rate of home ownership for skilled manual laborers and underestimated those effects for unskilled laborers. Furthermore, the information about the occupation of the respondents' parents was not of a kind because the survey asked each respondent to describe his or her parents at the same age the respondent was at the time of the interview.[26] Neither issue was a serious problem for us because we were interested in defining a proxy for the resources of the family of origin, not in investigating patterns of social mobility. The problem reasonably also had limited effects because our respondents were between ages 33 and 67: the information they gave about their parents' occupation at the same age pertained to a mature phase of the parents' employment.

Despite these problems and the need for caveats, we were confident that the SHIW data offered us a generally reliable picture of the relationship between social class and home ownership and at least a first answer to our research questions.

Models

We performed a dynamic analysis of the transition to home ownership. The data did not allow us to construct time-varying variables. Nevertheless, the advantage of a longitudinal analysis, instead of a standard cross-sectional logistic regression on the likelihood of being a homeowner in 1998, lay in the possibility of investigating the age of first-time home ownership while also taking into account right-censored observations (Blossfeld and Rohwer 1995). We considered the age of the male partner, measured in years, as the time axis for the analysis. More precisely, the time axis started at age 14 and ended at the age at which home ownership was achieved for those households that owned a home and at the time of the interview for those that did not (right-censored cases).

We started the analysis by computing the survivor functions of access to home ownership for selected social classes. Then we specified two types of event-history models: The first analyzes the rate of transition from not being a homeowner to becoming a homeowner, allowing us to investigate within a multivariate framework whether access to home ownership is class segmented. The second model is more specific and gets closer to the mechanism underlying the relationship between class and home ownership. This model also analyzes the transition rate to home ownership, but it does so by distinguishing among different methods of access to home ownership: purchase, self-development, inheritance, and gift. In this context, *self-development* refers to a set of informal practices largely based on the support of a family network.[27] *Gift* refers to the family's transmission *inter vivos* of property or of all the funds needed to purchase a home.[28] Both models are piecewise constant exponential models, with a single destination (becoming a homeowner) in the first case and with competing risks (different modalities of access to home ownership) in the second.[29]

Variables

Own and Family's Social Class and Resources

The key independent variables of our analysis refer to the socioeconomic resources of the couple and of the families of origin. We adopted Erikson and Goldthorpe's (1992) class schema, distinguishing among blue-collar workers (the urban working class), agricultural laborers, farmers, urban self-employed workers (including large employers), and middle-class and service-class workers (including people in higher-level white-collar occupations and lawyers, architects, and other professionals.)

We constructed the variable social class for both male and female partners. We also constructed a synthetic indicator of each couple's resources by combining the information on the partners' class position. Where the partners' class position differed, we employed a "prevalence principle," adopting the following ranking: (1) service class and professionals; (2) other urban self-employed workers/employers, self-employed farmers, and middle class; and (3) blue-collar workers and agricultural laborers.[30] The class position of the male partner prevailed in cases of heterogeneity within the same rank (for example, self-employed versus middle class).[31] We employed the same class schema and prevalence principle in defining the partners' class of origin.

Birth Cohort

Using the male partner's year of birth, we assigned each couple to one of three birth cohorts: 1931–1940, 1941–1955, and 1956–1965. This classification picked up the changes in the housing market described in the previous sections. Thus, the 1931–1940 cohort experienced the huge reconstruction boom of the post–World War II period. And members of this cohort, together with those of the 1941–1955 cohort, reached the mature phase of their careers at a time when there was little or no building regulation and few constraints on self-development, and when the rental sector offered a viable alternative to home ownership. These cohorts also benefited in the late 1960s from the privatization of public housing stock. The experience of the youngest cohort (born between 1956 and 1965) has been very different. This group entered a saturated housing market with a scant supply of private rental units and almost no supply of public ones. Many lacked the skills to work on their own homes—in recent decades, young people have been more likely to be clerks than carpenters; and those with the skills found legal constraints on self-development. For this group, home ownership increasingly has been driven by market forces; and, at the same time, the cost of housing was rising.

The three-part classification also reflects the socioeconomic realities of Italy in the second half of the twentieth century. Again, members of the 1931–1940 birth cohort entered the labor market during the postwar reconstruction era; they experienced the lowest levels of social protection and of labor market regulation. It would seem that members of the 1941–1955 birth cohort found the most favorable conditions when they entered the labor market: the Italian economic miracle occurred at the beginning of the 1960s; and in subsequent years, layoffs were limited and other regulations that protected workers were enforced. By the time members of the youngest birth cohort were entering and settling into the labor market, conditions had become more difficult. These workers faced very high rates of unemployment and a labor market in which fixed-term jobs and other nonstandard forms of employment were common (Bernardi 2000).

The labor market experiences of the three birth cohorts reflect the organizational, economic, and regulatory structures of the Fordist and post-Fordist eras. The 1931–1940 birth cohort and, in particular, the 1941–1955 birth cohort benefited from the value that Fordism placed on workers and their contribution to production and the economy; the 1956–1965 birth cohort came of working age after economic realities had begun to wreak havoc on workers' protections (Mayer 2001).

Community Size and Geographic Area

Finally, we defined two variables largely as controls. We used the size of respondents' community as an indicator of the relative importance of self-development. Our assumptions: that smaller communities are less likely to place constraints on land use generally and self-development specifically, and are more likely to foster informal support networks; and that major cities are a source of greater "housing stress," in that the market drives the availability and cost of housing. We defined respondents' geographic area using Bagnasco's (1977) schema (see note 5). Our purpose was to distinguish among the different housing and socioeconomic systems acknowledged in the literature.[32]

RESULTS

We start by presenting the survivor functions of the transition to home ownership. Then we move on to a discussion of our findings in the event-history analyses. We should stress that we present only the results for the couple's social class obtained with the prevalence principle and ranking criteria, not the detailed results for the male and female partners' social class separately.[33]

Survivor Functions of Access to Home Ownership

Figure 8.2 shows the class-specific survivor functions for entry into home ownership for the three birth cohorts considered in our study.[34] For each social class, these simple graphs show the proportion of members that have yet to become homeowners as a function of age. They immediately offer us answers to two of the research questions put forward at the beginning of this chapter: Does social class influence the likelihood of becoming a homeowner? And have class differences in the likelihood of becoming a homeowner changed over generations?

The answer to the first question is yes: in all three cohorts, the survivor function for blue-collar workers is consistently higher than that for other

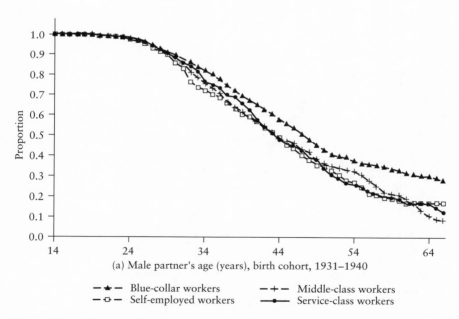

(a) Male partner's age (years), birth cohort, 1931–1940

— ▲ — Blue-collar workers   — + — Middle-class workers
— ▫ — Self-employed workers   ——•—— Service-class workers

Figure 8.2. Class-specific survivor functions for entry into home ownership, by birth cohort, Italy, 1998

SOURCE: Authors' calculations based on SHIW for 1998 (Banca d'Italia 2000).

Figure 8.2. (*Continued*)

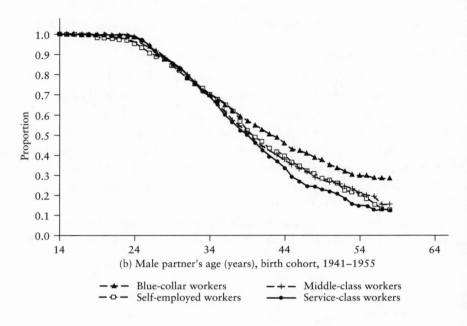

(b) Male partner's age (years), birth cohort, 1941–1955

— ▲ — Blue-collar workers   — + — Middle-class workers
— ◻ — Self-employed workers   —●— Service-class workers

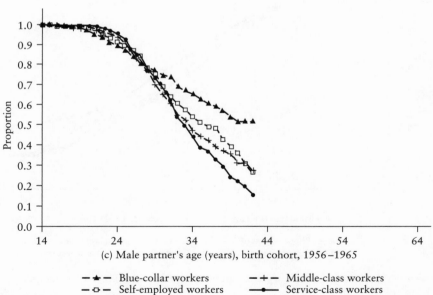

(c) Male partner's age (years), birth cohort, 1956–1965

— ▲ — Blue-collar workers   — + — Middle-class workers
— ◻ — Self-employed workers   —●— Service-class workers

classes of workers. This means that blue-collar workers are less likely to become homeowners than are workers in the service class, for example. The answer to the second question also seems to be yes. In the older cohorts, the difference in home-ownership rates between service-class workers and blue-collar workers at age 40 was about 10 percentage points (parts a and b); in the youngest cohort, the post-Fordist cohort, we found a difference of almost 35 points (part c).[35]

Notice that the slope of the functions generally is much deeper as we move from part a of Figure 8.2 to part c. Substantively, this means that households are becoming homeowners at increasingly younger ages. For members of the youngest cohort, this trend would seem to reflect the lack of viable alternatives in the rental market.

The Transition to Home Ownership

Using the results of the event-history models reported in Table 8.3, we expanded our initial analysis of the process that leads to home ownership within a multivariate framework. In model 1, we included the control variables and the couple's social class variable. In general, the effects for the control variables followed the expected pattern:

- As indicated by the effects of the age intervals, the likelihood of becoming a homeowner increased with age. We would argue that the delay in home ownership means the partners have more time to advance in their careers and so to earn more, and more time to save to buy a home (a necessity given the difficulty of accessing the credit market in Italy).
- Couples who lived in small towns were more likely to become homeowners than were couples who lived in larger communities. Cheaper land in rural areas, fewer restrictions on building, and the availability of support networks seem to be the underlying factors here.
- The analysis confirmed the finding described in Figure 8.2, a positive effect for the youngest cohort (born between 1956 and 1965): that is, people in Italy are becoming homeowners at an earlier age.[36] Given a lack of affordable alternatives in the rental sector for the youngest cohort, it's likely that new entrants in the housing market had fewer choices than in the past. In this sense, home ownership can be considered a strained choice.[37]

The analysis also confirmed the relationship between social class and home ownership: service-class workers and farmers are clearly at an advantage compared with other classes, while blue-collar workers and agricultural

TABLE 8.3

Transition to home ownership, Italy (piecewise constant exponential models)

Variable	MODEL 1		MODEL 2		MODEL 3	
	β	$\hat\alpha(\hat\beta)$	β	$\hat\alpha(\hat\beta)$	β	$\hat\alpha(\hat\beta)$
Age (years)						
15–23	-5.61^b	0.09	-5.54^b	0.11	-5.68^b	0.11
24–33	-3.12^b	0.05	-3.31^b	0.07	-3.45^b	0.08
34–43	-2.59^b	0.05	-2.76^b	0.07	-2.90^b	0.08
44–53	-2.39^b	0.07	-2.56^b	0.08	-2.69^b	0.09
54–67	-2.30^b	0.11	-2.45^b	0.12	-2.57^b	0.13
Community size						
≤20,000 inhabitants			Ref.			
20,001–40,000 inhabitants	-0.23^b	0.06	-0.23^b	0.06	-0.22^b	0.06
40,001–500,000 inhabitants	-0.32^b	0.05	-0.31^b	0.05	-0.29^b	0.05
>500,000 inhabitants	-0.61^b	0.08	-0.61^b	0.08	-0.59^b	0.08
Geographic area						
Third Italy			Ref.			
Industrial area	-0.10^a	0.05	-0.10^a	0.06	-0.09	0.06
South and islands	-0.07	0.05	-0.06	0.05	-0.08^a	0.05
Birth cohort						
Cohort 1 (born 1931–1940)	-0.30^b	0.05	-0.41^b	0.09	-0.42	0.09
Cohort 2 (born 1941–1955)			Ref.			
Cohort 3 (born 1956–1965)	0.39^b	0.05	0.15	0.11	0.19	0.11

Couple's social class

Blue-collar workers			Ref.			
Agricultural laborers	0.09	0.13	0.16	0.21	0.08	0.21
Farmers	0.49[b]	0.15	0.41[a]	0.24	0.29	0.23
Urban self-employed workers	0.27[b]	0.06	0.19[b]	0.09	0.19[b]	0.09
Middle-class workers	0.34[b]	0.05	0.22[b]	0.07	0.24[b]	0.07
Service-class workers	0.50[b]	0.06	0.40[b]	0.08	0.39[b]	0.09
*Cohort * social class*						
Cohort 1 * agricultural laborers			0.10	0.28	0.13	0.29
Cohort 1 * farmers			0.10	0.33	0.15	0.33
Cohort 1 * urban self-employed workers			0.12	0.14	0.15	0.14
Cohort 1 * middle-class workers			0.15	0.13	0.16	0.13
Cohort 1 * service-class workers			0.08	0.15	0.09	0.15
Cohort 3 * agricultural laborers			-0.73	0.47	-0.66	0.47
Cohort 3 * farmers			0.27	0.42	0.27	0.42
Cohort 3 * urban self-employed workers			0.23	0.16	0.22	0.16
Cohort 3 * middle-class workers			0.35[b]	0.14	0.32[b]	0.13
Cohort 3 * service-class workers			0.34[b]	0.16	0.33[b]	0.16

(*continued*)

TABLE 8.3
(*Continued*)

Variable	MODEL 1 β	MODEL 1 $\hat{\alpha}(\beta)$	MODEL 2 β	MODEL 2 $\hat{\alpha}(\beta)$	MODEL 3 β	MODEL 3 $\hat{\alpha}(\beta)$
Male partner's class of origin						
Blue-collar workers			Ref.			
Agricultural laborers					0.20[b]	0.07
Farmers					0.08	0.07
Urban self-employed workers					0.13[b]	0.06
Middle-class workers					0.03	0.06
Service-class workers					0.11	0.09
Female partner's class of origin						
Blue-collar workers			Ref.			
Agricultural laborers					0.07	0.07
Farmers					0.28[b]	0.07
Urban self-employed workers					−0.03	0.06
Middle-class workers					0.11[a]	0.06
Service class workers					0.09	0.09
Number of events	2,662		2,662		2,662	
Log-likelihood	−11,132		−11,122		−11,104	

SOURCE: Authors' calculations based on SHIW for 1998 (Banca d'Italia 2000).

[a]$p < .10$.
[b]$p < .05$.

NOTE: The models refer to couples in which the head of household is between ages 33 and 67.

laborers are particularly disadvantaged. The rate ratio comparing the likelihood of service-class workers' becoming homeowners versus blue-collar workers is about 1.65.[38] (It's roughly the same for farmers versus blue-collar workers.) This means that on average and over time, 1.65 service-class workers become homeowners for every blue-collar worker. In other words, the likelihood of becoming a homeowner for a service-class worker is about 65 percent higher than that for a blue-collar worker. In the case of service-class workers, this result seems to depend on having greater economic resources.

In model 2, we introduced the interaction of birth cohort and social class. We did this to test what we observed in our comparison of the survivor functions for the three cohorts—namely that class differences seemed to have increased in the youngest birth cohort. What we found was an increased advantage among service- and middle-class workers in the youngest birth cohort. For example, in the 1941–1955 cohort, members of the service class were 50 percent more likely than members of the working class to make the transition to home ownership. In the youngest cohort (born between 1956 and 1965), that difference more than doubled, to 109 percent.[39]

In model 3, we introduced the class-of-origin variables for the male and female partners. This model allowed us to address an aspect of our last research question: Does the social class of origin of the two partners directly influence the likelihood of their becoming homeowners? Model 3 shows that when considered separately from the couple's own resources (or the social class of the household), the assets associated with class of origin do play a role in achieving home ownership. Comparing the separate effects for male and female partners yielded a complex pattern.[40] On the whole, it seems that people coming from farming or self-employed families are the most advantaged. The most plausible explanation for this result seems to be that farmers and self-employed people own property that can be transferred to the next generation. We also found a positive effect for respondents whose parents were agricultural laborers or middle-class or service-class workers.[41] One final note, however: the size of these effects was not very large. For instance, considering the largest of the class-of-origin effects, the rate of transition to home ownership for couples in which the female partner came from a farming family was 32 percent higher than for couples in which the female partner came from a blue-collar family.

Ways to Become a Homeowner

To deepen the analysis and test some of the explanations put forward in the previous section, we distinguished four ways in which people become homeowners: purchase, self-development, inheritance, and gift. Purchase represents the market way to home ownership; while self-development and gifts are community- and family-supported paths. Inheritance is another family-supported means to become a homeowner, but is largely beyond the control of the prospective owner. Finally, both inheritances and gifts are forms of intergenerational transfers and so have the potential to contribute to the reproduction of inequality.

We used a competing-risk model to investigate whether there are class differences in the methods of access to home ownership and whether those differences are related to birth cohorts. Table 8.4 shows the results of that model for the control variables and the variable that refers to the couple's social class.

We found the following effects for the control variables:

- The impact of age varied by modality: it increased constantly for those who purchased or inherited their home; it increased sporadically for those who received their home as a gift; it increased and then decreased for those whose home was self-developed. The age effects seem to reflect the realities of the Italian housing system. Given the limits of the credit market, most families buy a home with savings accumulated over a period of years. Inheritances are likely to be received when the legatees are older; gifts, when the recipients are younger (ages 24 to 33). Lastly, self-development and in particular self-construction require physical capabilities and network support, both of which are likely to diminish as people age.
- Community size is negatively associated with access to home ownership via self-development, inheritance, and gift. These results seem to point to stricter planning in cities, which could limit self-development, and to the relative scarcity of housing and land to be passed down from one generation to the next.
- Planning regulations and the scarcity of property may also explain our findings for geographic area. Thus, in the industrial and urban areas of the country, self-development and gifts are less likely means to home ownership than they are in the South and, to a lesser degree, in the Third Italy.
- Finally, a comparison of the cohorts born between 1941 and 1955, and between 1956 and 1965 indicated that the younger cohort relied more on purchase and gift to achieve home ownership, and less on self-development.

TABLE 8.4

Transition to home ownership by method of access, Italy
(piecewise constant exponential models with competing risks)

Variable	PURCHASE		SELF-DEVELOPMENT		INHERITANCE		GIFT	
	β	$\hat{\alpha}(\beta)$	β	$\hat{\alpha}(\beta)$	β	$\hat{\alpha}(\beta)$	β	$\hat{\alpha}(\beta)$
Age (years)								
15–23	-6.85^b	0.15	-6.52^b	0.21	-6.54^b	0.22	-8.00^b	0.35
24–33	-4.45^b	0.09	-4.24^b	0.13	-4.86^b	0.16	-5.75^b	0.25
34–43	-3.70^b	0.09	-4.01^b	0.13	-4.38^b	0.16	-6.03^b	0.28
44–53	-3.44^b	0.10	-4.03^b	0.17	-4.03^b	0.19	-6.21^b	0.40
54–67	-3.26^b	0.15	-4.71^b	0.35	-3.53^b	0.27	-5.77^b	0.65
Community size								
≤20,000 inhabitants			Ref.					
20,001–40,000 inhabitants	0.07	0.08	-0.53^b	0.11	-0.43^b	0.13	-0.79^b	0.24
40,001–500,000 inhabitants	0.14^b	0.07	-0.97^b	0.11	-0.86^b	0.13	-0.61^b	0.18
>500,000 inhabitants	-0.04	0.10	-1.96^b	0.26	-1.33^b	0.24	-1.24^b	0.37
Geographic area								
Third Italy			Ref.					
Industrial area	0.03	0.07	-0.53^b	0.14	-0.13	0.15	-0.90	0.32
South and islands	-0.26^b	0.06	0.10	0.10	0.16	0.12	0.51	0.18

(continued)

TABLE 8.4
(*Continued*)

Variable	PURCHASE		SELF-DEVELOPMENT		INHERITANCE		GIFT	
	β	$\hat{\alpha}(\beta)$	β	$\hat{\alpha}(\beta)$	β	$\hat{\alpha}(\beta)$	β	$\hat{\alpha}(\beta)$
Birth cohort								
Cohort 1 (born 1931–1940)	−0.33[b]	0.07	−0.02	0.10	−0.50[b]	0.13	−0.75[b]	0.24
Cohort 2 (born 1941–1955)			Ref.					
Cohort 3 (born 1956–1965)	0.58[b]	0.07	−0.30[b]	0.13	0.19	0.14	0.72	0.17
Couple's social class								
Blue-collar workers			Ref.					
Agricultural laborers	−0.11	0.22	−0.12	0.27	0.10	0.30	0.91	0.34
Farmers	0.26	0.24	−0.06	0.36	1.20[b]	0.25	0.50[b]	0.60
Urban self-employed workers	0.38[b]	0.08	0.19	0.13	−0.00	0.15	0.33	0.25
Middle-class workers	0.47[b]	0.07	0.20[a]	0.12	0.06	0.13	0.34	0.20
Service-class workers	0.69[b]	0.08	0.30[b]	0.14	−0.04	0.18	0.45	0.26
Number of events	1,562		530		385		168	
Log-likelihood			−13,874					

SOURCE: Authors' calculations based on SHIW for 1998 (Banca d'Italia 2000).

[a] $p < .10$.
[b] $p < .05$.

NOTE: The models refer to couples in which the head of household is between ages 33 and 67.

When we considered the effect of the key variables that relate to the couple's social class, the results were particularly interesting. It turned out that workers in the service and middle classes and urban self-employed workers were more likely to buy a home than were blue-collar workers. Households in these classes also had a higher rate of access to home ownership via gifts and, to a lesser extent, self-development. Farmers were most likely to inherit a home; agricultural laborers, to be gifted with one by their parents or relatives. The size of these effects was particularly telling. For instance, the rate ratio comparing the likelihood of purchasing a home for service-class workers and blue-collar workers was 1.99: service-class workers were twice as likely to buy a home. In the case of self-development, the rate ratio was "only" 1.35.

In the final step of the analysis, we examined the interaction of birth cohort and couple's social class. Table 8.5 presents selected results of this modeling exercise.[42] The most notable finding: the social-class variable strengthened the disparity between service- and middle-class workers, and blue-collar workers in the youngest cohort. The rate ratio comparing the likelihood of purchase between service class and working class went up to 2.7—the rate of access to home ownership via the market for the former group is almost three times higher.

Three results here seem particularly relevant:

- *The cohort effect.* The market modality—purchasing a home—had become more important in the youngest birth cohort; the informal modality—self-development—was less important.
- *The class effect.* Class differences were largest in the case of home purchases.
- *The interaction of cohort and class.* Class differences in terms of home purchases increased considerably for the youngest cohort.

Together, these three results explain the aggregate strengthening of the relationship between social class and home ownership in the youngest birth cohort that we described in the previous section.

CONCLUSIONS

In Italy, almost 70 percent of households own a home. What we set out to determine in this chapter is whether it is possible that social inequalities limit

TABLE 8.5
The impact of social class on the transition to home ownership
through purchase or self-development, Italy
(piecewise constant exponential model with competing risks)

Variable	PURCHASE		SELF-DEVELOPMENT	
	$\hat{\beta}$	$\hat{\alpha}\,(\hat{\beta})$	$\hat{\beta}$	$\hat{\alpha}\,(\hat{\beta})$
Age (years)				
15–23	-6.90^{b}	0.16	-6.67^{b}	0.24
24–33	-4.50^{b}	0.11	-4.38^{b}	0.17
34–43	-3.74^{b}	0.11	-4.14^{b}	0.17
44–53	-3.47^{b}	0.12	-4.15^{b}	0.18
54–67	-3.28^{b}	0.16	-4.78^{b}	0.34
Community size				
<20,000 inhabitants		Ref.		
20,001–40,000 inhabitants	0.08	0.08	-0.47^{b}	0.11
40,001–500,000 inhabitants	0.16^{b}	0.07	-0.90^{b}	0.11
>500,000 inhabitants	-0.02	0.10	-1.83^{b}	0.27
Geographic area				
Third Italy		Ref.		
Industrial area	0.05	0.07	-0.52^{a}	0.14
South and islands	-0.27^{b}	0.06	-0.07	0.05
Birth cohort				
Cohort 1 (born 1931–1940)	-0.41^{b}	0.12	-0.27	0.17
Cohort 2 (born 1941–1955)		Ref.		
Cohort 3 (born 1956–1965)	0.34^{b}	0.15	-0.55^{b}	0.28
Couple's social class				
Blue-collar workers		Ref.		
Agricultural laborers	-0.26	0.36	-0.23	0.43
Farmers	-0.12	0.42	-1.51	1.01
Urban self-employed workers	0.34^{b}	0.12	0.07	0.19
Middle-class workers	0.36^{b}	0.10	0.21	0.15
Service-class workers	0.57^{b}	0.11	0.34^{a}	0.20
Interaction of cohort and social class				
Cohort 1 * agricultural laborers	0.31	0.47	0.28	0.55
Cohort 1 * farmers	0.65	0.53	1.66	1.09

(*continued*)

TABLE 8.5
(*Continued*)

Variable	PURCHASE		SELF-DEVELOPMENT	
	$\hat{\beta}$	$\hat{\alpha}\,(\hat{\beta})$	$\hat{\beta}$	$\hat{\alpha}\,(\hat{\beta})$
Cohort 1 * urban self-employed workers	0.08	0.18	0.46[a]	0.27
Cohort 1 * middle-class workers	0.16	0.16	0.13	0.25
Cohort 1 * service-class workers	0.01	0.19	0.31	0.32
Cohort 3 * agricultural laborers	−0.30	0.70	c	c
Cohort 3 * farmers	0.38	0.72	1.63	1.44
Cohort 3 * urban self-employed workers	0.12	0.21	0.52	0.41
Cohort 3 * middle-class workers	0.33[a]	0.18	0.43	0.35
Cohort 3 * service-class workers	0.41[b]	0.19	0.34	0.43
Male partner's class of origin				
Blue-collar workers	Ref.			
Agricultural laborers	0.20[b]	0.09	0.37[b]	0.14
Farmers	0.02	0.10	0.16	0.15
Urban self-employed workers	0.15[a]	0.08	−0.18	0.15
Middle-class workers	0.05	0.08	0.05	0.15
Service-class workers	0.14	0.11	−0.20	0.26
Female partner's class of origin				
Blue-collar workers	Ref.			
Agricultural laborers	0.10	0.09	0.03	0.14
Farmers	0.17[a]	0.09	0.60[b]	0.14
Urban self-employed workers	−0.10	0.08	−0.11	0.15
Middle-class workers	0.13[a]	0.08	0.05	0.15
Service-class workers	0.07	0.11	−0.20	0.16
Number of events	1,562		530	
Log-likelihood	−11,132			

SOURCE: Authors' calculations based on SHIW for 1998 (Banca d'Italia 2000).

NOTE: The models refer to couples in which the head of household is between ages 33 and 67. The results for inheritances and gifts are not shown.

[a]$p < .10$.
[b]$p < .05$.
[c]Not estimated.

access to home ownership in a housing system characterized by a high incidence of home ownership. More precisely, we addressed three questions:

- Does social class influence the likelihood of becoming a homeowner?
- Have class differences in the likelihood and the process of becoming a homeowner changed over generations?
- What role do intergenerational transfers and family support play in the attainment of home ownership?

The limitations of our data suggest that further research with retrospective data and better definitions of social and occupational classes are necessary. Still, on the basis of our findings, we would tend to answer yes to each of our research questions. The event-history analysis of the transition to home ownership shows that there are indeed class differences in the likelihood of becoming a homeowner in Italy, that blue-collar workers and agricultural laborers are less likely to become homeowners than are workers in other social classes. For instance, the likelihood of becoming a homeowner for a service-class worker is about 65 percent higher than that for a blue-collar worker. We did find, however, that the impact of social class varied by birth cohort. Social inequalities turned out to be less acute in the older cohorts than in the youngest. A case in point: service-class workers in the 1941–1955 birth cohort were 50 percent more likely to own a home than were blue-collar workers. In the youngest cohort (born between 1956 and 1965), that difference increased to 109 percent.

In the second step of our analysis, we examined the ways in which households acquire a home. We wanted to understand the mechanisms that underlie the increase in class differences observed for the youngest birth cohort. The competing-risk model showed that generally those differences are strong for people who buy or who are given a home. The market modality was particularly important for members of the youngest cohort. At the same time, self-development had become less so.

The increase in class differences for the youngest birth cohort has to be interpreted against a backdrop of economic and social conditions. First, in the late 1960s and early 1970s, the privatization of public housing stock benefited working-class households. Also, housing prices in Italy were keeping pace with inflation, and few regulations constrained self-developed housing. By the end of the 1970s, public housing stock was in very short supply, the price of housing was skyrocketing, and regulations were beginning to make it difficult for people to build or contract for new housing by themselves. Moreover, as those born between 1956 and 1965 came of homeowning age, conditions for them in the labor market changed dramatically: the semiskilled and unskilled workers among them faced higher risks of unemployment, and many of them were trapped in contract jobs (Bernardi 2000). In the absence of job security and earnings that keep pace with the cost of living, these working-class people find it increasingly difficult to finance a home purchase.

These results allow us to evaluate the different theories on the relationship between home ownership and social inequality, at least for the Italian case. According to consumption-class theory, home ownership, independent from social class, has become a divisive element in society. One of the pillars of that theory is the assumption that access to home ownership is no longer a function of social class. We would argue with that assumption. In our analyses, we found evidence that social class does affect the probability of becoming a homeowner and the method of acquiring a home, and so clearly affects individuals' life chances. Paradoxically, at a time when social scientists are talking about a classless society, we find evidence that at least in the area of home ownership, social inequalities are as much if not more a factor today than they were in the 1960s and 1970s, when the class structure in society was widely acknowledged.

Of course, these interpretations move from a subjective dimension that is important to consider. In his book *A Nation of Homeowners*, Peter Saunders presented a table on the relationship between home ownership and social class in the United Kingdom in the mid-1980s (1990, table 1.3). From that table, we learn that almost 88 percent of service-class workers (professionals, managers, and employers) owned a home, as did 66 percent of skilled workers, 46 percent of semiskilled workers, and 33 percent of unskilled workers. The rate ratios comparing the incidence of home ownership for service-class workers versus that of the other groups were 1.3, 1.9, and 2.7 respectively. In other words, members of the service class were almost two times more likely to become homeowners than were semiskilled workers, and almost three times more likely to own a home than were unskilled workers. It was in these figures that Saunders read evidence of the "blurring of class cleavages" (16).

Our data were not very different: we calculated a rate ratio of 1.7 in a comparison of service-class workers with blue-collar workers (skilled, semiskilled, and unskilled workers). What is different is our interpretation. We would argue that class cleavages are very much in evidence when one group has a 70 percent advantage over another. Before we leave our readers to draw their own conclusions, however, one last thought: anyone who turned down odds of almost 2 to 1 at the gaming tables would likely lose everything very quickly.

TABLE 8A.1
Composition of the 1998 SHIW sample by type of household

Type of household	Percentage of sample
Total sample	
Household head ages 33–67	28.2
Household head <33 or >67	71.8
TOTAL	100.0
Number observed	7,147
First sample selection: household head ages 33–67	
Single-family households: singles	
Divorced singles	2.0
Widowed singles	2.8
Other singles	4.3
Single-family households: couples	
Couples without children	12.7
Couples with children	62.1
Single-family households: single parents	
Divorced single parents	2.7
Widowed single parents	4.0
Other single parents	0.5
Multifamily households	
Couples (with and without children) living with relatives	5.2
Single parents living with relatives	0.8
Other multifamily households	2.9
TOTAL	100.0
Number observed	5,131
Final sample selection: household head ages 33–67, single-family household, couples)[a]	
Number observed	3,791

SOURCE: Authors' calculations based on SHIW for 1998 (Banca d'Italia 2000).

[a] A few cases were excluded from the analysis because of missing values or inconsistent data (for dependent variables).

TABLE 8A.2

Descriptive statistics for the independent variables (couples, household head age 33–67)

Variable	Description	Couples (%)	Other households (%)
Age at transition to home ownership	Age of male partner (household head) at time of home ownership attainment, increasing by 1 unit each year	Mean = 35.7 S.D. = 9.0 N = 2,662	Mean = 35.8 S.D. = 10.8 N. = 749
Couple's (household) social class			
Blue-collar workers	Dummy = 1 if prevailing occupation within the couple (household) was that of manual worker employed in industry or services [V; VI; VIIa]	27.1	26.2
Agricultural laborers	Dummy = 1 if prevailing occupation within the couple (household) was that of manual worker in agriculture or primary production [VIIb]	2.6	3.2
Farmers	Dummy = 1 if prevailing occupation within the couple (household) was that of self-employed in agriculture or in primary production [IVc]	1.6	2.6
Urban self-employed workers	Dummy = 1 if prevailing occupation within the couple (household) was that of self-employed or employer in commerce, services, craft activities, etc. [IV$_{a+b}$; I–II, employers component]	18.2	12.6
Middle-class workers	Dummy = 1 if prevailing occupation within the couple (household) was that of not-manual worker employed in administration, services, etc. [III]	31.7	28.3
Service-class workers	Dummy = 1 if prevailing occupation within the couple (household) was that of higher-level not-manual worker employed in administration, services, etc., or of a liberal profession [I–II, employed and professionals component]	16.5	8.1
Not employed/missing	Dummy = 1 if neither partner worked or information is missing	2.3	19.1

Male partner's (household head) class of origin

Blue-collar workers	Dummy = 1 if prevailing occupation of male partner's (household head) parents was that of manual worker employed in industry or services [V; VI; VIIa]	30.9	28.9
Agricultural laborers	Dummy = 1 if prevailing occupation of male partner's (household head) parents was that of manual worker in agriculture and primary production [VIIb]	14.7	16.9
Farmers	Dummy = 1 if prevailing occupation of male partner's (household head) parents was that of self-employed in agriculture or in primary production [IVc]	11.6	12.5
Urban self-employed workers	Dummy = 1 if prevailing occupation of male partner's (household head) parents was that of self-employed or employer in commerce, services, craft activities, etc [IV$_{a+b}$; I–II, employers component]	15.5	15.2
Middle-class workers	Dummy = 1 if prevailing occupation of male partner's (household head) parents was that of not-manual worker employed in administration, services, etc. [III]	14.1	12.7
Service-class workers	Dummy = 1 if prevailing occupation of male partner's (household head) parents was that of higher-level not-manual worker employed in administration, services, etc., or of a liberal profession [I–II, employed and professionals component]	6.9	6.7
Not employed/missing	Dummy = 1 if neither of male partner's (household head) parents worked or information is missing	6.1	7.2

Female partner's class of origin

Blue-collar workers	Dummy = 1 if prevailing occupation of female partner's parents was that of manual worker employed in industry or services [V; VI; VIIa]	32.4	Omitted
Agricultural laborers	Dummy = 1 if prevailing occupation of female partner's parents was that of manual worker in agriculture and primary production [VIIb]	14.5	Omitted

(continued)

TABLE 8A.2
(*Continued*)

Variable	Description	Couples (%)	Other households (%)
Farmers	Dummy = 1 if prevailing occupation of female partner's parents was that of self-employed in agriculture or in primary production [IVc]	10.6	Omitted
Urban self-employed workers	Dummy = 1 if prevailing occupation of female partner's parents was that of self-employed or employer in commerce, services, craft activities, etc. [IV$_{a+b}$; I–II, employers component]	15.2	Omitted
Middle-class workers	Dummy = 1 if prevailing occupation of female partner's parents was that of not-manual worker employed in administration, services, etc. [III]	15.0	Omitted
Service-class workers	Dummy = 1 if prevailing occupation of female partner's parents was that of higher level not-manual worker employed in administration, services, etc., or of a liberal profession [I–II, employed and professionals component]	6.0	Omitted
Not employed/missing	Dummy = 1 if none within female partner's parents does/did work or information is missing	6.3	Omitted
Control variables *Male partner's (household head) birth cohort*			
Born 1931–1940	Dummy = 1 if male partner (household head) is born in 1931–1940	24.3	35.2
Born 1941–1955	Dummy = 1 if male partner (household head) is born in 1941–1955	48.5	44.2
Born 1956–1965	Dummy = 1 if male partner (household head) is born in 1956–1965	27.2	20.7

Geographic area			
Industrial area	Dummy = 1 if couple (household) resides in the northwest of Italy	23.6	25.4
Third Italy	Dummy = 1 if couple (household) resides in the northeast or in the northern center of Italy	30.6	37.6
South and islands	Dummy = 1 if couple (household) resides in the south of Italy or in the islands	45.8	37.0
Community size			
<20,000 inhabitants	Dummy = 1 if couple (household) resides in a village with less than 20,000 inhabitants	24.5	30.1
20,001–40,000 inhabitants	Dummy = 1 if couple (household) resides in a city with 20,001–40,000 inhabitants	21.9	18.9
40,001–500,000 inhabitants	Dummy = 1 if couple (household) resides in a city with 40,001–500,000 inhabitants	42.5	36.7
>500,000 inhabitants	Dummy = 1 if couple (household) resides in a city with more than 500,000 inhabitants	11.1	14.3
Number of observations		3,791	1,291

SOURCE: Authors' calculations based on SHIW for 1998 (Banca d'Italia 2000).

NOTES: In the coding of social classes, we referred to the respondent's last known job (in cases of current employment, unemployment, or retirement). When information was missing for one partner, available information was used. References to the numbering of categories in the class scheme developed by Erikson and Goldthorpe (1992) are in brackets.

Bivariate summary table for housing tenure and independent variables
(couples, household head age 33–67)

| | PERCENTAGE OF | | | | |
Variable	Home-owners	Public-sector renters	Private-sector renters	Other[a]	Total
Couple's social class					
Blue-collars workers	60.9	7.9	21.7	9.5	100.0
Agricultural laborers	62.6	3.0	17.2	17.2	100.0
Farmers	81.7	3.3	3.3	11.7	100.0
Urban self-employed workers	71.4	2.3	16.1	10.2	100.0
Middle-class workers	73.9	2.2	15.7	8.2	100.0
Service-class workers	78.2	0.6	13.1	8.0	100.0
Male partner's (household head) class of origin					
Blue-collar workers	64.9	4.6	21.4	9.1	100.0
Agricultural laborers	73.7	4.8	13.1	8.4	100.0
Farmers	75.3	3.2	10.7	10.9	100.0
Urban self-employed workers	73.7	1.9	15.1	9.3	100.0
Middle-class workers	70.8	2.4	17.4	9.3	100.0
Service-class workers	72.9	1.5	16.8	8.8	100.0
Female partner's class of origin					
Blue-collar workers	66.1	4.9	19.1	9.9	100.0
Agricultural laborers	72.3	5.1	13.5	9.1	100.0
Farmers	78.6	2.7	10.2	8.5	100.0
Urban self-employed workers	69.7	3.1	16.3	10.8	100.0
Middle-class workers	71.9	2.1	16.9	9.1	100.0
Service-class workers	72.0	0.9	21.0	6.1	100.0

Variable	PERCENTAGE OF				
	Home-owners	Public-sector renters	Private-sector renters	Other[a]	Total
Male partner's (household head) birth cohort					
Born 1931–1940	78.7	5.0	12.3	4.0	10.00
Born 1941–1955	73.2	3.9	15.7	7.2	100.0
Born 1956–1965	57.4	2.1	23.3	17.2	100.0
Geographic area					
Industrial area	68.2	4.4	20.1	7.4	100.0
Third Italy	76.2	2.8	12.3	8.7	100.0
South and islands	67.3	3.9	18.4	10.4	100.0
Community size					
<20,000 inhabitants	77.9	1.9	10.9	9.3	100.0
20,001–40,000 inhabitants	70.5	3.0	15.4	11.1	100.0
40,001–500,000 inhabitants	68.9	4.6	18.1	8.4	100.0
>500,000 inhabitants	57.6	5.2	29.0	8.1	100.0
AVERAGE	70.2	3.7	16.9	9.2	100.0
Number of observations	2,662	139	642	348	3,791

SOURCE: Authors' calculations based on SHIW for 1998 (Banca d'Italia 2000).

NOTE: Totals may not sum to 100.0 because of rounding.
[a]Living rent-free.

Bivariate summary table for housing tenure and independent variables
(all households except couples, household head age 33–67)

	PERCENTAGE OF				
Variable	Home-owners	Public-sector renters	Private-sector renters	Other[a]	Total
Type of household					
Divorced singles	45.1	3.9	32.4	18.6	100.0
Widowed singles	60.6	5.6	16.9	16.9	100.0
Other singles	59.4	3.2	24.7	12.8	100.0
Divorced single parents	43.9	10.1	37.4	8.6	100.0
Widowed single parents	64.5	7.4	22.2	5.9	100.0
Other single parents	50.0	12.5	37.5	—	100.0
Couples (with or without children) living with relatives	82.1	2.6	10.4	4.9	100.0
Single parents living with relatives	65.1	16.3	14.0	4.7	100.0
Other multifamily households	74.2	5.3	15.2	5.3	100.0
Household's social class					
Blue-collar workers	59.8	10.1	21.6	8.6	100.0
Agricultural laborers	68.3	9.8	14.6	7.3	100.0
Farmers	85.3	2.9	—	11.8	100.0
Urban self-employed workers	68.1	1.8	19.0	11.0	100.0
Middle-class workers	65.8	2.5	22.7	9.0	100.0
Service-class workers	73.1	—	23.1	3.8	100.0
Household head's class of origin					
Blue-collar workers	58.4	7.2	25.2	9.1	100.0
Agricultural laborers	64.7	7.8	18.3	9.2	100.0

| Variable | PERCENTAGE OF | | | | |
	Home-owners	Public-sector renters	Private-sector renters	Other[a]	Total
Farmers	75.2	3.1	10.6	11.2	100.0
Urban self-employed workers	67.9	5.6	20.4	6.1	100.0
Middle-class workers	60.4	1.8	28.7	9.1	100.0
Service-class workers	68.6	1.2	20.9	9.3	100.0
Household head's birth cohort					
Born 1931–1940	65.6	4.4	19.4	10.6	100.0
Born 1941–1955	66.3	6.8	18.8	8.1	100.0
Born 1956–1965	56.2	5.2	29.6	9.0	100.0
Geographic area					
Industrial area	55.5	4.3	31.1	9.1	100.0
Third Italy	69.7	5.2	14.6	10.5	100.0
South and islands	64.0	7.1	21.1	7.7	100.0
Community size					
<20,000 inhabitants	71.4	4.1	13.1	11.3	100.0
20,001–40,000 inhabitants	69.3	4.9	16.8	9.0	100.0
40,001–500,000 inhabitants	61.2	7.2	23.8	7.8	100.0
>500,000 inhabitants	48.6	5.9	37.3	8.1	100.0
AVERAGE	64.0	5.7	21.2	9.1	100.0
Number of observations	826	73	274	118	1,291

SOURCE: Authors' calculations based on SHIW for 1998 (Banca d'Italia 2000).

NOTE: Totals may not sum to 100.0 because of rounding.
[a]Living rent-free.

Notes

1. Mulder and Smits (1999), for instance, make this point for the Netherlands; Choko (1995), for Canada; and Ricci (1997), for Italy.

2. *Imputed rent* is the in-kind rent that homeowners "receive as owners from themselves as tenants" (Headey 1978, 23). In investment terms, the concept is known as *implicit return* (Dornbusch and Fischer 1994, 354).

3. These two lines of research share other similarities as well. Briefly, both point to the same set of mechanisms that undermine class structure: the diffusion of different forms of households (dual-earner households versus traditional single-earner households, for example) and the generalization of employment risk. Moreover, both use *exclusion* to describe contemporary patterns of inequality. For a more detailed discussion of the risk society and for a critical evaluation of the assumed effects of unemployment and precarious work contracts on the class structure, see Bernardi (2000) and Kurz and Steinhage (2001). For a critique of the exclusion concept, see Goldthorpe (2002).

4. For example, Milan and Rome formally adopted comprehensive urban development plans in 1953 and 1964, respectively (Padovani 1984). Many other cities, including those in major suburbs, did not adopt plans until the 1970s (Ferracuti and Marcelloni 1982) or later. But even when planning was by and large enforced in the country, illegal building was widely tolerated.

5. The Third Italy includes regions in the northeast (Friuli Venezia Giulia, Veneto, Trentino-Alto Adige) and center (Emilia Romagna, Marche, Toscana and Umbria) of the country. The concept, which was introduced by Bagnasco (1977), revises the traditional dichotomy between the industrialized and economically developed North and the relatively underdeveloped South. The Third Italy is an area where economic development has been led mainly by small but dynamic businesses, often embedded in family and community networks where regulation is often informal and flexible. The decentralized character of production in this area, and hence of settlements, is particularly relevant to our purpose.

6. Unauthorized building is still common today but mainly in tourist areas, where people build vacation homes.

7. Figure 8.1 is based on data kindly provided by Nomisma, a private institute that conducts research on the real estate market; similar trends can be observed in the housing price index provided by the Centro Studi Investimenti Sociali (CENSIS; 2002, 409) of housing prices.

8. These subsidies today are available mainly to housing cooperatives.

9. There are conditions that restrict the availability of severance funds. First, to be eligible for a prepayment, an employee must have worked continuously for his or her employer for at least eight years. Second, employers are only required to make a severance prepayment to 10 percent of those who are eligible, up to a maximum of 4 percent of their employees.

10. Interest is considered to a maximum of about € 3,600.

11. No distinction exists in Italy between inheritance taxes and taxes on *inter vivos* transfers.

12. This is a departure from common practice in other European countries, where tenants cannot be evicted just because the term of their lease has ended.

13. The figure is an estimate based on data from editions of ISTAT's *Annuario Statistico Italiano*.

14. By 1998, affordability, not supply, had become the major housing problem in the rental market.

15. Funding for the Italian public housing sector comes almost entirely from the compulsory contributions of employees and their employers. But the government has systematically diverted these funds to other public expenditures—this notwithstanding a ruling of the Constitutional Court finding fault with the practice (Tosi 1994).

16. That some public-housing tenants should have the "right to buy" has been implicit in the policy since the 1950s. In fact, in 1949, the original proposal for the first public housing fund (INA-Casa) was to build low-cost houses for the purpose of selling them to assorted households in some kind of housing lottery. A compromise was reached, and the plan was amended: only half of the realized housing was sold (Ferracuti and Marcelloni 1982). In 1993, a law was passed that about half of the existing public housing stock should be sold to low-income households.

17. The *equo canone* made specific provisions for an allowance system, but that system was never implemented.

18. According to Guiso and Jappelli, *inter vivos* transfers are particularly relevant because they can target specific recipients at specific times in the life course (see also Kohli 1999). Bequests—albeit not irrelevant—are more random, and in modern societies tend to come later in life, when recipients' life chances already have been defined.

19. It is likely that Guiso and Jappelli's estimates understate the importance of intergenerational transfers because the SHIW data do not include transfers within a given household. According to SHIW data for 1998, about 9 percent of Italian households are both multifamily and multigenerational.

20. This classification scheme allows ISTAT to distinguish between people who are not married and who are still living with their family of origin, and people who are married and living with their parents in multifamily households. Because the ISTAT study focused on the delay in forming a family, there was no need to consider the latter group, those who formed their own family even though they were living in a multifamily household.

21. *Self-development* in this context refers to both commissioned house building (Martens 1985) and self-construction. In the former case, prospective homeowners commission a home from a building contractor, instead of buying a home in the housing market. In the latter case, prospective homeowners are directly involved in building their house. Both of these forms of housing provision are rela-

tively independent of housing and credit market dynamics, and both generally lower the cost of becoming a homeowner. They have the added advantage of giving would-be homeowners greater control over process and timing in terms of demands on their resources.

22. In Italy, 59 percent of people ages 18 to 34 live in their parents' home (ISTAT 2000). Given our selection, subjects older than 33 who were still living with their parents were not considered. We understood that if this group was large, our selected sample would be biased. However, among respondents ages 33 to 42 (our youngest cohort), just 10.4 percent were still living with their parents—a fairly small percentage that was not likely to affect our results. (The authors thank Wout Ultee for alerting us to this possible problem.)

23. We did not examine single, divorced, and widowed people because the SHIW data do not provide information on the characteristics of their possible or previous partners. Multifamily households were omitted because there are at least two heads of household when families share the same dwelling, and the SHIW data do not account clearly for intrahousehold transfers. More information on the composition of the SHIW sample and on the excluded cases is shown in Tables 8A.1 and 8A.4. If we compare the distribution of home ownership by social class in the excluded sample (Table 8A.4) with the one actually considered in the analysis (Table 8A.3), class differences decrease slightly, likely a function of the facts that (1) home ownership is less common among singles (Table 8A.4) and (2) members of both service and middle classes who are not living in a couple are more likely to be single.

24. To our knowledge, as we are writing this chapter, no research on housing history is available in Italy. The Italian Household Longitudinal Survey (ILFI) offers detailed retrospective information on education, employment, and family, but through at least the second wave did not make available information on the timing of home ownership or even collect data on self-development or intergenerational transfers. The "Multipurpose" survey carried out by ISTAT in 1998 and published in 2000 collected retrospective information on education, employment, and family, and focused on the first home couples shared.

25. Barbagli and Schizzerotto (1997) make this point on occupational categories.

26. In other social science research—studies of social mobility, for example—it is common to ask each respondent about his or her parents' condition when the respondent was a certain age.

27. The exact wording of the SHIW questionnaire is a home "specifically built by my family/in co-operative with others" (Banca d'Italia 2000, 106). We know that home ownership by way of cooperatives is marginal in Italy.

28. Financial help from the family to help cover costs are not considered here because this information was not collected in the SHIW survey for 1998.

29. The two models are nested: the first is a simplified specification of the second.

30. Here, too, we relied on the discussion on ranking classes in Erikson and Goldthorpe (1992, 45–46).

31. We recognize that our decision here is open to debate, but we believe this choice gave us a more consistent measure of the households' social class, considering the limited and discontinuous participation of Italian women in the labor market.

32. More details on coding schemes and descriptive statistics for the independent variables are presented in Table 8A.2. Bivariate descriptive statistics for the relationships among housing tenures and the independent variables are presented in Table 8A.3.

33. The substantive conclusions we were able to draw from the model where the couple's social class was included and the ones from the model with the individual effects for the male and female partners were almost identical. The model with the synthetic indicator for the couple's class actually was preferable according to a log-likelihood ratio test; and it allowed for much easier handling of the interactions with the cohort variable. The results of the specifications of the model that is not shown here are available from the authors on request.

34. *Social class* is the couple's social class as defined by the prevalence principle described above. The survivor functions for self-employed farmers and agricultural laborers are not shown.

35. We used age 40 in these comparisons because it was the oldest age observed for the youngest cohort.

36. Interestingly, when we used a logistic regression with the same set of independent variables, we found a *negative* effect for the youngest cohort (this result is not shown here). The reason is that the dependent variable changes: in the case of the logistic regression, it is the likelihood of being a homeowner in 1998; in the case of the event-history models, it is the rate of transition to home ownership from age 15 to age 67.

37. It also seems that support from the family network is crucial to the transition to home ownership for young people.

38. The rate ratio, or relative-risk ratio, for groups A and B is the ratio of the rate in group A to the rate in group B: rA/rB (Blossfeld and Rohwer 1995; Powers and Xie 2000). If groups A and B are equally likely to make the transition under study, the rate ratio is 1.0. If the rate ratio is greater than 1.0, the likelihood of making the transition in group A is higher than it is in group B. If the ratio is smaller than 1.0, the opposite is true. For instance, a rate ratio of 2.0 means that the likelihood of transition in group A is twice that of group B.

39. The variation in the transition rate is computed using a formula described in Blossfeld and Rohwer (1995, 92). In this case, the variation in the rate comparing the service class and the working class in the younger cohort is

$$[\exp(0.40) * \exp(0.34) - 1.00] * 1.00 \sim 1.09$$

40. It is important to note that there are differences in the effects of the male partner's class of origin versus the female partner's. For instance, home ownership is more likely for the sons of self-employed workers and employers but for the daughters of farmers. We could have speculated on the fascinating idea of gender differences in the intergenerational transfer of resources: the means of production and sites to sons, land to daughters. But that kind of analysis was further complicated by marriage patterns and the tendency toward homogamy. Given the purpose of this study, we chose to step back and leave this issue for a more-focused analysis of gender differences, like Barbagli, Castiglioni, and Della Zuanna's (2003) study on family formation in Italy, which examined the role of gender and family support in a couple's decision to set up their household near or at a distance from one or both sets of parents.

41. This last effect was not statistically significant when we considered both partners' families.

42. Given the limited number of events, we did not include in the table the effects for inheritance and gift. The full set of results is available from the authors.

References

Bagnasco, Arnaldo. 1977. *Tre Italie: La problematica territoriale dello sviluppo Italiano*. Bologna: Il Mulino.

Banca d'Italia (Bank of Italy). 2000. I bilanci delle famiglie italiane nel 1998. *Supplementi al Bollettino Statistico—Note Metodologiche e Informazioni Statistiche*, vol. 10, no. 22 (April 18).

Barbagli, Marzio, Mario Castiglioni, and Gianpiero Della Zuanna. 2003. *Fare famiglia in Italia. Un secolo di cambiamenti*. Bologna: Il Mulino.

Barbagli, Marzio, and Antonio Schizzerotto. 1997. Classi, non caste. Mobilità tra generazioni e opportunità di carriera in Italia. *Il Mulino* 371:547–57.

Beck, Ulrich. 1992. *Risk society. Towards a new modernity*. London: Sage.

Bernardi, Fabrizio. 2000. Globalization and social inequality: Changing patterns of early careers in Italy. GLOBALIFE Working Paper Series 7, Faculty of Sociology, University of Bielefeld, Bielefeld.

Bernardi, Fabrizio, and Teresio Poggio. 2002. Home-ownership and social inequality in Italy. Quaderni del Dipartimento 26, Department of Sociology and Social Research, University of Trento, Trento.

Blossfeld, Hans-Peter, and Götz Rohwer. 1995. *Techniques of event history modeling. New approaches to causal analysis*. Mahwah, NJ: Erlbaum.

Castles, Francis Geoffrey, and Maurizio Ferrera. 1996. Home ownership and the welfare state: Is Southern Europe different? *South European Society and Politics* 1 (2): 163–84.

Centro Studi Investimenti Sociali (CENSIS). 2002. *35° rapporto annuale sulla situazione sociale del Paese. 2001*. Milano: Angeli.

Chiuri, Maria Concetta, and Tullio Jappelli. 2000. Financial markets, judicial costs and housing tenure: An international comparison. Luxembourg Income Study Working Paper 230, Maxwell School of Citizenship and Public Affairs, Syracuse University, Syracuse, NY.

Choko, Marc. 1995. Home owners: Richer or not? Is that the real question? In *Housing and family wealth*, edited by Ray Forrest and Alan Murie, 133–47. London: Routledge.

Delle Donne, Marcella. 1978. *L'equo canone*. Napoli: Liguori.

Dornbusch, Rudiger, and Stanley Fischer. 1994. *Macroeconomics*. 6th ed. New York: McGraw-Hill.

Erikson, Robert, and John Goldthorpe. 1992. *The constant flux: A study of class mobility in industrial societies*. Oxford: Clarendon Press.

European Mortgage Federation (EMF). 1998. *Hypostat 1987–1997*. Bruxelles.

Ferracuti, Giovanni, and Maurizio Marcelloni. 1982. *La casa. Mercato e programmazione*. Torino: Einaudi.

Forrest, Ray, and Alan Murie. 1995. Accumulating evidence: Housing and family wealth in Britain. In *Housing and family wealth*, edited by Ray Forrest and Alan Murie, 58–85. London: Routledge.

Giddens, Antony. 1994. *Beyond left and right. The future of radical politics*. Cambridge: Polity Press.

Goldthorpe, John. 2002. Globalisation and social class. *West European Politics* 25 (3): 1–28.

Guiso, Luigi, and Tullio Jappelli. 1996. Intergenerational transfers, borrowing constraints and the timing of home ownership. Temi di Discussione 275, Bank of Italy, Rome.

Headey, Bruce. 1978. *Housing policy in the developed economy*. London: Croom Helm.

Istituto Nazionale di Statistica (ISTAT). 1997. *Rapporto annuale sulla situazione del paese nel 1996*. Roma.

———. 2000. *Le strutture familiari. Indagine multiscopo sulle famiglie, "Famiglia, soggetti sociali e condizione dell'infanzia" anno 1998*. Informazioni 17. Roma.

———. 2002a. *Annuario statistico Italiano 2002*. Roma.

———. 2002b. *Il valore della lira dal 1861 al 2001*. Informazioni 34. Roma.

———. 2003. *Famiglie, abitazioni e zona in cui si vive. Indagine multiscopo sulle famiglie, "Aspetti della vita quotidiana" anno 2002*. Informazioni 36. Roma.

Kohli, Martin. 1999. Private and public transfers between generations: Linking the family and the state. *European Societies* 1 (1): 81–104.

Kurz, Karin, and Nikolei Steinhage. 2001. Global competition and labour market restructuring: The transition into the labour market in Germany. Paper presented at the International Sociological Association (Research Committee 28) meeting in Mannheim, April 26–28.

Martens, Maartje. 1985. Owner-occupied housing in Europe: Postwar developments and current dilemmas. *Environment and Planning A* 17:605–24.

Mayer, Karl Ulrich. 2001. The paradox of global social change and national path dependencies. Life course patterns in advanced societies. In *Inclusions and exclusions in European societies*, edited by W. Woodward and M. Kohli, 89–110. New York: Routledge.

Mulder, Clara, and Jeroen Smits. 1999. First-time home-ownership of couples: The effect of inter-generational transmission. *European Sociological Review* 14 (3): 323–37.

Nomisma. 2001. *Prospects in the Italian real estate market*. Bologna.

Organisation for Economic Co-operation and Development (OECD). 2000. *OECD statistical compendium*. Vol. 1. Rheinberg: DSI Data Service & Information. CD ROM.

Padovani, Liliana. 1984. Italy. In *Housing in Europe*, edited by M. Wynn, 247–80. New York: Croom Helm.

———. 1996. Italy. In *Housing policy in Europe*, edited by P. Balchin, 188–209. London: Routledge.

Pisati, Maurizio, and Antonio Schizzerotto. 1999. Pochi promossi, nessun bocciato. La mobilità di carriera in Italia in prospettiva comparata e longitudinale. *Stato e Mercato* 56:249–79.

Powers, Daniel A., and Yu Xie. 2000. *Statistical methods for categorical data analysis*. San Diego: Academic Press.

Ricci, Renzo, ed. 1997. *Povertà abitativa in Italia, 1989–1993*. Commissione sulla Povertà e l'Emarginazione Sociale, Presidenza del Consiglio dei Ministri, Dipartimento per l'Informazione e l'Editoria. Roma: Istituto Poligrafico e Zecca dello Stato.

Saunders, Peter. 1990. *A nation of home owners*. London: Unwin Hyman.

Tosi, Antonio. 1987. La produzione sociale della casa in proprietà: Pratiche familiari, informale, politiche. *Sociologia e Ricerca Sociale* 22:7–24.

———. 1990. Italy. In *International handbook of housing policies and practices*, edited by W. van Vliet, 195–220. New York. Greenwood Press.

———, ed. 1994. *La casa: Il rischio e l'esclusione. Rapporto IRS sul disagio abitativo in Italia*. Milano. Angeli.

Villosio, Claudia. 1995. Mercato del credito, proprietà della casa, risparmio delle famiglie. *Annali della Fondazione Luigi Einaudi—Torino* 29:213–48.

CHAPTER NINE

Home Ownership and Social Inequality in Spain

Anna Cabré Pla and
Juan Antonio Módenes Cabrerizo

In demographic studies comparing European countries, often Spain is treated as a different reality, grouped together with other Southern European nations. And often the authors of those studies explain that treatment by claiming, with little or no evidence, that Spain shares social, economic, and cultural ties with Italy, Portugal, and Greece.

In much the same way, social scientists often cite a southern culture to explain the high rate of home ownership in Spain. Certainly it is true by all indicators that home ownership is much more common in Spain than in most other European countries: it is the primary form of occupancy in all regions and among all social classes. But high home-ownership rates in Spain are not the result of tradition; they are the product of the rapid social and economic changes that took place during the second half of the twentieth century. Like young people putting off leaving their parents' home, choosing to study for yet another degree, opting to set up a permanent household, or deciding to limit the size of their family, home ownership in Spain is just one of the strategies individuals and families adopt to achieve or maintain the social and economic status of average Europeans.[1]

In the past, home ownership was beyond the reach of the majority of Spanish families.[2] With important differences from one region of the country to another, a large part of the rural population lived under different forms of tenancy—in houses that belonged to landlords and that were loaned or rented to them together with the land they worked. With urbanization from the second half of the nineteenth century onward, upper- and middle-class urban families invested in housing for themselves and their relatives. They

233

built multistory houses in towns and cities, used what they needed for their family, and rented out any extra apartments out of the kinship network, usually to people they knew from work or socially. In popular neighborhoods, rental housing was built by private investors or by factory owners for their workers. Company-owned housing was also built in isolated industrial or mining colonies, where workers and their families lived in uniform houses, usually in lieu of additional wages, as a condition of their employment.

Low-income families—by the first decades of the twentieth century, the largest segment of the Spanish population—often lived in precarious conditions: eviction and homelessness were common problems for the poor, who had to rely on family or work as domestic servants to keep a roof over their heads.

Things changed dramatically after the Spanish Civil War (1936–1939). Responding to the disastrous state of the country and following the example of other European nations, the new regime took measures to protect tenants, passing laws to freeze rents (Ley de Protección de Vivienda, 1939) and to make eviction extremely difficult (Ley de Arrendamientos Urbanos, 1946). These laws had serious consequences for housing in Spain. With inflation outpacing rents, many landlords could not afford to maintain their buildings. Few buildings were being constructed, and existing buildings were falling into disrepair and being abandoned.

In 1954, a new measure was passed—Ley de Vivienda de Renta Limitada—to encourage private investment in rental housing; but it was not enough to meet the rapidly increasing demand for housing, a demand exacerbated by large migratory flows from rural areas to cities. Images of shantytowns, of people crowding into illegally sublet rooms, and of boarding houses are forever associated with this time in Spanish history. By the end of the decade, the government had taken more steps to preserve the current housing stock and to stimulate the housing market: it allowed the sale of houses and flats to their permanent tenants at very low prices. We would argue it was this policy that may well have been the first and most important step toward the generalization of home ownership in Spain.

A wave of sales led to passage of the Ley de Propiedad Horizontal in 1960. The objective was to regulate the sale of flats within a building; in effect, the law created a legal basis for massive investment in new buildings that would be sold by individual flats and apartments. Movement to the cities, high employment, the virtual absence of urban land use regulations and norms, and skyrocketing inflation did the rest. Rural migrants brought their savings and invested them in stone (or should we say concrete?). Young couples bought cheap and comparatively small apartments in new areas of the expanding cities. Middle-aged families left the historical centers and improved their standard of living by acquiring new and better-quality flats. And steady employment at inflated wages helped all of them pay their mortgage. In a matter of years, home ownership had become the goal of most Spaniards.

In the meantime, a moribund rental market was in large part restricted to housing occupied by long-term tenants paying very low rents.[3] There were few opportunities to rent to new tenants. In 1956 and again in 1964, the Ley de Arrendamientos Urbanos was modified to allow small rent increases with new leases, but the impact of the amendments was limited. Real change would not come until 1985, when the Decreto Boyer removed price controls and tenancy conditions from new rental contracts.[4] Rents immediately went up, giving new impetus to the home-ownership movement.

New tax policy also gave a boost to home ownership. Following a number of legal reforms during the late 1970s and the 1980s, for the first time, everyone in Spain had to pay income tax. That mortgage principal and interest were tax-deductible now figured into the financial plans of a large number of families.[5] When the law governing rentals was changed again in 1994, this time to offer relief to tenants, it was too late. The preference for home ownership was too deeply rooted to make renting anything more than a temporary solution at times of personal or family instability.

Home ownership was not a tradition in Spain; renting was. It was a combination of social and economic factors that led to the home-ownership culture, a culture that is still emerging.

HOME-OWNERSHIP RATES

Most families in Spain own their home. According to the 1991 census, 78 percent of primary residences in the country were owned by their occupants, and close to 82 percent of the population lived in those households.[6] More-recent data cite an ownership rate of 86 percent of homes (European Mortgage Federation 2000, cited in Trilla 2001) and 85 percent of households (according to Encuesta Contínua de Presupuestos Familiares, 2001 edition).

Married couples, the subject of our study, owned their homes in 82 percent of cases. The proportion of homeowners was also very high for other groups with the exception of separated and divorced persons. And, as discussed below, after marriage, ownership appears to be quite independent of the stage of the family life cycle.

The last Census on Population and Households (*Censo de Población y Viviendas*) for which all data are available was taken in 1991. Although more recent data on housing tenures in Spain was available from surveys, we used only census data in our analysis.[7] We wanted to be able to examine not just tenure but also the relationship between tenure and other demographic, social, and geographic variables.

In this section we examine the home-ownership patterns of couples married from the 1950s through the 1980s. To clarify those patterns, we divided the population into four birth cohorts based on the date of birth of the male partner:

- Born between 1931 and 1935 (ages 55 to 59 in 1991)
- Born between 1941 and 1945 (ages 45 to 49 in 1991)
- Born between 1951 and 1955 (ages 35 to 39 in 1991)
- Born between 1961 and 1965 (ages 25 to 29 in 1991)

Age and the Distribution of Home Ownership

Table 9.1 shows that the majority of married men in all cohorts owned their home. This held true even among members of the youngest cohort (61.0 percent), an indication not only that most married couples come to own their homes at some point, but that most of them own homes from the beginning of their married life. This appears to be a distinctive feature of home ownership in Spain.

The table also shows that the rate of home ownership increases with the age of the birth cohort: we found the highest rate—83.2 percent in the 1931–1935 cohort. A cross-sectional interpretation of the data would suggest that ownership is already predominant when households are created, and that the rate continues to increase over the years as families transfer from other tenure types.

The rental rate was highest in the youngest cohort but still well below the rate of home ownership (27.1 percent versus 61.0 percent). That renting is a temporary solution is clear from the sharp drop in the rate of rentals between the youngest cohort and the cohort born between 1951 and 1955

TABLE 9.1
TABLE 9.1
Housing tenure by husband's birth cohort, Spain, 1991

Husband's birth cohort	TENURE TYPE (%)		
	Own	*Rent*	*Other*[a]
1931–1935	83.2	11.3	5.4
1941–1945	82.9	11.6	5.4
1951–1955	76.4	16.3	7.3
1961–1965	61.0	27.1	11.9
NATIONAL AVERAGE	77.3	15.6	7.1

SOURCE: Authors' calculations based on Censo de Población de 1991.

NOTE: Because of rounding, rows may not total 100.0 percent.
[a]Includes, for example, borrowed housing and company housing.

(from 27.1 percent to 16.3 percent). Also, the youngest couples were more likely to borrow a residence, usually from a family member, again as a temporary measure.

The Regional Distribution of Home Ownership

Although Spain is a very diverse country by geography and culture, home-ownership rates throughout the nation are high. To assess regional variations, we examined six representative regions (*Comunidades Autónomas*). Andalusia and Extremadura are southern regions; both still have a significant agrarian population, and both experienced large migrations outward between the 1950s and the 1970s. Catalonia, Madrid, Valencia, and the Basque Country are the most urban regions of the country. Their economies are more diversified, and all have been an important destination for migrants from the south. Each of these regions has its own cultural traits; and three of them—Catalonia, Valencia, and the Basque Country—even have their own co-official languages.

Table 9.2 shows that almost without exception, a majority of families in every region owned their home, and that the proportion of homeowners increased with age. Clearly home ownership is not a function of culture so much as of economical and political conditions that are common to all regions.

TABLE 9.2

Home ownership by region and husband's birth cohort, Spain, 1991

	PERCENTAGE OF HOMEOWNERS BY HUSBAND'S BIRTH COHORT			
Region	1931–1935	1941–1945	1951–1955	1961–1965
Andalusia	83.9	83.9	76.3	62.9
Basque Country	89.1	91.0	87.6	72.1
Catalonia	76.1	78.4	74.3	62.8
Extremadura	88.8	82.7	71.8	48.1
Madrid	82.7	85.3	79.2	61.8
Valencia	87.3	87.0	82.6	70.9
NATIONAL AVERAGE	83.2	82.9	76.4	61.0

SOURCE: Authors' calculations based on Censo de Población de 1991.

The distinctly urban or rural nature of the regions we studied apparently had little impact on housing tenure. We found two exceptions in the cities of Madrid and Barcelona (Catalonia), where the percentage of homeowners was slightly lower in the oldest cohort. It may well be that these households were still benefiting from the sizable housing stock in the city centers with frozen rents. In Extremadura, a paradigm of rural life, nearly nine of ten married couples from the oldest cohort owned their home.

We observed the greatest regional variation in the behavior of young couples, particularly the 1961–1965 birth cohort. In Extremadura, for example, just 48 percent of younger couples owned their home. In the Basque Country, closely followed by Valencia, more than 70 percent of young couples were homeowners.

The relatively low rate of ownership among young people in Extremadura may be linked to the tradition of tenancy in Southern Spain. But it may also reflect the ready availability and affordability of rental housing in the wake of the large-scale exodus from rural areas. Still, even in Extremadura, the vast majority of older couples owned their home. In fact, the percentage of home ownership among members of the oldest cohort there was one of the highest rates we found.

The Basque Country and especially Valencia were very active urban residential markets during the 1980s (Cabré and Módenes 1999). Comparative studies show that for different reasons, Valencia offers the best quality-to-price relationship in real estate of all regions in Spain, which probably explains why younger people bought homes there so early.

Social Position and Home Ownership

In our analysis, we did not find a significant relationship between social position and housing tenure. In the two older cohorts, in particular, the rates were much the same across upper, middle, and lower classes (Table 9.3). The behavior of the middle class—the largest under this classification scheme—matched that of the upper class; the rates of ownership across birth cohorts were much the same for both classes.

In the younger birth cohorts, home ownership was less extensive in the lowest social category. There were fewer homeowners among newly married couples, and the transition from renting to buying happened at later stages of the family life cycle. This explains the relatively larger differences between this social group and the others in the 1951–1955 birth cohort. But by the end of the family life cycle, even couples with fewer economic resources were likely to own a home in almost the same proportion as were couples in the other categories.

We did not find a clear correlation between social position and home ownership; but it seems that social position may influence the timing of access to ownership: ownership at the time of marriage was significantly more likely among middle- and upper-class couples than it was among lower-class

TABLE 9.3
Home ownership by husband's social class and birth cohort,
Spain, 1991

Husband's social class	PERCENTAGE OF HOMEOWNERS BY HUSBAND'S BIRTH COHORT			
	1931–1935	*1941–1945*	*1951–1955*	*1961–1965*
Upper	85.5	85.5	78.9	63.1
Middle	84.3	84.0	78.1	63.3
Lower	82.2	79.3	69.4	56.0
NATIONAL AVERAGE	83.2	82.9	76.4	61.0

SOURCE: Authors' calculations based on Censo de Población de 1991.

TABLE 9.4

Home ownership by wife's employment status and
husband's birth cohort, Spain, 1991

Wife's employment status	PERCENTAGE OF HOMEOWNERS BY HUSBAND'S BIRTH COHORT			
	1931–1935	*1941–1945*	*1951–1955*	*1961–1965*
Not employed	83.4	82.9	75.6	59.2
Employed	82.6	83.1	77.8	64.0
NATIONAL AVERAGE	83.2	82.9	76.4	61.0

SOURCE: Authors' calculations based on Censo de Población de 1991.

couples. The transition to ownership was also faster for both middle- and upper-class couples.

Wife's Employment and the Distribution of Home Ownership

Table 9.4 shows that having two incomes did help couples in the youngest cohort to become homeowners. But, at least until recently, having two incomes was not essential to home ownership.[8] The 1960s saw the greatest growth in home ownership in Spain; that decade was also a period in which relatively few women worked outside the home. Couples in the three older cohorts achieved high rates of home ownership without relying on the wife's labor. And in the oldest cohort, those born between 1931 and 1935, the ownership rate was actually higher if the wife did not work.

FINANCING HOME OWNERSHIP

Except in cases of extreme poverty or social exclusion, socioeconomic differences do not seem to affect home-ownership rates in Spain. What they do affect is the timing of access to home ownership.[9] In this section, we explore that phenomenon among three groups of homeowners: those who have finished paying for their home, those who are still paying a mortgage or other loan, and those who inherited or were given their home. Here, too, our focus is on four variables: age, region, social class, and wife's employment.

Age and Home-Ownership Financing

Table 9.5 summarizes the relationship between financing situation and age. Not unexpectedly, the older the cohort, the greater the proportion of homes completely paid for. That the percentage of homes completely paid for increases with age—more than 75 percent of households in the 1931–1935 birth cohort—could well indicate a reluctance or inability to move. People who have paid off their home generally have lived there for many years.

What is striking about the data in Table 9.5 is that 41.1 percent of couples in the 1961–1965 birth cohort had completely paid off their home loans—this at a time (1991) when mortgage interest rates were historically high. In Spain, young people often begin saving for a home before they actually marry. But given their age and the cost of money at the time, clearly these young couples relied on more than a mortgage to buy their home. Some may have received financial help from their families; others may have been helped by the availability in the market of existing homes of lesser quality at lower prices.

Home ownership by means of inheritance or gift was relatively stable across birth cohorts, averaging just over 10 percent. That the rate was somewhat higher in the youngest cohort suggests wedding gifts in well-to-do families; that it was highest in the oldest cohort suggests legacies.[10] For young couples, an inheritance can be the means by which they become homeowners. For older couples, many of whom already own a home, inherited hous-

TABLE 9.5
Home financing by husband's birth cohort, Spain, 1991

Husband's birth cohort	PERCENTAGE OF HOMES		
	Completely paid for	*With payments pending*	*Inherited or received as a gift*
1931–1935	75.1	11.5	13.4
1941–1945	71.2	19.4	9.4
1951–1955	54.5	37.9	7.6
1961–1965	41.1	48.1	10.8
NATIONAL AVERAGE	63.7	25.9	10.3

SOURCE: Authors' calculations based on Censo de Población de 1991.

TABLE 9.6
Home financing by region and husband's birth cohort, Spain, 1991

| | HUSBAND'S BIRTH COHORT | | | | | |
| | 1951–1955 Percentage of Homes | | | 1961–1965 Percentage of Homes | | |
Region	*Completely paid for*	*With payments pending*	*Inherited or received as a gift*	*Completely paid for*	*With payments pending*	*Inherited or received as a gift*
Andalusia	50.9	43.2	5.9	42.9	46.3	10.8
Basque Country	57.6	38.2	4.2	37.8	55.4	6.8
Catalonia	58.7	36.4	4.9	40.6	52.4	7.0
Extremadura	48.4	38.0	13.6	49.2	33.1	17.7
Madrid	56.6	40.5	2.9	36.9	57.5	5.6
Valencia	54.0	37.0	9.0	42.6	46.3	11.1
NATIONAL AVERAGE	54.5	37.9	7.6	41.1	48.1	10.8

SOURCE: Authors' calculations based on Censo de Población de 1991.

ing allows them to purchase a new home or to help their adult children become homeowners. These effects are strongly suggested by the fact that couples in the 1961–65 birth cohort occupy a smaller proportion of inherited or donated homes.

Region and Home-Ownership Financing

From this point, our analysis of financing considers only the two younger birth cohorts because there was very little diversity in the older cohorts.

Table 9.6 shows similarities across all of the regions we studied. In the younger cohort, we did find higher rates of payments pending in the mainly urban regions (Madrid, the Basque Country, and Catalonia). High prices and a scarcity of housing stock in these areas translate into larger mortgages that take more time to pay off. Also, continuing to pay a mortgage can be a fiscal strategy: that is, even families that can well afford to pay off a home loan may choose to take advantage of the tax benefits associated with mortgage payments. Finally, the proportion of inherited housing is lower in these areas, probably because many urban families have only recently migrated to the city.

Social Position and Home-Ownership Financing

Although social position did not seem to have a strong impact on home financing, we did find the results for lower-class homeowners in the younger cohort particularly interesting (Table 9.7). A larger-than-average proportion of young couples had paid off their mortgages (44.4 percent versus 41.1 percent) and a significantly smaller-than-average proportion of them were still making payments (42.1 percent versus 48.1 percent). Our explanation: these households often find it difficult to meet the requirements of financial institutions and so are more likely to rely on savings and family support to buy a home. Notice, too, that inheritances and gifts are particularly important for this segment of the population.

The relative importance of pending payments may speak more to the quality of housing than to a household's ability to pay off its mortgage. That a higher rate of upper- and middle-class homeowners were still paying home loans in 1991 indicates that their homes were more expensive and of better quality than the homes of the lowest social group. Also at work here was the strategy higher-income households adopt to keep making mortgage payments because they can save money—via tax deductions—doing so. In the younger birth cohort, upper-class couples showed a slightly higher rate of inheritances and gifts than did middle-class couples. This may relate to differ-

TABLE 9.7

Home financing by husband's social class and birth cohort, Spain, 1991

| | HUSBAND'S BIRTH COHORT | | | | | |
| | 1951–1955 Percentage of Homes | | | 1961–1965 Percentage of Homes | | |
Husband's social class	Completely paid for	With payments pending	Inherited or received as a gift	Completely paid for	With payments pending	Inherited or received as a gift
Upper	55.5	37.5	7.0	38.5	49.7	11.8
Middle	53.3	39.7	7.0	39.1	51.1	9.7
Lower	57.3	32.9	9.8	44.4	42.1	13.5
NATIONAL AVERAGE	54.5	37.9	7.6	41.1	48.1	10.8

SOURCE: Authors' calculations based on Censo de Población y Vivienda de 1991.

TABLE 9.8

Home financing by wife's employment status and husband's birth cohort,
Spain, 1991

	HUSBAND'S BIRTH COHORT					
	1951–1955 Percentage of Homes			1961–1965 Percentage of Homes		
Wife's employment status	Completely paid for	With payments pending	Inherited or received as a gift	Completely paid for	With payments pending	Inherited or received as a gift
Not employed	56.3	35.3	8.4	44.2	43.5	12.2
Employed	51.3	42.7	6.1	36.0	55.3	8.6
NATIONAL AVERAGE	54.5	37.9	7.6	41.1	48.1	10.8

SOURCE: Authors' calculations based on Censo de Población de 1991.

ences in family wealth; but it also can be explained by the relative immobility of the upper class, whose members have lived in urban areas for many generations.

In the cohort born between 1951 and 1955, we found similar but smaller differences. In the two older birth cohorts, those differences had all but disappeared.

Wife's Employment and Home-Ownership Financing

The wife's employment appears to be an important factor in how young couples finance their home. As Table 9.8 shows, when the wife is working outside the home, the couple is more likely to be paying a mortgage. When she is not, the couple is more likely to have paid off their mortgage or to have received their home as an inheritance or gift. Again, these findings, in defiance of intuitive thinking, suggest that having mortgage payments is a positive situation.

Two incomes often makes the difference in meeting the requirements financial institutions establish for granting mortgages, and paves the path to tax savings, better-quality housing, and the accumulation of wealth. This strategy is even more obvious in the older cohorts, where we found a much higher proportion of households continuing to make mortgage payments when the wife was employed outside the home. This probably means that the wife's income provides couples with better-quality housing at later stages of the family life cycle.

Understanding intergenerational relationships is key to understanding the path to home ownership in Spain in recent times. To identify those relationships, we analyzed the changes undergone by men who had lived dependently (usually with their parents) in 1981 but were married and living in their own home in 1991.[11] As many as 71.5 percent of all couples who married during the 1980s in Spain were homeowners in 1991. That is one of the main characteristics of the Spanish housing system: couples tend to buy a home in the first stages of their union, very often at marriage or shortly after, before they have a child.

We found that parents' tenure is highly correlated with the tenure of their adult children. Of respondents whose parents were homeowners in 1981, 77 percent owned a home in 1991. But of respondents whose parents were tenants in 1981, only 50 percent were homeowners in 1991. Of course, this does not mean that tenants in 1991 were mainly the children of tenants. The rate of home ownership in Spain in recent decades has been so high—more than 81 percent of men married during the 1980s came from a family in which the parents owned a home—that even most of the married children who rented a home in 1991 (62.6 percent) had been living in a parent-owned home ten years earlier.

Age and the Intergenerational Transmission of Tenure

Table 9.9 shows the effect of age on the intergenerational transmission of tenure type. The older the man at marriage, the more likely he was to be a homeowner in 1991. In other words, we found a higher percentage of renters among the younger couples in our sample. This makes sense: younger couples have had less time to save money to buy a house and usually have more difficulty qualifying for a mortgage—a function of instability in the labor market for younger workers.

In all birth cohorts, parents' tenure conditioned their adult children's tenure. Even though ownership was less frequent among the youngest couples, the home-ownership rate of the couples whose parents owned a

TABLE 9.9
Parents' housing tenure and the tenure of married adult children,
by married son's birth cohort, Spain, 1991

| | PERCENTAGE OF ADULT CHILDREN WHO OWNED A HOME IN 1991 | | *Percentage of homeowners in 1991* |
| | Parents' tenure in 1981 | | |
Married son's birth cohort	*Homeowners*	*Tenants*	
1931–1935	84.5	55.3	78.8
1941–1945	79.5	56.0	74.9
1951–1955	73.4	44.6	67.8
1961–1965	64.0	36.1	57.4
NATIONAL AVERAGE	77.1	49.6	71.5

SOURCE: Authors' calculations based on Encuesta Sociodemográfica de 1991.

home was 77 percent compared to 50 percent among couples whose parents
were tenants.

Although the impact of parents' tenure on their adult children's tenure
is clear, the reason is not. Is the value of owning a home one of the values
that parents transmit to their children? Or are parents who own a home
more likely to help their children buy a home because the parents believe
that home ownership is important? Or is it simply that parents who own a
home are more likely to have the resources to help their children buy a
home? These are questions we could not answer with the available data.

Regional Differences in the Intergenerational Transmission of Tenure

In all of the regions we studied, we found a relationship between parents'
housing tenure and that of their adult children, although the strength of the
association varies (Table 9.10). In Extremadura, where rental housing is
more readily available, the proportion of homeowners was relatively low
even among the children of homeowners (57 percent).

In contrast, in Valencia and the Basque Country—regions with a high
ownership rate—more than 85 percent of the adult children of homeowners
were homeowners themselves in 1991, suggesting that the intergenerational
transmission of home ownership is very strong. At the same time, the high

proportion of homeowners among the children of renters indicates that the transmission of rental tenure is relatively weak in these regions. The findings for Catalonia and Andalusia were somewhere in the middle between Extremadura, a rural region, and the rest of the urban regions.

Social Class and the Intergenerational Transmission of Tenure

Is the intergenerational transmission of tenure influenced by the income level of young couples (measured by husband's social class)? When we examined the transmission of home ownership, social class did not appear to be important. There was only a 4-percentage-point difference between upper- and lower-class couples who came from home-owning families (Table 9.11), by far the largest group. However, the data told a different story about those who came from tenant families. In these cases, the married son's social class was significantly related to the transition to home ownership: more than 54 percent of the upper-class couples became homeowners versus 42 percent of the lower-class couples.

Obviously, to understand the impact of social class on the intergenerational transmission of housing tenure, we need more in-depth analysis. One

TABLE 9.10
Parents' housing tenure and the tenure of adult children,
by region, Spain, 1991

| Region | PERCENTAGE OF ADULT CHILDREN WHO OWNED A HOME IN 1991 | | Percentage of homeowners in 1991 |
| | Parents' tenure in 1981 | | |
	Homeowners	*Tenants*	
Andalusia	75.4	50.3	70.2
Basque Country	90.8	68.2	87.6
Catalonia	74.7	51.1	68.7
Extremadura	56.9	34.0	53.9
Madrid	81.5	48.4	75.3
Valencia	85.1	54.5	79.6
NATIONAL AVERAGE	77.1	49.6	71.5

SOURCE: Authors' calculations based on Encuesta Sociodemográfica de 1991.

TABLE 9.11

TABLE 9.11

Parents' housing tenure and the tenure of married adult children,
by married son's social class, Spain, 1991

| Married son's social class | PERCENTAGE OF ADULT CHILDREN WHO OWNED A HOME IN 1991 | | *Percentage of homeowners in 1991* |
| | Parents' tenure in 1981 | | |
	Homeowners	*Tenants*	
Upper	79.4	54.2	74.9
Middle	77.6	52.5	72.4
Lower	75.2	42.0	68.8
NATIONAL AVERAGE	77.1	49.6	71.5

SOURCE: Authors' calculations based on Encuesta Sociodemográfica de 1991.

TABLE 9.12

Parents' housing tenure and the tenure of married adult children,
by the social class of the married son's father, Spain, 1991

Social class of married son's father	*Percentage of homeowners in 1981 who were homeowners in 1991*	*Percentage of tenants in 1981 who were homeowners in 1991*	*Percentage of homeowners in 1991*
Upper	74.1	42.9	68.6
Middle	77.2	50.2	71.2
Lower	77.6	51.8	73.0
NATIONAL AVERAGE	77.1	49.6	71.5

SOURCE: Authors' calculations based on Encuesta Sociodemográfica de 1991.

possibility is to take into account the parents' social class. Table 9.12 shows an interesting fact: the children of upper-class parents are more likely to rent if their parents rented. Again, this seems counterintuitive. It may be that the children of well-to-do families more often live in dwellings that belong to their families, housing that they may or may not pay rent for and that they may or may not eventually own. It could be that these young people more often choose professions that require them to travel, so they choose to rent, at least for a while. Or it may be that they have better access to high-quality rental opportunities in urban centers, especially if their parents and grand-parents were tenants there as well. Finally, it is possible that members of rich families have more information and a wider range of possibilities for invest-ment and tax savings, and so focus less on home ownership as a financial strategy.

Wife's Employment and Housing Tenure

Again, having two incomes increases a couple's access to home owner-ship. This effect was stronger when the married son's parents were tenants (Table 9.13). Also, the wife's employment in the labor market was a factor when low-income couples made the transition from renting to owning. Only 46.7 percent of single-earner families with tenant parents owned a home; in two-income families, 53.9 percent of them became homeowners.

THE QUALITY OF HOUSING

In Spain, social class seems to make little difference in the rate of home own-ership, the financing situation of homeowners, or the transmission of tenure type from parents to their adult children. But social class makes a significant difference in the quality of both owner-occupied and rental housing. Among

TABLE 9.13
Parents' housing tenure and the tenure of married adult children,
by wife's employment status, Spain, 1991

| | PERCENTAGE OF ADULT CHILDREN WHO OWNED A HOME IN 1991 | | |
| | Parents' tenure in 1981 | | *Percentage of homeowners in 1991* |
Wife's employment status	*Homeowners*	*Tenants*	
Not employed	76.2	46.7	70.3
Employed	78.6	53.9	73.6
NATIONAL AVERAGE	77.1	49.6	71.5

SOURCE: Authors' calculations based on Encuesta Sociodemográfica de 1991.

TABLE 9.14
Average size of owner-occupied housing by husband's birth cohort
and social class, Spain, 1991

Husband's birth cohort	AVERAGE SIZE (M^2)			Average (m^2)
	Husband's social class			
	Upper	Middle	Lower	
1931–1935	111.4	98.6	89.8	98.1
1941–1945	111.5	99.4	92.6	100.0
1951–1955	106.0	97.3	90.9	97.4
1961–1965	95.9	90.2	86.4	89.9
NATIONAL AVERAGE	107.3	96.7	90.0	96.7

SOURCE: Authors' calculations based on Encuesta Sociodemográfica de 1991.

the factors that indicate housing quality are age, state of repair, fixtures, and size (floor area in square meters). For example, the data in Table 9.14 show the effect of birth cohort and social class on the relative size of housing.

Notice that the crucial factor here is social class. In 1991, the average size of housing for upper-class households was 107.3 square meters; for middle-class households, 96.7 square meters; for lower-class households, 90.0 square meters. The differences explained by husband's birth cohort (the last column in the table) were much smaller. Even if we were to interpret the differences among cohorts as a function of respondents' age, social class clearly plays an important role over time in improving the quality of housing. Under that condition, over a thirty-year period, upper-class families would gain 15.5 square meters (the difference between the dwelling size of the 1931–1935 cohort and the 1961–1965 cohort); while middle-class families would gain 8.4 square meters, and lower-class families would gain just 3.4 square meters.

CONCLUSIONS

In the second half of the twentieth century, home ownership became the housing tenure of choice in Spain (Gaviria 1996). Today, four out of five families own their home. Of those who do not, one-third live rent-free in housing borrowed from family or friends. Family networks also play a role in what is left of the rental sector: that is, we expect a reasonable portion of tenants rent from family or friends.

In this context, social class seems to have little bearing on home-ownership rates. The main differences we found concerned the timing of the transition to ownership; the proportion of owners who were still paying home loans; and the quality of housing and its improvement over time. The unexpected relationship between pending payments and social position suggests that homeowners from different social groups adopt very different strategies for investing in real estate.

In Spain, the family network is crucial to the transition to ownership. One of ten owner-occupied homes is a legacy or a gift from family. And the financial help of parents is probably a very important source of funds for first-time homeowners. Family also supports home ownership in a less direct way, through the intergenerational transmission of housing tenure. In fact, family tradition in this instance seems more important than social class: the adult children of tenants, for example, are much more likely to be tenants themselves, whatever their social position. Even so, a majority of tenants' children move from their parents' rented home to a home they have purchased. In switching from tenancy to ownership, social class is a factor but a less important factor than the wife's employment outside the home.

We would expect a second income to increase the likelihood of home ownership, and it does for the adult children of tenants and for younger couples. But some of the data on two-income households surprised us. For example, the wife's employment actually had a small negative effect on the incidence of home ownership in the older birth cohorts. And in results that are not reported here, we found that a second income had only a very small positive effect on housing quality (measured by floor area), which supports the argument that housing quality is primarily related to social class.

In Spain, home ownership is almost universal. That is especially interesting because ownership is not a tradition in the country. Instead it is a relatively new investment strategy and a response to a world in which nothing —not employment, not marriage, not old-age pensions—is certain.

Home ownership in Spain is also a response to the negative consequences of the government's regulation of housing. Over time, laws that were passed to protect tenants depleted the stock of rental housing. The result has been the extension of property to people in all social classes. The social distinction today is not between owners and renters; instead, it centers on the quality and the quantity (second homes, investment property) of housing.

It is common among policymakers in Spain to point to home ownership as one of the main causes of workers' unwillingness to move and, so, of a stubbornly high unemployment rate.[12] They ignore the fact that some of the most mobile populations in the world exist in societies where the rate of home ownership is increasing steadily, as is the case in much of Northern Europe (Trilla 2001). Their response, instead, is to encourage the construction of rental units and to promote tenancy as an alternative for young couples. Certainly the government has an interest in the housing of its citizens. And should owner-occupancy be used to restrict the growth or opportunities of certain segments of the population, government at all levels must intervene. But here the government is fighting a trend that has evolved over time and that is most remarkable in its inclusion of people from all socioeconomic groups. For most Spaniards, home ownership is a choice, a strategy implemented with family and quality of life in mind. Given the overwhelming prevalence of home ownership in the country, it will be interesting to see if the government's new policies are adopted and how they are received.

Notes

1. For an introduction to the topic of residential strategies in Europe, see Bonvalet and Brun (1998), Bonvalet and Gotman (1993), and Cuturello (1992).

2. For a well-documented introduction to the historical evolution of housing in Spain with respect to social trends and housing policies, see Cortés (1995). A remarkable work focused on urban housing planning in Spain is Leal and Cortés (1995).

3. In fact, very often these tenants were permanent, their tenancy having almost hereditary status; and their rents were still frozen.

4. *Decreto Boyer* is the popular name of the Real Decreto-Ley. Miguel Boyer, then the minister of economy, proposed the reform. Its main innovation: landlords would no longer be forced to extend tenancy contracts; all leases signed after the decree could freely set both rent and duration.

5. The Spanish system of tax relief for housing was finalized in 1978. Taxpayers with a mortgage are able to deduct the interest part of their payments; they also can deduct their principal payments up to a maximum of 15 percent of their

annual tax. There is wide evidence that this system is fiscally regressive. The more expensive a home, typically the higher the mortgage and the larger the deduction. During the 1980s, 59 percent of the taxpayers who claimed this tax relief came from the upper 40 percent of the income distribution. Only 9 percent of beneficiaries fell into the lowest 30 percent of the income distribution (Cortés 1995). And the system has not become much more equal over time.

6. Much of the data we relied on in our analysis of housing and social inequality in Spain were taken from the 1991 census and a sociodemographic survey that same year conducted by the Instituto Nacional de Estadística.

7. Two surveys, for example, are the Family Budget Survey (*Encuesta de Presupuestos Familiares*) and the Social Inequality Survey (*Encuesta de Desigualdad Social*).

8. Even in the youngest cohort, the majority of wives did not work outside the home. Just 40 percent of young homeowning households were dual-income households; the equivalent rate among renters and others was 35 percent.

9. They also have an impact on the quality of housing—for example, on the average size of dwellings.

10. The rate of inherited homes is particularly high in rural areas.

11. Biographical data from the 1981 and 1991 sociodemographic surveys allowed us to compare the tenure in the family home (where the respondent lived in 1981) with that of the respondent in his own home in 1991.

12. One of the classic solutions to high unemployment is to encourage workers to move from areas where the labor market is depressed to areas where it is buoyant.

References

Bonvalet, Catherine, and Jacques Brun, eds. 1998. *Logement et habitat: L'état des savoirs*. Paris: La Découverte.

Bonvalet, Catherine, and Anne Gotman, eds. 1993. *Le logement, une affaire de famille. L'approche intergénérationnelle des status résidentielles*. Villes et Enterprises. Paris: L'Harmattan.

Cabré, Anna, and Juan A. Módenes. 1999. *Aspectos demográficos de las necesidades de vivienda en la Comunidad Valenciana*. Papers de Demografia. Bellaterra: Centre d'Estudis Demogràfics.

Cortés, Luis. 1995. *La cuestión residencial. Bases para una sociología del habitar*. Ciencias-Serie Sociología 205. Madrid: Fundamentos.

Cuturello, Paul, ed. 1992. *Regards sur le logement: Une étrange marchandise*. Villes et Enterprises. Paris: L'Harmattan.

European Mortgage Federation. 2000. *Mortgage and property markets in the European Union and Norway. Comparison and trends*. HYPOSTAT 1989–1999. Brussels.

Gaviria, Mario. 1996. *La Séptima Potencia: España en el mundo*. Barcelona: Ediciones B.

Leal, Jesús, and Luis Cortés. 1995. *La dimensión de la ciudad*. Monografías 145. Madrid: Siglo XXI, CIS.

Trilla, Carme. 2001. *La política de vivienda en una perspectiva europea comparada*. Barcelona: Fundación La Caixa.

CHAPTER TEN

Home Ownership and Social Inequality in Britain

John Ermisch and Brendan Halpin

In this paper we study first-time home ownership in Britain in the 1990s. We take a dynamic approach, looking at the effect of life-course developments on the rate of house-buying decisions. And we pay special attention to the role of social class: Does social class still matter for housing tenure in the United Kingdom?

Whether and when people become homeowners is important for a number of reasons. First, home ownership is a long-term commitment. Although some homeowners do sell their homes and then rent, these are mainly transitional moves into private rental housing for short periods. Permanent moves are much less common. For instance, among the two-thirds of British people born in 1958 who became owner-occupiers by age 33, only about 3 percent had bought homes and subsequently sold them and moved into public housing (Ermisch and Di Salvo 1996).[1] Thus, how much of their lives people spend as homeowners is strongly associated with when they first buy a home.

Second, the tax system in Britain offers homeowners large tax-exempt returns on their investment, thereby contributing directly to their accumulation of wealth. Third, homeowners have at least one asset: Their equity in their home. They also are much more likely to have financial assets (other than real estate), particularly riskier investments, and higher average levels of wealth (Banks and Tanner 1999, tables 5.2 and 5.5). For example, among working-age individuals who do not contribute to a private pension, 22 percent of those who do not own a home have no financial assets compared with 4 percent of homeowners. The non–homeowners in this group have mean financial wealth of £1,200 compared with £6,900 for homeowners. It appears that those who do not accumulate housing wealth do not compensate by accumulating more of other types of wealth.

Fourth, home ownership affects geographic mobility. Although undoubtedly self-selection plays a part here, the residential mobility rates of private-sector tenants are five times those of owner-occupiers.[2] Their reluctance to move may limit the ability of owner-occupiers to respond to changes in labor market conditions—for example, a job loss or a better opportunity elsewhere.[3]

BACKGROUND

Housing Policies

At the start of World War I, just 10 percent of households in Great Britain owned their home; fully 90 percent rented from private landlords. With the exception of subsidies for private-sector building in the 1920s, housing policies since have featured subsidies for new building in the public sector and rent controls in varying degrees in the private sector. Slum clearance was an adjunct to subsidies for new building in the public sector; it was particularly important in the 1930s and from 1956 to 1975. The main thrust of housing policy, then, was to clear slums and to encourage the construction of local-authority housing, which could be let at rents low-income people could afford. By 1961, about 45 percent of households owned their own home, 25 percent rented from local authorities, and 30 percent rented from a private landlord.

Home ownership has increased steadily since. At the time of the 1981 census, nearly 60 percent of households owned their home, nearly 30 percent rented from local authorities, and just 10 percent rented from private landlords. Ten years later, 67 percent of households were owner-occupiers, and 24 percent were public tenants. The latter are primarily people who rent their home from local authorities, but they also include those who rent from housing associations (3 percent of households), charitable organizations whose purpose is to provide cheap housing to targeted groups (for example, the elderly or low-income families). The remaining 9 percent were private tenants. According to the British Household Panel Survey (BHPS 1991–1998), only 6 percent of people ages 35 to 54 are private tenants, but this tenure still plays an important role for younger people. Among those under age 25 who are not living with their parents, 45 percent are private tenants. Even in this group, though, 35 percent are owner-occupiers.[4]

Today, then, the main alternative to owning a home is renting in the public sector. Public housing is allocated not by price but by administrative procedures that limit both access and consumer choice. In terms of access, priority is usually given to families with children and to the elderly; household income is less a factor. Once a household enters public housing, it can remain there even if its circumstances change.

A number of fiscal policy developments contributed to the redistribution of housing tenure over time. One had to do with changes in tax policies that affected owner-occupiers' cost of housing. Tax relief on mortgage interest was not designed to encourage home ownership; it was simply one provision in an income tax system that offered relief for all interest payments. In 1969, however, personal income tax relief for interest paid was restricted to interest on loans for certain purposes, the principal one being the purchase and improvement of property. This restriction was removed in 1972 and then reinstated in 1974—a change that made the deduction for mortgage interest appear special. In the 1990s, tax deductions for mortgage interest were gradually reduced; they disappeared completely in 2000.

Two other fiscal policies also affected owner-occupiers' cost of housing. Before 1963, owner-occupiers and landlords paid income tax on *imputed rent*, the assessed rental value of their property. In 1963, the tax on owner-occupiers was repealed, and the tax on landlords was amended: they would be taxed on actual rental income net of allowable business costs, not assessed value. Second, when a capital gains tax was enacted in 1965, gains on taxpayers' primary residence were specifically exempted.

During the 1980s there were important changes in policies toward local-authority housing and financial markets (Ermisch 1991). The 1980 Housing Act withdrew central government subsidies from local-authority housing. Although there was no compulsion to raise rents, there was a strong incentive for local authorities to do so: rents went up in real terms by 44 percent between 1980 and 1982. By the end of the 1980s, real rents rose another 16 percent, but that increase was well below the rate at which average earnings were growing, and local-authority tenants still received considerable public subsidy throughout the decade (Hills 1991). In addition, the capital-spending plans of local authorities came increasingly under the control of the central government during the 1980s. The result: the construction of local-authority housing fell dramatically, reaching the lowest level in the postwar period.

Another provision of the 1980 Housing Act was the right to buy granted to tenants of local-authority housing. That right came with discounts ranging from 33 percent to 70 percent of a property's value. By the end of the decade, about 1.3 million public-sector dwellings were sold under the right to buy. It is generally agreed that most of the units sold were from better-quality public housing stock.

Britain has benefited from a well-developed housing finance market for a long time. However, there have been periods of mortgage rationing, when households could not borrow the amount they wanted because lenders had reduced the percentage of house value that they would finance. As a consequence of policy changes affecting financial markets, mortgage rationing ended during the early 1980s. Mortgages with high loan-to-value ratios—from 95 percent to 100 percent—were common during the house price and consumption boom of the 1980s. But when the boom ended in the early 1990s and the price of houses fell sharply, many people lost their homes and many lenders lost their investment. Today, the maximum mortgage has fallen back to about 90 percent of house value.

Intergenerational Transfers

The importance of intergenerational transfers to first-time homeowners is difficult to gauge. Di Salvo and Ermisch (1997) found that members of the 1958 cohort whose parents were homeowners were more likely to become owners themselves, but they were unable to distinguish the relative importance of direct transfers (via inheritance or gift) and indirect transfers (the influence of aspirations). Evidence from the 1958 birth cohort indicates that only a few first-time homeowners received financial help from their parents when they purchased their house, which suggests the importance of aspirations.[5] But parents can transfer resources to their adult children in other ways (for example, by helping them with expenditures after the purchase is made). Furthermore, homeowning parents may be more able and willing to make contingent transfers should their adult children have financial difficulties.

The Cost of Housing

Since 1970, there have been large fluctuations in the price of houses (and land) relative to annual disposable income per capita. The peaks have been as high as 10.5 times disposable income, and the troughs as low as 7.4. The peaks occurred in 1973, 1980, and 1989; the troughs, in 1977, 1982, and 1995. For example, during the last downturn (1989–1995), house prices in southern England fell by as much as 20 percent. Expectations about future price inflation or deflation, then, are an important influence on the house-purchase decision, along with current income, interest rates, and housing prices. The rate of change in the incidence of home ownership is jointly determined with house prices, making simple comparisons of the two not very meaningful.

Life-Course Changes

About one-third of women born in the 1950s cohabited in their first partnership; that proportion more than doubled for women born since. Not surprisingly, this trend is largely responsible for an increase in the median age at marriage: from 22 for women (25 for men) born in 1956 to 26 for women born ten years later (more than 29 for men).[6] The increase in cohabitation, then, is also responsible for the increase in the average age at motherhood, from 25 to 27, between the 1956 and 1966 cohorts.

Still, long-term cohabiting unions are rare. On average, they last about two years before the partners marry or separate. Within ten years, about 60 percent of cohabiting unions have turned into marriage, and 35 percent have dissolved (Ermisch and Francesconi 2000).

Estimates using BHPS data, which refer mainly to people born in the 1970s, indicate that just over half of young women leave home by age 21 (Ermisch 1999); young men, by about age 22. Almost 40 percent of young people move from their parents' home to live with a partner. A comparison of these estimates with the observations made by Ermisch and Di Salvo (1997) for the 1958 birth cohort tells us that women's median leaving age has stayed about the same, but that young men are leaving home about a year earlier. The real change between the 1958 cohort and the younger group has to do with the reason they left home. In the 1958 cohort, 60 percent of the women and about 55 percent of the men moved out to live with a partner. Today, most young people leave their parents' home to live independently: just 41 percent of women and 36 percent of men leave to live with a partner.

We expect that entering a cohabiting union or getting married is associated with becoming a homeowner. The association with marriage is likely to be stronger because of the short duration of most cohabiting unions.

DATA

In the fall of 1991, the BHPS interviewed a representative sample of 5,500 households, containing about 10,000 persons. The same individuals have been interviewed again in each successive year (the survey is ongoing). If participants split off from their original household to form a new household, all adult members of the new household are also interviewed. Similarly, children in original households are interviewed when they reach age 16. So the sample remained broadly representative of the population of Britain as it changed through the 1990s.

The core questionnaire elicits information about income, labor market behavior, housing conditions, household composition, education, and health at each yearly interview. In most respects, the data collected are similar to the data gathered by the American Panel Study of Income Dynamics and the German Socioeconomic Panel.

Our analysis used the BHPS data from the period 1991 to 1998. According to those data, 80 percent of respondents ages 35 to 54 were owner-occupiers, and another 15 percent were public tenants. Life table estimates suggest that the median age of the transition to home ownership is 25 for women and 27 for men.[7]

Using survey data versus retrospective data presented certain difficulties for us in analyzing first entry to owner occupation. There is the initial-conditions problem, the left censoring caused by the lack of information on housing history and exogenous variables before the survey was first taken. The data we were using were drawn from eight waves of the survey, at eight annual observation points approximately between late 1991 and late 1998. In our case, we did not know if the non–homeowners in any wave had ever owned a home. Remember, we were looking for information on first-time homeowners. We minimized this problem by restricting our working sample to individuals who were ages 16 to 24 the first time they appear in the data. We know that this was not a perfect solution—11 percent of this population already owned a home when they were first observed. It was a compromise between being more certain about having the proper risk set and losing too many observed entries.

Still, the panel data do have advantages over retrospective data. They do not suffer from recall problems, and they include rich information on demographic, social, and economic variables that vary over time.

Housing tenure is a concept that attaches to the dwelling in which a household lives; it is therefore a household-level concept. For our purposes, it was not adequate to simply map this variable to individuals. We were interested in the acquisition of home ownership, which is different from living in a house that is owned. In particular, we did not want to consider individuals living with their parents in their parents' house to be owner-occupiers; nor did we want to include lodgers, people renting a room in an owner-occupied house. To deal with this, we defined a category we called *dependent residence*, in which one or both of the individual's parents are members of the household (subcategory: with parents), or the individual's relationship to the homeowner is other than self or spouse/partner (subcategory: other dependent). Although this may be inaccurate as a general treatment—in a multigenerational household, for example, the adult child, not the elderly parents, may be the homeowner—we felt it was acceptable in this case because we wanted to observe the movement of young people into independent ownership. In our sample of individuals under age 25 at their first observation, 65 percent were living with their parents at first observation, and another 5 percent were otherwise dependent.

The restrictions discussed above reduced the sample considerably from the full BHPS sample of more than 10,000 individuals. A further restriction—that we needed to observe individuals in at least two consecutive waves—reduced the numbers more. When we limited our sample to individuals under 25 when first observed, who did not own a home when first observed and whom we could observe for at least two consecutive waves, we were left with just 2,376 individuals, a total of 8,827 person-years.

FIRST RESULTS

We began with a preliminary analysis. Table 10.1 shows the effect on entry to owner occupation of four variables. The first was housing tenure in the previous year. We found the highest percentage of new owners among those

TABLE 10.1
Entry to owner occupation by tenure, partnership change,
marital status, and education in the previous year,
Great Britain, 1991–1998

Variable	Annual rate of entry	Percentage of entries	N
Housing tenure in the previous year			
Public housing	4.1	8.8	1,078
Private rental	11.1	33.7	1,519
With parents	4.3	50.4	5,922
Other dependent	11.7	7.2	308
AVERAGE/TOTAL	5.7	100.0	8,827
Partnership change during the year			
Married	56.3	13.4	119
Cohabited	11.1	39.5	473
Partnership dissolved	4.6	1.4	154
Stayed partnered	13.0	32.5	1,254
Stayed single	1.1	15.5	6,827
AVERAGE/TOTAL	5.7	100.0	8,827
Marital status in previous year			
Married	9.6	11.8	614
Cohabiting	14.0	22.1	794
Divorced	1.5	0.2	66
Separated	6.7	0.8	60
Never married	4.5	65.1	7,293
AVERAGE/TOTAL	5.7	100.0	8,827
Highest educational attainment in previous year			
O-level and below	3.8	38.0	4,810
A-level and nursing	6.3	27.7	2,129
Above A-level	10.6	34.3	1,561
AVERAGE/TOTAL	5.7	100.0	8,500

SOURCE: Authors' calculations based on the BHPS, waves 1–8.

NOTE: Totals may not sum to 100.0 because of rounding.

who were in private rental housing in the previous year (11.1 percent) or among the other-dependent group, those who lived as part of another household other than one headed by a parent (11.7 percent). Despite the relatively low rate of entry among those living with their parents (4.3 percent), the strong representation of these individuals in the risk set meant that 50.4 percent of first moves into owner occupation were directly from the parents' home. Our finding was consistent with Di Salvo and Ermisch's (1997) finding, based on retrospective data, that 55 percent of first entries to a major tenure (home ownership or public-sector rental) coincided with a first move from the parental home. If we had conditioned our analysis on people's living independently of their parents in the preceding year, we would have missed half of the entries to home ownership.

The second variable we examined was change in partnership status over the same period. We found the highest rate of entry (56.3 percent) among those who had married during the previous year (see Table 10.1). Although only a small number of respondents formed partnerships during the year —marrying or entering a cohabiting union—they accounted for one-half of the first movements into home ownership. Thus, partnership formation often coincides with buying a first home. Close to a third of first home purchases (32.5 percent) were made by those who were already partnered (either married or cohabiting) in the previous year and remained so. If we had limited our analysis to respondents who had a partner in the previous year, we would only have accounted for 35 percent of the first entries to home ownership.

The third variable was marital status in the previous year. Table 10.1 shows that those in cohabiting unions had the highest rate of entry to owner occupation. Although the entry rate was quite low for those who had never been married, this group contributed 65.1 percent of the observed entries because of its large representation in the population at risk. Of course, as our data on partnership change suggest, many of these entries accompanied movement into a partnership during the same year.

The fourth variable was respondents' highest educational attainment in the previous year. As shown in Table 10.1, the likelihood of becoming an owner-occupier in any given year increased with educational level. Actually, to the extent that some of these young people had not completed their education, our findings may understate the gradient with respect to final educational attainment, a factor that is strongly related to lifetime income prospects.

Our preliminary analysis showed effects for a number of other variables too. For example, we found that the rate of entry to owner occupation was much higher if a woman or her partner held a job in the previous year, and that among those with jobs, the average monthly pay of women who became owners during the year was higher than that of women who did not buy a first home. Among women with partners, the average monthly pay of their partner was also higher for those who became owner-occupiers.

Of particular interest here is the influence of social class on the likelihood of becoming a homeowner. The class definitions we used were taken from the Office for National Statistics Socio-Economic Classification (ONS-SEC; see, for instance, Rose and O'Reilly 1998). That classification was recently adopted for official purposes by the British government and is strongly and explicitly influenced by the Goldthorpe class scheme (Erikson and Goldthorpe 1992). It assigns people to categories on the basis of their current or last occupation, with special treatment of the never employed and the long-term unemployed. It differs from conventional class categorizations, then, by giving weight to certain aspects of employment status, but its conceptual base is clearly social class. We chose to use a nine-category version of the system. Table 10.2 gives the person-year distribution in our sample.

From Table 10.3 it is clear that the rate of entry to owner occupation generally increases with social class position: about one in five of the higher professional and managerial group became a homeowner for the first time each year; the rate for those effectively outside the labor market—the people who had never worked or who had been unemployed for more than a year, and full-time students—was less than one-tenth that. More than 50 percent of first-time homeowners were members of the three highest social classes; still, members of the working class (those in supervisory and craft-related occupations and manual laborers) accounted for nearly 30 percent of the observed entries into owner occupation.

MODELING BECOMING A HOMEOWNER

We modeled the probability of becoming a homeowner in a given year conditioned on respondents' never having owned a home before. Because ours was a household sample, it was often the case that a respondent's spouse or

TABLE 10.2
Class distribution (in person-years) by gender, working sample, Great Britain

Description	MEN		WOMEN		TOTAL	
	N	Percentage	N	Percentage	N	Percentage
Higher professional and managerial occupations	200	4.5	127	3.0	327	3.8
Lower professional and managerial occupations	303	6.9	269	6.4	572	6.6
Intermediate occupations	305	6.9	657	15.5	962	11.1
Small employers and self-employed	144	3.3	38	0.9	182	2.1
Supervisory and craft-related occupations	501	11.4	103	2.4	604	7.0
Semiroutine manual occupations	796	18.0	487	11.5	1,283	14.8
Routine manual occupations	205	4.7	250	5.9	455	5.3
Never worked and long-term unemployed[a]	929	21.0	1,224	28.9	2,153	24.9
Full-time students	1,030	23.3	1,084	25.6	2,114	24.4
TOTAL	4,413	100.0	4,239	100.0	8,652	100.0

SOURCE: Authors' calculations based on the BHPS, waves 1–8.

NOTE: The class definitions were taken from the ONS-SEC (see, for example, Rose and O'Reilly 1998).
[a]The long-term unemployed have been unemployed for more than a year.

partner was also in the sample. It was not always the case though: the spouse or partner may not have been present for the interview, or may have been excluded from our sample because he or she was too old, had not been interviewed the previous year, or had owned a home before. People living with a partner do not make two independent contributions to the likelihood of entering owner occupation, so we did not want to include both partners in the analysis. In the case of couples, then, we chose to normalize on one partner: the woman. Our reasoning: because women leave their parents' home earlier than men do (on average, at age 21 versus age 22), they have more time in which to purchase a home by age 24 (given our restriction that individuals had to be under 25 when first observed). So our sample excluded person-years for married or cohabiting males but included person-years for all single persons and for all women in partnerships.

TABLE 10.3
Entry to owner occupation by social class in previous year,
partnered women, Great Britain

Social class in previous year	Annual rate of entry	Percentage of entries	N
Higher professional and managerial occupations	19.3	12.7	327
Lower professional and managerial occupations	12.9	14.9	572
Intermediate occupations	13.8	26.7	962
Small employers and self-employed	8.2	3.0	182
Supervisory and craft-related occupations	8.4	10.2	604
Semiroutine manual occupations	5.4	13.9	1,283
Routine manual occupations	4.8	4.4	455
Never worked and long-term unemployed[a]	1.7	7.4	2,153
Full-time students	1.6	6.8	2,114
AVERAGE/TOTAL	5.8	100.0	8,652

SOURCE: Authors' calculations based on the BHPS, waves 1–8.

[a]The long-term unemployed have been unemployed for more than a year.

When we included partners' characteristics in the model, we dropped the person-years of those without partners. That is, the sample included only married or cohabiting women, and the impact of their individual partner's characteristics were easily interpreted as those of the man in the partnership. In principle, we could have retained single women in this analysis, but the results may have been misleading and hard to interpret, and the increase in sample size would have been illusory. For comparison, we did do an analysis of couples that was based on the male partner.

We measured time-dependent covariates (marital status, for example) in the year previous to the observation, to preserve the possibility of causal interpretation. However, in some circumstances we included markers of change between $t - 1$ and t in recognition of the fact that annual observations are too infrequent to allow adequate observation of causal processes. For instance, if the event of marriage does "cause" home ownership, the period between the cause and the effect is likely to be much less than the year or so that our observational scheme demands. If there is a causal relationship between getting married and buying a first home, and we leave it out of the model (because we cannot distinguish it from a causal relationship in the opposite direction—buying a first home "causes" marriage), then our estimates of the effect of marital status as a state would be biased. For example, suppose that most people get married and within a short period buy a first home. If people are already married when we observe them but do not own a home (a condition of our study), then some other factor must be at work that makes them less likely to buy a home. (Symmetrically, people who do move soon after marriage are more likely to have been single in the previous year.)

The models we estimated were discrete-time transition-rate models. The resulting log-likelihood function was identical to that of a binary logit model (see Allison 1982, 74–75). The transition rate to home ownership (conditional on never having been an owner-occupier at $t - 1$) for person j, p_{jt}, was assumed to take the form $\log[p_{jt}/(1 - p_{jt})] = \beta X_{jt-1}$, where X_{jt-1} is a vector of explanatory variables measured at $t - 1$ (or earlier), or as a change between $t - 1$ and t. It includes the person's age, which was the duration variable in this analysis. β is a vector of parameters to be estimated. Some of the observations came from spells in progress at the beginning of the panel (1991). The contribution to the likelihood function of such observations, therefore, must condition on the respondent's never having been an owner-occupier up to the time the panel started. Jenkins (1995) shows that because terms are canceled in the conditional-survivor probability, their likelihood contribution depends only on transition rates and data for the years since the beginning of the panel, provided the total elapsed spell duration is an element of X_{jt-1}.[8] In this application, spell duration is the age of the person.

One note: if there is unmeasured person-specific heterogeneity (for example, preferences favoring owner occupation), this convenient canceling in the likelihood does not occur. In general, the distribution of the unobservable that shifts the transition rate differs between the persons whose spell was in progress in 1991 and those who started their spell between 1991 and 1998. The model assumes that there is no residual heterogeneity.

The first set of models is reported in Table 10.4. Model 1, the simplest model, contains only the social-class variable along with the person's age (and its square) and gender, and interactions between the two. The age and gender coefficients imply that the rate of entry to owner occupation peaks at

TABLE 10.4

Modeling the hazard of entry to owner occupation,
all women and single men, Great Britain

Variables	MODEL 1		MODEL 2		MODEL 3		MODEL 4	
	β	pᵃ	β	pᵃ	β	pᵃ	β	pᵃ
Gender female	4.01	0	1.39	0.239	1.26	0.319	-1.04	0.187
Age								
Linear	1.95	0	1.20	0	1.19	0	0.02	0.167
Squared	-0.04	0	-0.02	0.001	-0.02	0.001		
By female	-0.14	0.001	-0.04	0.405	-0.03	0.536		
Social class								
Higher professional and managerial occupations			Ref.					
Lower professional and managerial occupations	-0.28	0.205	-0.72	0.022	-0.62	0.062	-1.92	0.026
Intermediate occupations	-0.03	0.870	-0.55	0.044	-0.43	0.173	-0.92	0.211
Small employers and self-employed	0.56	0.126	-0.80	0.113	-0.30	0.619	-1.66	0.195
Supervisory and craft-related occupations	-0.27	0.238	-0.59	0.068	-0.62	0.075	-2.57	0.083
Semiroutine manual occupations	-0.79	0	-1.34	0	-1.11	0.001	-2.46	0.015
Routine manual occupations	-1.03	0	-1.62	0	-1.33	0.001	-1.53	0.116
Never worked and long-term unemployed[b]	-1.98	0	-2.48	0	-1.78	0	-2.64	0.032
Full-time students	-1.53	0	-2.02	0	-1.47	0.004	-2.27	0.115
Change in social-class position								
Upward			1.09	0	0.79	0.007	0.73	0.376
No change			0.95	0	0.78	0.001	0.30	0.635
Downward			Ref.					

Marital status						
Married or cohabiting	Ref.					
Single, divorced, widowed, or separated	-2.80	0	-2.74	0		
Change in marital status						
No change	Ref.					
De-partners	-0.93	0.051	-0.8	0.098	-0.73	0.319
Marries	4.50	0	4.52	0		
Starts cohabiting	3.92	0	3.89	0		
Any kids at $t-1$	-1.20	0	-1.12	0	-0.81	0.123
Acquires kids at $t-1$ to t	-0.29	0.286	-0.11	0.701	-0.22	0.767
Educational level						
High			Ref.			
Medium			0.33	0.058	0.68	0.156
Low			0.03	0.860	-0.39	0.411
Employment status						
Employed			Ref.			
Unemployed			-0.82	0.063	-0.52	0.682
Other			-0.28	0.286	-0.11	0.866
Monthly gross income						
Own			0.47	0.136	0.14	0.844
Partner's					0.50	0.208
Partner's social class						
Higher professional and managerial occupations					Ref.	
Lower professional and managerial occupations					0.09	0.899
Intermediate occupations					-1.42	0.042

(continued)

TABLE 10.4
(Continued)

Variables	MODEL 1		MODEL 2		MODEL 3		MODEL 4	
	β	p^a	β	p^a	β	p^a	β	p^a
Partner's social class (continued)								
Small employers and self-employed							-2.02	0.025
Supervisory and craft-related occupations							-0.50	0.527
Semiroutine manual occupations							-0.48	0.535
Routine manual occupations							-2.36	0.048
Never worked and long-term unemployed[b]							-1.48	0.133
Full-time students							0.59	0.548
Father's social class								
Professional and managerial occupations			Ref.					
Intermediate occupations							-1.00	0.081
Self-employed							0.54	0.279
Supervisory and craft-related occupations							-0.27	0.641
Manual laborers							-0.02	0.971
N	8,111		8,111		7,840		528	
df used	12		20		25		33	
Log-likelihood	-1,405.2887		-938.626		-892.858		-137.867	

SOURCE: Authors' calculations based on the BHPS, waves 1–8.

[a]Significance based on robust Huber/White sandwich standard errors.
[b]The long-term unemployed have been unemployed for more than a year.

age 24 for men without partners and at age 23 for women. At all ages below 28, women are more likely to become owners than are men without a partner. At any given age, manual laborers, those outside the workforce, and full-time students are much less likely to become homeowners than are members of other classes. For example, the transition rate is about 85 percent lower than the reference category for those who have never worked and the long-term unemployed, the most extreme category. By way of illustration, according to this model, the median age of new homeowners among women who were students until age 22 and then went into higher professional and managerial occupations was about 24, and 81 percent of these women became owners before their twenty-ninth birthday. In contrast, for women in routine manual occupations at all ages (16 to 28), only 56 percent became homeowners before their twenty-ninth birthday.

In light of the fact that women enter partnerships earlier than men and the strong association between partnership formation and first-house purchase indicated in Table 10.1, the gender differences in the age pattern of house purchase could mainly reflect the gender difference in partnership formation. Furthermore, people from working-class occupations also tend to form partnerships earlier.

The second model is somewhat richer, bringing in marital status and children. It also allows for change between $t - 1$ and t in class position, marital status, and the presence of children on the grounds that the year between surveys is too long to be confident that the state at $t - 1$ is necessarily the causally relevant one. The effect of being in a partnership at $t - 1$ is nonetheless clearly positive. When we considered change in marital status, we found that a partnership breakup has a strong negative effect, but that a new partnership (marriage or cohabitation) has a dramatic effect: people who formed a partnership between $t - 1$ and t were far more likely to buy a first home than were those already married at $t - 1$. The rate for those who married in the previous year was higher than that for those beginning a cohabiting union, but both groups showed very strong effects: partnership formation and house purchase are very closely associated.

We might have speculated that the effect of children would be positive, but this was not the case. Respondents with children at $t - 1$ were 70 percent less likely to move into a first home. Were we to argue that what we were seeing here was largely an effect of the arrival of children, we would also be mistaken: the arrival of a first child in the intersurvey period had no significant effect. Post hoc reasoning leads us to suggest that the association may work in the other direction: young couples who want to buy a home tend to do so before they have children; therefore those who already have children have characteristics that make them less likely to buy. A more direct effect may be that people with children are more likely to be allocated public housing, the main alternative to owner occupation as a largely absorbing destination.

The logic of allowing for change in the class position is that an occupational change large enough to cross a class boundary is likely to have significant consequences for the household's income stream, either negative in the short term (so people postpone large decisions, among them buying a house) or positive. Given the age range of our sample, positive moves were likely to involve either entry into the labor market or career advancement via a new job. When we allowed for such changes—by the admittedly crude means of treating the class categories as a hierarchy and partitioning the transitions into upward, no change, and downward—we found clear evidence of the former effect: dropping down the hierarchy reduces the rate of purchase by about 60 percent. However, there was little difference between those whose social class remained stable and those who moved up.

The addition of this set of variables strongly moderated the effect of gender—a change that may be related to the effect of marriage and the younger age at which women marry. The effect of age was also reduced, but not dramatically. On the whole, the effect of class at $t - 1$ was increased: members of every other category were less likely to buy a first home than were members of the higher professional and managerial group.

The third model introduced variables that might be thought to relate to individuals' ability to make an investment in a home: education, employment status, and current gross pay. Education showed a very weak effect that at first glance was surprising: those with medium-level education (defined as A-level or equivalent) were more likely to buy a first home than were those with higher-level education.[9] On reflection, this effect must be seen in the context of the age of our sample (16 to 31, with the mean a little above age 21): those with higher qualifications would have had relatively little time to convert them into labor market advantage. It is also possible that the extent to which education is a proxy for economic status is overwhelmed by the effect of occupation inherent in the class variable.

Unemployment also had a negative effect, but again not a particularly strong one. This may be the result of overlap with the long-term unemployed component of the class variable and collinearity with own income, the effect of which is positive but insignificant.

On the grounds that the class variable may have its effect through factors like these, we wanted to see to what extent class weakened in this model. We found that it did not change very dramatically. Parameter estimates fell for the never worked and long-term unemployed and for students; but the overall pattern was little affected. Manual laborers and those outside the workforce clearly were less likely to buy a first home, even taking the other factors into account. It appears that longer-term labor market position has a stronger impact on the decision to buy a home than do short-term considerations like current pay and employment status. This could be because the pattern and stability of earnings over the life course are important bases for decision making here.

The final model in Table 10.4 brings in information on partner and class of origin. Because partner information required that the respondent be married or cohabiting, and that her partner be in the sample, and because information on class of origin (that is, father's class) was collected only in 1991 and 1998, we lost a very high proportion of our cases, which in turn led to significance falling. However, we did find that having a partner in an intermediate occupation, self-employed, or doing routine manual work significantly reduced the rate of house purchase. The partner's pay was not significant. Class of origin (based on a simplified version of the classification scheme, one that uses occupation only) had one marginally significant effect: people whose father worked at an intermediate occupation were less likely to buy a first home than were those whose father was a professional or manager.

We reworked this model for the sample with partners, men and women separately, dropping the class-of-origin variable. Our findings are shown in Table 10.5. We anticipated an asymmetry in the effect of class and economic characteristics: to the extent that men on average have better positions, we expected to see weaker partner effects in the male sample.[10] Although that generally appeared to be the case, few of the effects were significant. Two effects that were significant were also puzzling: the man's being a student had a positive effect in the male sample; and moving upward in class position had

TABLE 10.5
The effects of partners' characteristics, men and women, Great Britain

Variable	MEN		WOMEN	
	β	p^a	β	p^a
Intercept gender female	−13.60	0.300	10.43	0.104
Age				
Linear	0.95	0.375	−0.91	0.097
Squared by female	−0.02	0.376	0.02	0.115
Social class				
Higher professional and managerial occupations		Ref.		
Lower professional and managerial occupations	0.15	0.814	−1.67	0.014
Intermediate occupations	0.38	0.587	−0.67	0.273
Small employers and self-employed	0.16	0.868	−0.55	0.662
Supervisory and craft-related occupations	0.95	0.210	−1.28	0.220
Semiroutine manual occupations	0.54	0.442	−1.54	0.050
Routine manual occupations	1.02	0.263	−0.87	0.261
Never worked and long-term unemployed	1.57	0.156	−1.65	0.089
Full-time students	2.21	0.075	−1.82	0.143
Change in social-class position				
Upward	−1.43	0.042	0.52	0.364
No change	−0.45	0.388	0.54	0.248
Downward		Ref.		
Change in marital status				
No change		Ref.		
De-partners	−0.69	0.206		
Any kids at $t − 1$	−0.54	0.220	−0.62	0.110
Acquires kids at $t − 1$ to t	−0.58	0.464	−0.28	0.618
Educational level				
High		Ref.		
Medium	−0.28	0.525	0.53	0.167
Low	−0.02	0.961	−0.27	0.498

TABLE 10.5
(*Continued*)

Variable	MEN		WOMEN	
	β	p^a	β	p^a
Employment status				
Employed		Ref.		
Unemployed	−2.85	0.007	−0.11	0.894
Other	−1.89	0.119	−0.27	0.616
Monthly gross income				
Own	1.21	0.012	0.72	0.269
Partner's	1.31	0.065	0.61	0.065
Partner's social class				
Higher professional and managerial occupations		Ref.		
Lower professional and managerial occupations	−0.14	0.831	−0.28	0.66
Intermediate occupations	−0.33	0.584	−1.03	0.101
Small employers and self-employed	−1.36	0.064		
Supervisory and craft-related occupations	−0.66	0.572	−0.70	0.286
Semiroutine manual occupations	−0.71	0.292	−0.73	0.267
Routine manual occupations	−1.01	0.292	−1.36	0.113
Never worked and long-term unemployed[b]	−1.49	0.274	−1.49	0.075
Full-time students	0.14	0.906	−0.01	0.988
N	322		768	
df used	27		29	
Log-likelihood	−121.63		−210.37	

SOURCE: Authors' calculations based on the BHPS, waves 1–8.

[a]Significance based on robust Huber/White sandwich standard errors.
[b]The long-term unemployed have been unemployed for more than a year.

a significant negative effect. Partner's pay also had a positive effect on the male sample, as did own pay, and both effects were of similar size. Being partnered with a woman who was self-employed had a negative effect. It may well be that in this age range, self-employment is less likely to be associated with significant commercial assets than with a more precarious labor market position.

For partnered women, we saw significant negative effects for own class among lower-level professionals and managers, semiroutine manual workers, and those outside the workforce. Having children had a marginally significant negative effect, and partner's working at an intermediate occupation or routine manual labor, or being outside the workforce, had a negative effect. Both own and partner's pay had positive effects.

We did find that partnered people were more likely to become homeowners; but these models were hampered by the small size of the sample. Again, we were looking at a subsample that was reduced even more by the loss of individuals whose partner was not in the sample. Also, the really strong effect of being partnered is temporally local to the time the partnership forms, which means it had decayed for most of the people in this subsample.

PUBLIC HOUSING AS AN ALTERNATIVE DESTINATION

Class effects on housing tenure reflect different economic advantages across class categories; and, as mentioned earlier, home ownership seems to be strongly associated with other forms of asset accumulation. However, the institutional context also must be taken into account. The main competitor to owner occupation as a long-term tenure is public housing, and here the factors that affect inflow are administrative and, in many respects, the reverse of those that affect entry to owner occupation. Low income, poor occupational position, unemployment, and the presence of children all have negative effects on the decision to buy a house; it makes sense, then, that they should have positive effects on the decision to move into public housing.

To explore this thesis, we reconstructed the sample with public housing as the destination instead of owner occupation, and refitted models analogous to models 1 and 3 in Table 10.4. The gender and age effects were broadly similar to those we observed for owner occupation, and the class effects, as expected, were reversed. Practically all groups were significantly more likely than higher professionals and managers to move into public housing, with those who had never worked or who had been unemployed for more than one year and the less skilled manual classes leading the way. With the exception of the reference category, students had the lowest rate of entry to public housing. The fuller specification of model 2 reduced the class effect, but we still saw strong positive effects for those who had never worked and the long-term unemployed and less-skilled manual workers. But change in social-class position, which had a significant positive effect in the owner-occupation model (see Table 10.4), had no effect here. Marital status had a similar effect: forming a partnership or being in a partnership had a large positive effect. In this respect, public housing is like owner occupation in that it represents a stable, long-term tenure. It is diametrically unlike owner occupation in the effect of children: having children at $t - 1$ or acquiring them by t increases the transition into public housing very substantially. In fact, this is so large an effect—remember that families with children are given priority in the allocation of public housing—that we can assume it was responsible for much of the negative effect in the owner-occupation models.

Finally, although we did not find an effect for education, we did see a positive effect for unemployment. Unemployment, then, is associated not only with the lack of financial resources to buy a house but also with greater access to public housing.

CONCLUSION

There are several different types of housing tenure in Great Britain; the most important—and the most stable—are owner occupation and renting in the public sector. Access to home ownership depends on the household's economic resources, its assets and its prospects of a good and steady income stream. In the absence of those resources, the working class and people outside the workforce are clearly less likely to buy; and, with the exception of students, they also are more likely to enter public housing.

The economics of buying or renting a home is important; but other factors also enter the tenure decision. Individual and family life cycle has a very important influence on the extent to which the stability of tenure is important. People who are single and students have different needs from couples, and the flexibility of a private rental or of continuing to live in the parental home is more likely to meet those needs in the short term. Acquiring a partner or, in the case of public housing, a child changes the individual's needs, and with them the likelihood of entry into a more stable tenure.

In the discussion of our analyses, we described the problem we had drawing causal inferences from data collected simultaneously with the observation of the outcomes. But it is not clear that when the event in question is a process—as forming a partnership and choosing a tenure are—that even continuous observation would help substantially. Here the observed events (a marriage, the completion of a house purchase) are the culmination of processes that have been operating over a long period.

The relevance of class for contemporary societies has been actively challenged in recent years. In fact, Pakulski and Waters (1996) famously declared class was dead several years back. But these arguments seem to be motivated more by an interest (often postmodernist) in identity and lifestyle than in the more traditional concern with life chances; they also seem driven more by speculation than by empirical evidence. When we focus empirically on the determinants of life chances—for example, on the accumulation of assets or on housing tenure, as we did in this study—we find that class still has a strong and clear effect, that it is not simply a proxy for income or education. The individual's structural position within British society, indexed empirically as a function of occupation and employment, continues to influence legitimate expectations about the future in terms of security and access to resources. Those class-structured expectations, in turn, affect life plans not only for the long term but also for the short term—in particular, the decision to commit to a partner or to have a child. Those with social-class and other advantages are likely to have easier access to home ownership, which, in turn, gives them easier access to wealth in the form of housing equity and other assets. And all of it perpetuates the differences among social classes.

In our study, we found that after controlling for current social class, parents' class had little effect on first-time home ownership (see model 4 in Table 10.4). But the United Kingdom has a pattern of intergenerational social mobility that is entirely typical of Western industrial societies (see, for example, Erikson and Goldthorpe 1992), which is to say that there is a reasonably strong association between class of origin and own class. We can assume, then, that parents' social class has at least an indirect effect on home ownership. Moreover, although we did not have the data to confirm our thinking, we would argue that parents have direct influence on their adult children's transition to home ownership through the transmission of parental assets and values. What the analysis makes clear is that the first entry into a stable housing tenure—home ownership or public housing—is most immediately affected by life cycle developments and strongly modulated by current class position.

Notes

1. The study was conducted in 1991, when participants were age 33. Among those who became homeowners, the median age at first purchase was 23. This finding is consistent with evidence from the general population from the British Household Panel Study (BHPS), analyzed by Ermisch and Di Salvo.

2. The rates are based on the authors' calculations from the BHPS. We describe that study in detail below, in the discussion of our data.

3. Still, homeowners are more mobile beyond their local area than are tenants in the public sector.

4. Di Salvo and Ermisch (1997), in their study of people born in 1958, found that 42 percent had been a private tenant at least once before their thirty-third birthday, and that the median time as a private tenant was just over two years.

5. The BHPS data indicate that in each year, about 5 percent of all households that became outright homeowners (without a mortgage) did so primarily through an inheritance.

6. Live-in partnership is also being postponed by young people today, particularly for those just reaching adulthood (Ermisch and Francesconi 2000). The median age at first partnership has risen to about 23 for women and 25 for men, from 21 and 23, respectively, for those born in the 1950s.

7. This was based on the assumption that the age-specific annual movement rate between other housing tenures (treating living with parents as a separate tenure category) and owner occupation represents the first entry rate for people under 28.

8. This convenient canceling result does not carry over to analogous continuous-time transition models (see Lancaster 1990, chap. 8).

9. The parameter for those with lower levels of education was insignificant.

10. This may have been complicated by the fact that we had fewer partnered males in the sample.

References

Allison, Paul D. 1982. Discrete-time methods for the analysis of event histories. *Sociological Methodology*, 61–98.

Banks, James, and Sarah Tanner. 1999. Household saving in the UK. Working paper, Institute for Fiscal Studies, London.

Blossfeld, Hans-Peter, and Goetz Rohwer. 1995. *Techniques of event history modelling*. Mahwah, NJ: Erlbaum.

Di Salvo, Pamela, and John Ermisch. 1997. Analysis of the dynamics of housing tenure choice in Britain. *Journal of Urban Economics* 42:1–17.

Erikson, Richard, and John H. Goldthorpe. 1992. *The constant flux*. Oxford: Clarendon Press.

Ermisch, John. 1991. Housing policy and resource allocation. *Oxford Review of Economic Policy* 7:41–49.

———. 1999. Prices, parents and young people's household formation. *Journal of Urban Economics* 45:47–71.

Ermisch, John, and Pamela Di Salvo. 1996. Surprises and housing tenure decisions in Great Britain. *Journal of Housing Economics* 5:247–273.

———. 1997. The economic determinants of young people's household formation. *Economica* 64:627–44.

Ermisch, John, and Marco Francesconi. 2000. Cohabitation in Great Britain: Not for long, but here to stay. *Journal of the Royal Statistical Society* Series A 163:153–71.

Hills, John. 1991. *Unravelling housing finance: Subsidies, benefits and taxation*. Oxford: University Press.

Jenkins, Stephen P. 1995. Easy estimation methods for discrete time duration models. *Oxford Bulletin of Economics and Statistics* 57:129–38.

Lancaster, Tim. 1990. *The econometric analysis of transition data*. Cambridge: Cambridge University Press.

Pakulski, Jan, and Malcolm Waters. 1996. *The death of class*. London: Sage.

Rose, David, and Karen O'Reilly. 1998. *The ESRC review of government social classifications*. London/Swindon: Economic and Social Research Council/UK Office for National Statistics.

CHAPTER ELEVEN

Home Ownership and Social Inequality in Ireland

Tony Fahey and Bertrand Maître

Although precise data on home ownership in Ireland at the close of the nineteenth century are not available, it is clear that the vast majority of households at the time, both rural and urban, rented their home. One hundred years later, most Irish households own their home, and Ireland has one of the highest rates of home ownership in the developed world. The purpose of this chapter is, first, to describe this revolution in housing tenure and the forces that drove it, and, second, to examine its impact on present-day inequalities in housing wealth and living standards.

THE EVOLUTION OF TENURE PATTERNS

Table 11.1 sets out the evolution of tenure patterns in Ireland over the period for which comprehensive data are available—from 1946 to 2002. The home-ownership rate rose continuously from the 1940s to the 1980s, but plateaued at just under 80 percent in the 1990s. This was in a context where the number of housing units approximately doubled, from 662,600 in 1946 to almost 1.3 million in 2002. A sharp increase in the use of mortgage financing as a way of accessing housing occurred during the 1970s and 1980s. In 1971, just 22 percent of Irish households, about 161,000 in number, had mortgages; by 1991, 41 percent—more than 413,000 households—did so. By 2002, the proportion of households with mortgages remained at 41 percent, but the number had risen to almost 530,000.

What caused home-ownership rates in Ireland to rise steadily over the second half of the twentieth century? Certainly, generic factors like rising

TABLE 11.1
Housing tenure, Ireland, 1946–2002

| | PERCENTAGE OF DWELLINGS | | | | | |
| | Year | | | | | |
Type of tenure	1946	1961	1971	1981	1991	2002
Owner occupied	52.6	59.8	68.8	74.4	79.3	77.4
With mortgage	—	—	22.2[a]	34.2	41.3	41.4
Without mortgage	—	—	46.6[a]	40.2	38.0	36.0
Public rental	42.7[b]	18.4	15.5	12.5	9.7	7.9
Private rental	—	17.2	13.3	10.1	8.0	8.9
Rent-free or missing	4.6	4.7	2.4	3.0	3.0	4.6
TOTAL DWELLINGS (1,000s)	662.6	676.4	726.4	896.1	1,019.7	1,279.6

SOURCES: Population censuses 1946–2002.

NOTE: Columns may not sum to 100.0 percent because of rounding.
[a]Interpolated from the 1973 Household Budget Survey.
[b]Data for 1946 do not distinguish between private and social renting.

income and a growing capacity to save (Chevan 1989) were as important in Ireland as elsewhere. Here, however, we want to concentrate on two broad sets of factors that operated with unusually strong effect in Ireland: public policy measures that promoted or subsidized home ownership, and a system of mortgage financing that made housing credit widely available at low interest rates. Of course, the second set of factors overlaps with the first: public policy shaped the mortgage credit system as a whole, and the government played a direct role, too, by providing loans through a system of local-authority mortgages. Nevertheless, for our purposes it is helpful to treat these two sets of factors separately.

Public Housing Policies

Land Reform and Tenant Purchase

The historical foundation of the state's promotion of home ownership can be traced to the rural land reform program carried out in Ireland under British rule from the 1890s to the 1920s (Fahey 2002). This program transferred ownership of about 85 percent of the agricultural land in Ireland, and the dwelling stock that went with it, from some 19,000 landlords to approximately 400,000 tenant smallholders.[1] Essentially, the tenants bought out the landlords' holdings with the help of heavy subsidies from the British government.[2] The purchase annuities payable by the former tenants were set at a large discount on what they had been paying in rents; the government made up the difference so that landlords received satisfactory compensation for their loss of ownership and rental income. Advances from the Treasury to fund land reform amounted to £101 million in the years before Irish independence (1921), which was well in excess of half the Irish gross national product at the time. The consequence of this reform was that the system of farm rentals disappeared: owner occupation had become the dominant housing tenure in rural Ireland well in advance of World War II.

Another important strand of public policy that promoted owner occupation of housing was a direct outgrowth of the land reform program. It began as a public housing program in rural areas; later it would become an alternative and heavily subsidized route to home ownership for working-class households, both rural and urban. The program crystallized in the first decade of the twentieth century as a means to placate farm laborers for their exclusion from the largesse granted tenant farmers under the land reform program. Every piece of land reform legislation passed in this period was paralleled by the provision of generously subsidized public housing for rural laborers—and eventually the category "rural laborers" would include the entire working class outside the major towns and cities in Ireland (Fahey 2002; Fraser 1996). By World War I, this program had endowed the rural working class with high-quality low-cost public housing and had created a public housing sector that was precociously large for its time (Fraser 1996).

In the 1920s, inspired by the example set by former tenant farmers, rural public housing tenants began to campaign for the right to buy their homes at discounted prices. A government commission set up to inquire into this issue in 1933 enthusiastically recommended the purchase option, and in doing so reflected the ideological significance that had come to be attached to home ownership:

> It appears to us that it is scarcely necessary to argue the advantages of ownership. The history of our country has been one of continuous struggle both on the land and in the town to gain the freedom and security that go with ownership. This we regard as a basic and essential principle in any Christian state that bases social order on justice. In the security that it gives better citizenship is de-

veloped, and men are encouraged to improve their holdings. (Saorstát Éireann 1933, 14)

Arising from the commission's report, a generously subsidized tenant purchase scheme for rural public housing was introduced in 1936, with purchase annuities initially set at 75 percent of prepurchase rents. In the early 1950s, purchase annuities were reduced to 50 percent of rents, imitating the give-away terms farmers had enjoyed since the 1933 Land Act (Walsh 1999). Not surprisingly, by 1964, 80 percent of the housing built under the rural public housing program to date had been sold to sitting tenants (Minister for Local Government 1964, 35).

In large towns and cities, public housing projects had expanded through the slum clearance programs of the 1930s and 1940s. Tenants' demands to be allowed to purchase their home were resisted until the 1950s, when limited purchase options were introduced. The 1966 Housing Act opened the way for a more generous approach by combining the urban and rural local-authority housing programs and by adopting the rural pro-sales philosophy on the question of tenant purchase. Purchase prices set under the new legislation were typically extremely favorable to tenants, and urban workers took full advantage.[3] From the early 1970s onward, older public housing was sold as fast as new public housing was built. By the mid-1990s, more than two-thirds of the public housing stock built over the preceding century had been purchased by tenants (Table 11.2). Moreover, these dwellings accounted for about one in four of owner-occupied units: if they had not been sold—if they were still being rented in 1991, for example—the home-ownership rate that year would have been just 60 percent rather than the 79 percent it actually was.

Grants and Tax Breaks for Private Housing

The state also supports home ownership by offering grants and tax breaks to households buying privately built housing. These provisions tend to be less generous than the subsidies bestowed on individual households through rural land reform programs or sales of local authority housing; but they have affected a larger proportion of house buyers, particularly since the 1960s, when private housing construction began expanding rapidly. These programs are so numerous and complex and have changed so often over time that it is difficult to summarize their character or impact.

TABLE 11.2

Local authority housing construction and sales, Ireland, 1898–1998

Period	Housing built[a]	Housing sold to tenants	Housing owned by local authority at end of period
1898–1963	178,368	74,400	103,900
Urban	91,437	4,400	—
Rural	86,931	70,000	—
1964–1998	151,700	156,600	99,000
TOTAL 1898–1998	330,000	231,000	99,000

SOURCES: Minister for Local Government (1964, 35); and *Annual Housing Statistics Bulletins.*

[a]Includes flats.

Grants for private house building were introduced in the 1920s. The scale of public loans, grants, and public housing expenditures rose to high levels in the 1950s: 97 percent of new dwellings received some form of direct grant aid (Ó hUiginn 1959–1960, 49, 64; Pfretzschner 1965, 37). Since then, housing subsidies have been at moderate levels by European standards (Joumard 2001). The scope of grants has steadily narrowed; today they primarily target first-time buyers of new houses, who also benefit from certain stamp duty exemptions (see below).

In recent decades, as interest and tax rates increased significantly, tax breaks for private homebuyers have become more important than direct grants. In 1988, the National Economic and Social Council (NESC) estimated that of a total of £552 million in public subsidies to housing in 1987, £218 million (almost 40 percent) went to owner-occupiers and £175 million (80 percent) of that took the form of tax relief on expenditures related to the purchase of housing (NESC 1988, 60). The principal forms of tax subsidy in Ireland are widely known in other countries: the state does not tax the imputed rent arising from home ownership; it offers relief for home mortgage interest payments; and it exempts capital gains arising in connection with the sale of the household's principal residence (Joumard 2001).

Imputed rent is the rental value of owner-occupied housing. In the early decades of income taxation, this notional value was added to homeowners' taxable income. However, estimates of imputed rent were generally low, so the tax yielded little revenue and had little impact on home-buying behavior.[4] Taxation on imputed rent from housing was abolished in 1969. The tax burden on residential property was further lightened in 1978, when domestic dwellings were exempted from rates (local property taxes).

Until 1974, all home mortgage interest paid was taxed at marginal rates. That year, the amount of interest allowable was capped (albeit at a high level); still the significance of this subsidy remained large until the late 1980s.[5] Since the late 1980s, the importance of mortgage interest relief as a subsidy has fallen sharply, in part because inflation has eroded the value of allowable interest payments and in part because tax rates have fallen. Furthermore, in the mid-1980s, the tax relief on mortgage interest was reduced from the marginal rate to the standard rate, which is now at 20 percent.

Capital gains from the sale of a principal residence are entirely exempt from taxation. The precise value of this exemption is difficult to estimate: it is greatly influenced by how capital gains are quantified (depending, for example, on whether and how allowances are made for inflation, interest payments, and depreciation) and the rate at which they are taxed. The capital gains tax in Ireland was reduced from 40 percent to 20 percent in 1997, thus halving the implicit benefit arising from the exemption.

Although owner-occupied housing is lightly taxed in most ways, it is subject to one significant form of taxation—a stamp duty on housing transactions that must be paid by the purchaser. Current rates of stamp duty range from zero for properties worth less than €127,000 to 9 percent for properties worth more than €635,000. The average rate is about 4 or 5 percent.[6] First-time homebuyers are exempt from stamp duty for lower-cost housing and receive a 25 percent discount on stamp duty for medium-cost housing. For other homebuyers, the stamp duty, in conjunction with legal fees and other transaction costs, creates a significant disincentive to housing mobility.

Mortgage Financing

The government's direct intervention in the housing market has been an important contributor to the rise of home ownership in Ireland; but a case can be made that since the 1960s, the system of mortgage financing has been equally important. Reliance on mortgage credit to finance new home construction and purchase is high. Of the new homes built for owner occupation between 1988 and 1998, 80 percent carried mortgages in 1998 (Central Statistics Office 2000, 9).

The private mortgage market was for a long time shared by building societies (deposit-taking institutions that have flourished in Ireland since the late nineteenth century) and insurance companies. Mortgages granted by both of these kinds of institutions enjoyed various forms of preferential tax treatment until the 1980s (Commission on Taxation 1982, 167–69, 173–76, 389–90), which encouraged private mortgage financing. Deregulation of the financial markets in the 1980s, however, ended the differential treatment of credit institutions and loans. It also enabled the retail-banking sector to enter the mortgage market. This intensified competition in that market, particularly after the advent of the European Monetary Union (EMU) in 1999 enabled non-Irish lending agencies to enter the market, and contributed to a downward push in interest rates.

The state also played an important role in mortgage lending up to 1987. Under the Small Dwellings Acquisitions Acts, the first of which was enacted in 1899, local authorities were empowered to provide mortgages for private housing.[7] Until 1955, local-authority mortgages were open to all (subject to applicants' meeting lending criteria); they focused increasingly on lower-income households after that date. Before the economic takeoff in the 1960s, local authorities were often the primary source of mortgage financing. In the mid-1970s, they still accounted for nearly half of all new mortgage loans by number and more than a third by value. Even by the mid-1980s, they accounted for more than a quarter of new loans by value. Although the interest rates on these mortgages were at best only marginally more attractive than commercial rates, local authorities offered higher loan-to-value ratios than did commercial lenders (usually up to 95 percent) and took a more flexible approach to eligibility criteria, repayment schedules, and repayment terms. The flexibility of these loans gave low-income households added incentive to buy a home over and above that provided by the sale of local-authority housing. Fiscal retrenchment in 1987 sharply reduced the funds available to local authorities for lending purposes; and by the early 1990s, their share of the mortgage market had fallen below 2 percent.

The mortgage system in Ireland has effectively promoted home ownership because more often than not it has provided borrowers with very low real interest rates. This is as true of commercial mortgages as of local-authority mortgages. As Figure 11.1 shows, inflation reduced real mortgage

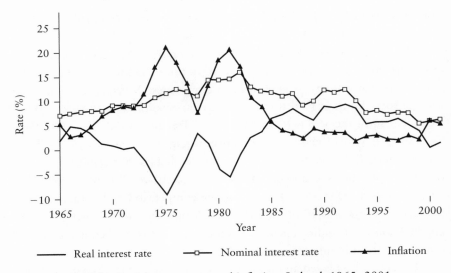

Figure 11.1.   Mortgage interest rates and inflation, Ireland, 1965–2001

SOURCES: NESC (1976, 94); Central Bank of Ireland *Quarterly Bulletin* (various years); and Central Statistics Office (2000).

interest rates in Ireland to low or even negative levels from the late 1960s to the early 1980s and again in the late 1990s. Between 1965 and 2001, real interest rates in Ireland exceeded 5 percent in just one period, from the mid-1980s to the mid-1990s. The impact of the EMU was evident at the end of the 1990s, when real interest rates fell more or less to zero despite the overheated state of the housing market in Ireland at that time (see below). Inflation reached particularly high levels in the mid-1970s and again in the early 1980s, more than compensating for high nominal mortgage interest rates. These bouts of inflation proved a boon to borrowers because they rapidly eroded the real value of outstanding mortgage debt. Between 1978 and 1983, for example, the cumulative increase in the consumer price index (our measure of inflation) was 108 percent, which means that the real value of mortgages held over the period was more than halved. In real terms, then, inflation did more to "clear" mortgages than householders' mortgage payments did.

The losers in this system were depositors, the source of the funds lending agencies were giving out in mortgages, who provided those funds at low or even negative rates of return. When real interest rates dropped very low, deposits would fall off and private mortgage funds would be scarce. As a result, private lenders periodically were forced to ration housing credit. Mortgage funds were particularly scarce in the mid-1970s, when real interest rates plummeted and exchange rate risk inhibited foreign borrowing by private credit agencies. It was during these periods that local-authority mortgages played an important role. Because they were funded by government borrowing, they depended on international capital markets that were less constrained by the level of savings in the Irish economy. This ensured a flow of funds to Irish homebuyers that would not have been available in a wholly private mortgage system. Since the EMU came into being in 1999, interest rates in Ireland and the amount of capital available for lending there have been determined by broader European patterns: they are no longer tied to supply-and-demand factors in the domestic financial market. And with abundant and cheap credit in the private sector, the need for public-sector mortgages has largely disappeared.

In sum, the Irish system of mortgage financing of private housing has undergone continuous change since the mid–twentieth century. But with the exception of a period of moderately high real interest rates from the mid-1980s to the mid-1990s, the system usually has managed to combine low real interest rates with reasonably abundant supplies of funds for lending. It has extended mortgage credit to households well down the income ladder (although not to those at the very bottom of the ladder). In effect, the progressive distribution of interest-rate benefits amounted to a form of hidden subsidy for homebuyers. Although the value of that hidden subsidy is difficult to quantify, it may well have exceeded the value of the grants and tax breaks described above and so should be recognized as another important factor in the high rate of home ownership in Ireland.

Prices, Inflation, and Affordability

Housing assets are often thought of as a hedge against inflation; and in a high-inflation environment, this provides strong motivation for buying a home. But data on house prices in Ireland since 1970 suggest that until the recent economic boom, prices did little more than keep pace with inflation (Figure 11.2). Real house prices rose somewhat in the late 1970s but then fell back slightly; by the late 1980s, they were only marginally higher than they had been in 1970. In consequence, any impression of capital gain that homeowners might have had over this period was largely illusory. After

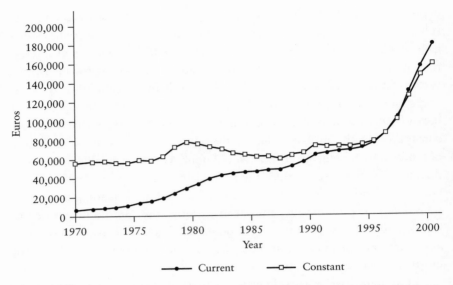

Figure 11.2. Trends in house prices in current and constant (1996) euros, Ireland, 1970–2000

SOURCES: Department of the Environment *Annual Bulletin of Housing Statistics* (various years); and Central Statistics Office (2000).

NOTE: Prices adjusted by the consumer price index. The price series makes no adjustment for quality and includes the prices of both new and second-hand houses.

1994, an unprecedented surge of economic growth, a rise in disposable income (fueled in part by income tax cuts), a fall in interest rates, and a large increase in the size of the young-adult population led to explosive growth in the demand for housing. As a result, the average house price went up 240 percent in nominal terms (204 percent in real terms) between 1995 and 2000.[8] This growth occurred despite the declining significance of mortgage interest tax relief as a form of subsidy and the quite high level of stamp duty on house purchases. It suggests that shifts in tax incentives, which would tend to discourage home buying and the demand for housing, were overridden in this period by broader economic factors that supported home ownership.

Although housing prices exploded in the late 1990s, a combination of falling interest rates and rising after-tax income meant that the affordability of housing—the cost of servicing a typical mortgage as a percentage of disposable income—remained remarkably stable. By 1999–2000, as Figure 11.3 shows, homeowners on average spent a slightly lower share of their total household expenditures on mortgage payments than they had before the 1994–1995 boom in housing prices (see also Bacon and associates 1998; Downey 1998; and McLaughlin 2002, 10–11).[9]

Which Factors are Important?

There are so many possible contributors to the long-term increase in home ownership in Ireland that it is difficult to identify which were the more important. Rural land reform was crucial in the early part of the twentieth century. The growth of local-authority housing and the widespread sale of that housing were a major source of home ownership for working-class households and accounted for about a quarter of all home ownership by the early 1990s. Low real interest rates on mortgages also have been an important factor in recent decades, in effect providing a hidden subsidy to homebuyers.

The impact of other factors on home-ownership patterns is less clear-cut. In the 1950s, grants and tax breaks in Ireland for the construction and sale of private homes were higher than they were in other countries (Ó hUiginn

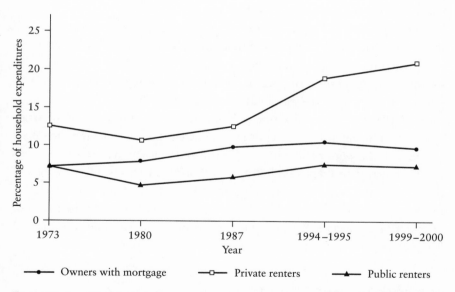

Figure 11.3.   Weekly rent or mortgage payments as a percentage of total housing expenditures, Ireland, 1973–2000

s o u r c e : Authors' calculations based on Household Budget Surveys (1973, 1980, 1987, 1994–1995, 1999–2000).

1959–1960), but they do not seem to have been particularly high since then (Joumard 2001). Even in the Irish case, it is difficult to assess their impact on home-ownership levels. They may have pushed house prices up; and, because they came at the expense of higher tax levels in the economy as a whole, they also may have reduced disposable income. Furthermore, over much of the past four decades, subsidies for home purchase have competed with subsidies for other kinds of saving. Until 1974, for example, interest on all personal borrowing—including but not confined to mortgages—was fully tax-deductible, and contributions to life insurance savings policies remained tax-deductible into the 1980s. Today, contributions to private pensions are tax-deductible to quite high limits and absorb much higher levels of tax expenditures than does mortgage interest relief. Home ownership, then, rarely has had the tax relief field to itself. What all of this means is that the actual support provided by state subsidies for home ownership is complex, difficult to determine, and constantly in flux. In the absence of what would need to be a complex and exhaustive tracking of their effects through time, it is impossible to draw conclusions on what the overall impact of state subsidies on home-ownership levels has been.

The same difficulties arise in trying to determine whether supports for home ownership, taken together, have been on balance regressive or progressive.[10] Certain individual subsidies undoubtedly have been regressive. For example, tax relief for mortgage interest generally is regressive, particularly when it is allowed at the marginal tax rate as was the case in Ireland until the mid-1980s. The subsidization of home ownership through sales of local-authority housing also is regressive to the extent that it benefited the upper segment of the pool of low-income households rather than the lower segment. The same could be said for local-authority mortgages. However, given the number and diversity of subsidies and the constant change in the relative importance of different subsidies, it is difficult to characterize their overall distributional effects. All we can say for certain is that together, they helped bring about the very high levels of home ownership found in Ireland today.

THE ROLE OF INHERITANCE

There has been little systematic research on the role inheritance plays in the level of home ownership in Ireland. Still, the rise in home ownership means that intergenerational transfers likely do have some influence on the distribution of housing wealth. Ireland has an inheritance tax, but it is designed to impose little or no burden on the vast majority of within-family inheritances.[11]

The direct inheritance of a dwelling is likely to be most prevalent in rural areas, given the long history of owner-occupied farms there. For the country as a whole, however, it should be noted that more than 70 percent of the present housing stock has been built since 1960 (Central Statistics Office 2000, 9), limiting the degree to which these houses have yet entered the inheritance cycle. Inheritance patterns are also likely to be affected by the persistence of large families in Ireland into the 1960s. Consider, for example, the cohort born in 1960: 44 percent of the births in this cohort were fourth- or higher-order births (Fahey and Russell 2001). This could mean considerable dispersal of inheritance benefits across adult children or other descendants. A further complication is a by-product of historically low marriage rates in Ireland. More than one in five people over age 65 in the 1990s had never married or had children—an exceptionally high proportion by the standards of other countries (Fahey 1995). These people are likely to leave bequests to nephews, nieces, and other remote relatives, again dispersing the effects of the inheritance.

The pattern of housing development in Ireland over recent decades means that the transfer of buildable land may be as important a form of housing-related transfer for many families as is the bequest of a house. In fact, in instances where a structure is old, the house may have less real value than the site it occupies. Ireland is a sparsely populated country—it has half the land area of England but only 8 percent of the population—and it experienced a long-term population decline until the 1960s. In consequence, it has been possible to sustain low housing density. Only 6 percent of housing units in 1998 were flats or apartments; 43 percent were detached houses; and the balance were semidetached or terraced houses (Central Statistics Office, 2000). The construction of single-family homes dispersed over the rural hinterlands of towns and cities has long been tolerated by planning policy and continues to be common. This phenomenon has been driven in part by the transfer of housing sites on family-owned farmland to other family members.

TABLE 11.3
Household housing wealth by income quintile, Ireland, 2000

Income quintile	Percentage of total standardized income	Percentage owner occupied	MEAN VALUE OF OWNER-OCCUPIED (1,000 EUROS)		Net value as percentage of gross value	Percentage of total housing wealth
			Gross	Net of mortgage debt		
1 (lowest)	7.3	69.6	128.3	124.1	96.7	15.2
2	11.3	80.6	138.2	130.6	94.5	16.1
3	17.0	87.3	169.1	156.0	92.3	19.2
4	23.8	88.7	218.9	198.1	90.5	24.3
5 (highest)	40.7	87.0	244.0	205.7	84.3	25.3

SOURCE: Living in Ireland Survey, 2000.

NOTE: Columns may not sum to 100.0 percent because of rounding.

THE IMPACT OF HOME OWNERSHIP
ON SOCIAL INEQUALITY

The Distribution of Housing Wealth

We begin our assessment of the impact of home ownership on social inequality in Ireland with a look at the distribution of housing wealth. Given the limitations of space, we confine our attention to observations made in the year 2000. For data, we rely on the Living in Ireland (LII) Survey, the Irish version of the European Community Household Panel, with a sample of approximately 4,000 households.[12] The advantage of the LII for the purpose of our analysis is that the survey gathers in-depth information on a range of housing variables, including tenure, the respondent's estimate of market value, and the amount outstanding on any mortgage. It also collects extensive data on income, characteristics of household members, and other aspects of the life in the household.

Obviously, housing wealth is not distributed as equally as income: almost 20 percent of Irish households in 2000 had no housing wealth, while all households had at least some income. But, as Table 11.3 shows, the distribution of housing wealth in 2002 cut across income quintiles: we found high levels of home ownership throughout the income distribution.[13] In the highest quintiles, the proportion of homeowners approached 90 percent; but even the lowest quintile had a rate of almost 70 percent. Furthermore, average housing wealth even in the lowest income quintile was quite high, with a mean net value of €124,100—60 percent of the mean net value of houses in the top income quintile (€205,700). This indicates that inequalities in housing wealth between the bottom and top income levels are reasonably narrow. Furthermore, households in the lowest income quintile had only 7 percent of total disposable income but had 15 percent of net housing wealth. At the other extreme, the households in the highest income quintile had 41 percent of total disposable income but only 25 percent of housing wealth. What these patterns show is that those who are disadvantaged with respect to income are much less disadvantaged with respect to housing wealth, even though they have a somewhat smaller share of housing wealth than they ought to in strict proportional terms. So we can say that the distribution of housing wealth has a certain equalizing effect in that it counters—at least to a degree—social inequalities arising from the distribution of income.

Table 11.4 shows the distribution of housing wealth by the age of the head of household. This table clarifies the patterns in the previous table by

TABLE 11.4
Housing wealth by age of head of household, Ireland, 2000

| Age of head of household | Percentage of total standardized income | Percentage owner occupied | MEAN VALUE OF OWNER-OCCUPIED (1,000 EUROS) | | Net value as percentage of gross value | Percentage of total housing wealth |
			Gross	Net of mortgage debt		
<35	25.4	56.7	164.9	109.3	66.3	14.1
35–44	20.0	86.9	186.3	158.4	85.0	19.4
45–54	21.7	88.0	206.7	189.1	91.5	23.9
55–64	15.0	88.5	175.8	172.2	98.0	16.8
65–74	10.7	95.0	181.2	180.8	99.8	14.7
≥75	7.3	91.1	161.9	160.6	99.2	11.0

SOURCE: Authors' calculations based on the Living in Ireland Survey, 2000.

NOTE: Columns may not sum to 100.0 percent because of rounding.

showing a link between income and housing patterns on the one hand and life cycle stage on the other.[14] Young households (those headed by a person under age 35) have a larger share of income than of housing wealth: 25 percent versus 14 percent. Elderly households are in the opposite situation: those aged 65 to 74 have 11 percent of income and about 15 percent of housing wealth; while those aged 75 and older have 7 percent of income and 11 percent of housing wealth. For households in the intermediate age ranges (ages 35 to 64), there is less divergence between shares of income and of housing wealth; but even in this group there is a slight tendency for the balance to shift toward housing wealth as age increases. Clearly, housing wealth tends to accumulate with age, whereas income does not, at least when it comes to the divide between work and retirement. Here, too, housing wealth tends to counter income inequalities because it is most concentrated in the elderly, who have low incomes, and least concentrated in younger people, who have higher incomes.

We should make mention of the relatively low level of housing wealth among the youngest households in Table 11.4. First, although this group's level of home ownership (57 percent) was high by international standards, it was substantially lower than that of the older age groups in Ireland. Second, the gross value of this group's housing was less than that of all the other age groups bar those 75 and over. This may indicate that a large number of young households buy relatively inexpensive starter homes. Third, younger households had higher levels of mortgage debt on their houses: they owned, on average, only 66 percent of the equity in their homes, compared with virtually 100 percent equity ownership among the elderly. It may seem that 66 percent equity ownership is quite high for young households, which have not had enough time in the housing market to clear a significant portion of their mortgage debt. However, the house price boom between 1995 and 2000 dramatically altered loan-to-value ratios among mortgagees, bestowing on them large windfall gains in equity value.

Housing Expenditures, Income, and Poverty

Housing tenure has important consequences for expenditures on housing and, through those expenditures, on the real value of income. Homeowners who own their house outright need less income to achieve a given standard of consumption than do those with expenditures on mortgage or rent. The precise advantage bestowed by the different tenure categories varies enormously, depending on both current and historical housing prices, mortgage interest rates, inflation, housing subsidies, and rates of return on alternative uses of capital. Even outright homeowners, who in a proximate sense are better off because they do not have to pay mortgage or rent costs, can lose out in the longer term if the capital they invested in their house would have yielded a higher rate of return in some other investment. This is particularly true if the added return would have been sufficient to cover the cost of renting a home and would have left a surplus for higher consumption.

In place of the complex analysis that a full understanding of housing tenure and all these other variables would entail, we adopt a simpler approach that concentrates on the direct, proximate links among housing tenure, housing expenditures, and income levels. The housing-expenditure data relate to mortgage payments in the case of owners and rent payments in the case of tenants. In looking at income levels in this context, the key measure we focus on is the *poverty rate*, the percentage of households that fall below 60 percent of median income.

Table 11.5 shows relevant data for the main tenure groups. Mean housing expenditures were highest in absolute terms for owners of private housing with a mortgage and for private renters (at close to €100 per week in each case). However, as a proportion of household income, these expenditures were much higher for private renters (at 24 percent of household income) than for private mortgagees (15 percent of household income). Outright owners, of course, had zero expenditures (remember that the focus here was solely on mortgages and rents), and renters in the public sector also had relatively low expenditures (less than 9 percent of household income).

The last two columns of Table 11.5 provide one indication of the impact of housing expenditures on living standards by comparing poverty rates before and after deducting mortgage and rent payments from household income. The before-housing poverty rate is the poverty rate as normally calculated; we arrived at the after-housing poverty rate by subtracting mortgage or rent payments from household income and recalculating the 60 percent poverty line and associated poverty rates on the basis of the adjusted income.[15]

Poverty rates before housing expenditures were lowest (at almost 9 percent) for owners of private housing who were paying a mortgage and much the highest (at 66 percent) for renters of public housing. The poverty rate for renters in the public sector was high both before and after adjusting for

TABLE 11.5

Housing expenditures (mortgage payments or rent)
and poverty rates by tenure, Ireland, 2000

Type of tenure	Mean housing expenditure (euros per week)	Housing expenditure as percentage of household income[a]	POVERTY RATE[b]	
			Before housing expenditure	After housing expenditure
Owns private housing				
Without mortgage	0.0	0.0	33.0	28.9
With mortgage	101.7	15.1	8.7	10.8
Owns former public housing				
Without mortgage	0.0	0.0	34.9	29.4
With mortgage	52.7	13.1	25.1	27.1
Rents				
Private housing	97.2	24.2	20.3	30.4
Public housing	21.7	8.7	66.3	66.2
AVERAGE OF ALL HOUSEHOLDS	44.6	8.1	26.1	25.7

SOURCE: Living in Ireland Survey, 2000.

[a]The denominator is total household income (not standardized).
[b]Percent below 60 percent of median income.

rents. For the other categories, however, subtracting mortgage or rent payments reduced the differential in poverty rates among groups to some extent. As we expect, the greatest impact was on private renters because housing expenditures account for such a large share of their income: their poverty rate went up from 20 percent to 30 percent. Among outright owners (of both private and what was formerly public housing), having no housing expenditures improved their relative position somewhat: for both groups, the rate dropped 4 or 5 percentage points, to around 29 percent. In both groups of mortgagees, we found a small worsening in poverty rate, on the order of 2 percentage points.

Table 11.6 shows similar comparisons between a selection of households from each tenure category and at different ages. These comparisons again show a modest narrowing of poverty differentials among the categories when housing expenditures were taken into account.

The analysis of housing costs, household income, and poverty rates confirms the point made earlier: that housing tends to moderate inequalities that arise from income distribution. Outright ownership reduces household expenditures and so increases the percentage of income available for nonhousing consumption. But this tenure is particularly prevalent among the elderly, who generally have low incomes. Private renting is at the other extreme, in that high rent-to-income ratios worsen the financial situation of many renting households—even though average income levels among households in this category are not particularly low.[16] Other tenure categories fall somewhere in between.

CONCLUSION

Ireland made a transition during the twentieth century from a society of renters to a society of homeowners, and it now has one of the highest rates of home ownership in the developed world. That position can be traced back in the first instance to agrarian land reform that began in the 1890s. This program, which subsidized the purchase of farms by tenant farmers, had the

TABLE 11.6

Income levels, poverty rates, and housing expenditures (mortgage payments or rent) by housing tenure and age of head of household, Ireland, 2000

Type of tenure and age	Mean housing expenditure (euros per week)	Housing expenditure as percentage of household income[a]	POVERTY RATE[b]	
			Before housing expenditure	After housing expenditure
Outright owner				
44–55	0.0	0.0	23.4	21.4
>65	0.0	0.0	46.5	40.0
Owner with mortgage, 35–44	91.2	16.2	15.4	18.3
Private renter, <35	106.6	25.8	15.7	26.4

SOURCE: Authors' calculations based on Living in Ireland Survey, 2000.

[a]The denominator is total household income (not standardized).
[b]Percent below 60 percent of median income.

direct effect of making owner occupation the dominant tenure in rural Ire-land before World War II; it had equally important indirect effects in both the early promotion of public housing and the subsequent conversion of that housing into owner-occupied homes for working-class households.

Ireland has deployed a full range of state subsidies to promote home ownership, including a complex and ever-shifting array of grants and tax breaks. It seems obvious that these policies have encouraged households to buy homes. But given market distortions and the unpredictable effects of-ten produced by subsidies, their actual impact on home ownership is hard to calculate and may on balance have been less than is usually assumed. It is possible, although difficult to establish, that the accessibility and low cost of mortgage credit in Ireland had a greater impact than direct state subsi-dies did in promoting home ownership. Intermittent periods of high infla-tion were particularly important in this regard: inflation eroded the value of mortgage debt and kept real interest rates very low, conferring a hidden subsidy on mortgage borrowers. When low interest rates made mortgage funds scarce in the private market, local-authority mortgages, which were funded by government borrowing, filled much of the gap, widening access to mortgage credit among low-income households. This meant that the benefits of low interest rates and the debt-reducing effects of inflation were widely shared.

The present-day distribution of housing wealth indicates that high levels of home ownership in Ireland tend to moderate income inequalities. Low-income households, on average, have a considerable amount of housing wealth, and are less disadvantaged in terms of that wealth than they are in terms of income. Conversely, high-income households have less of an ad-vantage in housing wealth than their pro rata income position would lead us to expect. This equalizing impact of home ownership is in part a life cycle effect: elderly households tend to have low income but a large holding of housing assets, while younger households tend to have higher income but fewer housing assets.

Home ownership also has implications for housing expenditures, most obviously in that outright homeowners pay neither rent nor mortgage and so need less income to achieve a given standard of living than do tenants or mortgagees. It seems that the equalizing effect of home ownership extends, at least to a degree, to living standards. We cannot characterize that effect as extremely strong, but it is significant enough to be taken seriously in analyses of social inequalities in Ireland.

Many larger questions about the significance of home ownership in Ireland have yet to be answered. What difference does the high level of home ownership make to Irish society? Has it helped or harmed Ireland's economic performance in the long run? Has it made Ireland more stable politically? Has it made society there more cohesive? More conscious of family? Happier? Is it the best—or even a good—way for households to build economic security over the life course? Some authors attribute powerful effects to home ownership in these and many other areas; but the social sciences have yet to provide robust answers to these questions.[17] Only in recent decades has housing tenure become the subject of social science research: data before the 1950s are rare. It is well, then, to be skeptical about the many supposed benefits of home ownership until research reveals the reality of its economic, political, and social impact.

Notes

1. The precise number of landlords and tenants varied each year, but the numbers of both were in steady decline over the period.

2. The government's objective was to defuse Irish nationalist antipathy to the union with Britain by yielding to popular demands on the land question—a strategy of "killing home rule with kindness." For an overview, see Bull (1996).

3. One program implemented by the Dublin Corporation in the late 1980s, for example, entailed discounts on the market value of housing of up to 60 percent (Lord Mayor's Commission on Housing 1993).

4. The tax yield from this source in 1961 was estimated at £325,000, about 1 percent of the total yield from income taxes that year (Kaim-Caudle 1965; see also Commission on Taxation 1982, 133–34; and NESC 1976, 40).

5. For a brief overview of the complex history of these reliefs, see Commission on Taxation (1982, 173–76).

6. In 2002, the average house price in Ireland was €180,000 (see below).

7. The funds came from state-backed borrowing.

8. The nominal increase was from €76,000 to €180,000.

9. The figure also shows that the people who suffered from housing shortages and the rising cost of house prices in this period were those who rented their home in the private sector.

10. For discussions on this topic, see NESC (1976, 1988); and Drudy and Punch (2001).

11. Thus, for example, bequests to children are tax-exempt up to a bequest value of €381,000.

12. We used unpublished microdata from the survey here. For a full description, see Callan et al. (1996).

13. The equivalence scale used here to standardize income across households of different sizes and structure was 1 for the first adult, 0.66 for each subsequent adult, and 0.33 for each child (under age 14).

14. For further analysis of this issue, see Fahey (2003).

15. For a discussion of the validity of this procedure, see Fahey, Nolan, and Maître (2004).

16. This may explain in part why just 9 percent of the population in Ireland rent in the private sector.

17. See, for example, Saunders (1990).

References

Bacon, Peter, and associates. 1998. *An economic assessment of recent house price developments*. Report submitted to the Minister for Housing and Urban Renewal. Dublin: Stationery Office.

Bull, Philip. 1996. *Land, politics and nationalism: A study of the Irish land question*. Dublin: Gill and Macmillan.

Callan, T., et al. 1996. *Monitoring poverty trends: Data from the 1997 Living in Ireland Survey*. Dublin: Stationery Office/Combat Poverty Agency.

Chevan, Andrew. 1989. The growth of home ownership: 1940–1980. *Demography* 26 (2): 249–65.

Central Statistics Office (CSO). 2000. *Quarterly National Household Survey: Housing and households, 3rd quarter 1998*. Release 12. Dublin.

Commission on Taxation. 1982. *First report of the Commission on Taxation: Direct taxation*. PL 617. Dublin: Stationery Office.

Downey, Daithi. 1998. *New realities in Irish housing. A study on housing affordability and the economy*. Dublin: Consultancy and Research Unit for the Built Environment, Dublin Institute of Technology.

Drudy, P. J., and Michael Punch. 2001. Housing and social inequality in Ireland. In *Rich and poor. Perspectives on tackling inequality in Ireland*, edited by S. Cantillon, C. Corrigan, P. Kirby, and J. O'Flynn. Dublin: Oak Tree Press.

Fahey, Tony. 1995. *Health and social care implications of population ageing in Ireland, 1991–2011*. Dublin: National Council for the Elderly.

———. 2002. The family economy in the development of welfare regimes: A case study. *European Sociological Review* 18:1.

———. 2003. Is there a trade-off between pensions and home ownership? An exploration of the Irish case. *Journal of European Social Policy* 13:2.

Fahey, Tony, Brian Nolan, and Bertrand Maître. 2004. Housing expenditures and income poverty in EU countries. *Journal of Social Policy* 33:3.

Fahey, Tony, and Helen Russell. 2001. *Family formation in Ireland. Trends, data needs and implications*. Policy Research Series Paper 43. Dublin: Economic and Social Research Institute.

Fraser, M. 1996. *John Bull's other homes. State housing and British policy in Ireland, 1883–1922*. Liverpool: Liverpool University Press.

Joumard, Isabelle. 2001. *Tax systems in European Union countries*. OECD Economics Department Working Papers 301. Paris: Organisation for Economic Co-operation and Development.

Kaim-Caudle, Peter R. 1965. *Housing in Ireland: Some economic aspects*. Paper 28. Dublin: Economic and Social Research Institute.

Lord Mayor's Commission on Housing. 1993. *Report*. Dublin: Dublin Corporation.

McLaughlin, Daniel. 2002. Affordability. *Irish Property Review*, January.

Minister for Local Government. 1964. *Review and report on progress (housing)*. Dublin: Stationery Office.

National Economic and Social Council (NESC). 1976. *Report on housing subsidies*. Dublin.

———. 1998. *A review of housing policy*. Dublin.

Ó hUiginn, Padraig. 1959–1960. Some social and economic aspects of housing—an international comparison. *Journal of the Statistical and Social Inquiry Society of Ireland*, vol. 20, pt. 3.

Pfretzschner, Paul A. 1965. *The dynamics of Irish housing*. Dublin: Institute of Public Administration.

Saorstát Éireann. 1933. *Final report of the Commission of Inquiry into the Sale of Cottages and Plots Provided under the Labourers (Ireland) Acts*. Dublin: Stationery Office.

Saunders. 1990. *A nation of home owners*. London: Unwin Hyman.

Walsh, Anne-Marie. 1999. Root them in the land: Cottage schemes for agricultural labourers. In *Ireland in the 1930s*, edited by Joost Augusteijn. Dublin: Four Courts Press.

CHAPTER TWELVE

Home Ownership and Social Inequality in the United States

George S. Masnick

Home-ownership differentials are both a consequence and a cause of social inequality in the United States. Differences in income, wealth, education, family structure, and racial identity have all been shown to contribute to differences in rates of home ownership, and varying ownership opportunities help sustain differences in wealth, education, access to jobs, and overall quality of life. In particular, home-ownership differentials have played a pivotal role in creating and sustaining social inequality between whites and blacks across a wide range of social indicators.

The best discussion of housing inequality in the contemporary United States is found in Myers and Wolch (1995). It describes a study that focused on emerging housing trends between 1980 and 1990. Myers and Wolch titled their essay "The Polarization of Housing Status" and developed their narrative around that theme:

> [The] effects of polarization [are] spread unevenly, both socially and spatially. As younger persons struggled to reach their aspirations, and even to fill their most basic needs, an older generation rose to levels of economic success that were unmatched in this century. And, predictably, minorities, women and less economically advantaged citizens suffered most. Thus we find evidence of a growing "generation gap" and "diversity gap" in [the] realization of the American Dream. (271)

That dream is of owning a home.

In our own examination of inequality in home ownership in the United States, we focus on racial inequality, which we believe is the most important weakness in the American social fabric. To be sure, we address emerging generational differences here, and the importance of education in determining housing tenure. But we do not systematically present and explain other factors that underlie inequality in home ownership—for example, social class, occupation, and geographic location—factors that figure more directly in other chapters of this volume. We focus on race because racial differences in home ownership transcend social class and labor market status, and because those differences are the target of important housing policy initiatives today.

In the following pages we review long-term trends in home-ownership rates and the pattern of owner occupancy among whites and blacks in the United States during the twentieth century.[1] We then summarize the research that has attempted to understand the black–white home-ownership gap. We say "attempted" because we could not find a broad consensus about the degree and causes of inequality in black–white home ownership. Although studies have identified demographic, economic, and policy-related forces that explain certain racial differences in home-ownership trends, often their failure to examine birth cohorts in their analyses leaves their conclusions wanting.

By speaking to one particular inequality in one specific country outside Europe, we have tried to raise important conceptual and methodological issues for future housing research everywhere. The methodological message with which we end the paper is perhaps the most important product of our exercise. Although we demonstrate some of the specific insights that can be gained through the use of a cohort perspective in analyzing differences in home ownership by race, more important is the recognition that this type of approach is required when investigating inequalities in home ownership along other social dimensions as well.

LONG-TERM TRENDS IN HOME OWNERSHIP

Home-ownership trends in the United States over the past century have rarely been stable for any length of time (Figure 12.1).[2] During the early part of the twentieth century, demographic and economic factors in large part determined the course of these trends. Rates moved steadily downward during the early decades of the century, as immigrants from Europe swelled the ranks of the U.S. population, and as the resident population became ever

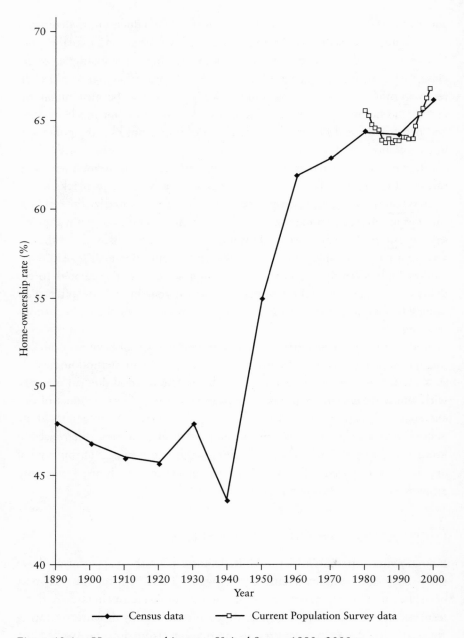

Figure 12.1. Home-ownership rates, United States, 1890–2000

SOURCE: U.S. Census Bureau, decennial census data (1890–2000) and Current Population Survey (1983–2000).

more concentrated in urban locations, where opportunities to own a home tended to be more limited.

Home-ownership rates remained below 50 percent early in the century because large down payments and short-term mortgages put owning a home beyond the reach of most households, native or foreign born. Winnick (1957) reported that the average down payment in a sample of twenty-two cities ranged from two-thirds of the purchase price (between 1911 and 1914) to about half (between 1925 and 1929). Mortgage contracts were short term, typically six to eleven years. The result: few people could afford to finance a home; and a significant proportion of homes—Winnick estimated between 25 percent and 50 percent—were acquired debt-free.

Public policy played little or no role in addressing housing shortages or the affordability of housing until the 1930s. Throughout the first three decades of the twentieth century, when tremendous demographic pressure was put on the housing stock by immigration and urbanization, government was reluctant to address emerging housing needs directly. The United States lagged far behind European nations in developing a national housing policy. The prevailing philosophy was that local initiative and the free market would best meet the growing demand for housing.

The booming economy of the 1920s and large investments in housing by entrepreneurs appeared to support the government's free-market philosophy: the private sector was adding almost a million units annually to the housing stock during the peak years of the 1920s (Listokin 1991). As a consequence, the home-ownership rate reversed its downward drift of the previous decades and began to move sharply upward.

But the stock market crash in 1929 abruptly put the brakes on the growth in home ownership. The bank failures, personal bankruptcies, and high unemployment that characterized the Great Depression caused rates to drop by more than 4 percentage points (from 47.8 percent to 43.6 percent) between 1930 and 1940.[3] During the early 1930s, mortgage foreclosures soared to around one thousand a day, and half of the country's homeowners were in default (Listokin 1991).

The New Deal forever changed the role of the national government in addressing America's housing needs. Multiple interventions in the 1930s in financial and housing markets eventually boosted home-ownership rates. The establishment of the Federal Home Loan Bank system in 1932 and passage of the National Housing Act of 1934, which created the Federal Housing Administration (FHA), were critical first steps in what would eventually become a much broader federal housing initiative. Other agencies established during the 1930s included the Federal National Mortgage Association (Fannie Mae), the Federal Savings and Loan Insurance Corporation (FSLIC), and the Reconstruction Finance Corporation (RFC) (Listokin 1991).

With the establishment of these federal agencies, and the private housing efforts they stimulated, Americans increasingly were able to rely on the availability of long-term government-insured mortgages. Depression-era housing programs were directed at making home ownership more dependable and affordable; but a secondary goal, support for the construction industry as a means of putting people back to work, was equally important. Support for the construction and real estate industries continues to be an important objective of national housing policy in the United States even today.

The home-ownership rate climbed dramatically during the 1940s and 1950s, a response to a number of reinforcing trends:

- Government-backed mortgages had placed the long-term cost of home ownership at affordable levels for many households.
- The booming war economy of the 1940s and the prosperity of the 1950s boosted household earnings, which again made housing more affordable.
- The federal government guaranteed war veterans low-interest mortgages to help them move quickly into home ownership. Other national programs that supported the education and employment of veterans also facilitated the transition to home ownership for many American households.
- After the war, couples were marrying and having children earlier, providing strong motivation to buy a house with a big yard on a safe street near a brand-new school.
- The ascendancy of the automobile and federal support for cheap gasoline opened up vast areas of cheap land to housing development, and the modern automobile-dependent suburb was born.
- The expansion of the interstate highway system under the Eisenhower administration (1953–1961), ostensibly to improve military preparedness during the cold war, also improved access to suburban housing developments across the country.

Certainly low-cost loans, higher incomes, early marriage, and access to less-expensive tract housing had an enormous impact on the growth of owner occupation between 1940 and 1960. But these factors don't explain all of the unprecedented increase in home-ownership rates—almost 20 percentage points—over that twenty-year period. It wasn't just that owning a house became easier; it was also that renting became more difficult. To be sure, the booming economy and affordable mortgages helped many renting households make the transition to owning, releasing a "pent-up demand" for ownership from the 1930s and early 1940s. But rental occupancy also fell because of national, state, and local urban-renewal programs that set about clearing the slums (often in conjunction with highway construction). These programs severely reduced the availability of affordable rental housing in urban America.

The free market was slow to address the needs of renters, particularly low-income renters. Although urban renewal usually called for the replacement of demolished private rental units with public rental units, these projects were also slow getting going. For example, in 1950, just 32,000 public housing units were started nationally, a drop in the bucket compared with the number of housing units being demolished and with the almost 2 million private housing starts that year (Listokin 1991). With affordable houses being built in the suburbs and the deficit of rental units everywhere, it should come as no surprise that new households made the choice to buy rather than rent.

In the 1950s, federal housing policy began to move slowly away from the free-market model that characterized the first half of the century. The 1949 Housing Act articulated a goal of "a decent home and a suitable living environment for every American." This pronouncement would affect housing policy for decades. The 1954 Housing Act recognized the need to broaden the federal initiative beyond the demolition of substandard housing and support for new construction: it addressed the rehabilitation of deteriorating housing units and of neighborhood infrastructure in general. By signing the Housing Act of 1961 into law, President John Kennedy created the first FHA-insured program for low-income rental housing. In 1965, the Department of Housing and Urban Development (HUD) was elevated by President Lyndon Johnson to a Cabinet-level agency; and in 1968, the Housing and Urban Development Act privatized Fannie Mae and established the Government National Mortgage Association (Ginnie Mae). Also in 1968, HUD initiated programs to help low-income families buy (Section 235) or rent (Section 236) homes.[4]

Throughout the 1960s, the interaction of economics, demographics, and public policy took on a new synergy that boosted the formation and stability of renter-occupied housing and that caused home-ownership growth to slow dramatically. By the middle of the decade, the oldest of the baby-boom generation were beginning to form their own households; but unlike their parents, they increasingly chose not to marry and start families at a young age. By the 1970s, those who had married were divorcing at record rates. With the growth in single-person and single-parent households came a shift to renter occupancy.

In the mid-1960s, the national government had become much more concerned about addressing the housing needs of low-income households, most of which rented their home. Widespread urban riots left no doubt about the seriousness of racial inequality in America. A blue-ribbon commission appointed by President Johnson to investigate the causes of the riots began its final report with a now-famous quote: "Our nation is moving toward two societies, one black, one white—separate and unequal" (National Advisory Commission on Civil Disorders 1968). The commission, recognizing the need for dramatic improvement in the quality of life in central-city neighborhoods, recommended marked increases in federal spending for education, housing, employment, job training, and social services (Yinger 1995). President Johnson recommended nothing less than a war on poverty to address these problems.

On the housing front, the government's focus shifted to the construction of new rental units: in 1960, only 425,000 rental units were subsidized by federal housing programs for the poor; by 1970, that number had more than doubled; by 1975, it had jumped to 2.4 million units; and by 1985, it was at 4.6 million units (Listokin 1991). The greater availability of rental housing boosted new renter households and had a dampening effect on the rise in the home-ownership rate.

Finally, the 1973 oil embargo touched off inflation that slowed economic growth and eventually boosted mortgage interest rates into the double digits. Housing inflation in the 1970s and early 1980s motivated those who could afford to "invest" in home ownership to purchase houses and to move up into bigger and more expensive housing. However, many would-be home-buyers were unable to afford the higher down payments or monthly mortgage payments created by the inflationary housing market. In addition, many young workers were impacted by the restructuring of older rust-belt industries that began in the late 1970s and the Reagan recession of the early 1980s, and this weakened home ownership further.

These demographic and economic explanations of the decline in home ownership rates in the 1980s are not the whole story. Yes, a continued shift away from marriage was responsible in part for the slipping demand for owner-occupied housing in the 1980s, but ownership rates for young and middle-aged married couples also fell during this period (Masnick, McArdle, and Belsky 1999). High unemployment and high real housing costs certainly depressed home ownership in the early 1980s, but improvements in both indexes later in the decade did little to boost owner occupation. Despite the baby-boom generation's moving into the peak years for home ownership, and despite a generally favorable economy and affordable interest rates, owner-occupancy rates remained stuck near 64 percent from the mid-1980s to the mid-1990s. Housing analysts now recognize that other economic and demographic factors also were operating in that period, among them a widespread drop in the real earnings of young men (Schrammel 1998) and a simultaneous rise in the importance of wives' earnings (Myers 1985a, 1985b), and the increasing role of immigrants from Asia and Latin America in many of the larger U.S. housing markets (Joint Center for Housing Studies 1988–1999).

It is against this broad sweep of home-ownership trends that we now turn to examine black–white differentials. For the most part, the demographic, economic, and public policy factors that produced these trends also have affected both black and white home-ownership rates, moving them in the same direction. But the differences in the upward and downward movement of those rates for blacks and whites is significant: they tell us that the rates at which blacks and whites own their home have not been affected equally.

WHITE AND BLACK DIFFERENTIALS IN HOME OWNERSHIP

There is perhaps no greater indicator of the persistence of social inequality in the United States than the enduring racial inequality in home ownership. And there is no greater challenge to addressing racial inequality in the United States than that provided by long-term differences in black and white home ownership. Yet, despite more than fifty years of attention to the insidious consequences of racial segregation and discrimination, research on ownership differentials has not figured prominently in the debate on racial inequality in America.[5] Concern with black–white inequality traditionally has focused on such social indicators as per capita income, average wage levels, poverty rates, unemployment, labor force participation, household composition, education, out-of-wedlock birth rates, infant mortality, and life expectancy.

In retrospect, the factors that helped create differences between white and black home-ownership opportunities also promoted differences in well-being between the races across the range of social indicators. In fact, the economic and psychic well-being of individuals, households, and the nation at large might be linked to trends and differences in home ownership. In their comprehensive review of the literature on home ownership in the United States, Megbolugbe and Linneman (1993) put forth a long list of reasons that policymakers who address health and welfare now consider home ownership to be especially worthy of attention. They make a strong case that people tend to associate home-ownership opportunities with better housing, safer and more pleasant neighborhoods, better schools, better jobs, and more opportunities to save and see capital appreciate. These aspects of home ownership are what Americans think of as the core of the American dream (Myers 1981; Rossi 1980). From a societal perspective, broad-based home ownership promotes greater community involvement, leads to the upgrading of the nation's housing stock, and helps stimulate local and national economies.

Figure 12.2 plots the broad trends in white and black home-ownership rates between 1890 and 2000.[6] For the most part, the curves run parallel, which supports the contention that the same demographic, economic, and policy factors influence home ownership in both racial groups. But a different picture emerges when we examine the differences between the two curves. Figure 12.3 plots the gap between black and white home-ownership rates. Notice that the gap narrowed between 1890 and 1940, stayed relatively stable until 1950, and then began widening. On average, throughout the twentieth century, white home-ownership rates exceeded black home-ownership rates by about 25 percentage points.

Decade by decade, the gap in home-ownership rates by race went through noteworthy ups and downs. The narrowing of the gap during the first half of the century was briefly interrupted between 1920 and 1930, when the gap widened slightly. Not surprisingly perhaps, whites appeared to have benefited more than blacks from the booming economy. But when the boom ended, whites were hurt more than blacks: during the Depression decade, white home ownership fell by 5 points (10 percent) compared to a

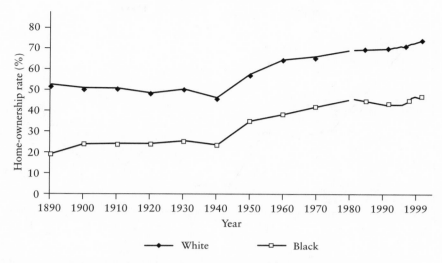

Figure 12.2.   Trends in home ownership by race, United States, 1890–1999

SOURCE: U.S. Census Bureau, decennial census data (1890–1999) and Current Population Survey (1983–1999).

NOTE: Census data before 1980 generally reported housing tenure by two categories, white and non-white. Because the proportion of blacks in the nonwhite population of the United States between 1890 and 1980 was relatively high, nonwhite and black trends over that period were almost synonymous. The data shown here for the period from 1983 to 2000 were reported for non-Hispanic blacks.

1-point drop (4 percent) for nonwhites. The majority of nonwhite home-owners during the Depression were black farmers, a group that was better able to maintain its status quo than were more urbanized whites.

During the 1940s, both blacks and whites made strong gains in home ownership, so there was little change in their relative positions. But during the economic boom of the 1950s, white home-ownership rates increased significantly faster than black rates did, just as they had during the 1920s. Whites clearly fared better at claiming new home-ownership opportunities during the rapid suburbanization that was part of the post–World War II economic expansion. The ongoing movement of displaced black agricultural workers from the rural South to the urban North, where ownership opportunities were more limited, reduced the increase in black home ownership even as blacks' economic status was improving dramatically.

During the 1960s and 1970s, the gap once again narrowed as the cumulative effect of economic growth and the Great Society's social programs

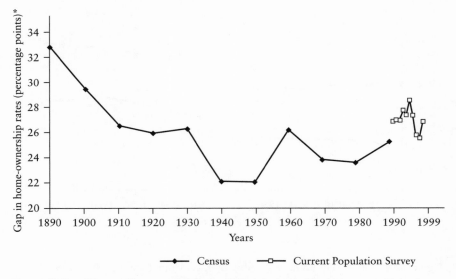

Figure 12.3.   The gap between white and black home-ownership rates, United States, 1890–1999

SOURCE: U.S. Census Bureau, decennial census data (1890–1999) and Current Population Survey (1983–1999).

NOTE: Census data before 1980 generally reported housing tenure by two categories, white and nonwhite. Because the proportion of blacks in the nonwhite population of the United States between 1890 and 1980 was relatively high, nonwhite and black trends over that period were almost synonymous. The differential shown here for the period from 1983 to 2000 was calculated using data reported for non-Hispanic blacks.

* The white home-ownership rate less the black home-ownership rate.

began to benefit working-class blacks. During the 1980s and early 1990s, blacks once again lost significant ground to whites; but in the late 1990s, black ownership gains outstripped those of whites.

Government policies in midcentury played a role in preserving home-ownership inequality for blacks. The FHA in its early *Underwriting Manual* discouraged loans to would-be homeowners in all black or racially mixed neighborhoods under the pretext that housing in those neighborhoods was unlikely to hold its value (Oliver and Shapiro 1995). Redlining and other practices and laws that prompted discrimination in lending were struck down by the U.S. Supreme Court in 1948. Analysts would characterize the narrowing of the home-ownership gap in the 1960s and 1970s as one of the major achievements of judicial and legislative actions to protect civil rights and ensure fair housing. The widening of the black–white home-ownership gap that took place between 1980 and 1995 was especially disturbing: it represented a step backward after two decades of hard-won progress. In fact, although the Court's decision in *Shelly v. Kramer* had made redlining illegal in 1948, many banks and mortgage companies quietly continued to adhere to discriminatory lending practices (Galster 1993a). It was not until 1990 that fair-housing audits of banking practices began to force change in the way mortgage lending was done. In particular, the HUD-sponsored Housing Discrimination Study (Yinger 1991b) and the Federal Reserve Bank's decision to void a bank merger where discriminatory mortgage lending was documented appear to have had the largest impact on reversing discrimination in mortgage lending (Yinger 1995). Still, racial "steering" by real estate agents hardly diminished in most places, and it contributed to the persistence of housing segregation throughout the 1980s and early 1990s.

The strong gains in black home ownership in the last years of the twentieth century suggest that another chapter is being written in the continuing narrative of racial inequality in home ownership in the United States. In the summer of 1994, for the first time in U.S. history, a presidential administration developed and implemented a policy targeted at increasing the overall home-ownership rate for those who had been ill served by housing markets.[7] The program had four goals: to make home ownership more affordable; to eliminate barriers to home ownership; to enable families to better manage the responsibilities and rewards of home ownership; and to make it easier to complete the paperwork to buy a home (U.S. Department of Housing and Urban Development 1994). Initiatives were undertaken by the FHA, Fannie Mae, the Federal Home Loan Mortgage Corporation (Freddie Mac), and others to lower required down payments, to recognize multiple income sources in qualifying a household for a housing loan, to reward prompt and regular monthly mortgage payments, to translate mortgage applications into languages other than English, and to work with realtors and banks to end discrimination in marketing and lending. Through these initiatives, the Clinton administration set a goal of reaching a national home-ownership rate of 67.5 percent by 2001, and it succeeded: the rate that year was 67.8 percent. The effort was remarkable in that it did not leverage an existing upward trend in the home-ownership rate; it did not depend on any major new legislation; and it did not recommend any large funding initiatives. The strategy was simply to focus on groups with low home-ownership rates and to vigorously enforce fair-housing and banking laws that were already on the books. The subsequent increase in home ownership has been particularly strong for minorities; and the minority population in the suburbs, where opportunities for home ownership are greater, has also grown markedly (Frey 2001). The George W. Bush administration, in an initiative announced in 2002, has sustained President Clinton's commitment to boost minority home ownership. It has set a goal of adding 5.5 million minority homeowners by 2010, a level of growth that would significantly raise the rate of home ownership among minorities.

EXPLAINING BLACK–WHITE HOME-OWNERSHIP DIFFERENCES

Modern studies of racial differences in income and wealth go back to the 1960s;[8] studies of racial differences in home ownership, to the early 1970s. In a paper presented in 1969 and published several years later, Kain and Quigley (1972) were among the first to attempt to measure the effects of discrimination on home ownership among blacks. In a sample of St. Louis residents interviewed in 1967, they found that the black home-ownership rate would have been almost 30 percent higher if blacks had been able to purchase homes at the same rate as whites at similar life-cycle stages and with similar income, education, and employment characteristics. They also found that blacks who had recently moved were no more likely to own their homes, indicating that barriers to home ownership were not falling (at least in St. Louis). In addition, their results showed that black homebuyers paid more than whites for equivalent housing. They concluded that restriction on the supply of housing—a function of segregation and housing market discrimination—was the root cause of both the home-ownership deficit and higher ownership costs for blacks.

Kain and Quigley's paper stimulated a series of studies that attempted to verify and clarify the measurement of differences between black and white rates of owner occupancy. McDonald (1974) found similar results in a sample of Detroit households; he attempted to show that mortgage discrimination in the black ghetto was as important as restrictions on movement out of the ghetto in keeping black home-ownership rates low. Roistacher and Goodman (1976) also found lower home-ownership rates for blacks in a sample of households living in the country's twenty-four largest metropolitan areas in 1971. In fact, they found a substantially larger "unexplained" black–white ownership gap than Kain and Quigley had found in St. Louis; but they did not find significant differences in home-ownership rates by race when they accounted for other family characteristics of new homeowners. This latter finding suggested to the authors "a reduction in the barriers to home ownership for blacks in terms of segregation and mortgage market discrimination, but not necessarily an elimination of these problems" (69). Silberman, Yochum, and Ihlanfeldt (1982) revisited the data used by Roistacher and Goodman, and showed that recent entrants into the housing market (newly formed households) had a much lower residual unexplained variance in the black–white gap, and that the gap had narrowed between 1974 and 1978.[9] Their conclusion: "racial discrimination in the housing market is gradually declining over time, and the households with limited (past) experience in housing markets are more likely to take advantage of the changing environment than those households with human capital acquired in the past" (452).

This early literature underscored that a significant portion of the gap between black and white home-ownership rates could be explained by differences in economic, social, and demographic variables; but at least part of the gap could not. Efforts to close the gap, then, would need to address, not only the causes of black–white differences in income, employment, education, family structure, and the like, but also the aspects of the housing market that directly discriminated against blacks. A distinctly positive note was sounded: it looked as though the unexplained home-ownership gap was disappearing for newly formed households and new homeowners. But the record over the past twenty years has proved that conclusion to have been premature at best.

Although recognizing that both recent entrants into the housing market and recent homebuyers might behave differently from longer-established households, the early studies failed to develop a fully articulated life-cycle perspective on housing. They gave no attention to possible trends among age cohorts. Furthermore, although suggesting that trends might differ by region of the country, the early literature failed to specify why this should be so; it also neglected to hypothesize why the racial gap in home ownership widened or narrowed in different decades.

Beginning in the 1990s, studies of racial inequalities generally and in terms of home ownership took a more historical perspective. Within this new research, there was—and continues to be—greater focus on cohort dif-

ferences. There are several reasons for this shift in emphasis. First, the widening home-ownership gap by race in the 1980s, along with the relative stagnation of the aggregate home-ownership rate during that period, was a significant new development, and one that relied for its explanation on offsetting
trends in the home-ownership rates of younger and older cohorts (see below). Social scientists often commented that the people in this younger generation would be the first in American history to do less well than their parents, and cohort differences in home ownership were often singled out to
support that thinking (Myers et al. 1992; Myers and Wolch 1995). Second,
more attention was being paid to other fundamental differences between the
generations as the baby-boom cohorts aged and were replaced by a younger
generation that was different not only in size but also in culture, psyche, and,
most important, ethnic composition. Third, wider availability of census data,
in the form of public-use microdata samples (PUMS), allowed for greater detail in the analysis of cohort housing consumption across time and space.

A "bridge" study between early and more-recent analyses of home-
ownership trends is that of Long and Caudill (1992). Their findings showed
a narrowing of the gap in home ownership between white and black married
couples between 1970 and 1980, and again between 1980 and 1988. Black
couples living in suburban and nonmetropolitan areas owned homes at
85 percent of the white rate. And when racial differences in economic and
demographic characteristics were controlled, black home ownership rose to
97 percent of the white rate, closing the gap almost entirely. When Long and
Caudill turned their attention to housing wealth, however, they found much
less convergence between whites and blacks in the suburban–rural subsample, and a divergence in the entire sample, which included city dwellers.
They concluded that the primary consequence of racial discrimination that
has not been ameliorated by economic trends or public policy is the disadvantage blacks face in the accumulation of wealth through home equity. And
they argued that to achieve greater parity here, blacks must be able to buy
homes in areas where housing values are stable or appreciating.

Long and Caudill's conclusion that suburban black couples had nearly
achieved ownership parity with comparable suburban white couples, thereby
obviating the need for new or intensified antidiscrimination policies to boost
home ownership, appears to have been wide of the mark. They did not examine generational differences in household composition: by failing to consider those differences in marriage patterns and single parenthood, their

sample of black married couples in the younger generation was not typical of all black households. In addition, the first wave of black suburbanization was highly selective. But Long and Caudill's conclusions about the effects of ghettoization on the accumulation of housing wealth were more on target. Housing discrimination has reduced the ability of black parents to accumulate wealth through home equity and to pass that wealth on to their children, to help get them started in the housing market (Oliver and Shapiro 1995). Home equity not only allows people to move up to better housing; it often serves as a cushion to help households through financially difficult times. Home equity also allows people to remain homeowners when financial stress might otherwise propel them to become renters.

Oliver and Shapiro (1995) conducted the most far-reaching study of black–white wealth differentials but only for one point in time. They used 1987 data from the Survey of Income and Program Participation (SIPP) to examine differences by race in home ownership and home equity. They found that home equity is the largest asset of a majority of American households; in fact, it is practically the only asset for blue-collar and low-level white-collar households. Their summary of the literature on housing discrimination and on the differences by race in the critical social and economic factors that affect home ownership is perhaps the best discussion of the topic in print. According to Oliver and Shapiro, blacks accumulate less wealth because a smaller proportion of them own homes; and even those who own homes are financially disadvantaged because blacks have more difficulty obtaining standard mortgages, they pay higher mortgage interest rates, and their houses appreciate at a slower rate. The authors attributed the interest-rates differential in part to the fact that banks have abandoned black neighborhoods, forcing the people in those neighborhoods to turn to finance companies and other lenders that charge higher interest. They also suggest that blacks might be less sophisticated about choosing between a variable- or fixed-rate mortgage or about refinancing when appropriate. Fear of losing their mortgage makes blacks more hesitant to take advantage of lower costs when interest rates go down. And they document that blacks have less ability to "buy down" a mortgage with a larger down payment or the payment up front of points. At work here is also a lack of parental resources, resources that first-time homebuyers often rely on to help them come up with a down payment and the transaction costs of buying a house. Finally, they claim that banks doing business in black neighborhoods often charge a premium for "small" mortgages (mortgages on housing with a low purchase price) because of the greater costs that banks incur in selling small mortgages to the secondary mortgage market.

A recent study by Immergluck (1998) tracked the late 1990s upswing in black home buying in the Chicago area using Home Mortgage Disclosure Act (HMDA) data. The study confirmed many of Oliver and Shapiro's and Long and Caudill's conclusions. It showed high concentrations of recent house purchases by blacks in neighborhoods where most homeowners are black or in integrated neighborhoods that are quickly turning black. These patterns reinforce segregation and exert downward pressure on the wealth that might be accumulated through appreciation.

Collins and Margo (1999) examined black–white differences in the home-ownership rates of male householders between the ages of 20 and 64 who were not enrolled in school. They used census data from PUMS files from 1900 to 1990. Their tabulation of the home-ownership gap for these restricted subgroups of households showed smaller differences in the early 1900s than those shown in Figure 12.3. They also found a significantly smaller gap in both 1980 and 1990 — under 20 percent in each of those years compared with under 24 percent and more than 25 percent, respectively, in the general population of households.[10] What this finding in the male-headed-household sample implies is that households headed by women play an important part in determining overall patterns of black home ownership.

Collins and Margo found that fully 63 percent of the widening gap between 1940 and 1960 could be explained by changes in demographic and geographic variables linked to the likelihood of home ownership, but that those factors explained only 39 percent of the narrowing gap between 1960 and 1980. The movement of blacks from the rural South to urban centers in the Northeast and Midwest was the largest contributor to the widening gap in the earlier period. Increases in black educational attainment and occupational status were important factors in the gap's narrowing in the later period; but their effect was limited by increases in the proportion of blacks who were not married and in households headed by women.

Another important finding from the Collins and Margo analysis concerns the contribution of birth cohort to the overall gap in home ownership between whites and blacks. During the early decades of the twentieth century, the gap was wider for older cohorts than for younger cohorts. For example, in 1900, the home-ownership gap by race for those born between 1846 and 1855 was about 30 points; for those born between 1861 and 1870, the gap was closer to 20 points. The differential between older and younger cohorts persisted until after 1940. In 1960, the first year in the post–World War II period for which tenure data are available in the PUMS files, the gap between the under-40 cohorts began to exceed the gap between cohorts over age 50.[11] This turnabout occurred because the cohorts with the smaller gaps in the early decades of the century had become the older cohorts in the middle of the century, and they had maintained their more-favorable position. Also, for the younger cohorts entering the housing market after World War II, the racial gap in home ownership had widened to nearly 30 percentage points by 1960. By 1990, the gap for younger cohorts had dropped to between 21 points and 24 points; by then, the gap for older cohorts of male householders was between 16 points and 19 points, preserving the older cohorts' advantage. Although they identified these cohort differences, Collins and Margo failed to explain them. In that omission, they were in good company with most of the authors conducting research on black–white home-ownership gaps, especially before 1990.

Smith and Welch (1989) did use a cohort perspective to examine black–white differences in the economic status of men. Their analysis covered the period from 1940 to 1980. Although home ownership was not one of the variables they studied, the thoroughness with which they tracked birth cohorts on other social and economic variables, and the implications of their findings for home-ownership trends justify its inclusion here. Smith and Welch began by documenting that the gap between black men's and white men's wages between 1940 and 1980 had narrowed considerably. By tracking cohorts' wages over time, they showed that within defined educational levels, the wages of black men rose more rapidly than did the wages of white men. They also showed that within levels of education, younger cohorts had narrowed the wage gap more than older cohorts had, and that progress toward closing the wage gap, particularly since 1960, was in large part a function of younger blacks' having more education. Although they acknowledged that most education takes place by age 25, they found evidence that a significant upgrading of educational status continues to take place during middle adulthood, as cohorts age.

Smith and Welch concluded that much of the reduction in the black–

white wage differential in the first half of the period (1940–1960) reflected the relocation of black males from the South to the North, where wages were higher. They attributed the improvement in the second half of the period (1960–1980) to the restructuring of the Southern economy and educational system. The importance they attached to birth cohorts, education, geographic location, and migration patterns established their study as a guide for how we might best undertake research to understand black–white differences in home ownership.

Recent research that emphasizes the post-1980 decline in segregation in certain parts of the country and the rise of a black middle class across the country (see Cutler, Glaeser, and Vigdor 1999; and Kain, forthcoming) has not been able to reconcile these newer developments with the increase in the black–white home-ownership gap between 1980 and 1995. The drop since the late 1970s in the relative percentage of black high school graduates ages 18 to 24 enrolled in college, the high cost of college and the high student debt that college graduates typically carry, and the stagnation of black–white income ratios over the same time period (Farley 1996) are factors that may well explain the widening gap in black–white home-ownership rates between younger cohorts.

GENERATIONAL DIFFERENCES IN HOME OWNERSHIP
BY RACE AND EDUCATION

The cohort-related differences in the home-ownership rates of blacks between 1980 and 1990 reflected a larger trend in the aggregate rate: home ownership among younger cohorts generally—both blacks and whites—was falling (Myers and Wolch 1995). The generational differences by race and ethnic origin are shown in Table 12.1. Whatever the causes, home-ownership rates for those ages 25 to 34 fell during the 1980s, while the rates for those ages 65 to 74 went up. Underlying that general effect were significant differences in rates by race. That is, the rates for younger blacks and Hispanics fell by 20 percent and 17 percent respectively, more than twice the 8 percent drop experienced by white men ages 25 to 34.

Gyourko and Linneman (1996) also documented an increase in the generational gap in home ownership between 1980 and 1990. They followed up that research a year later with an analysis of PUMS data from the four de-

TABLE 12.1
Home-ownership rates by race and ethnic origin,
selected ages, United States, 1980 and 1990

Age and race and ethnic origin	HOME OWNERSHIP RATE (%)		Change (%)
	1980	1990	
Ages 25–34			
White, non-Hispanic	57	52	−8
Black	30	24	−20
Asian	38	36	−5
Hispanic	35	29	−17
AVERAGE	52	46	−12
Ages 65–74			
White, non-Hispanic	76	82	+8
Black	59	64	+8
Asian	63	66	+5
Hispanic	56	59	+5
AVERAGE	74	80	+8

SOURCE: Adapted from Myers and Wolch (1995, table 6.2).

cennial censuses between 1960 and 1990. They wanted to clarify the contribution of age groups to trends in home ownership and to examine how those trends are influenced by the interaction of age group with education, family structure, and race. They concluded that the "absolute and relative decline in ownership for the least educated represents one of the largest asset shifts in the postwar era" (1997, 1). They also found that especially for younger cohorts (under age 35), delays in marriage and having children are no longer the impediments to home ownership that they once were. Finally, by examining statistically adjusted white and nonwhite home-ownership levels, controlling for the usual economic and demographic variables, Gyourko and Linneman confirmed that the racial gap in home-ownership rates for the youngest cohorts had widened during the 1980s.[12]

An alternative to the statistical treatment of age-specific data employed by Gyourko and Linneman involves graphing trajectories of home ownership by cohort. This technique, which was first used by Pitkin and Masnick

(1980), summarizes differences in home-ownership rates by cohort and often reveals patterns obscured by other approaches.[13] Figure 12.4 shows trajectories of home-ownership rates by birth cohort and race (non-Hispanic whites and non-Hispanic blacks) based on 1980 and 1990 PUMS data. The tails of the arrows represent the home-ownership rate for cohort age x in 1980; the heads of the arrows, the rates for cohort age $x + 10$ years in 1990. With this method of presenting data on home-ownership rates, we can readily see several important trends during the 1980s:

- Whites under age 45 made the transition to home ownership much faster than blacks did; but blacks over age 45 narrowed that gap somewhat, indicating that a larger percentage of older-cohort blacks move into their own homes later in the life cycle.
- Successive cohorts of those over age 45 in 1980 were tracking on higher ownership trajectories for both whites and blacks. The opposite was true for cohorts under age 45 in 1980: they appear to be falling further and further behind.
- The youngest cohorts of blacks lost ground between 1980 and 1990 in relation to their white counterparts.

How much of the racial differences in home ownership can be explained by differences in factors we know are associated with home ownership—for example, education, income, family structure, region, and nature of residence (urban versus rural)? This is the question that researchers from Kain and Quigley to Gyourko and Linneman have asked, but that no one has answered without qualification. None of the studies cited above fully understood that the answer to this question would depend on birth cohort and the period under consideration. To illustrate this latter point, we plotted a series of trajectories by birth cohort, race, and education level for the years 1988 through 1998. Part a of Figure 12.5 shows the average impact of education on home-ownership rates by age group and race. The trajectories here indicate that home-ownership rates for the white cohorts under age 45 were accelerating faster than the ownership trajectories for black cohorts of the same ages. They also show that successively younger cohorts under age 45—especially the black cohorts—were tracking on higher ownership trajectories (the heads of the arrows are above the tails of the arrows immediately to the right). This was the opposite of what we observed in Figure 12.4 for the 1980–1990 period.

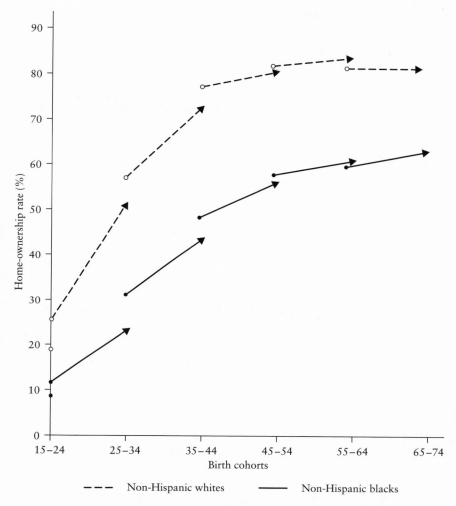

Figure 12.4. Home-ownership trajectories by birth cohort and race, United States, 1980–1990

Author's calculations based on Census public-use data files (1980, 1990).

NOTE: The single points for the 15–24 age group represent the starting ownership levels of the youngest cohorts in 1990. That is, these points would be the tails of the arrows that represent this cohort's transition to home ownership between 1990 and 2000, when members of these cohorts move into the 25–34 age groups.

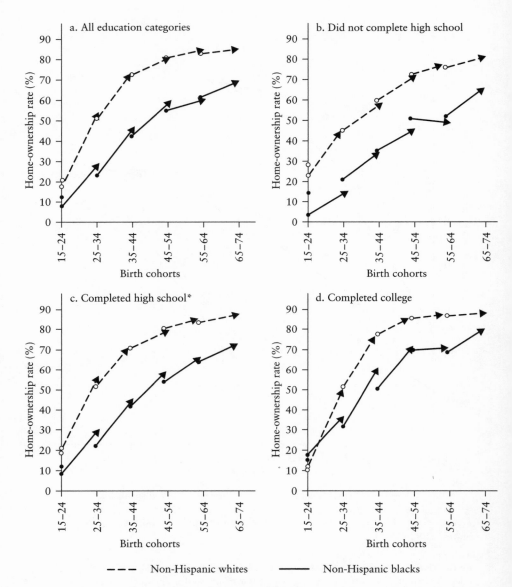

Figure 12.5. Home-ownership trajectories by birth cohort, race, and education of householder, United States, 1988–1998

Author's calculations based on Current Population Survey public-use data files (1988, 1998).

In parts b through d of Figure 12.5, we looked at the householders' level of education. The trajectories tell us that it was black high school and college graduates who boosted their rates the most between 1988 and 1998 (parts c and d). Younger cohorts with less than a high school education in both racial groups (part b) were actually falling further behind (the heads of the arrows are below the tails of the arrows immediately to the right).[14] One explanation for the lower ownership rates among the least educated is the higher incidence of female-headed households in this population: households headed by women typically have lower home-ownership rates (Myers and Wolch 1995). This is particularly true of households headed by young black women. However, household type does not explain all of the black–white differences within educational categories. Many of those differences remain even when the analysis is confined to married couples (Masnick and Di 2001).

That home ownership increased over the period for young better-educated blacks stands in stark contrast with the persistent slippage in home ownership experienced by younger blacks without a high school education. These patterns suggest that it was primarily the better-educated households that were able to take advantage of the extremely favorable economic conditions and housing policies in the United States during the mid- and late 1990s. Even a favorable economic climate and supportive programs were not sufficient to reverse the trends for those with an educational handicap.

SUMMARY AND CONCLUSIONS

How can we best characterize the differences between white and black home-ownership levels in the United States throughout the twentieth century? First, we must acknowledge that the home-ownership gap by race was exceedingly durable for long periods: that gap averaged between 25 and 30 percentage points throughout most of the century. Second, we must recognize that shifts in demographics, economic conditions, and public policy have made certain decades more or less favorable to closing the home-ownership gap. We should therefore be cautious about anticipating trends in all but the near term. Third, we must understand that the measurement of inequality in home ownership is sensitive to geographic location, type of household included in the analysis, the age of the household head, and the changing mix of nonwhite households. Fourth, we must recognize that variables like education and occupation cannot be equalized statistically for whites and blacks because segregation and racial discrimination have fundamentally influenced the quality of education and the labor market opportunities that have been available to blacks. The average high school diploma or college degree for blacks is still not equal to the average diploma or degree for whites in terms of the knowledge and skills that it is meant to certify; and we cannot expect parity here until classroom infrastructure, curriculum, teachers' qualifications, student–teacher ratios, and household involvement in children's education are the same for black and white students. Also, blacks do not have the income or the occupational mobility that whites with similar education and in similar occupational categories do. Moreover, blacks and whites for the most part still do not buy houses in the same markets, which means we cannot control for housing quality and costs when we examine differences in home ownership by race. These facts of white and black life define the very essence of what we are trying to measure, which is why race matters in the U.S. experience.

Looking at differences in white and black home ownership in the United States over the last century, we can say that much has changed and much has remained the same. Socioeconomic, demographic, and geographic realities combine with public policy to determine housing outcomes. Research on this subject has just recently recognized the importance of adopting a cohort perspective, of understanding that the transition to home ownership is different at different stages of life—whatever the individual's race. Still, there is no question that within birth cohorts, conditions that affect racial groups differently early in life establish different trajectories of home ownership that endure throughout life. The largest influences are manifest when cohorts first enter the housing market. The success of younger educated blacks in raising their home-ownership rates in the mid- to late 1990s should elevate their level of home ownership later in life. In much the same way, the falling level of home ownership among the least educated weighs heavily on their ability to achieve higher levels of home ownership as they age.

The evidence that blacks appear less able to tap into housing markets where housing values appreciate significantly over time also should give us pause. This inequality translates into the failure of home ownership as a mechanism for wealth accumulation; it also deprives succeeding generations of financial support in their own transition to home ownership. Ultimately, it is the legacy of discrimination that is most troubling. In the absence of equal education and parity in the labor market, in the absence of the equity that should accumulate through owning a home, the inequalities that characterized home ownership in the United States throughout the last century are unlikely to be resolved in this one.

TABLE 12A.1

Home-ownership trends by race, census and Current Population
Survey data, United States, 1890–2000

| Data source | HOME-OWNERSHIP RATES (%) | | | | | | |
	Total	White	Nonwhite	Non-Hispanic White	Non-Hispanic Black	Hispanic	Total minority[a]
Census							
1890	47.8	51.5	19.0				
1900	46.7	49.8	23.6				
1910	45.9	50.2	23.7				
1920	45.6	48.2	23.9				
1930	47.8	50.2	25.2				
1940	43.6	45.7	23.6				
1950	55.0	57.0	34.9				
1960	61.9	64.4	38.2				
1970	63.3	65.4	42.0				
1980	64.4			69.0	45.3	44.1	45.8
1990	64.2			69.1	43.9	42.1	44.5
2000	66.2			69.0	45.4	44.2	45.7
Current Population Survey							
1975	64.9			68.6	43.7	43.9	44.4
1976	65.1			68.9	44.4	42.7	44.2
1977	64.9			68.7	44.2	42.3	44.2
1978	65.0			68.9	44.7	42.6	44.6
1979	n.a.[b]			n.a.	n.a.	n.a.	n.a.
1980	n.a.			n.a.	n.a.	n.a.	n.a.
1981	n.a.			n.a.	n.a.	n.a.	n.a.
1982	n.a.			n.a.	n.a.	n.a.	n.a.

Data source	HOME-OWNERSHIP RATES (%)						
	Total	White	Nonwhite	Non-Hispanic		Hispanic	Total minority[a]
				White	Black		
1983	64.9			69.1	45.6	41.2	45.3
1984	64.5			69.0	46.0	40.1	44.8
1985	64.3			69.0	44.4	41.1	44.1
1986	63.8			68.4	44.8	40.6	44.1
1987	64.0			68.7	45.8	40.6	44.5
1988	64.0			69.1	42.9	40.6	43.1
1989	64.0			69.3	42.1	41.6	43.0
1990	64.1			69.4	42.6	41.2	43.1
1991	64.0			69.5	42.7	39.0	42.6
1992	64.1			69.6	42.6	39.9	43.1
1993	64.1			70.2	42.0	39.4	42.4
1994	64.2			70.1	42.8	41.6	43.6
1995	64.7			70.8	42.2	42.4	43.4
1996	65.4			71.6	44.3	41.2	44.2
1997	65.7			71.7	46.0	43.1	46.1
1998	66.2			72.2	46.6	44.9	47.1
1999	66.7			73.0	46.1	45.2	47.0
2000	67.2			73.6	47.6	45.5	47.8

source: U.S. Census Bureau, decennial census data (1890–2000) and Current Population Survey (1975–2000).

[a]Includes all groups except non-Hispanic whites.
[b]n.a. = not available

Notes

1. In this paper, we follow the convention in the United States of defining *home-ownership rate* as the proportion of households that are owner occupied.

2. See Table 12A.1 for detailed home-ownership rates.

3. The rate of home ownership at its low point between 1930 and 1940 was probably larger than Figure 12.1 indicates. It is not possible to measure annual trends with decennial censuses.

4. See Listokin (1991), Keith (1973), and Mitchell (1986) for further discussions of early federal housing policy.

5. See Myrdal (1944), Massey and Denton (1993), and Jargowsky (1997). Only two researchers—Galster (all years) and Yinger (all years)—have done sustained work on the home-ownership gap between blacks and whites. Their early collaboration (Yinger et al. 1979) set a research agenda that each of them has pursued with determination for the past two decades.

6. Census data on tenure collected before 1980 often categorized race by white or nonwhite only. Before 1980, the relatively low proportion of Asians, American Indians, and especially Hispanics, who can be of any race, meant that nonwhite and black trends were almost synonymous. Since 1980, increases in Asian and Hispanic immigration and in the number of people who claim American Indian ancestry have made the nonwhite category less useful for analysis. Increasingly, the categories non-Hispanic white, non-Hispanic black, non-Hispanic Asian/other, and Hispanic are being used.

7. In developing the program, the Clinton administration had partnered with more than two dozen public and private organizations that served as national housing advocates.

8. See Collins and Margo (1999) for a concise summary of this literature.

9. Roistacher and Goodman's data were taken from the Panel Study of Income Dynamics, a longitudinal study of a nationally representative sample of families that began in 1968 and continues today.

10. By extension, then, there was no widening of the gap between 1980 and 1990 like that shown in Figure 12.3 for all households.

11. Tenure data are not available in 1930 and 1950 PUMS files because parts of the original census records have been lost.

12. Gyourko and Linneman's results were contaminated by their failure to distinguish among the various nonwhite races. Blacks and Asians, for example, have very different patterns of home ownership over the life span.

13. Recently, analysts have begun to integrate statistical and graphic presentations of cohort data that preserve the best of both techniques (see, for example, Myers 1999).

14. The exception: the rates for the youngest cohort of both blacks and whites in 1998 exceed those in 1988. This seems out of line with other cohort trends, and

these data points should be viewed with suspicion. Work by Masnick et al. (1999) suggests that changes in the methodology of the Current Population Surveys after 1993 might account for some of the sharp increases observed in black and white ownership rates, especially among younger households.

References

Collins, William J., and Robert A. Margo. 1999. *Race and homeownership, 1900 to 1990*. National Bureau of Economic Research Working Paper 7277, www.nber.org/papers/w7277.

Cutler, David M., Edward L. Glaeser, and Jacob L. Vigdor. 1999. The rise and decline of the American ghetto. *Journal of Political Economy* 107 (3): 455–506.

Farley, Reynolds. 1996. *The new American reality*. New York: Russell Sage Foundation.

Frey, William H. 2001. *Melting pot suburbs: A census 2000 study of suburban diversity*. Washington, DC: Brookings Institution Center on Urban and Metropolitan Policy.

Galster, George. 1986. More than skin deep: The effect of housing discrimination on the extent and pattern of segregation. In *Housing desegregation and federal policy*, edited by John M. Goering, 119–38. Chapel Hill: University of North Carolina Press.

———. 1987a. The ecology of racial discrimination in housing: An exploratory model. *Urban Affairs Quarterly* 23 (September): 84–107.

———. 1987b. Residential segregation and interracial economic disparities: A simultaneous equations approach. *Journal of Urban Economics* (January): 22–44.

———. 1988. Residential segregation in American cities: A contrary view. *Population Research and Policy Review* 7:93–112.

———. 1989. Residential segregation in American cities: A further response. *Population Research and Policy Review* 8:181–92.

———. 1990a. Federal fair housing policy: The great misapprehension. In *Building Foundations*, edited by Denise DiPasquale and Langley C. Keys, 137–156. Philadelphia: University of Pennsylvania Press.

———. 1990b. Neighborhood racial change, segregationist sentiments, and affirmative marketing policies. *Journal of Urban Economics* 10:344–61.

———. 1990c. Racial discrimination in housing markets during the 1980s: A review of the audit evidence. *Journal of Planning Education and Research* 9 (3): 165–75.

———. 1990d. Racial steering by real estate agents: Mechanisms and motives. *Review of Black Political Economy* 19 (summer): 39–63.

———. 1990e. Racial steering in urban housing markets: A review of the audit evidence. *Review of Black Political Economy* 18 (winter): 105–29.

———. 1990f. White flight from racially integrated neighborhoods in the 1970s: The Cleveland experience. *Urban Studies* 27 (3): 385–99.

———. 1991. Housing discrimination and urban poverty of African Americans. *Journal of Housing Research* 2 (2): 87–122.

———. 1992a. The case for racial integration. In *The metropolis in black and white: Place, power and polarization*, edited by George C. Galster and Edward W. Hill, 270–85. New Brunswick, NJ: Center for Urban Policy Research.

———. 1992b. Research on discrimination in housing and mortgage markets: Assessment and future directions. *Housing Policy Debate* 3 (2): 639–83.

———. 1993a. The effects of lending discrimination cannot be argued away by examining default rates. *Housing Policy Debate* 4 (1): 141–46.

———. 1993b. Polarization, place and race. *North Carolina Law Review* 71 (June): 1421–26.

———. 1999. The evolving challenges of fair housing since 1968: Open housing, integration, and the reduction of ghettoization. *Cityscape: A Journal of Policy Development and Research* 4 (3): 123–38.

Gyourko, Joseph, and Peter Linneman. 1996. Analysis of the changing influences on traditional households' ownership patterns. *Journal of Urban Economics* 39 (3): 318–41.

———. 1997. The changing influences of education, income, family structure and race on homeownership by age over time. *Journal of Housing Research* 8 (1): 1–25.

Immergluck, Daniel. 1998. Progress confined: Increases in black home buying and the persistence of residential segregation. *Journal of Urban Affairs* 20 (4): 443–58.

Jargowsky, Paul A. 1997. *Poverty and place: Ghettos, barrios and the American city*. New York: Russell Sage Foundation.

Joint Center for Housing Studies, Harvard University. 1988–1999. *The state of the nation's housing*. Annual reports. Cambridge, MA.

Kain, John F. Forthcoming. *Racial and economic segregation in U.S. metropolitan areas*.

Kain, John F., and John M. Quigley. 1972. Housing market discrimination, home-ownership, and savings behavior. *American Economic Review* 62 (March): 263–77.

Keith, Nathaniel S. 1973. *Politics and the housing crisis since 1930*. New York: Universe Books.

Listokin, David. 1991. Federal housing policy and preservation: Historical evolution, patterns and implications. *Housing Policy Debate* 2 (2): 157–85.

Long, James E., and Steven B. Caudill. 1992. Racial differences in homeownership and housing wealth, 1970–1986. *Economic Inquiry* 30 (January): 83–100.

Masnick, George S., and Zhu Xiao Di. 2001. Cohort insights into the influence of education, race and family structure on homeownership trends by age: 1985 to 1995. Research Note N01-1, Joint Center for Housing Studies, Harvard University, Cambridge, MA.

Masnick, George S., Nancy McArdle, and Eric S. Belsky. 1999. *A critical look at rising homeownership rates in the United States since 1994.* Working Paper W99-2, Joint Center for Housing Studies, Harvard University, Cambridge, MA.

Massey, Douglas S., and Nancy A. Denton. 1993. *American apartheid: Segregation and the making of the underclass.* Cambridge, MA: Harvard University Press.

McDonald, John F. 1974. Housing market discrimination, homeownership, and savings behavior: Comment. *American Economic Review* 64 (March): 225–31.

Megbolugbe, Isaac F., and Peter Linneman. 1993. Homeownership. *Urban Studies* 30 (4/5): 659–82.

Mitchell, J. Paul. 1986. *Federal housing policy and programs: Past and present.* New Brunswick, NJ: Rutgers University Center for Urban Policy Research.

Myers, Dowell. 1981. Housing progress in the seventies: New indicators. *Social Indicators Research* 9: 35–60.

———. 1985a. Reliance upon wives' earnings for homeownership attainment: Caught between the locomotive and the caboose. *Journal of Planning Education and Research* 4 (3): 319–29.

———. 1985b. Wives' earnings and rising costs of homeownership. *Social Science Quarterly* 66:319–29.

———. 1999. Cohort longitudinal estimation of housing careers. *Housing Studies* 14 (4): 473–90.

Myers, Dowell, Richard Peiser, Gregory Schwann, and John Pitkin. 1992. Retreat from homeownership: A comparison of the generations and the states. *Housing Policy Debate* 3 (4): 945–75.

Myers, Dowell, and Jennifer R. Wolch. 1995. The polarization of housing status. In *State of the union: America in the 1990s*, Vol. 1, edited by Reynolds Farley, 269–334. New York: Russell Sage Foundation.

Myrdal, Gunnar. 1944. *An American dilemma: The Negro problem and modern democracy.* New York: Harper.

National Advisory Commission on Civil Disorders. 1968. *Final report.* Washington, DC: U.S. Government Printing Office.

Oliver, Melvin L., and Thomas M. Shapiro. 1995. *Black wealth–white wealth.* New York and London: Routledge.

Pitkin, John, and George Masnick. 1980. *Projections of housing consumption in the U.S., 1980 to 2000, by a cohort method.* Annual Housing Survey Studies 9, U.S. Department of Housing and Urban Development, Office of Policy Development and Research, Washington, DC.

Roistacher, Elizabeth A., and John L. Goodman Jr. 1976. Race and homeownership: Is discrimination disappearing? *Economic Inquiry* 14 (March): 59–70.

Rossi, Peter H. 1980. *Why families move.* 2nd ed. Beverly Hills: Sage.

Schrammel, Kurt. 1998. Comparing the labor market success of young adults from two generations. *Monthly Labor Review* 121 (2): 31–39.

Silberman, Jonathan, Gilbert Yochum, and Keith Ihlanfeldt. 1982. Racial differentials in home purchase: The evidence from newly formed households. *Economic Inquiry* 20 (July): 443–57.

Smith, James P., and Finis R. Welch. 1989. Black economic progress after Myrdal. *Journal of Economic Literature* 27 (June): 519–64.

U.S. Census Bureau. Various years. *Current population survey.* Public-use microdata files.

————. Various years. *Decennial census of the United States.* Washington, DC: U.S. Government Printing Office.

U.S. Department of Housing and Urban Development. 1994. *Homeownership strategy, memorandum for Robert E. Rubin from Henry G. Cisneros, August 17, 1994.* Washington, DC.

Winnick, Louis. 1957. *American housing and its use: The demand for shelter space.* New York: Wiley.

Yinger, John. 1976. Racial prejudice and racial residential segregation in an urban model. *Journal of Urban Economics* 3 (October): 383–96.

————. 1979. Prejudice and discrimination in the urban housing market. In *Current issues in urban economics,* edited by Peter Mieszkowski and Mahlon Straszheim, 430–68. Baltimore: Johns Hopkins University Press.

————. 1986. Measuring discrimination with fair housing audits: Caught in the act. *American Economic Review* 76 (December): 881–93.

————. 1987. The racial dimension of urban housing markets in the 1980s. In *Divided neighborhoods: Changing patterns of racial segregation,* edited by Gary A. Tobin, 43–67. Urban Affairs Annual Reviews 32. Newbury Park, CA: Sage.

————. 1991a. Acts of discrimination: Evidence from the 1989 Housing Discrimination Study. *Journal of Housing Economics* 1 (December): 318–46.

————. 1991b. *Housing Discrimination Study: Incidence of discrimination and variation in discriminatory behavior.* Washington, DC: U.S. Department of Housing and Urban Development.

————. 1992. An analysis of the efficiency of urban residential structure, with an application to racial integration. *Journal of Urban Economics* 31 (May): 388–407.

————. 1993. Access denied, access constrained: Results and implications of the 1989 Housing Discrimination Study. In *Clear and convincing evidence: Testing for discrimination in America,* edited by Michael Fix and Raymond J. Struyk, 69–112. Washington, DC: Urban Institute Press.

———. 1995. *Closed doors, opportunities lost: The continuing costs of housing discrimination.* New York: Russell Sage Foundation.

Yinger, John, G. C. Galster, B. A. Smith, and F. Eggers. 1979. The status of research into racial discrimination in American housing markets: A research agenda for the Department of Housing and Urban Development. *Occasional Papers in Housing and Community Affairs* 6 (December): 55–175.

CHAPTER THIRTEEN

Home Ownership and Social Inequality in Israel

Noah Lewin-Epstein, Irit Adler,
and Moshe Semyonov

Housing has obvious merits in that it provides shelter and safety. Although most families purchase housing to live in, housing also is a means of wealth accumulation and of improving material well-being. For most families, housing equity is their single most important asset. Furthermore, wealth accumulated in a family home has substantial implications for the next generation, not only as an inheritance but also as a source of funds with which parents can help their adult children buy their own home. Not owning a home has substantial implications too: it can mean the persistence into the next generation of inequality. That rates of home ownership differ from one social group to another, then, reflects not only current disparities, but also the potential for disparities over generations (Dreier 1982; Spilerman, Lewin-Epstein, and Semyonov 1993).

Until the mid-1980s, the dominant ideology in Israel was collectivist, and the economy was highly centralized; still, it is not easy to fit the Israeli welfare system into the welfare regime typology outlined in the introductory chapter in this book. Throughout the first four decades of its independence, Israel combined certain features of the social democratic welfare model with those of the corporatist—conservative—model. At the same time, Israel shares with the Southern European countries not only the Mediterranean Sea but also certain institutional attributes, especially a strong family-oriented social structure. As is common in Spain and Italy, family support in Israel plays a significant role in promoting the welfare of individuals. But unlike Spain and Italy, Israel has been a major provider of welfare services and has had a dominant effect on the distribution of housing tenure in the country. The role of the state in this regard is strongly linked to certain features of Israel as an immigrant society in which ethnonationalism is more salient than class in the stratification system. Hence, the Israeli case provides an opportunity to explore inequality in housing in a multiethnic society that differs from both North American immigrant societies with market economies (the United States and Canada, for example) as well as European welfare states.

The chapter consists of three substantive parts. In the first, we outline the politics and economics of housing in Israel and their relationship to ethnic inequality. In the second, we investigate the social patterns of home ownership in recent decades. The third section examines the extent to which inequality in home ownership is maintained from one generation to the next. We end with a discussion of our findings and conclusions about the role of housing in structuring social inequality in Israel.

SYSTEMIC CHARACTERISTICS

Emergent Stratification

It is not possible to comprehend stratification in general, and housing inequality in particular, without considering the processes that have shaped Israeli society and the composition of its population. Israel is a multiethnic society consisting of a majority Jewish population (81 percent of the total population) and a substantial minority of Arabs (approximately 19 percent of the total population).[1] The Jewish population, which numbered approximately 650,000 at the time of independence in 1948, recently crossed the 5 million mark. The nearly eightfold increase was largely the result of a continuous flow of immigrants. Jews who arrive in Israel are commonly viewed as returnees from the Diaspora, and the state assumes responsibility for helping them settle and integrate into society. Immigrants receive citizenship on arrival and are entitled to various forms of support. The role of the state in incorporating immigrants is evident in all spheres of life, from language instruction and job training to financial assistance with renting or purchasing a home.

Jews have migrated to Israel from practically every country on the globe. They are often distinguished by their national origin: European Jews (and their descendants who arrived in Israel via the Americas); North-African Jews, who came primarily from Morocco, Algiers, and Tunisia; and Middle

Eastern Jews, most of whom arrived from Iraq, Iran, and Yemen. A combination of social and political processes that are beyond our scope here have resulted in social and economic inequalities among the immigrant groups and their descendants, and so a strong overlap of ethnic origin and social status. Jews of European origin dominate culturally and politically, and their advantaged position is also manifested in higher levels of education, occupational prestige, and economic well-being. As a group, Jews of North African origin have the lowest standing, and those who originated in the Middle East fall somewhere in between (Khazzoom 1998).

The Arab citizens of Israel are for the most part descendants of Palestinian villagers who remained in Israel after the 1948 war for independence. Although the Arab population grew considerably over the second half of the twentieth century—from approximately 150,000 in 1949 to 1.1 million in 1999—it remains highly segregated from the Jewish population: most Arabs still live in villages and small towns. The Israeli Arab population is subordinate to the Jewish population in terms of education, labor market position, and economic well-being. This subordinate position is shaped and maintained by complex institutional processes.

Immigration and Housing

In 1948, Israel emerged from the war for independence with thousands of vacant housing units—the homes of Palestinians who had fled or been evacuated. These dwellings were assigned to the large number of Jewish refugees who had just arrived from the European Diaspora and the Moslem countries of the Middle East. The new immigrants, after being housed temporarily in transition camps, flocked to the larger cities in the center of the country, where job opportunities were more abundant. There they were accommodated in housing units that had been vacated by Arab residents (Lewin-Epstein, Elmelech, and Semyonov 1997). Once the homes in these cities were occupied, immigrants were directed to formerly Arab towns, all of which were in or near the coastal plains (Golan 1993; Morris 1990). As the flow of immigration continued in the early 1950s, most vacated Arab dwellings were occupied; and "new immigrants were placed in temporary tent cities—and these in turn were located near existing [Jewish] cities and towns, so that it would be possible to provide employment and basic health and educational services" (Matras 1973, 6).

By the mid-1950s, the government of Israel began to implement a comprehensive settlement program that had been designed to alter the geographic distribution of the population. This policy of population dispersion set out to establish new communities in the hinterland, in areas away from the center and the coastal plain. The focus of this policy was newly arrived immigrants, people who were not yet settled in the country and so were more easily moved. The immigrants who arrived in Israel shortly after the war were likely to live in the center of the country; those who came to Israel between the mid-1950s and the early 1960s, mostly Jews from North Africa, were forced to establish residence in peripheral towns that were generally less attractive and that offered few employment opportunities (Golan 1993; Gonen 1975; Matras 1973).

Immigration from the early 1960s to the early 1990s was sporadic, usually the result of political events in countries of origin. In the late 1980s, when the Soviet Union lifted restraints on emigration, Soviet Jews began to arrive in large numbers. In less than a decade, more than 750,000 of them immigrated to Israel, increasing the population there by approximately 15 percent. These immigrants were met with new government absorption policies. The state no longer attempted to settle immigrants according to a grand plan of national development; instead, they were encouraged to make their own decisions about where to live and whether to rent or buy housing. At the same time, they were not shielded by state agencies from market forces, as previous generations of immigrants had been.

Home Ownership and Housing Policy

The rate of home ownership in Israel exceeded 75 percent at the end of the twentieth century.[2] About 12 percent of households rent in the private sector; and about the same percentage rent in the public sector (Carmon 1998; Werczberger 1991). This distribution is very different from the situation that existed before 1948. Although information on housing in the Jewish population of Palestine during the British mandate (1920–1948) is sketchy, drawing on a number of sources we can piece together a fairly reliable picture. A labor union survey conducted among salaried Jewish workers just before World War II revealed that 90 percent of the Jews who were living in urban areas rented their home. The entire rental sector at the time was private (Sagiv 1986).

A rapid rise in rents during the 1930s led British authorities to establish tenant-protection regulations. These regulations froze rents and prohibited the eviction of tenants from rental units. When the State of Israel was established, the regulations were carried over: they suited the socialist ideology of the dominant political authorities. The effect of these regulations was to stifle the private rental sector. Another factor that contributed to the diminishment of the private rental market was the asymmetry of resources available to the private and the public rental sectors in the years following independence. Most residents of Israel were refugees who had fled their land of origin with few belongings. Although the new state had limited economic resources, it was helped by large transfers of funds from the U.S. and German governments and from Jewish organizations in North America and around the world. In large part it was these funds that made it possible for Israel to cope with its enormous increase in population and the needs of new settlers.

Almost from the outset, housing policy was used as an instrument for achieving three major goals:

- The expedient absorption of the immigrants who arrived in large numbers after 1948
- The rapid settlement of land, especially the frontier territories, where Jewish sovereignty was disputed
- The dispersion of the population away from the heavily populated urban center and coastal plain, to the northern and southern peripheries of the country

The government was able to harness housing policy to meet national goals because it has extensive control over land use. Furthermore, zoning is highly centralized, which gives the state substantial control over planning and implementing development and construction. Indeed, in the first two decades decisions governing when to start a housing project, where to locate it, and what it should look like were made for the most part by the government.

During the 1950s and 1960s, thousands of housing units were constructed with public funds. The state played a central role during this time, not only planning and regulating, but also funding and at times acting as developer and contractor. Most housing units constructed at the state's initiative eventually ended up in the private ownership of households through a variety of subsidized arrangements (Golan 1998). Several factors were at work here. First, private ownership of housing, combined with state control of the land, was viewed as an effective means of establishing a Jewish presence and dominance (Carmon 1998). Second, land and housing were used as resources in the political arena to reward favored groups, as was the case with labor leaders and army veterans (Rabinowitz 2000). Third, through the sale of public housing, the government regained part of its investment and was able to build still more housing (Werczberger and Reshef 1993). Fourth, private ownership ties people to the land, a commitment that is particularly important in an immigrant society (Gonen 1975). Fifth, widespread ownership of housing was viewed by the state as a means of creating an economic base for households and so of mitigating socioeconomic inequalities.

In the second half of the 1960s, the state began to reduce its direct engagement in the construction and marketing of housing, choosing instead to subsidize private contractors and buyers. This shift permitted the expansion of the private construction sector, which now accounts for practically all of the new housing in Israel. But even today, by guaranteeing contractors minimum prices and by offering buyers higher-subsidized mortgages, the government uses its resources and near-monopoly over land to direct construction to particular areas.

Since the early 1970s, housing policy in Israel has consisted primarily of subsidizing mortgage loans to various population groups. The government still helps new immigrants; but throughout much of this period, the rate of immigration has been down considerably. The focus of housing policy, then, has shifted to young couples and to socioeconomic bases of entitlement. Subsidized housing loans are based on a number of eligibility criteria. Although the guidelines have changed somewhat over the years, the essential features remain intact: a social component, a civic-virtue component, and a location component.

The goal of the *social component* is to facilitate home ownership among disadvantaged population groups. People who already own a home are not eligible for housing assistance. The amount of aid received by those who are eligible increases with the duration of marriage and family size.[3] Nonetheless, buying a home requires considerable private funds because mortgage loans generally cover just 30 percent of the sale price (Yechezkel 1998). Most would-be homeowners rely on their family of origin for purchase funds—a practice that contributes to the reproduction of inequality.

The second component—*civic virtue*—refers primarily to a record of military service. Military service is compulsory in Israel. As a means of rewarding veterans, the state gives them grants and subsidized loans for housing. This policy acts as an exclusionary mechanism: Most non-Jews are not called up for military service and so are not eligible for the full amount of state support.[4]

The third component—*location*—links the amount of state support and the terms of mortgage loans to the location of housing. This is the primary instrument the state uses to encourage housing purchases in areas designated a national priority.[5] Not surprisingly, lower-income groups are most responsive to state settlement programs: housing in peripheral areas is likely to be cheaper, and it comes with more state assistance. Through its control of land resources as well as mortgage loans, the state retains an important role in the distribution of housing and its ownership.

SOCIAL PATTERNS OF HOME OWNERSHIP

Again, ethnicity and country of origin are two characteristics that define social status in Israel. Hence, we began our analysis with an examination of home-ownership rates by these two characteristics. We focused on recent decades, utilizing data from the Census of Housing and Population from 1983 and 1995.

Ethnic and National Differences

Table 13.1 presents home-ownership rates and housing-density ratios for population groups by ethnicity and national origin. Before we turn our focus to group differences, however, it is important to remember that the rate of home ownership in Israel is very high—averaging over 75 percent across population groups in 1995. Indeed, this rate places Israel on par with the social democratic welfare regimes of the Scandinavian countries. This is particularly remarkable in light of the fact that Israeli society consists mostly of immigrants and their offspring.

The comparison of home ownership and housing density in 1983 and 1995 reveals an improvement for most population groups. In both years, immigrants from the Middle East had the highest rates of home ownership among Jews. Native-born Israelis of European origin also exhibited high rates, followed by the offspring of immigrants from the Middle East. It is noteworthy that the rate of home ownership among European immigrants

TABLE 13.1
Home ownership and housing density by ethnicity
and national origin, Israel, 1983 and 1995

Ethnicity and national origin	1983		1995	
	Percentage of homeowners	*Housing density[a]*	*Percentage of homeowners*	*Housing density[a]*
Arabs	81.6	2.26	87.1	1.87
Israeli-born Jews				
Israeli	69.3	1.09	63.4	0.98
European[b]	76.1	1.04	79.6	0.95
Middle Eastern	68.9	1.25	75.1	1.18
North African	55.4	1.18	63.7	1.18
Immigrant Jews				
European[b]	76.1	0.89	70.2	0.88
Middle Eastern	77.5	1.29	86.4	0.99
North African	57.5	1.28	74.3	1.06

SOURCE: Authors' calculations based on census data.

[a] *Housing density* is defined as the ratio of the number of all household members divided by the number of rooms in the housing unit (excluding kitchen and bathrooms). It is calculated for all households regardless of ownership status.

[b] Includes those of European ancestry who arrived in Israel by way of the Americas.

fell from 76.1 percent in 1983 to 70.2 percent in 1995—reflecting the influx of immigrants from the former Soviet Union in the early 1990s. At the time the data shown in Table 13.1 were collected (in 1995), many of the 750,000 recent arrivals had lived in Israel for less than three years.

In 1983, Jews of North African origin, both immigrants and native born, had the lowest rates of home ownership—57.5 percent and 55.4 percent, respectively. Although these groups exhibited the largest growth in home ownership, by 1995 they had failed to close the gap with Jews of Middle Eastern origin. The relatively low rate for second-generation North African Jews in 1983 was a function of demographics: most North African Jews immigrated to Israel in the late 1950s and early 1960s, so their offspring born in Israel would have been under 30 in 1983; by 1995, many of these young people had come of home-buying age.[6] But this does not explain the increase in home ownership among immigrants from North Africa—a subject we address in a later section.

Also of interest in Table 13.1 is the loss of home-ownership share among second-generation Israelis, from 69.3 percent to 63.4 percent. Here, too, age may be a factor. This group was the youngest of the groups we studied, and its members may have chosen to put off marriage and so home ownership. Later in the analysis, using age cohort analysis, we examined the complex relationship between home ownership and the family life cycle.

A curious finding in Table 13.1 is the high rate of home ownership among Arabs.[7] In 1995, more than 87 percent of Arab households, up from almost 82 percent in 1983, lived in housing they owned. These extremely high rates are all the more interesting in light of the fact that Israel's housing policies over the years consistently have given preference to Jews through eligibility criteria for public housing and subsidized housing loans. Also, the repeated expropriation of land by the state has made land an extremely scarce resource.[8] Compounding these difficulties are town planning and zoning policies that have further limited building opportunities in Arab communities (Rozenhek 1996). In response to economic, political, and regulatory obstacles to home ownership, Israeli Arabs have relied on their traditional paths to home ownership. Adult children frequently add rooms to an existing family dwelling; they look to members of their extended family for funds to buy housing; and many turn to family members to carry out the work of building or rehabilitating housing (Peled 1986; Shmueli, Schnell, and Sofer 1986).

Housing density is a measure of the number of household members per room in the household's home. A lower ratio here suggests more space per individual and implies a higher standard of living. In Western societies, the minimum acceptable housing density is 2.0—a ratio of 2 people per room (Lu-Yon and Kalush 1994). All population groups in Israel, including the Arab population, exceeded this standard in 1995. Still, from the data in Table 13.1, there seems to be a large gap in favor of native-born and immigrant Jews. But these ratios should be interpreted with caution. This measure is not sensitive to differences in the size of rooms, which makes a comparison of Jews and Arabs problematic: the rooms in Arab housing are larger than the standard-sized rooms in the apartments in which most Jews live. Also, the fertility rate is higher in the Arab (mostly Moslem) population, which accounts for much of the gap in housing density between Arabs and Jews.

Time of Immigration and Home Ownership

Immigrants arrived in Israel over an extended period. Figure 13.1 provides evidence of the relationship between their time of arrival and the likelihood of home ownership in 1983 (part a) and in 1995 (part b). Two patterns emerge. The first is the positive relationship between early arrival and home ownership. The rates were highest—exceeding 70 percent when examined in 1983 and exceeding 80 percent when examined in 1995—among immigrants who arrived before Israel's independence in 1948, and lowest—between 40 percent and 50 percent—among immigrants who entered the country shortly before the data were collected.

The second pattern that emerges from these data is the persistent disadvantage of immigrants from North Africa. Clearly, the timing of their arrival is not the sole cause of their lower rates of home ownership. Looking at those who arrived in Israel between 1953 and 1966, for example, immigrants from Europe and the Middle East had very similar rates of home ownership, while immigrants from North Africa lagged behind. The gap was quite substantial in 1983, although it did narrow somewhat by 1995.

Aging and the Transition to Home Ownership

Home ownership has important implications for the intergenerational transfer of resources, which means inequality among immigrant groups is likely to affect access to home ownership in successive generations of native-born Israelis. We addressed this issue in Figure 13.2. Using data from the 1983 and 1995 censuses, we plotted our estimates of home-ownership rates of native-born married heads of households by ethnic origin and age. We decided to focus on native-born groups to limit the effects of immigration; and we chose to look only at married heads of households to limit the effects of changing marriage patterns over time. Each of the parts in Figure 13.2 provides a rough estimate of the interactions of age, period, and home ownership for one ethnic group.[9]

For native-born Jews of European origin (part a), we found a steady increase in home ownership with age, from about 75 percent in the youngest age group (25 to 36 years old) to over 90 percent in the older age groups. Ownership continued to grow with age albeit at a decreasing rate. From the trajectories here, we find evidence that the slight increase in home ownership observed in Table 13.1 for this group of Israelis was the result of aging: for

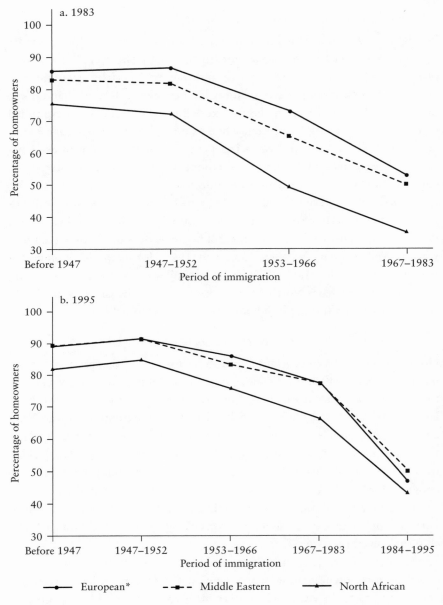

Figure 13.1. Home ownership among immigrants by national origin and period of immigration, Israel, 1983 and 1985

* Includes those of European ancestry who arrived in Israel by way of the Americas.

all age cohorts, home-ownership rates in 1995 were roughly equal to the rates in 1983 with one exception—a slightly higher rate in 1995 among people ages 61 to 72.

A similar pattern is evident for descendants of immigrants from the Middle East (part b of the figure), except that the trajectory of home owner-ship levels off around age 50 at about 90 percent. We did not estimate rates for the older cohorts here because there were too few cases of Israeli-born Jews of Middle Eastern origin over age 60 to allow reliable estimates.

Part c shows the relationship of age and home ownership over time for native-born Jews of North African origin. Once again, we can see an increase in ownership with age. But in this population, there is also a clear shift over time. The rate of home ownership in the ages 37–48 cohort in 1995 was 10

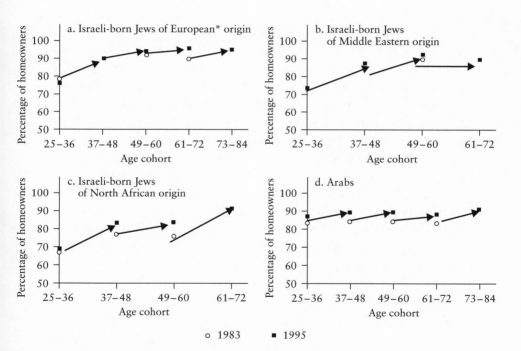

Figure 13.2. Home-ownership trajectories among native-born married heads of household by ethnicity, Israel, 1983–1995

NOTE: Synthetic cohort analysis allowed the authors to estimate the trajectories of changes in homeownership be-tween 1983 and 1995.

* Includes those of European ancestry who arrived in Israel by way of the Americas.

TABLE 13.2
Home ownership by community size,
Israel, 1983 and 1995

| | PERCENTAGE OF OWNERS | |
Community size	1983	1995
Metropolitan centers[a]	68.7	65.6
100,000–199,999 inhabitants	81.2	75.8
20,000–99,999 inhabitants	71.8	75.7
2,000–19,999 inhabitants	63.8	85.9

SOURCE: Authors' calculations based on census data.

[a]Jerusalem, Tel Aviv, and Haifa.

percentage points higher than it was for the same age population in 1983. The same is true for the ages 49–60 cohort. Evidently, Israeli-born Jews of North African descent experienced real growth in home ownership, although at any given age they still lagged behind the other Jewish groups.

Turning our attention to the native-born Arab population (part d), we find yet another pattern. The trajectories form what is essentially a flat line, suggesting no relationship between age and home ownership. In 1983, 83 percent of native-born Arabs ages 25 to 36 reported owning their housing, as did approximately the same percentage in the older cohorts. There was an increase in all age groups—to approximately 90 percent—between 1983 and 1995. Because our data pertained to married persons, we cannot explain the difference between the Arab and Jewish trajectories by the tendency of Arabs to marry earlier. More likely, the patterns reflect the different paths to home ownership taken by Arabs and Jews.

Changing Patterns of Home Ownership Across Communities

In many countries, private home ownership is more a rural phenomenon than an urban one. With their substantial population, high rate of mobility, and generally higher housing prices, large cities usually provide a high proportion of rental units. But in Israel, where state authorities planned, constructed, and populated many communities, development for the most part did not follow the usual pattern. As Table 13.2 shows, more than 65 percent of households in the country's metropolitan centers owned their own home in 1995. But the most interesting information in the table is the change that took place between 1983 and 1995. In 1983, the highest rate of home ownership was found not in the metropolitan centers but in communities of 100,000 to 200,000 residents. All of these communities—among them, Rishon Le-Zion, Ramat-Gan, and Holon—are Jewish communities established before 1948, and most are on the outskirts of Israel's three largest cities, especially Tel Aviv. These cities often serve as bedroom communities, which explains their high rate of home ownership. The lowest rate of home ownership in 1983 (about 64 percent) was found in the smallest communities. By 1995, however, these communities had the highest rate of home ownership (almost 86 percent). In the early 1980s, the state encouraged settlement in the northern and, to a lesser extent, southern peripheries, with the goal of increasing the Jewish presence in those areas. This was accomplished by means of generous mortgage loans, which had the effect over time of raising home-ownership rates in these smaller communities. Also a factor in the growth of home ownership in the smaller communities was suburbanization: that is, young families and recent immigrants have been moving to the outer ring of the metropolitan centers, to areas where housing is more affordable.

Labor Market Position and Home Ownership

We also examined the link between labor market position—defined by the occupation of the head of household—and home ownership. Our findings, shown in Table 13.3, can be summarized in two statements. First, there is a positive relationship between occupational status and the likelihood of home ownership, which translates into inequality in home ownership between those in higher and lower occupational categories. Second, the degree of that inequality fell dramatically between 1983 and 1995: the difference in home-ownership rates between managers and unskilled manual workers (the highest and lowest occupational groups) was 20 percentage points in 1983 and only 10 points in 1995.[10]

In 1983, the proportion of managers who owned their own home exceeded 85 percent. They were followed by academic professionals, with a home-ownership rate of 80 percent. The lowest rate of home ownership was found among unskilled workers: just 65 percent of them owned their housing. In 1995, the distribution of home ownership was more compressed. Home ownership among managerial and professional groups had fallen

TABLE 13.3
Home ownership by occupational category,
Israel, 1983 and 1995

	1983		1995	
Occupational category	Percentage of homeowners	Housing density[a]	Percentage of homeowners	Housing density[a]
Academic professional	80.3	0.99	78.1	0.92
Associate professional and technician	74.5	1.11	74.0	1.02
Manager	85.6	1.04	83.0	0.93
Clerical worker	77.1	1.08	77.1	1.01
Agent, sales worker, and service worker	69.5	1.32	70.6	1.12
Industry, construction, and other skilled worker	76.3	1.44	81.1	1.32
Unskilled manual worker	65.0	1.89	72.8	1.30

SOURCE: Authors' calculations based on census data.

[a] *Housing density* is defined as the ratio of the number of all household members divided by the number of rooms in the housing unit (excluding kitchen and bathrooms). It is calculated for all households regardless of ownership status.

somewhat, changes that in part reflected the influx in the early 1990s of technicians and professionals from the former Soviet Union. At the lower end of the occupational categories, we saw a substantial increase in home ownership among skilled and unskilled manual laborers. This was in line with the findings reported in Table 13.1, that the rates of home ownership increased considerably among Arabs and Jews of North African origin. Both population groups are overrepresented among manual laborers.

Another indication of the growing equality in housing was the narrowing of the gap in housing density. In 1983, housing density ranged from approximately 1 person per room among academic professionals to almost 2 persons per room among unskilled workers. By 1995, housing-density ratios were lower for all occupational categories, but especially for workers in the service industry (from 1.32 in 1983 to 1.12 in 1995) and for unskilled workers (from 1.89 to 1.30, a density roughly equivalent to that of skilled workers). The pattern here, like the pattern of home ownership, indicates less inequality: the gap between the top and bottom of the occupational categories has narrowed significantly. At least part of that equalization was a function of decreasing fertility in the lower-status occupational categories; but part of it was produced by a real increase in the average size of these workers' housing units.

SOCIOECONOMIC DETERMINANTS OF INEQUALITY IN HOUSING

Data for this section of the analysis were collected in the 1994/95 Survey of Families in Israel (Lewin-Epstein et al. 1996). The survey sampled 1,607 randomly selected Jews, all married, between the ages of 30 and 65.[11] One focus of the survey was parental assistance, and housing was the focal point of that analysis. Many items in the survey instrument, then, addressed the purchase of housing. In addition, comprehensive social and demographic data were collected on both spouses (provided by the one spouse randomly selected for an interview) and on their parents (including the socioeconomic characteristics of the parents when the spouses were age 16). In our analysis, we looked primarily at that point in the life cycle when the family of origin intersects with the family of destination—namely, the time of marriage. It marks the beginning of a new household and the time at which many couples make the decision to purchase a house. Our focus was on the ownership of the first housing unit in which the couple lived after marriage.

Intergenerational Corollaries of Home Ownership

A simple examination of the impact of parental help on the purchase of a home reveals that the rate of home ownership at marriage was considerably higher for those who received help from their parents than for those who did not (Table 13.4). This pattern held regardless of the time of marriage. On average, almost half of the couples who received parental help were able to purchase a home within one year of marriage; less than a third of those who received no assistance from their parents had bought a home within the same period. Although these data underscore the persistence of inequality from one generation to the next, the fact that parental assistance increased the rate of home ownership for newly married couples should come as no surprise. More surprising is that at least a quarter of those couples who got no help were able to buy their own home at this early stage of the family life cycle.

TABLE 13.4

Home ownership at marriage by parental assistance and
period of marriage, Israel, 1994–1995

Received parental assistance	PERCENTAGE OF HOMEOWNERS MARRIED IN THE PERIOD				
	Before 1961	1961–1970	1971–1980	After 1980	Average
Yes	44.4	60.4	47.2	47.3	49.4
No	27.0	42.4	25.7	25.1	29.6

It is noteworthy that the rate of home ownership at marriage among those who married between 1961 and 1970 was considerably higher that the rate among those who married in other periods, irrespective of whether they received help from their parents. Although we do not have direct evidence of this, a reasonable explanation is that during the 1960s, many Israelis of European origin received large sums of money in reparations from the German government, and there is evidence that a large portion of that money was used to purchase housing (Landsberger 1967).

Table 13.5 presents data on the percentage of home ownership at marriage by parents' housing tenure and husband's place of origin. The rate of home ownership at marriage clearly depends on whether or not one or both sets of parents owned a home when the spouses were growing up. The same basic pattern holds for the three groups, although disparities are evident. Among couples in which the husband was of North African origin, home ownership at marriage ranged from 19.2 percent (neither set of parents owned a home) to 39.1 percent (both sets of parents owned a home). Couples in which the husband was of European descent were much more likely to own a home whatever their parents' tenure. Moreover, the findings point to the fact that these couples were better able to overcome the disadvantage of their parents' lack of housing assets better than those couples in which the husband was North African or Middle Eastern.

It is noteworthy that the rate of home ownership at marriage was quite similar for Jews of North African and of Middle Eastern descent. In Table 13.1, we saw that the overall rate of home ownership among Jews originating in the Middle East was similar to the rate among Jews of European descent. It seems that the timing of the transition to home ownership in these two groups is different: young couples of European origin are much more likely to become homeowners at marriage.

The Timing of Home Ownership

In view of the high rate of home ownership overall in Israel, it could be concluded that owner occupancy there among most population groups is approaching saturation. The issue, then, is not simply whether a family owns a home; also important is how the experience of home ownership differs among households. Here we examine one aspect of home ownership—the timing of the transition to owner occupancy—and how it is affected by family background and other variables.

For the sake of this analysis, we took the time of marriage as the "natural" point at which couples purchase their own housing.[12] We calculated the duration of time to home ownership as the difference between the year housing was purchased and the year of marriage.[13] We also assumed a strong normative predilection toward owning rather than renting a home, so that delayed transition derives primarily from barriers to ownership, not from lack of motivation. Our dependent variable was the rate of transition to home ownership from the time of marriage. The independent variables included the husband's ethnic origin, age, and education; the parents' home ownership and standard of living when the respondents were growing up; and the spouses' employment status right after marriage, immigration sta-

TABLE 13.5

Home ownership at marriage by parents' housing tenure
and husband's place of origin, Israel, 1994–1995

| | PERCENTAGE OF HOMEOWNERS AT MARRIAGE | | |
| | Husband's place of origin | | |
Parents' housing tenure[a]	North Africa	Middle East	Europe[b]
Parents did not own	19.2	21.9	35.6
Parents of 1 spouse owned	24.2	27.1	43.2
Parents of both spouses owned	39.1	36.5	47.1

[a]Parents' housing tenure when respondent was age 16.
[b]Includes those of European ancestry who arrived in Israel by way of the Americas.

tus, and number of siblings.[14] Cox regression was used to estimate the coefficients.

The results of the analysis are shown in Table 13.6. Because ethnic origin is central to social stratification in Israel, the initial model (model 1) looked only at the husband's ethnic origin and age at marriage (to control for different patterns of marriage). The coefficients for the two indicators of ethnicity—contrasting North African and Middle Eastern origin individually with European origin—were negative and significant (B = −0.314 and B = −0.182 for the two groups, respectively). On the whole, then, couples in which the husband is of European origin make the transition to home ownership more rapidly.[15]

Model 2 introduced into the equation indicators of the socioeconomic standing of the family of origin. Parental home ownership had a positive effect on couples' transition to home ownership. As we expected, the family of origin's standard of living also had a positive effect on the transition to home ownership, but the effect did not reach conventional levels of statistical significance. Another indicator of the socioeconomic status of the family of origin is the father's occupational category. As is evident from model 2, father's occupation had no direct effect on the rate of transition to home ownership. It is also evident from model 2 that both ethnic origin and age at marriage have an impact on the rate of transition to home ownership even after controlling for the economic well-being of the families of origin. Hence, the family of origin's socioeconomic status, which we used as an indicator of the likelihood of parental help in the transition to home ownership, does not by itself explain the transition to home ownership.

In model 3, we added specific characteristics of the spouses, including socioeconomic standing at the time of marriage as measured by the spouses' work status in the first three years of the marriage and the husband's education. We also included variables that distinguished immigrants from native-born Jews, and the number of siblings of both spouses.

Several aspects of this model are noteworthy. First, the coefficients for ethnic origin dropped substantially and were no longer statistically significant. Second, the effects of parental home ownership were no longer significant. Third, the husband's age at marriage still had a positive effect on the transition to home ownership: the older the husband at the time of marriage, the more rapid the couple's transition to home ownership. Finally, couples who worked during the first three years of marriage were likely to make

TABLE 13.6

Predicting the rate of transition to first-time home ownership from the time of marriage, Israel (Cox regression, hazard function)

Variable	MODEL 1		MODEL 2		MODEL 3	
	Unstandardized coefficient	Standard errors	Unstandardized coefficient	Standard errors	Unstandardized coefficient	Standard errors
Husband's ethnicity						
North African	−0.314[a]	.067	−0.260[b]	.073	−0.059	.087
Middle Eastern	−0.182[a]	.067	−0.196[b]	.070	−0.018	.082
European[c]			Ref.			
Family of origin's housing tenure and standard of living						
Husband's parents' home ownership			0.210[a]	.087	0.122	.088
Wife's parents' home ownership			0.238[b]	.083	0.149	.084
Spouses' parents' standard of living			−0.113	.066	−0.119	.068
Controls for missing data						
Husband's parents' home ownership			0.166	.107	0.124	.107
Wife's parents' home ownership			−0.025	.120	−0.018	.121
Husband's father's occupation						
Academic professional, associate professional or technician, or manager			−0.038	.084	−0.076	.085
Clerical worker or agent, sales worker, or service worker			0.112	.067	0.106	.068
Unskilled manual worker			−0.116	.096	−0.090	.096
Skilled manual worker			Ref.			

(continued)

TABLE 13.6
(Continued)

Variable	MODEL 1		MODEL 2		MODEL 3	
	Unstandardized coefficient	Standard errors	Unstandardized coefficient	Standard errors	Unstandardized coefficient	Standard errors
Wife's father's occupation						
Academic professional, associate professional or technician, or manager			-0.068	.082	-0.092	.084
Clerical worker or agent, sales worker, or service worker			0.022	.066	0.047	.066
Unskilled manual worker			-0.095	.102	-0.120	.103
Skilled manual worker			Ref.			
Spouses' attributes						
Husband's age at marriage	0.015[a]	.006	0.014[a]	.006	0.014[a]	.006
Worked during first 3 years of marriage					0.216[b]	.062
Husband's education					0.024[b]	.009
Husband's immigration status					-0.089	.094
Wife's immigration status					-0.273[b]	.103
Number of siblings					-0.027[b]	.009
−2 log-likelihood	17,661.26		17,141.91		17,064.00	

[a] $p < .05$.
[b] $p < .01$.
[c] Includes those of European ancestry who arrived in Israel by way of the Americas.

the transition to home ownership more rapidly than couples who did not (B = 0.216). Husband's education had a similar impact. Indeed, education is the best proxy for lifetime earnings: higher education suggests increased access to the loans that generally are necessary for the purchase of housing.

Two other results of the analysis are of interest. The wife's being an immigrant had a negative effect on the transition to home ownership; this was not the case, however, for immigrant husbands. Also important was the negative effect of the number of siblings (B = −0.027) on the rate of transition to home ownership: the more siblings the couple had, the longer it took to buy a home. In fact, a more-detailed investigation revealed that this factor is the most important intervening variable between ethnic origin and the rate of transition to home ownership.[16]

DISCUSSION AND CONCLUSIONS

Our objectives here were to review recent trends in home ownership in Israel and to examine the extent to which inequality in housing passes from one generation to the next. Given that the absorption of immigrants is a defining characteristic of Israeli society, our focus was on the relationship between immigrant status and home ownership in the Jewish population of Israel. Before we began our analysis of that relationship, however, we compared home-ownership rates in the Jewish and Arab segments of Israeli society. We found that despite the political, social, and economic subordination of Israeli Arabs, their rate of home ownership is somewhat higher than that of the Jewish population. Of course, the rate of home ownership in Israel generally is high. But for Jews, that in large part is a function of state support, support that is withheld from the country's Arab population. Arabs have achieved their high rate of home ownership by living in rural areas, where housing and land are less costly, and by relying on extended family for both financial and physical help.

Our findings when we examined ownership rates for the Jewish population led us to conclude that position in Israel's housing market is strongly linked to the timing of immigration: In both 1983 and 1995, immigrants who had been in Israel longer were more likely to own their home. Yet, we found disparities in home-ownership rates even among people who had come to the country at the same time. These disparities were related to country of origin, and those most affected by these differences were Jews of North African origin or ancestry. Although North African Jews experienced the largest growth in home ownership between 1983 and 1995, at the close of the twentieth century they were still disadvantaged in relationship to other groups of Jews.

A comparison of home-ownership rates by occupational categories in 1983 and 1995 also revealed a narrowing of the gap separating higher and lower occupational groups. The difference in ownership rates between managers and unskilled laborers in 1983 was more than 20 percentage points; by 1995, it was just over 10 percentage points.

It is against this background that we examined individual and intergenerational factors that affect home ownership. Our interest here in particular was the extent to which inequality in home ownership is linked to the characteristics of the family of origin. Because approximately 40 percent of married couples in Israel make the transition to home ownership at the time they marry, we focused our attention on the factors that determine home ownership at this juncture in the life span. One indication of the importance of family of origin for home ownership is the fact that 50 percent of couples who had received help from their parents owned a home at the time of marriage, compared with less than 30 percent of those who received no parental aid. Another indication of the "family connection" was the positive relationship between parents' home ownership and the likelihood of their children owning a home at marriage.

Family socioeconomic status, measured by the occupational status of the father, did not have a consistent effect on offspring's likelihood of home ownership. This could be the result of difficulties measuring occupational status; or it might be that occupational status is not a reliable indicator of the household wealth that parents transfer to their children in the form of gifts or inheritance. These difficulties are further exacerbated in an immigrant society like Israel because migration often severs the link between family standing in the place of origin and family standing in the place of destination.

The two factors associated with family of origin that appear to have an impact on the transition to home ownership are the parents' possession of housing assets and the couple's number of siblings. Because buying a home requires substantial expenditure, even when state support is available, parental assistance is essential for most young couples. The extent to which families can provide financial support depends on their resources and how they must be divided. In fact, family size may well explain why households of European descent have higher rates of transition to home ownership than do other Jewish households. Until recently, Jews from North Africa and the Middle East tended to have considerably larger families than did Jews of European origin. Even after controlling for the socioeconomic status of the family of origin and the socioeconomic characteristics of the respondents, then, we found that having a larger number of siblings reduced the likelihood of home ownership for couples of North African or Middle Eastern descent.

Although inequality in home ownership clearly exists in Israel, we must acknowledge the very high rate of home ownership there. That rate is all the more remarkable when we consider the fact that a large proportion of the Israeli population is made up of immigrants and their children, the first generation to be born in Israel. Home-ownership rates and their growth can be understood only in the context of the decommodifying role played by the Israeli welfare state, at least for the Jewish population.

The State of Israel, through subsidies and planning strategies, has come close to meeting its goal of making every Jewish citizen a homeowner. Its housing policies have narrowed social and economic gaps in the ownership of housing. The result, some say, is that housing inequality today has less to do with home ownership than with the value of housing. Indeed there is large variation in the value of housing and in the wealth accumulated by means of home ownership. This variation is associated with the size, location, and type of housing unit. It may well be that today the study of differences in housing wealth is the key to understanding the unequal distribution of opportunity and the persistence of inequality across generations.

Notes

1. Moslems comprise 15.5 percent of the Israeli population; Christian Arabs, about 2 percent; and Druze, 1.5 percent.

2. When we speak of the *rate of home ownership*, we refer to the percentage of households that own the housing unit in which they live. A housing unit can be a house or an apartment in a multiunit building. In fact, owner-occupied flats constitute the overwhelming majority of housing units in Israel. It should be noted that in most cases, ownership relates to the structure but not the land on which it is situated. Over 90 percent of the land in Israel is owned by the state, which leases it to homeowners. (The lease is a long-term contract called a *lease for generations*.)

Consequently, transactions involving housing property require the approval of state agencies. The purpose of this process is to ensure that the land will remain under the ownership of the Jewish people (Barak-Erez 1998; Kedar 1998; Rabinowitz 2000).

3. In the past, attempts were made to determine the economic welfare of married couples and their families of origin as a basis for differential support. When that proved to be administratively and politically problematic, the government began using number of siblings, duration of marriage, and number of children as proxy measures of economic need.

4. Certain Jewish populations—most notably, the Ultraorthodox religious groups—are also exempt from military service, but a variety of legal machinations have made them eligible for state housing assistance.

5. These are areas where the government wants to increase the Jewish population. At various points in time, the northern and southern peripheries as well as the occupied territories of the West Bank and the Gaza Strip were designated priority areas.

6. Most native-born Jews to parents from Middle Eastern countries were also quite young in 1983, so the growth in ownership rates for this group by 1995 may also reflect the process of aging.

7. Israel's immigration policy limits the immigration of non-Jews; foreign-born Arabs are only rarely allowed to immigrate. Hence, the figures in Table 13.1 show home-ownership rates and housing-density ratios only for native-born Arabs.

8. This is true even in the rural areas where much of the Arab population lives.

9. Israeli-born heads of household whose fathers were also Israeli born were omitted from this analysis because of the small number of cases.

10. We should note that although home-ownership rates among occupational groups equalized somewhat, it is still possible that large differences existed among occupational groups in the value of housing assets. Unfortunately, information on the price of housing was not available in the census data.

11. The study focused only on the Jewish population. It was believed that the extended family structure common in the Arab population would call for a different study design and survey instrument. As a result of their interest in family structure and parental assistance, the authors limited the population studied to couples in a first marriage. Also, one or both spouses had to have lived in Israel for at least ten years.

12. Very few single people purchase housing in Israel. In 1995, only 5 percent of singles owned a home compared with about 78 percent of married people, 6 percent of divorced people, and around 13 percent of widowed people.

13. Couples who attained home ownership at the beginning of marriage were assigned a value of 0.5 because they could have purchased their own home anytime during the first year of marriage.

14. Immigration status was coded 1 if the respondent was age 16 or older when he or she arrived in Israel, and 0 if the respondent was born in Israel or immigrated there as a child. Standard of living was a subjective measure on a 5-point scale. We converted it to a dichotomous variable, assigning a code of 1 if the husband's or wife's parents had a higher-than-average standard of living, and of 0 if the parents' standard of living was average or below average.

15. A test of the difference between the two coefficients (North African and Middle Eastern) found that it was not significantly different from zero. Evidently, the main divide is between European origin and the other origin groups.

16. Details are available from the authors on request.

References

Barak-Erez, Dafne. 1998. Israel land authority between conflicting interests. *Iunei Mishpat* 21 (3): 613–36 (Hebrew).

Carmon, Naomi. 1998. *Housing policy in Israel: The first 50 years*. Haifa: Research Center of City and Region, Technion (Hebrew).

Census of housing and population. 1983. Stage B, demographic version. Jerusalem: Social Science Data Center, Hebrew University.

———. 1995. Stage B, demographic version. Jerusalem: Social Science Data Center, Hebrew University.

Dreier, P. 1982. The status of tenants in the United States. *Social Problems* 30:179–98.

Golan, A. 1998. Jewish nationalism, European colonialism and modernity: The origins of the Israeli public housing system. *Housing Studies* 13:437–505.

———. 1993. Changing the settlement map in areas vacated by the Arab population as a result of the war of independence, in the territory where the State of Israel was established, 1948–1950. Ph.D. dissertation, Hebrew University, Jerusalem (Hebrew).

Gonen, Amiram. 1975. Locational and ecological aspects of urban public sector housing: The Israeli case. In *The social economy of cities*, edited by G. Gappert and H. M. Rose, 275–97. Berkeley, CA: Sage.

Kedar, Sandi. 1998. Majority time, minority time. *Iunei Mishpat* 21 (3): 665–746 (Hebrew).

Khazzoom, Aziza. 1998. The origins of ethnic inequality in Israel. Ph.D. dissertation, University of California, Berkeley.

Landsberger, Michael. 1967. The distribution of assets in Israel, 1963/64. *Bank of Israel Review* 28:3–14.

Lewin-Epstein, Noah, Yuval Elmelech, and Moshe Semyonov. 1997. Ethnic inequality in homeownership and the value of housing: The case of immigrants in Israel. *Social Forces* 75:1439–62.

Lewin-Epstein, Noah, Moshe Semyonov, Seymour Spilerman, and Nira Shmidt Manor. 1996. *Consequences of intergenerational transfers of wealth for living standards and social inequality.* Tel Aviv: Institute for Social Research.

Lu-Yon, Hubert, and Rachel Kalush. 1994. *Housing in Israel: Policy and inequality.* Tel Aviv: Adva Center (Hebrew).

Matras, Judah. 1973. Israel's new frontiers: The urban periphery. In *Israel: Social Structure and Social Change*, edited by M. Curtis and M. S. Chertoff, 3–14. New Brunswick, NJ: Transaction Books.

Morris, Benny. 1990. *1948 and after: Israel and the Palestinians.* Oxford: Clarendon Press.

Peled, N. 1986. *Population and residence in the Arab sector of Israel.* Jerusalem: Ministry of Housing and Construction (Hebrew).

Rabinowitz, Dan. 2000. The forgotten option: Cooperative urban housing. *Teoria Bikoret* 16:101–27 (Hebrew).

Rozenhek, Zeev. 1996. *The housing policy toward the Arabs in Israel in the 1950s–1970s.* Jerusalem: Floersheimer Institute for Policy Studies.

Sagiv, Moshe. 1986. *The development of the rental housing market in Israel.* Jerusalem: Ministry of Housing and Construction (Hebrew).

Shmueli, Amir, Yitzchak Schnell, and Arnon Sofer. 1986. Changing patterns of housing in the communities of the "Little Triangle," 1949–1980. In *Residential patterns and internal migration among Israeli Arabs*, edited by Arnon Sofer, 13–32. Haifa: Haifa University (Hebrew).

Spilerman, Seymour, Noah Lewin-Epstein, and Moshe Semyonov. 1993. Wealth, intergenerational transfers and life chances. In *Social theory and social policy: Essays in honor of James S. Coleman*, edited by A. B. Sorensen and S. Spilerman, 165–86. New York: Praeger.

Werczberger, Elia. 1991. Privatization of public housing. Discussion paper 5-91, Sapir Center for Development, Tel Aviv (Hebrew).

Werczberger, Elia, and Nina Reshef. 1993. Privatization of public housing in Israel: Inconsistency or complementarity? *Housing Studies* 8 (3): 195–206.

Yechezkel, Y. 1998. *The new mortgage program of the Ministry of Housing and Construction.* Tel Aviv: Adva Center (Hebrew).

CHAPTER FOURTEEN

Summary and Conclusions

Karin Kurz and
Hans-Peter Blossfeld

In this book, we have brought together studies of twelve countries, studies that focus on the relationship between access to home ownership and social inequality. Here we summarize some of the main findings, paying particular attention to a possible relationship between home-ownership rates and inequality patterns on the one hand and welfare regime type on the other.

We begin by examining each country's housing system and welfare regime. We then focus on the question of how class or income position influences access to home ownership in different welfare regimes. Have opportunities for all classes become relatively equal across birth cohorts in these countries? Can we indeed speak—with respect to home ownership—of "individualized" societies? Or is the likelihood of home ownership still structured by traditional class patterns? As outlined in Chapter 1, most countries under study in this book experienced increasing risks of unemployment and decreasing economic prospects over the past twenty years (Blossfeld et al. forthcoming). Because becoming a homeowner typically requires a steady income stream, the transition to home ownership presumably has become more difficult. To the extent that job security is linked to occupational class, then, the dependence of home ownership on class may well have increased. In addition to our review of the role class plays in home ownership, we examine the findings on the relevance of intergenerational transfers, which reflect how inequality accumulates across generations.

WELFARE REGIMES AND HOUSING POLICIES

The discussions of housing policies throughout this book make it abundantly clear that a crucial element of government intervention in housing is how it influences the relative costs of renting versus owning (see Megbolugbe and Linneman 1993; and Mulder and Wagner 1998). Where public and private rental sectors are regulated in such a way that they offer affordable and high-quality housing, home-ownership rates are relatively low. A clear example is West Germany, with a home-ownership rate of 42 percent (Chapter 2). In this country, an important objective of housing policy has been to maintain affordable rental housing. To do so, the country established a relatively large public housing sector and regulated rents in the private sector — this despite the unambiguous rhetoric supporting home ownership voiced by all governments in office since the 1950s.

The strategy of keeping rents low, however, is not without pitfalls. If governments do not build up a large public rental sector, but regulate rents in the private sector instead, in the long run they may inadvertently raise home-ownership rates. That is, if rent controls discourage landlords from investing in new buildings and maintaining existing buildings, eventually there is going to be a shortage of rental housing, and the quality of the housing that is available is going to deteriorate over time. These conditions, in turn, increasingly force new households into private ownership. Witness the experience of the United Kingdom, Israel, Spain, and Italy, all of which froze rents at one time or another in the twentieth century.

Despite the possible unintended effects of housing policies, it is clear that political ideology shapes the types of housing tenure governments support. In this book, we did not intend to systematically test the viability of Esping-Andersen's (1990, 1999) classification of welfare regimes for housing. Nor did we expect a simple opposition—private ownership in liberal countries versus a large public rental sector in social democratic countries—to emerge. Nevertheless, the analyses of national housing policies in the chapters here suggest that regime type can be used to understand the general thrust of housing policies.

Consider the social democratic regime. In Chapter 1, we hypothesized that housing costs are collectivized to a greater degree in this regime type than in the other regimes. Collectivization, in theory, can be realized through different forms of housing tenure. In Denmark, for example, the government has fostered a large nonprofit rental sector; accordingly, the proportion of home-owning households is, at 53 percent, rather low (Chapter 6). But in Norway, the government's interest in high-quality housing for all took the form of "combat[ting] the property rights of the few (the landlords) by spreading ownership among the many (the tenants)" (Chapter 7, 160). This policy was supported by highly subsidized state loans (linked to limits on the size and cost of homes) and by cooperative forms of ownership. It was extremely successful, producing ownership levels of around 80 percent. Cooperative housing also plays a role in Denmark, but it appears to be of no significance in any of the other countries under study.

The Netherlands is an ambiguous case within the welfare regime classification. On the one hand, a tradition of a large public rental sector, rent controls, and low home-ownership rates clearly would qualify Dutch housing policy as social democratic or collectivist. On the other hand, since the 1980s, the country has cut back on the construction of public housing and has abolished rent controls. Moreover, the Dutch government has facilitated access to ownership through access to home mortgages that cover up to 100 percent of housing prices and a tax code that allows homeowners to deduct all mortgage interest payments. In 1982, the home-ownership rate in the Netherlands was 42 percent; by 1999, it had risen to 52 percent. Given, however, that almost all rental housing is public, the country still exhibits social democratic traits. Furthermore, self-building activities like those in the conservative countries are not common (Chapter 5).

Israel might well be considered a collectivist regime with respect to its housing policies: through generous subsidies of home ownership for its Jewish population, the home-ownership rate is approaching 80 percent. Israel, then, like Norway, could be considered an example of a country whose collectivist goals in the field of housing have been achieved by facilitating home ownership. The crucial difference, however, is that housing policies in Israel have been closely linked to immigration policies (Chapter 13). The state's objective was to incorporate large numbers of immigrants socially as well as economically by enabling them to become homeowners. This strategy was also meant to mitigate economic inequalities among groups in the Jewish population.

The United States has the purest example of liberal housing policy: the government supports private home ownership—mainly by way of tax relief—and generally relies on market forces to meet the demand for housing;

public housing traditionally has played only a marginal role (Chapter 12). Although some administrations have explicitly committed themselves to the goal of decent housing for the whole population, this has not resulted in housing policies of a range comparable to those in most European countries.

Until the end of the 1970s, Great Britain quite clearly followed a collectivist path: high subsidies for public housing and little specific support for private home ownership. That changed in the 1980s, as the government began to rely more on the market (Chapter 10). Council houses were sold to their tenants on a large scale, and subsidies for public housing were cut, which had the effect of raising rents toward market values (cf. Barlow and Duncan 1994). Since the 1980s, then, the British housing system has become more "liberalized."

Ireland's high home-ownership rate today—about 80 percent—cannot be attributed to housing policies that supported market mechanisms or to a persistent agrarian tradition. Instead, the prevalence of home ownership has its roots in a land reform program that started at the end of the nineteenth century (Chapter 11). At that time, most farmers occupied their holdings on leases; the land reform enabled them to buy their holdings at low prices. In the first decade of the twentieth century, a public rent program for farm laborers was put into place. By the 1920s, a campaign for the right to buy public housing led to a further increase in ownership rates. Although the high level of home ownership in Ireland is rooted in public programs intended to improve the living conditions of the population, the result—a private home-ownership sector without restrictions on land or house prices (except for public housing sales) and a small residual public housing sector—clearly shows traits of a liberal housing system.

Are there any distinguishing characteristics of the housing systems in the countries classified as conservative in Esping-Andersen's typology? The home-ownership rates range from 42 percent in Germany, to 54 percent in France, to a high of more than 70 percent in Belgium (Flanders). Germany is probably closest to a social democratic regime: it has a relatively large public housing sector and a regulated private rental sector, which has kept renting an attractive alternative, particularly in urban areas (Chapter 2). But cooperative forms of tenure, like those that are prevalent in Denmark and Norway, are not supported by state measures and are of minor importance in Germany (Häußermann and Siebel 1996). In Belgium, the housing system seems to be quite close to the liberal model: the public rental sector is small;

and private rents, which have not been regulated, are relatively high. This has made home ownership an attractive alternative for households. In addition, various public policies have supported home ownership. Although officially these policies target low-income households, in practice they have had the most impact on middle-class households (Chapter 4).

What truly distinguishes conservative regimes is probably the role homeowners themselves play in building their homes. By contrast, in social democratic and liberal regimes, private construction companies or nonprofit organizations are the primary actors (cf. Barlow and Duncan 1994). We come back to this point later, when we discuss the effects of occupational class on access to home ownership.

What are the characteristics of the housing systems in the two Southern European countries studied here? We would expect state involvement in housing to be weak and family involvement to be strong. Also, the market should play a more important role than it does in conservative regimes (cf. Barlow and Duncan 1994). The housing policies in Italy and Spain do not suggest that there is no government regulation of the housing market: at times, both countries have regulated rents. But what is generally lacking is a large-scale policy promoting public housing, a sector that has remained residual in both countries. Italy and Spain also conform to the Southern European model in another area: in both nations, the extended family typically plays a central role in helping younger members become homeowners. In Italy, one reason for this is that the mortgage credit sector has developed at a slower rate than it has in other European countries (Chapter 8). The data for Spain reveal that a sizable proportion of young homeowners are mortgage-free (Chapter 9). This is possible only where there is family support. Furthermore, the high home-ownership rates in Italy (about 70 percent) and Spain (more than 80 percent) are not simply a consequence of an agrarian tradition that has persisted longer than it has in other European countries. Instead, in both countries, rent regulations—in particular, rent freezes—seem to have played a crucial role in boosting the ownership sector. The withdrawal of private investors from the rental market has not left new households with options. This is surely also one of the reasons why young adults leave their parents' home relatively late in Italy and Spain by comparison with other European countries (Jurado Guerrero and Naldini 1996).

CLASS AND INCOME DIFFERENCES IN THE
ACHIEVEMENT OF HOME OWNERSHIP

The first, and not unexpected, result is that class and income are still factors in the transition to home ownership. There are very few signs that the importance of class or household income is shrinking; that is, there seems to be no pervasive trend toward individualization of home ownership. Several analyses reveal that class and income matter more for young adults today than for older generations. In most of the countries under study, those households that have entered the housing market since the early 1980s have faced higher risks of unemployment and generally more difficult economic conditions (Blossfeld et al. forthcoming). Almost all of the studies that investigated the development of class differences across birth cohorts or periods —namely, those for Belgium, Denmark, France, Germany, the Netherlands, Italy, and Israel—found evidence that the likelihood of home ownership for members of lower socioeconomic groups has deteriorated.[1] In Norway— where the housing market was deregulated in the 1980s—opportunities for home ownership have become less dependent on the household's economic position (Chapter 7). Similarly, home ownership became more evenly dispersed among occupational groups in Israel from 1983 to 1995 (Chapter 13).

Furthermore, the overall likelihood of home ownership has declined for younger cohorts in a number of countries. For example, there seems to be a growing delay in the transition to owner occupancy in France, Denmark, and Spain.[2] In general, we would expect two factors to contribute to delay here: First, young people today are spending more time in school, which means they are putting off marriage and having children—events that often signal a readiness to buy a home. Second, the increase in labor market problems makes it more difficult for young people to undertake a long-term commitment to home ownership. If, however, the transition to home ownership has been eased in some way—for example, by a change in regulations—or if renting is not a viable alternative, earlier transition to home ownership is plausible. The former situation applies to the Netherlands, where the requirements for down payments have eased considerably; the latter is true of Italy, where access to rental units has decreased greatly over time.

Is there a relationship between welfare regimes and class patterns in access to home ownership? We hypothesized in the introduction that in a social democratic country—like Denmark or Norway—differences in class or income should matter little, given the government's explicit commitment to equal living conditions and life chances (cf. Esping-Andersen 1990, 1999). The opposite pole, we believed, would be occupied by liberal countries, where the market would place households with few economic resources at a disadvantage. We expected class differences in conservative and Southern European countries to lie in between the two poles, with Southern European countries being closer to the liberal end.

What we found, again, is that class and income matter in all countries, including Denmark, Norway, and the Netherlands. That is, even in social democratic regimes, the transition to home ownership is more likely for households with greater financial resources. In addition, the analysis for Norway confirms that the value of housing increases with household income (Chapter 7). At the same time, however, the study for Norway shows that cooperative ownership helps reduce differences in home ownership among income groups: lower-income households, which are disadvantaged on the private housing market, are able to compensate through easier access to cooperative ownership.

Most of the results in the different chapters of this book are not strictly comparable, given differences in birth cohorts and periods studied as well as the specific explanatory variables used in the statistical models. The analyses for Denmark and Great Britain are roughly comparable, though, which gives us a clue about the extent of inequality in Great Britain, a liberal welfare regime.[3] When we compare the results of roughly similar transition-rate models, we find that the effect of class is decisively stronger in the British sample than in the Danish one. In Great Britain, the estimated odds of home ownership are more than 2.2 times greater for higher-level professionals and managers than they are for unskilled or semiskilled manual workers.[4] In contrast, the transition rate to home ownership in the Danish sample is about 1.6 times greater for higher-level white-collar workers than it is for unskilled workers.[5] As expected, then, the results suggest that class differences are greater in the liberal regime.

Unfortunately, the results of the empirical analyses for the conservative and the Southern European regimes cannot be compared with those from Denmark and Great Britain. The birth cohorts studied in Germany were older; and the studies of France and Italy made no differentiation between skilled and unskilled workers.[6] But we can compare the findings for France and Italy.[7] The results from event-history models for married men show that the transition rate to home ownership in France is about 1.8 times higher for service-class employees than for manual workers, and that the rate in Italy is about 2.1 times higher.[8] Clearly, we do not find the decisively greater inequality we had expected to find in Italy, a Southern European regime. Of course, a more meaningful comparison would demand standardized tests across a number of welfare regimes.

INTERGENERATIONAL TRANSFERS AND THE ACHIEVEMENT OF HOME OWNERSHIP

We now turn to the question of what role family and intergenerational transfers play in the transition to home ownership. As argued in the introductory chapter, we would expect self-building and family support to be relevant primarily in conservative and Southern European regimes, where the family is still considered a major service provider. Often, family support in those regimes is a crucial component of self-building, a means to home ownership that we expect is particularly important for working-class households: those households can compensate for their lack of financial resources, at least in part, by their own labor and the practical help of extended family, friends, and neighbors. In countries where self-building is common, the home-ownership rates of manual workers—in particular, skilled manual workers (given their higher income)—should approach those of lower- and middle-level white-collar workers, who have higher income on average.

The empirical results from the country studies do not provide a clear picture. In the German study, we do indeed find that the transition rates to home ownership are similar for skilled manual workers and lower- and middle-level nonmanual workers (Table 2.6). But we also find this pattern in Great Britain and Denmark (however, for younger birth cohorts)—two countries where self-building is less prevalent.[9] In contrast, in the Netherlands, the rate of home ownership for skilled manual workers (and similarly for unskilled manual workers) is noticeably lower than the rate for lower- and middle-level nonmanual workers (Table 5.8). We noted above that the analyses for France and Italy make no distinction between unskilled and semiskilled manual laborers, and skilled manual laborers. In France, a conservative regime, manual workers did not fare worse (in fact, they may have fared somewhat better) than office and service workers (Table 3.3). This was not the case in Italy, a Southern European regime, where manual workers displayed a significantly lower rate of owner occupancy than did lower- and middle-level white-collar workers.[10]

Taken together, the results suggest that the mechanisms that produce differences or similarities between blue-collar and white-collar workers are too complex to be reduced to the question of self-building in a specific national context. For example, in their study of France, Meron and Courgeau attribute the gap they found between manual workers and clerical/service staff in young birth cohorts to the changing composition of the two groups: manual workers today tend to be more qualified (and, by implication, better paid); clerical and service workers, on the other hand, are increasingly less qualified and their jobs have become less secure. To understand the role occupational class plays in home-ownership trends across countries, then, we need more information. In particular, we need direct measurements of how households become homeowners—though purchase, self-construction, inheritance, or gift. This information was available in the Italian study (Chapter 8), and the analysis revealed that the working class can catch up to some extent through self-building. But it also found that self-building has become less common today, a function of communities' enforcing planning and building regulations and of cost.

One consistent result did emerge from the studies of Denmark, Germany, and France: manual workers (and, more generally, low-income households) are more likely to become homeowners when they live in rural areas. This relationship points to the fact that land prices are typically lower in rural areas than in urban areas, making home ownership more accessible. It also reflects the fact that support networks are more common in rural communities.

Our findings on the relevance of intergenerational transfers come from the studies of West Germany, the Netherlands, Denmark, and Israel.[11] These studies controlled for father's (and sometimes father-in-law's) social class and parents' home ownership. We expected intergenerational transfers to be most important in West Germany and less important in the Netherlands and Denmark (both of which we classify as social democratic welfare regimes), given the stronger commitment to equal opportunity in those countries.[12] In the West German sample (three cohorts born in the periods 1929–1931, 1939–1941, and 1949–1951), parents' home ownership increases the transition to owner occupancy significantly, by about 60 percent (Table 2.9). Blue-collar workers and lower- and middle-level white-collar workers seem to profit more from their parents' assets than do members of other occupational groups. In contrast, in the analysis for the Netherlands (which examined a wide range of birth cohorts), any effect of parents' home ownership disappears as soon as parents' occupational class is controlled for in the statistical model (Table 5.8). However, in the Danish analysis (which followed a cohort of 18- to 20-year-olds from 1980 through 1993), ownership in the family of origin increases the rate of transition to home ownership by about 40 percent—even when parents' occupational class is included in the model (Table 6.2).

Our findings, then, are ambiguous. Although the comparison between Germany and the Netherlands seems to confirm that parents' assets matter less in a social democratic regime, the results from Denmark indicate the opposite. Mulder and Wagner (1998)—and Mulder in Chapter 5 of this volume—suggest a number of possible reasons for the higher relevance of the family of origin in West Germany. The most important are probably that parent–child transfers are taxed less in Germany and that down payments are more flexible in the Netherlands, which makes Dutch households less dependent on long-term savings and the financial support of family. We can only speculate on the reasons behind the findings for Denmark. One important difference between the Danish study and the other two studies is that the Danish analysis focused on a relatively young cohort, people who were starting their housing career during an economic downturn. Also, the proportion of homeowners in the parents' generation was greater than it was for the parents of the older birth cohorts. Hence, there was a greater likelihood of parental support. The empirical result suggests that even in an institutional context where reliance on the family of origin is less common—as we would expect in Denmark—the importance of intergenerational transfers might increase when the economic situation is difficult. To test this proposition, however, we would need a comparison of several birth cohorts.

Regarding the results on the relevance of intergenerational transfers, a caution is in order. Where we find an effect of parents' ownership on the likelihood of their adult children's transition to home ownership, several mechanisms may be at work.[13] Probably the two most important for first-time ownership are the direct transfer of financial resources to adult children who want to buy a home and the socialization toward home ownership. People who grew up in a home their parents owned may well have acquired a "taste" for home ownership (Henretta 1984). Certainly, at first glance, we cannot preclude the possibility that the results for West Germany, the Netherlands, and Denmark are the product, at least in part, of socialization. However, we cannot think of a reason why socialization effects should vary among these three countries. So, differences in the relevance of parents' home ownership probably are caused by differences in the importance of intergenerational transfers within the various country contexts.

In contrast to the studies of Germany, the Netherlands, and Denmark, the analysis for Israel explicitly rules out parents' home ownership as simply an indicator of socialization effects. In addition to parents' social class and home ownership, this study included the number of siblings in the statistical model. In an examination of married men whose parents had immigrated to Israel, parents' home ownership increases the rate of transition to home ownership by about 20 to 30 percent (Table 13.6, model 2). But that effect is reduced considerably as the number of siblings is taken into account (Table 13.6, model 3). This suggests that the financial resources of the family of origin do indeed play an important role in the transition to home ownership.

PERSPECTIVES FOR FUTURE RESEARCH

The country-specific studies in this book are only a first step in understanding how a household's labor market position and the resources of the family of origin influence access to owner occupancy in different national contexts. Still, they make two important contributions to that understanding. First, contrary to the rhetoric of increasing individualization in contemporary society, labor market position continues to be of major importance for access to owner occupancy. This is true for all countries under study, even those with social democratic housing policies that extensively involve the state and nonprofit organizations in the provision of housing. Second, with the economic problems of the 1980s and 1990s, access to home ownership became increasingly dependent on labor market position in almost all of the countries where this aspect was studied. This is particularly troubling because being a homeowner is associated not only with better living conditions but also with the increased opportunity to accumulate assets that can be transferred to the next generation.

On the basis of the country studies, we were able to identify links between welfare regime types and social inequalities in access to home ownership. Future research, however, will need to work with more comparable data across countries to produce more conclusive results on the connections between welfare regime type and housing policies on the one hand and patterns of inequality on the other. In particular, the influence of the family and of intergenerational transfers in the transition to home ownership—two areas that only rarely have been studied—deserve closer investigation.[14]

Of the country-specific studies here, only the study of Ireland tackled the question of how home ownership *itself* affects the inequality structure. This question, too, warrants further research with systematic comparisons of countries. Another issue raised by the studies on Israel and the United States is the role immigration status, race, and ethnicity play in access to home ownership. The results of these analyses make clear that social class and labor market position are by no means the only dimension of inequality that merit study. Immigration status, race, and ethnic origin are important factors in the housing biographies of households whatever their labor market position or the resources of the family of origin.

Notes

1. In Germany, the analysis of birth cohorts did not show a reduction in the likelihood of becoming a homeowner. But the cohorts studied were relatively old, and the analysis followed them only until the beginning of the 1980s, when the macroeconomic situation was just beginning to deteriorate. Cross-sectional data did show that the working classes fared worse than the middle class from the 1980s on (Table 2.1).

2. Differences in the birth cohorts studied mean that the results are not strictly comparable across the three countries.

3. The study of Denmark (Chapter 6) followed a sample of young men, ages 18 to 20 in 1980 and living in couple relationships, until 1993; the British analysis (Chapter 10) examined couples and single people who were under 25 in 1991, and followed them until 1998. Although the birth cohorts, the relationship status, and the periods studied varied somewhat, both analyses covered a period when macroeconomic conditions had worsened: the 1980s to early 1990s for Denmark, and the 1990s for Great Britain.

4. The odds are 2.2 in the comparison with workers in semiroutine manual occupations and 2.8 in the comparison with workers in routine manual occupations. They are calculated by exp(coefficient) (Table 10.4, model 1).

5. The odds are calculated from the respective coefficient in Table 6.1 as exp(0.4419).

6. Comparisons are also not possible with Belgium and Spain because the analyses are cross-sectional and have a somewhat different focus.

7. The French analysis followed a 1952–1963 birth cohort (men, living in couple relationships) through 1997 (Chapter 3); in the Italian analysis, the youngest cohort—married men born between 1956 and 1965—was followed until 1998 (Chapter 8).

8. Calculated from Tables 3.3 and 8.3 (model 2) by exp(coefficient).

9. See Tables 10.4 (model 2) and 6.1 (model 2).

10. For Italy, again, we refer to the youngest cohort (born between 1956 and 1965), which compares best to the 1952–1963 cohort for France. (See Table 8.3, model 2, the interaction effects with cohort 3.)

11. Unfortunately, in the country studies of the liberal and Southern European welfare regimes, information about the housing tenure of the family of origin was not available in the data sets employed for the analyses.

12. We had no hypothesis for Israel because we did not assign it a welfare regime type.

13. See Chapter 5 for a full list.

14. Although Forrest and Murie (1995) have taken a step in this direction, they did not link their findings to welfare regime type and the housing policies in different countries.

References

Barlow, James, and Simon Duncan. 1994. *Success and failure in housing provision.* Trowbridge, UK: Redwood Books.

Blossfeld, Hans-Peter, Erik Klijzing, Melinda Mills, and Karin Kurz. Forthcoming. *The losers of globalization: Becoming an adult in uncertain times.*

Esping-Andersen, Gøsta. 1990. *The three worlds of welfare capitalism.* Princeton, NJ: Princeton University Press.

———. 1999. *Social foundations of postindustrial economies.* Oxford: Oxford University Press.

Forrest, Ray, and Allan Murie, eds. 1995. *Housing and family wealth. Comparative international perspectives.* London: Routledge.

Häußermann, Hartmut, and Walter Siebel. 1996. *Soziologie des Wohnens. Eine Einführung in Wandel und Ausdifferenzierung des Wohnens.* Weinheim: Juventa.

Henretta, John C. 1984. Parental status and child's home ownership. *American Sociological Review* 49:131–40.

Jurado Guerrero, Teresa, and Manuela Naldini. 1996. Is the South so different?

Italian and Spanish families in comparative perspective. Special issue, *Southern European Society & Politics* 1:42–66.

Megbolugbe, Isaac F., and Peter D. Linneman. 1993. Home ownership. *Urban Studies* 30:659–82.

Mulder, Clara H., and Michael Wagner. 1998. First-time home-ownership in the family life course: A West German–Dutch comparison. *Urban Studies* 35 (4): 687–713.